The Retail
Loss Prevention Officer

The Retail Loss Prevention Officer

The Fundamental Elements of Retail Security and Safety

Anthony D. Manley

Upper Saddle River, New Jersey 07458

Cataloging-in-Publication Data is available at the Library of Congress.

Publisher: Stephen Helba
Executive Editor: Frank Mortimer, Jr.
Assistant Editor: Korrine Dorsey
Production Editor: Denise May, UG / GGS Information Services, Inc.
Production Liaison: Barbara Marttine Cappuccio
Director of Manufacturing and Production: Bruce Johnson
Managing Editor: Mary Carnis
Manufacturing Buyer: Cathleen Petersen
Creative Director: Cheryl Asherman
Cover Design Coordinator: Miguel Ortiz
Cover Designer: Cheryl Asherman
Cover Image: gettyimages
Editorial Assistant: Barbara Rosenberg
Marketing Manager: Jim Peyton
Formatting and Interior Design: UG / GGS Information Services, Inc.
Printing and Binding: R. R. Donnelley & Sons

Pearson Education LTD
Pearson Education Singapore, Pte. Ltd
Pearson Education, Canada, Ltd
Pearson Education–Japan
Pearson Education Australia PTY, Limited
Pearson Education North Asia Ltd
Pearson Educaçion de Mexico, S.A. de C.V.
Pearson Education Malaysia, Pte. Ltd

10 9 8 7 6 5 4 3 2 1

0-13-039475-0

This book is dedicated to my wife, Emily,
who has encouraged me in all my professional and educational endeavors

Contents

Preface xvii

Introduction xxi

Criminal and Civil Law for the Loss Prevention Officer

PART 1: Law and Liability 2

Introduction to Law 2
Statutory Law 2
Common Law 4
Case law, 4
Precedent, 4
The rule of Stare Decisis in judicial decisions, 4
The right for redress, 4
The Liability That Retail Personnel May Encounter 5
Criminal law, 6
Civil law, 6
The contrast between criminal and civil law, 7
Endnotes 8

CHAPTER 1: Civil Liability 9

Intentional and Negligent Wrongs Defined 9
Premises Liability 12
The question of security negligence, 12
Negligence, 13
Vicarious Liability 14
Scope of employment defined, 14
Products Liability 15

CHAPTER 2: Criminal Law and Liability 17

False Arrest and False Imprisonment 17
The elements of false arrest, 18
The Presence of Probable Cause 20
Probable cause defined, 21
Reasonable grounds defined, 22

Reasonable time and manner defined, 23
Presumptions and the burden of proof, 23
Factors leading to a probable cause conclusion, 24
Malicious Prosecution 25
The elements of malicious prosecution, 25
Damages 28
Compensatory damages, 28
Punitive damages, 29
Damages for malicious prosecution, 29
Malicious prosecution and vicarious liability, 30
The awarding of damages, 30
Defamation 31
The elements of defamation, 31
Libel and slander, 31
Assault and Battery 31
Definition of assault, 32
Definition of battery, 32
The elements of assault and battery, 32
General Releases 33
Payment in lieu of release, 33
Endnotes 34

CHAPTER 3: Criminal and Civil Litigation 35

The Criminal Justice System 36
Pre-litigation 36
The court system, 36
The trial process, 37
Preserving physical evidence, 38
Obtaining confessions, admissions, and witness statements, 38
Interview attempts by unknown parties and damaging remarks by others, 41
Litigation 42
The civil lawsuit, 42
The role of loss prevention, 44
Discovery, 45
Testifying at examinations before trial, 46
Testifying at trial, 47
Rules of Evidence 49
Definition of evidence, 49
The exclusionary rule, 50
Motion to suppress evidence, 50
Reasonable doubt and the preponderance of evidence, 50
Endnote 50

PART 2: Criminal Law and the Retail Loss Prevention Officer 51

CHAPTER 4: Legal Powers and Limitations 52

Security and Civil Law 52
The Arrest 53
Definition, 53
Evidence to support an arrest, 53
Authority to Arrest by a Security Officer 55
Offenses defined, 55
The security officer and the "private citizen" concept, 57
In conclusion, 58
The Use of Force in Effecting an Arrest 59
Justification of physical force by a private citizen, 59
Aiding a police officer, 62
Resisting arrest, 62
Search and Seizure 62
The search after the arrest, 62
Civil Rights 66
The "Color of State Law," 68
Sexual Harassment and Privacy Rights 69
Sexual harassment conduct, 69
Sexual harassment and its effects, 70
Prevention of sexual harassment, 70
Invasion of or the right to privacy, 71
Juvenile Apprehension Procedures 71
Juvenile and delinquency defined, 72
The courts, 72
Juvenile Custodial and Detention Procedures 74
Custodial and questioning procedures, 75
Parental notification retarding a written record, 76
Conclusion, 76
Endnotes 77

CHAPTER 5: Applicable Laws and Alternative Charges 78

Larceny 78
Larceny defined, 79
Culpable conduct, 79
Value of stolen property, 79
Defense by a criminal defendant, 80
Anti-security item, 80
License and Privilege 81
Trespass defined, 82
Burglary defined, 82
Attempt to Commit a Crime 84
Criminal Possession of Stolen Property 85

Theft of Services 86
Credit Cards and Debit Cards 86
Confiscation of cards, 88
Endnotes 88

The Fundamental Elements of Retail Security and Safety

PART 3: The Retail Loss Prevention Officer 90

CHAPTER 6: Loss Prevention 92

Retail Loss Prevention 92
Other concerns for loss prevention, 93
Defining the security officer, 94
The security officer's role in security and safety, 95
The Security Officer and the Employee 99
The Use of Weapons, Devices, and Controls 100
Possession and use of firearms, 100
Handcuffs, 100
Batons and jacks, 101
Chemical sprays and electronic devices, 101
Radios and public address systems, 102

CHAPTER 7: Risk Analysis and Threat Potential 103

Identification of the Areas of Loss 103
Loss prevention surveys, 103
The responsibility of loss prevention, 106
Deterrence as a factor in crime control, 108
Reactive vs. proactive, 109
Endnotes 110

CHAPTER 8: Investigative Techniques 111

Investigation of Loss, Theft, and Shrinkage 111
Conducting and Internal Investigation 112
Concluding the Investigative Process 114
Informants, 115
Closed circuit television, 115
Covert surveillance, 116
Wiretaps and the Recording of Telephone Conversations 117
Eavesdropping defined, 117
Wiretaps, 118
Employee Searches 118
Invasion of Privacy and Defamation 119
Defamation, 119
Disclosure of confidential information, 120
The Investigation at a Scene of Occurrence 121
The scene, 121
The collection and preservation of evidence, 122

Accident Investigation and Insurance Fraud 123
Cons, scams, and flim-flams, 123
Interviews and Interrogations 125
Routine investigations, 125
Criminal investigations, 126
The Miranda Warning and Other Issues 127
Juveniles, 128
Unions, 128
Conclusion, 129
Endnotes 129

CHAPTER 9: Loss Prevention Contractual Services 130

Undercover Detectives and Operations 130
The role of the undercover detective, 130
The use and operation of the undercover detective, 131
Honesty shoppers, 132
Complementary Contractual Services 133
Watchclock systems, 133
Armored car services, 135
Polygraph services, 135
Insurance and fidelity bonding, 137
Other essential services, 139
Endnotes 140

CHAPTER 10: Other Responsibilities and Considerations 141

Exterior Patrols 141
Parking fields, 141
Safes 144
Safe access and security, 145
Drugs on Premises 146
Drug testing, 146
Lost and Found Children 148
Lost or missing child, 148
Found child, 150
Lost and Found Property 150
Police Officers 151
Obstructing governmental administration, 151
Police cooperation, 151
Police officers hired as security officers, 152
The Media 153

PART 4: External and Internal Retail Theft: Loss from Theft and Fraud 155

The Shoplifter and the Dishonest Employee 155
Inventory Loss 156
The Relation of Cost, Benefit, and Value to the Retailer 157
Endnotes 158

CHAPTER 11: The Shoplifter 159

Classification 159
Social Issues 159
The profile of the shoplifter, 162
The art of shoplifting, 163
The characteristics of a shoplifter, 164
Actions That Encourage Shoplifters 165
Actions That Discourage Shoplifters 166
Protective devices and systems, 166
Control of ticket switching, 167
Additional support in theft control, 168
Endnote 168

CHAPTER 12: The Primary Rules in Determining Probable Cause in a Shoplifting Arrest 169

Witnessing the Crime 169
The Stop 171
Detaining and Detention 172
Accomplices, 173
The Role of Loss Prevention and Selective Prosecution 174
Cautionary arrest and release procedures, 175
The Role of the Employee 176
Employee training, 177

CHAPTER 13: The Dishonest Employee 179

Employee Theft 179
The Employee as a Security Risk 182
Why they steal, 183
Where they steal, 184
How they steal, 185
Some indicators of employee theft, 186
Covert actions in curtailing internal theft, 186
Types of Internal Theft 187
Embezzlement, 187
Theft of services by an employee, 188
Insurance fraud by an employee, 189
Cashier theft, 189
Pilferage, 190
Damage, 191
Computer theft and sabotage, 191
The Dishonest Security Professional 194
Endnotes 197

CHAPTER 14: External Crimes and Frauds Affecting the Retail Establishment 198

Burglary 198
The protection of the facility and its assets, 199
Robbery 200
Anti-robbery procedures, 202
Employee procedures in the event of a robbery, 203
Larceny from the Person without Force 205
Schemes and Scams 206
Returns and refunds, 206
Till taps and scams, 207
Bad Checks and Credit Card Fraud 208
Bad checks, 209
Credit card fraud, 211
Check and credit card identification procedures, 212
Civil Recovery 214
Counterfeit Currency 215
Contractor and Vender Larceny 216
Sidewalk Delivery 217
Endnotes 217

CHAPTER 15: Loss Prevention and Control: Tactics and Procedures 218

Loss Control Procedures 218
The hiring process, 218
Awareness and training, 220
Asset control, 221
Internal and External Theft Control 222
Loss Prevention Systems and Security Personnel, 222
Employees, 223
Cashiers and cash rooms, 225
Stock control, 227
Physical security, 228
Shipping and receiving areas, 232
Electronic article surveillance, 234
Anti-shopping signage, 235
Helpful Management Techniques for Security and Safety 237
The role of loss prevention, 237
The role of management, 237
The role of human resources, 239
Endnote 242

PART 5: Emergencies, Threats, and Hazards 243

CHAPTER 16: Emergencies 244

The Emergency Procedure Plan 244
Emergency planning, 244
Emergency response team, 245
Natural and Man-made Disasters 247
Categorizing disasters, 247
Fire emergency, 248
Gas leaks, 251
Bomb threats, 252
Bomb threat procedure, 257
Terrorism, 258
Retail Issues 260
Other Serious Business Threats 263
Sabotage, 263
Espionage, 263
Natural and accidental events, 264
Evacuations 264
Endnotes 266

CHAPTER 17: Accidental Injuries or Serious Illnesses 267

Customer, Visitor, or Employee 267
Legal duty, 268
Workers' compensation, 269
Accident records, 270
Occupational Safety and Health Act 272
Infectious and health hazards, 273
The Safety Committee 276
Establishment of a safety committee, 277
Endnotes 278

CHAPTER 18: Strikes, Violence, Unruly Persons, and Crowds 279

Strikes and Picketing 279
Unruly Crowds 280
Abnormal, Disturbed, and Disgruntled Persons 281
Workplace Violence 282
Employee violence, 284
Endnote 286

PART 6: Alarms and Inspections 287

Introduction 287
Maintenance of alarm hardware, 287

CHAPTER 19: Alarm Systems 288

Burglar Alarms 288
Alarm design, protection, and hardware, 288
Types of burglar alarm systems, 292
Fire Alarms 293
Alarm design and hardware, 293
Sprinkler Alarm Systems 294

CHAPTER 20: Systems Inspection, Testing, Maintenance, and Recordkeeping 296

Fire Inspections 296
Areas of inspection, 297
Alarm Systems Testing 299
Alarm records, 299
Alarm System Response 300
Burglary and fire response: after hours, 300
Robbery and fire response: during business hours, 301

PART 7: Relevant Topics of Concern for the Retail Loss Prevention Department 302

CHAPTER 21: Report Writing 303

Preparation and Maintenance of Incident or Case Reports 303
Recordkeeping 304
The Significance of the Report 305
Custodial responsibility of the report, 306
The time record, 307

CHAPTER 22: Training 309

The Loss Prevention Manger's Role in Training 309
Required training for employees, 309
Safety training, 313
Loss prevention officer training, 313
Performance Evaluation 314

Appendix 317

Glossary 336

Selected References 343

Websites of Interest 345

Index 347

PREFACE

The first recorded endeavor regarding retail security took place in England in about 1663 during the emergence of mercantile establishments. Specifically this consisted of a privately paid force of constables designed to patrol and protect business property at night. As the need arose, various private police groups began to concentrate and specialize by taking various forms as merchant police, dock police, and warehouse police. As paid organized police forces in the United States were beginning to appear during the mid-1800s, private security had its beginnings as a recognized entity when Alan Pinkerton formed a private security and detective agency specializing in investigative and security services on a nationwide basis.

Presently, within our society there are two broad areas of security and safety. The first is the legal or public sector, which includes the police, varied law enforcement agencies, and the prosecutors. These institutions along with the courts and corrections share a common goal to preserve the peace, prevent crime, and keep the community and its citizens safe. This public sector is commonly known as the criminal justice system.

Second, there is the private sector, which includes various contractual and proprietary types of private security, private investigators, executive protection and bodyguards, security alarm protection, and security consultants among others. They are employed by business and industry to protect the varied assets of a company. As an alternate to public law enforcement, there are thousands of private security companies that offer "contractual services" to business and industrial establishments. These services may include armed or unarmed personnel, with the hired officers attired in a uniform or not.

In addition, many firms employ their own security personnel as a means of more personal control and supervision. Such a security force can be tailored to a specific need or service. These "proprietary" security forces can encompass a one-person security unit up to a large security guard force that could include hundreds of officers.

For the police to provide protection for all the security needs of private business would entail large expenditures for police personnel, equipment, and ancillary services. The tax base would have to be enormous, and the general public would consider it excessive. Concerning private security, however, the cost of security protection is surreptitiously passed on to the public. Customers may not be aware that they pay for this security service along with loss by theft and damage as part of their purchase price. But if they were mindful of it, they would realize that the cost of service between a police officer and that of a security officer is great indeed. Along with salaries, benefits, and part-time employment, the cost to business in making use of private security is a cost benefit. Moreover, the possibility of conflicts could cause serious problems if there is a sense of favoritism by public officers toward one business over another.

As demands for police services along with their tasks are being increased daily, the need for protection in business and industry, and the community in general has heightened in proportions that are simply beyond the capabilities of the police alone. The focus on specialization and community policing has created a situation where police presence has been reduced in or toward the business community. In many areas of the country we find that the attention of the police has shifted from the prevention of crime to responding and investigating crimes that have already occurred. The businesses, in an attempt to secure and protect their investment, have turned to private security, so that they have some control over the losses they may suffer both internally and externally. Unfortunately, the cost of this control must be passed on to the consumer.

Because of its size in the workforce and the significance on business establishments, the security industry has drawn the attention of the legislatures, the courts, and the insurance sector. Although the security profession has become more refined technically and professionally in recent years, there are those instances where poor self-restraint and legal considerations are many times neglected.

In the last few years, some states had come to the conclusion that there were too many instances in which security guards were involved in unlawful circumstances, and in many cases, instances where they had little or no training. Numerous situations have come about where guards who were hired had questionable backgrounds, some with very serious criminal histories and who were placed in sensitive security positions. Employers complained that poor selection and training led to an increase in civil liability and litigation, especially so in recent years as the public in general became more forthright and aware of their right to sue, and the protection of their civil rights in particular. Some of these states realized that in an effort to correct this problem there should be some type of background check and training for all security guards employed in that state.

Subsequently, a few legislators found it was in the state's interest to require proper screening and hiring of all security guards, with guards meeting minimum standards in recruitment, investigation, training, certification, and licensing. Security guard companies, guard schools, and instructors have also come under scrutiny and are now obligated to some type of minimum requirements and certification.

Fundamentally, these concerns produced legislation to some degree now found in many states, and affects all security guards, including security officers, loss prevention officers, store detectives, guard and watch companies both contractual and proprietary operating within that state's boundaries.

The author would be neglectful if one particular subject was not covered at this juncture. Those states that have established guidelines and regulations concerning the hiring, training and licensing of security guards are to be commended. However, in recent years the acceptable applicant pool for guards has been reduced because of several factors. The most important factor being low wages, which cause qualified applicants to look elsewhere and find better paying jobs. Entry-level guards with law enforcement or military background are becoming harder to attract because of these low wages and poor benefits.

In many parts of the country, security firms or proprietary guard services offer little more than the minimum wage to begin employment. Moreover, it is not unusual for security guard firms to fall into bankruptcy or be dissolved after attempting to renew a contract at a lower rate, and then failing.

Low pay equals low standards and as long as the business establishment accepts these lowered requirements, the profession will suffer. So it should not come as a surprise for businesses to hear of increasing talk about unionizing security officers and guards. There have been some inroads in the area of proprietary services with demands of better pay and benefits. Contractual security guard firms will surely follow as guards affiliate with each other for a common goal, especially when enhanced responsibilities are added and hi-tech services and equipment become the norm.

Because business and industry wish to pay as little as possible for security services, excessive competition becomes the standard behavior. Consequently, security firms competing with each other by bidding low for a contract, inevitably result in cutting insurance costs, overhead expenses, and guards' salaries. Because of this competition, the service and the quality of the people offered have remained stagnant, if not lowered. Businesses that attempt to employ guards above the average in education and training soon discover that they may be able to get the "best offered" for the "cheapest price." Unfortunately, in an effort to cut costs and save money, a business soon learns that the security guards offered are poorly educated and trained, meet minimum dress standards, care less for their responsibilities, have little job satisfaction, and have limited loyalty to anyone.

As we have seen during the latter part of 2001, there has been a failure of appropriate safety in airport security checks of airline passengers. Many states have no restrictions or regulations concerning security guards, and until recently there had been no central agency that controls security guards employed at our airport terminals. Because of public exposure of the poorly trained guard at these locations since 9/11, the federal government has taken steps to federalize, train, regulate, and set a wage standard that will attract a higher level of applicant. However, the rest of the industry has failed to encourage the need for broad national or state requirements of trained security officers.

In the State of New York, which has licensing and training requirements for security officers, the New York Security Guard Advisory Council, whose members include security professionals in the field, are attempting to elevate the security industry as a whole. In effect, the council is considering the possibility of a "super guard" designation that would guarantee to businesses an officer with above average capabilities. Wackenhut Security, a national security firm, offers business corporations "traditional," "upscale," and "custom" security officers, with each designation guaranteeing different levels of training and background. Unfortunately, most businesses at this time choose the "traditional" guard and its lower cost.*

Today, technology is advancing at a rapid pace. Along with the ever-changing needs of our society and the possibility of loss due to numerous threats or risks, the security officer must be familiar with a vast category of rules, requirements, services, and criminal and civil law that the sworn police officer never had to experience fifty years ago.

Regulation has given rise to the standards of a security guard. The time of the "warm body" assigned to a fixed post and who is of no use when called upon has been relegated to the past. Business has come to realize, though somewhat slowly, that an inept and poorly trained security guard causes more problems financially and image-wise than not. As responsibility, training, certification, and ethical conduct become the norm, effective security officers will be well regarded and sought after, and the security profession will certainly attain compensation commensurate to their abilities and worth.

*Stephanie McCrummen, "Doing Business with Security Firms," *Newsday*—Long Island Business; Executive Edition, December 14, 1998.

ACKNOWLEGMENTS

The author would also like to thank the following reviewers: Alex del Carmen, University of Texas, Arlington, TX; Holly Dershem-Bruce, Dawson Community College, Glendive, MI; Shaun Gabbidon, Penn State University—Capital College, Middletown, PA; and Robert McCrie, John Jay College of Criminal Justice, New York, NY.

SPECIAL NOTE FROM THE AUTHOR

Nothing should be construed about how one should act or react based upon what is read or contained herein. The author accepts no liability of any type of damages, real, inferred or imagined, or for any professional injury, personal injury or property damage that might result from the use or misuse of any of the information, techniques, or applications presented or implied in this book. This book is intended as an educational and training publication and should not be considered a substitute for advice and consultation with your own attorney; only an attorney can give legal advice. New laws are enacted routinely, and court decisions are handed down daily. The author suggests that you use this book in conjunction with accepted procedures, current law, and legal advice from your counselor.

The commentary, citations, and case law described in this book have been summarized in most cases to illustrate a point under examination and are taken from previous holdings. For a full review of a particular case, the reader should refer to the published case citation.

Regarding state citations noted herein and elsewhere, precedent may be offered to the court when a holding has been handed down on a previous similar case from another state, and only when that state has no case for precedent, *may* the court defer to a decision from that other state. However, federal holdings or judgments handed down to a state court will be binding on all states.

In an endeavor for clarification, the term *security guard,* although generally accepted as pertaining to the uniformed security guard, is also identical in meaning to the term *security officer* when found in all case notes, law citations, and court decisions represented herein, and will be comparable to both designations unless so noted.

However, about retail security management in particular, there is a distinction concerning the functions and tasks between the security officer and the security guard as indicated in the following narrative.

Note also, that throughout this book, the author has used *italics* or ***bold italics*** for emphasis in order to highlight certain law citations, words, issues and/or topics of importance.

Introduction

A society legislates and adjudicates laws to control and regulate behavior for the common good. It is administered fairly with certain rights and recourse granted to anyone facing a legal action, and therefore within our society no one is above the law. Today, society in general and the individual in particular, are more aware and conscious of their personal and civil rights, and ready to impose sanctions on activity that will impair or damage those rights. In response to this, Americans have become much more litigious in the protection of their personage and the punishment of the offender.

Because of their positions and the circumstances that may befall them, the security officer and the police officer may be considered more susceptible to criminal and/or civil action against them and their employer than that of the average citizen. It is hoped that the contents of this book will make the security officer more aware of his or her conduct and actions, and how both may affect the officer criminally and civilly.

This book includes topics that should be part of the retail security officer's training curriculum, and is tailored to that specific field of security. Moreover, it will explain how security functions in a retail business environment, no matter how the retail establishment may differ in service, merchandise, or customer demographics. Think of this book as providing a general background into the retail security profession. More importantly, look upon it as a guide to your objectives, thought process, and performance.

Also, consider this book as a reference work. It is a compilation of the thoughts, ideas and procedures experienced and collected from various professional groups that the author has come in contact with. Along with the criminal intellect and nefarious inclination of some of our citizens, these groups include the police, security professionals, consultants, lawyers, criminal justice professors and security instructors.

In addition, it is hoped that this book will serve a second purpose. As noted above, the text was originally written for the reader who is about to enter or has some prior experience in retail security. It was written essentially as a primer or manual for the retail security officer where the present body of knowledge is lacking. Whether employed as a proprietary or contractual security officer, or as security supervisor, these officers should be able to relate and apply the narration contained in this book to their routine duties in any retail establishment. However, in the enhancement and prevailing interest of private security and its administration, we have seen a growing interest in academic instruction and training in recent years. Accordingly, this book is also directed to the student of security management and administration, who has little or no experience or understanding concerning retail loss prevention or private security in general. Although the student should be able to gain some knowledge and a broad perspective regarding the tasks and functions required of retail security, the law and the security principles described herein may be applied to all security employment. Moreover, it will lend an understanding of the legal process and the perils regarding criminal and civil litigation.

The law, narrative, and commentary described in this book are enumerated for the purpose of clarification in interpreting the law—or the law as it has been adjudicated. The security officer may relate the incidents or interpretations described herein to his or her own particular employment as a reference to mind-set and conduct in similar circumstances. If you wish to delve into a particular area of study, there are many associations, organizations, trade groups, agencies, and public institutions in which the security officer may research in detail any security subject that is contained within these pages. Remember that your eventual decision on how to act or react in a given situation, no matter how serious it may be, should in the final analysis be based on your actions within the law, your training, and your employer's policies and procedures. Other than your actions being subject to civil litigation, consider also that if you act in violation of your employer's directives regarding your actions, though legal and without criminal fault on your part, you may place yourself in jeopardy of termination.

Criminal and Civil Law for the Loss Prevention Officer

Part 1

LAW AND LIABILITY

INTRODUCTION TO LAW

American jurisprudence had its beginnings in English common law. After the Norman Conquest around 1066, William the Conqueror and his successors attempted to unite the country under a common rule. The Normans wanted a system of unity and control so that governing was made easier and accountable, but they also wanted to curtail the power and unrestrained private warfare among the various "manors" and "kingdoms" throughout the country. Before that period, the feudal lords of the land had full authority to render whatever judgment they deemed necessary for control of the populace, obedience to the lord, and ultimately to the king. There was no clear-cut differentiation between customs, religion, morality, and criminal offenses. Judgments, punishment, and sentences were haphazard and many times without fairness. Relinguishment of property, mutilation, and branding were common forms of punishment, and torture coupled with a death sentence was not uncommon. Although an offense in one part of the land may be a capital crime, the same crime may not be seen as such in another part of the country. Moreover, there was no established remedy for the common citizen concerning restitution for property loss or injury by another, and redress in any case was practically nonexistent.

Under the direction of William, the King's Court (*Curia Regis*) began to develop into a system of royal courts throughout England. Important decisions rendered in one county or shire by the justices of the King's Courts were written down in books. These books were called *reported cases* and included the key facts about the case, the issue of law, the legal principles expressed by the justices, their decisions, and the reasons for their decision. These reported cases became appropriate and applicable to the country as a whole and were known as *common law* because of their acceptance throughout England. Initially, this arrangement covered only actions where property, money, or injury was in question, and where money was sought as restitution. The king and his lords still had the power to mete out whatever punishment they wished upon the masses who may have committed some criminal act. It wasn't until the signing of the *Magna Carta* by King John in 1215 that the administration of justice and the relationship of the Crown (the exercise of royal power) was delineated to the people.

When the English began to settle in North America, they brought common law with them. As time passed, common law was incorporated into laws that were enacted and published for the common good. These laws were called *statutes* or *statutory law*, and were established by federal, state, or local authorities to control and regulate society. Because common law was adaptable to varied conditions in the North American colonies, the principles developed in that common law became the basic law of the entire United States. Common law is largely *case law*, which developed in the decisions of judges in actual cases tried before them. The terminology of common law and case law are many times used interchangeably. Because *statutory law* is legislative in its process, the terminology now used to differentiate both is statutory law and case law.

American jurisprudence is basically a legal process that is based on evolutionary law—a process in which a government develops a system of rules and regulations enforceable by penalties or sanctions to control the conduct of its people, all for the common good. Law as a process also includes court interpretation of state and federal laws by a judge who determines the meaning or the "spirit" intended by the enactors of the law, and how that law applies to a particular case before the court. This "law," at any given moment, is an ever-changing process. What may be considered a crime today may not be a crime tomorrow. Social, political, and business relationships are changing daily, so that a flexible system is required to accommodate the various problems and situations that are constantly arising.

Laws are rules that govern society. They are guidelines established by the people for the good of the inhabitants within that society. Society, as the state, will determine what constitutes a crime, and once determined, laws will be enacted by the lawmakers (legislators) of that society.

Whether state or federal government, the legislature (members elected by the people) will write and establish law for the benefit of all; the executive branch (police, prosecutors, and corrections) will enforce those laws; and the judicial branch (the courts) will punish the offenders. In essence, our legal system sets down our obligations to each other, prescribes the penalties for violating these obligations, and establishes the procedure to enforce these obligations.

Our laws are founded on the following:

STATUTORY LAW

Statutory law are the laws that are written down, enacted, and promulgated by society through their legislators. These laws may be enacted by local, town, city, county, state, or the federal government. They may apply to control crime, a person's actions or behavior, or a practice of a business or an agency, all for the good of that society. Laws are constantly being drawn and mandated, amended and repealed as society deems necessary. Again, what may be a crime today may not be a crime tomorrow.

Note that despite the importance of statutes and regulations, many areas of our law still consist almost entirely of court decisions (case law).

COMMON LAW

Common Law is law carried over to our country from English common law prior to our present and ever-changing justice system, when most if not all inhabitants were illiterate and there was no written law. Therefore, consistency of decisions was needed and categorically written down. Common law is distinguished from statutory law in that it is a body of law that develops and evolves through *judicial decision*—a case-by-case tradition. The courts are empowered to interpret statutes when a dispute arises about their meaning or intent, or a point of law comes into question, so that many areas of our law consist almost entirely of court decisions. Common law plays a strong role in our present legal system because common law provides authority not set down in statutory law, affords defenses, and renders an interpretation of those statutes. Basically, court opinions serve as authority or *precedent*, which is often binding and always of importance to subsequent court decisions.

Case Law

Case law is the principle that a court must stand by its previous decisions. It is usually referred to as precedent, and lawyers will search for these precedents in previously rendered decisions to help their present case before the court. However, application to the case will depend on a few factors:

- Whether the present court has the same legal jurisdiction (state or federal).
- The level of the court in which the decision was made (a lower or an appeals court).
- The similarity of facts in both cases.

Precedent

Precedent as defined means that a previously decided case, which is recognized as authority, may be applied to the disposition of future cases. However, attorneys for each side may find conflicting precedents to support their client's position. The courts are not bound to follow a precedent case in which the key facts are distinguishable from those in the case under consideration. Although appellate courts may follow their earlier case precedents, they also may reverse a long-standing decision if warranted by a change in social or economic circumstances. If so, the new precedent will negate the old precedent concerning the same principle of law.[1]

The Rule of Stare Decisis in Judicial Decisions

Applied throughout the United States, the *stare decisis* rule is that if a decision is rendered by a higher court of *the state in which a case is being tried*, and that decision could be applied to the case presently before the lower court, then the decision of the higher court is binding on the lower court and must be followed. But a higher court in one state could render a decision that may also be applicable to a case being tried in different state and taken into consideration, but need not be followed even with strong arguments by an attorney. This may occur because courts in different states may express different viewpoints as to the principles or the spirit of the law involved and to the application of that law. Any decision by the United States Supreme Court, the highest court in the land, found to be applicable in a case being tried in a lower federal or state court, must also be binding.

The Right for Redress

The United States has the highest proportion of lawsuits to population of any industrial nation in the world. California has more lawyers than all of Great Britain. There were more than ten million civil suits pending in federal and state courts in 1988,[2] and the numbers are growing yearly. There is no doubt that it is becoming easier and more readily acceptable than ever before to seek redress for some fault or perceived fault that may happen upon the average citizen.

Our country is based upon the rule of law that every citizen has the right for redress under the law, whether it is a criminal offense or a civil action. In recent years however, it is most popular to denounce our litigious society, and to condemn lawyers and claimants seeking some type of compensation in the courts as overzealous and greedy. The civil suit seeking compensatory and punitive damages for wrongful conduct is the most effective weapon against abuse and indifference by government entities, business corporations, insurance companies, and ordinary citizens. Nevertheless, it should also be noted that outrageous claims and frivolous lawsuits could cause more harm than good to the legal system. Because of this perception by the public, insurance companies have used those examples of frivolous suits to benefit their cause in order to make their case for insurance reform, and thereby watering down or taking away valuable rights.[3]

In any event, we must be more cognizant of the fact that more and more people are seeking civil redress. It is becoming more commonplace, and notably, with the courts awarding damages considered excessive in nature in many instances. Because of this, security officers must be more aware of their actions or reactions in the course of their duties and when dealing with the public.

With those precautions in mind, the following is presented to enlighten loss prevention officers to the law, their actions, and how it might effect them professionally and financially. Keep in mind that the criminal and civil law detailed here is based on statutory and case law and generalized for security officers throughout the United States.

THE LIABILITY THAT RETAIL SECURITY PERSONNEL MAY ENCOUNTER

Unless one becomes involved in the criminal or civil law process, distinction between the two may be somewhat nebulous to the average citizen. In actuality, there is a great difference between the two. It is a most important job-related responsibility that security officers become aware that there are two types of law that control their actions and make them subject to criminal charges or civil litigation if they commit a wrongful act. Loss prevention officers must have some background in the law and how it is enforced. To act without such knowledge places officers in legal jeopardy.

There are two types of law:

Criminal Law

Criminal law defines those offenses against the state (the people), and prescribes the punishment for their commission or omission. Crimes are circumscribed by legislation (written or statutory law) enacted by the U.S. Congress (federal law, rules, and regulations), and the various state legislatures (penal law, criminal code). Most criminal law is set by the states, but this past century has seen the federal government adopt its own criminal code to a great degree dealing with concerns outside of state boundaries or those that cross state boundaries.

These criminal laws define certain behavior as being illegal and upon conviction in court, such activity is punishable by a fine or imprisonment. If a crime has in fact been committed, the state must prove that the person charged (the defendant) did act as intended, or did not act as required.

Criminal law includes four basic offenses. Offenses may include infractions, violations, and the two levels of a crime. Infractions are those minor deeds that are usually found in the state's vehicle and traffic laws. Violations are usually those local village, town, county, or city ordinances that regulate certain behavior in certain areas such as environmental, health, conservation, or safety. A transgression of an infraction or a violation will usually result in a citation and a fine, and rarely, if ever, jail time. Violations are usually not classified as crimes, unless the ordinance notes that subsequent violations may raise the offense to the level of a crime. Only crimes are enumerated in criminal law and these crimes are classified as *misdemeanors* or *felonies*. For a full description of crimes, see OFFENSES defined in Chapter 4.

Civil Law

Civil law refers to that law relating to private rights and remedies sought by a party who has suffered a "wrong" or has been "damaged" in some manner. It is a noncriminal lawsuit involving an act that is considered a civil wrong.

When a person commits an act or fails to act as required, when there is no right or privilege to do so, and such an act or failure to act injures the person, property, or reputation of another, either directly or indirectly, it is a *civil wrong*. This is also called a *tort*, and the commission of a tort is a civil act and not a criminal act. Although a tort and a crime may be the same or similar in many cases, the parties, burden of proof, and damages are different. Civil (tort) law is produced by judges in their decisions handed down (common law), and by laws enacted by the legislatures (statutory law).

A wrong may consist of an injury or a harm to an individual or a group, and is classified as an *intentional* or a *negligent wrong*. There is another wrong that is categorized as a *strict liability tort*, which is a liability for making, selling, or presenting a defective product where a injury has occurred or may occur because of such product. See PRODUCTS LIABILITY in Chapter 1 for information on this tort.

The aim of the civil lawsuit is to seek relief for the damages that were suffered (*compensatory damages*) and to punish and/or deter another from committing the same or similar act (*punitive damages*). Recovery may be sought for loss of earnings, defamation, emotional distress, injury, pain and suffering, medical expenses, false arrest, and imprisonment. These compensatory damages are intended to compensate the injured or wronged party for any losses or injury he or she may have suffered. Damages sought and received are usually in the form of money, but action may also be brought against a person or business establishment in an effort to change a practice or a procedure. Punitive damages are awarded to punish the wrongdoer.

The following definitions are important to understanding the differences in legal terminology and how it applies to our comprehension of the law.

The Contrast between Criminal and Civil Law

Throughout this book, note that in civil law we will refer to the retailer, owner, agent, or security officer as the *defendant* or *defendants*. The person or group "falsely" arrested, injured, harmed, or damaged in some way is referred to as the *plaintiff* or *plaintiffs*. The plaintiffs are represented by their attorney, and the defendants are represented by the company's attorney or one provided by the insurance carrier.

This is in contrast to criminal law where the person accused, arrested, and charged is the *defendant*, and the retailer, owner, agent, or security officer, as the case may be, is the *complainant*. The defense attorney represents the criminal defendant and the prosecutor or district attorney represents the people of the state through the complainant.

The burden of proof in a civil case is a *preponderance of the evidence* (clear and convincing evidence), and if found for the plaintiff by a judge or jury, the plaintiff is entitled to money damages to compensate him for the injury or offense against him. In a criminal action, it may be said that the plaintiff is the state (the people) represented by the prosecutor or district attorney and the person charged is the defendant. The injured party or the victim of the crime is the complaining witness or the complainant, and the state must prove its case *beyond a reasonable doubt*. The burden of proof is much more demanding than in a civil trial. If found guilty, the defendant may be sentenced to pay a fine or to a term of incarceration. This sentence is paid to the state, and the injured party or victim receives nothing, other than the knowledge that justice has been served.

If a person commits a crime which may also be a tort, he or she may be tried separately in either or both the criminal and civil courts. The outcome of one court will not affect the outcome of the other court.

The implications and consequences, which can occur because of the actions or inactions of a security officer, can be harmful both criminally and financially, not only to the individual officer, but also to his or her employer and/or to the company he or she may be contracted to serve. Without a doubt, we can assume that most security personnel will be placed in some type of a liability or litigious situation at some time in their career, where some remedy will be sought by a litigant for some wrong or perceived wrong committed against them.

The security officer should be aware that people don't care if a badge signifies the term "security" or "police." If they can, they will claim that their constitutional rights were violated or some damage had been caused, and will attempt to seek some sort of remedy.

Remember that an action in criminal court does not negate an action in civil court. A person may be acquitted in criminal court for an offense, and subsequently sue the party who initiated that criminal action in civil court for damages. However, if the criminal defendant is found guilty, he may have a difficult time proving damages in civil court. Conversely, a complainant may charge a person for a crime and also sue in civil court for damages. The civil case may be bolstered by the fact that the criminal defendant pled or was found guilty.

Because civil and criminal liability is so important an issue, the purpose of the narration contained herein is to familiarize security personnel with the legal significance and consequences of certain aspects of the work they conduct on a daily basis.

Unless security officers have some familiarity and knowledge of the law, and are aware of the limitations of the law placed on their actions, any responsibility or duties required of them will be without foundation.

We will cover civil liability first since the culpable actions by security officers and the defensive remedies favorable to them can be readily defined in civil law, and easily applicable to criminal law. In addition, we will present an introduction into the process of civil litigation.

ENDNOTES

1. J. David Reitzel, et al., *Contemporary Business Law—Principles and Cases*, 4th ed. (New York: McGraw-Hill Publishing Co., 1990), p. 20.
2. Ibid., p. 6.
3. Ibid., pp. 5–7.

Chapter 1
Civil Liability

Before we consider criminal law and how the security officer should act in enforcing the law, it is essential that we understand civil liability and its financial effect on that officer.

Civil law may be defined as a body of laws that deal with the relationship between individuals, whereas criminal law deals with offenses against the state. Within civil law, civil liability includes the procedures for civil law actions based on *a violation of a legal duty or standard of care* (which may result from an accident), *an omission of an act or duty*, and *an intentional or a criminal act* (in which the plaintiff may have suffered).

INTENTIONAL AND NEGLIGENT WRONGS DEFINED

If a person suffers from some act, or a failure to act, when no privilege or right exists, and such act or failure injures the person, property, or reputation of another, directly or indirectly, it may be considered a *civil wrong*.

There are two types of "wrongs"—*intentional wrongs* (willful torts), and *negligent wrongs* (negligent torts). The plaintiff's complaint will note intentional and negligent wrongs, and it is possible that the security officer or other employee committed an intentional wrong, while the company may have committed a negligent wrong.

Consequently, a tort is a private or civil wrong for which the court will provide a remedy in the form of an action for damages. A personal tort involves an injury to the person or to the person's reputation and psyche, as distinguished from an injury or damage to real or personal property.

Several ways in which a company, an institution, or a person may be held liable in a civil action are described as follows:

A negligent tort.

During a report of a premises evacuation, which was a result of a fire in the building, the plaintiffs attempted to exit the building via a fire exit visibly marked as such, but found it to be locked and blocked by merchandise, thereby causing severe injuries to the plaintiffs because they were unable to exit safely.

Negligent hiring practices (negligent tort).

The company can be held liable if they hire an employee without a thorough background check or overlook certain prior behavior during the hiring process, and the employee thereafter commits a violent act while at work.

Negligent retention practices (negligent tort).

The company can be held liable if they have information regarding violent actions, possible violent acts, or threats by an employee, and no action or very little action is taken. Subsequently, the employee commits a violent act upon another.

Premises liability (negligent tort).

The company or institution can be held liable for damages in a civil court for any security issue where any *foreseeable act* can be established. A *foreseeable act* is a situation in which the owner or lessee of the premises failed to use *ordinary care* to reduce or eliminate an unreasonable risk of harm, one that was or may have been created by a condition on the premises the owner or lessee knew or should have known about so as to exercise reasonable and *ordinary care* (see *ordinary care* under NEGLIGENCE DEFINED on page 13).

Various intentional torts.

Concerning the actions by a security officer:

- A security officer arrested or placed the plaintiff into custody without cause.
- The security officer failed to have probable cause for the arrest and detention, but continued with the process and falsely requested of the police that the subject be charged with a crime, when in fact the security officer committed the crime of malicious prosecution.
- Prior to requesting the presence of the police, a security officer detained the defendant for an excessive amount of time causing emotional trauma.
- A security officer used derogatory and/or racial epithets against the plaintiff.
- The security officer, by his actions while consummating the arrest, embarrassed the plaintiff in front of family, friends, and/or passersby, thereby causing emotional trauma and a loss to the plaintiff's reputation.
- A security officer unnecessarily used excessive physical force upon the subject causing an injury.

To further clarify intentional and negligent wrongs, consider the following:

1. The employer was negligent in hiring the security officer with a known unfavorable background and propensity toward violence.
2. The employer was negligent in the training and supervision or lack thereof of the security officer.
3. The retailer in question kept disorderly, unsafe, and cluttered premises, causing the plaintiff to trip and fall over boxes and assorted trash placed or left in the aisle, thereby causing a severe injury to the plaintiff.

4. A security officer becomes angry with a customer and looses his temper. Without lawful motive or purpose, he strikes the customer in the face with his fist, causing a broken and bloody nose. The officer had no reason to strike the customer, and had not acted under any authority or duty required by his employer. Therefore, he acted outside of *the scope of his employment.*
5. The plaintiff was falsely arrested by the security officer invoking the processes of criminal law. The security officer realizes that the arrest he made was unlawful or without merit. However, he continues with the arrest and detention and requests police assistance to further process the subject. Upon arrival the police officer decides that after investigation and inquiry there is no basis for an arrest and prosecution, and to continue such an arrest would constitute *malicious prosecution.* The police officer is duty bound to refuse the security officer's "arrest" or to not proceed any further, and releases the subject.
6. By bringing criminal charges against the plaintiff, the security officer (by committing perjury) did enter and continue a malicious prosecution against the plaintiff. The jury does not believe all the facts as given by the security officer, and finds that there was no basis for an arrest and prosecution. The plaintiff was acquitted after trial, and subsequently initiates a civil action.
7. The security officer caused a battery upon the plaintiff in touching and/or striking the plaintiff with his hands and fists.
8. The plaintiff was falsely imprisoned, and improperly restrained and confined without probable cause and legal justification.
9. The security officer defamed the plaintiff by loudly calling him a "thief" in public, which was heard by a large crowd that had collected, and because of this, the plaintiff suffered a "loss of his reputation."
10. The plaintiff's civil rights were violated because he was called racial and derogatory names in public and in the privacy of the security office.
11. The plaintiff suffered "embarrassment" and "emotional distress" at the time of the incident and subsequently thereafter, and still has psychological issues that require ongoing medical attention.

In the above illustrations, numbers 1, 2, and 3 would be considered *negligent torts*, and numbers 6 through 11 would be *intentional or willful torts*. Regarding illustration number 4, the plaintiff could also possibly sue the security officer (intentional tort) and the company that employed that officer (poor supervision and training, and acting outside the scope of his employment—negligent tort). In illustration number 5, the security officer and the retailer is now placed in civil jeopardy for a false arrest.

The plaintiff could ask that *compensatory damages* (injury or harm to self, or damage to property only) and *punitive damages* (punishment of the wrongdoer for the wrong committed) be found against the store and/or the employees.

Regarding willful torts (intentional wrongs), the retailers' insurance carrier has the right in some states to refuse to become involved in a defense in this type of action, and therefore could leave the defendant in a civil suit without protection.

In a negligent tort (e.g., an auto accident, personal injury to a customer), the insurance carrier will cover the retailer as defined in the policy contract.

PREMISES LIABILITY

The Question of Security Negligence

A businessperson who maintains a premises upon which another can be expected to enter is under the affirmative duty to make every reasonable effort to remedy conditions that could *foreseeably* create or contribute to a dangerous hazard or crime-inducing risk. Essentially this has been interpreted as meaning that a *legal duty* is due to those persons who enter a business owner's property by taking certain care in protecting those persons against harm and injury. If as a result of this legal breach of duty, actual damages may have been suffered, the plaintiff may seek redress in a civil court.

Courts have awarded damages against business and property owners for injuries sustained under dangerous and threatening conditions, in addition to harm received at the hands of criminal assailants on the common law theory of negligence. The relationship between the party who suffers an injury or some type of damage (the plaintiff) and the property/business owner (the defendant) will depend on the degree of care expected by the damaged party and the care required by the property/business owner.

The plaintiff, in order to initiate a civil action, had a legal right to enter and remain on or within the company's establishment. The establishment may be considered a *public place* open to the public in that the company may invite the general public at large to enter the premises for the purpose of selling the company's products. Therefore, a plaintiff may fall into three categories—an invitee, a licensee, or a trespasser.

The Invitee. An *invitee* may be described as a customer, browser, or visitor who enters the premises open to the general public. The public, whether a customer who is on the premises ready and willing to purchase merchandise, just "browsing," or a visitor who is present legally for whatever reason is considered an invitee, and has *license and privilege* to be on the premises. A museum, a library, a supermarket, and a retail establishment would fall into this category of a place of public access. Moreover, a *business visitor* is a person who enters upon a business establishment for the purpose of some type of business dealing(s) or a business appointment with the retailer or the retailer's agent. An example might be a salesperson who enters for the purpose of selling or offering a product or service. The business visitor also has license and privilege. Both the public and the business visitor are protected under the invitee concept. The greatest degree of protection is given to the invitee in regard to negligence that may cause some harm or injury.

The Licensee. The *licensee* would include contractors or workers who are hired, contractually or not, to come on the premises for the purpose of repair, renovation, or other improvements. These workers enter the business establishment with an implied or express consent, and are considered licensees and do not have the same protection as the invitee. A licensee has less protection since any knowledge of a dangerous condition will prevent any recovery for damages if such would occur. Licensees are expected to accept the property as they find it and look out for their own welfare. In addition, the knowledge of any danger that may be known to that licensee, who then enters the premises, may preclude the licensee from any type of recovery. However, the retailer/business owner has a legal duty to advise the licensee of any danger or dangerous condition the owner is aware of prior to that licensee coming aboard.

The Trespasser. The *trespasser* is a person who enters upon a property unlawfully. This person does not have the implied or express consent of the business owner. In other words, the trespasser does not have license or privilege to enter thereon or therein.

Those who enter on or within a premise without consent, and without the right and privilege to do so, have no legal recourse if some injury or damage befalls them. Persons who fall into this category are trespassers as defined in the law, or persons who enter the premises for the purpose of committing a crime such as larceny, burglary, or assault. The owner or possessor of the property cannot be held liable for any harm or injury that may befall the trespasser. Although there have been some very rare instances in which a plaintiff, while committing a crime on a business premises, suffered some injury, whether caused by the trespasser's actions or not, and after a civil action subsequently was awarded damages in court. See TRESPASS in Chapter 5 for further details.

Negligence

Anytime there is the question of an injury or damage that a victim can attribute as being caused by negligence on the part of the retailer, we can be sure that there is the possibility of civil litigation against that retailer in the near future.

Negligence Defined. It is important at this point to define what the term *negligence* means as it relates to civil law. As defined in *Black's Law Dictionary*, negligence is the *omission* to do something that a reasonable person, guided by those considerations that ordinarily regulate human affairs, *would do*, or the doing of something that a reasonable and prudent person *would not do*. It can also be the failure to use such care as a reasonably prudent and careful individual would use under similar circumstances.

Negligence can be characterized chiefly by inadvertence, thoughtlessness, and inattention—an unintentional act by a person, which does not come within the standards established by law for the protection of the public at large (*negligent wrong*).

This is contrary to *wantonness* and *recklessness*, which is characterized by *willfulness or full awareness*—a voluntary or intentional act, either committed or omitted (*intentional wrong*).

Negligence can be further defined in the sense that the retailer, owner, or the lessee of the premises failed to use *ordinary care* to reduce or eliminate an unreasonable risk of harm, which was created by a condition on the premises that the retailer, owner, or lessee knew or should have known about so as to exercise reasonable and ordinary care.

Ordinary care may be defined as the retailer, owner, or lessee who *acted in a reasonable manner* in light of what he or she knew or should have known about a condition, and the risks that may be or have been caused by that condition. Moreover, the failure of the owner/lessee to use such ordinary care is *proximate cause* for the injury and/or damage, because a natural and continuous sequence may produce an event, and without such cause, the event would not have occurred. Further, the plaintiff must show that for a *proximate cause* to be present, the act or omission that occurred and complained of must be such that an ordinary person would or should have foreseen that injury or damage might reasonably result from that event, and failed to use ordinary prudence or care under the circumstances.

Actions such as those described above show how important reports and documented routine audits and inspections within a retail establishment are in providing *ordinary care* in identifying and correcting security and safety problems.

Basis for the Lawsuit. In order to show a claim for security negligence, the plaintiff must basically show the following:

- The retailer has a *legal duty* to take certain care and actions for the protection of customers and visitors coming onto the premises.
- The retailer knew or should have known that a crime or risk of injury and/or damage was *foreseeable* in the eyes of a reasonable person.
- The retailer failed to provide security, or a reasonable level of adequate security to prevent such a crime, risk of danger, or injury suffered by the plaintiff.
- The retailer's failure was a *proximate cause* for the damage suffered in the claim by the plaintiff.
- The plaintiff suffered actual damages and seeks redress because of the retailer's breach of *legal duty*.
- The plaintiff suffered damages because of the actions of a security officer acting within or outside of the *scope of his employment*.

VICARIOUS LIABILITY

Essentially, the intent of an action for vicarious liability is that damages awarded to the plaintiff against a security officer may not be as great as it would have been if the higher echelon and/or the corporation are included in the lawsuit. Basically, *vicarious liability* is the ability to include and lay a claim of liability against as many defendants as possible in the lawsuit so as to gain as much monetary damages as conceivable.

Vicarious liability may be considered a form of *strict liability*, because it is a liability without fault. This is somewhat different from a liability such as *negligence* where such form of liability *requires a breach of duty*, and *intentional liability*, which requires *intent or a willful act*, where such intent gives rise to an injury or a wrong.

But if the plaintiff was harmed or wronged by an employee in the *scope of his employment*, redress may be sought against that employee *and* his superiors. Therefore, vicarious liability may be imposed on one person or a company based on a civil wrong committed by another person. In retail loss prevention, vicarious liability will most assuredly arise if the plaintiff can show that the retailer is or may be liable for the willful conduct of a security officer employed to protect the company's assets, and acts within the *scope of his employment*.

Scope of Employment Defined

If a security officer commits an act that may be considered a wrong, the person who has been offended may seek redress in civil court for damages as a plaintiff. If there is no *breach of duty* by the business establishment, but the security guard did *act within the scope of his employment* by which there was an intentional or willful act where a wrong and some harm was suffered, the plaintiff may sue the security officer, manager, trainer, and employer.

Further, the term *scope of employment* may be defined as any act or action that is intended to benefit or further the employer's business. But if a security officer acts unlawfully, without reason, in violation of company policy and procedures, and without authority and duty required of his or her employer, that officer acts outside of his or her scope of employment. Be aware also that acts forbidden by the employer or outside of the confines of company policy may be found to be within the scope of employment. As an example the question may arise—at what point does the threat or use of force by a security officer in the performance of an arrest become excessive, and departs from the protection of a company's assets? Such an argument may have to be settled by the court.

DEFENSE BY A RETAILER IN A LAWSUIT

The best defense against liability for any business establishment regarding their employees, particularly security officers, is that *due diligence* be made in . . .

- The hiring process,
- The training process, and
- The subsequent effective supervision of that employee with written documentation of each process.

pPRODUCTS LIABILITY

Other than the negligence noted under premises liability, the question of other vulnerabilities by a retailer obtainable as damages by a plaintiff are not uncommon. One of the more litigious areas of liability a retailer may face is some loss or injury sustained by a customer after the purchase, which was caused by a product, article, or substance sold and carried by the merchant. This would include harm to a would-be customer while still on the retail premises caused by that product, article, or substance on display, offered for sale, or carried by the merchant.

Products liability refers to all parties along the chain from manufacturer to retailer of any product that may have caused damage (injury) to another. This "chain" includes the manufacturer, assembler, wholesaler, and retailer, whether already sold or on display. Any product that is proven to contain inherent defects causing harm to a consumer or user of the product, whether loaned, given, or sold, may be subject to a products liability lawsuit. The claim may be based on *negligence*, *strict liability*, or *breach of warranty*. The injured party must prove that the product was in fact defective based upon a design defect, a manufacturing defect, or a marketing defect.

The liability of a product may be defined as the legal responsibility that a manufacturer, distributor, or retailer has to compensate persons who are injured as a result of using the product. This liability allows a person to sue for damages when they have been injured or their property has been damaged because the product was *defective*.

The plaintiff must prove that there is a *causal connection* between the product's defect and the injury or harm suffered by the plaintiff, and that such defect did in fact exist when the product left the hands of the defendant. Also consider that it is not uncommon today for the retailer to be held strictly liable for product-related injuries, even when the product had been purchased years ago, was abused in some manner, was used other than designed, or was altered and made unsafe after the sale.

If the plaintiff suffers a misfortune based on a product, the plaintiff's attorney will attempt to attach liability regarding the product onto the manufacturer, distributor, or retailer (or all three vicariously), under the following general areas:

1. ***Design defect***—the product was defective or deficient in its manufacture or design, or was inappropriate for the purpose intended. Liability may also be based merely on the *negligent conduct* of the defendant in either the manufac-

ture or sale of the product. In addition, the manufacturer, distributor, and/or retailer may be held strictly liable for the *unreasonable dangerous nature of the product*. Unreasonable dangerous nature may include usefulness and desirability of the product, availability of other safer products that meet the same need, the likelihood of injury, and common knowledge and normal expectation of the danger among others.

2. ***Failure to warn***—the manufacturer or retailer failed to warn the consumer of known faults or defects that could harm the user, and failed to reclaim, recover, and/or remove from sale the defective product in a timely manner. This may include the continued marketing of a product that is known or should have been known to be unsafe.
3. ***Foreseeable misuse***—the manufacturer and/or retailer should have known that the product may be used other than intended or may be used more severely than the purpose designed. This may include the probability of counteracting the *implied warranty* of the product, where the manufacturer or retailer warrants that the goods or product is of good quality and fit for its ordinary purpose.

Chapter 2

Criminal Law and Liability

FALSE ARREST AND FALSE IMPRISONMENT

The essence of America's declaration of "life, liberty and the pursuit of happiness" is a citizen's freedom of movement. The taking away of a person's liberty, placing him in custody, and detaining him for a period of time is a serious matter that cannot be taken lightly under any circumstance. It doesn't matter whether the arrest was by a police officer, security officer, or an ordinary citizen, certain elements must be present to justify a legal arrest. Whatever justification exists, the actions of the person who makes the arrest will be carefully examined later at length in order to determine if such action was warranted and legal. Be assured that if unwarranted, there will be forthcoming litigation against the person who made the arrest.

A security officer is a private person, whether acting alone or in the employ of someone else. As a private person, he or she has minimal rights when it concerns the arrest of another, whereas a police officer has certain powers of arrest over that of the ordinary citizen. Therefore, the security officer (a private person) should be particularly cognizant that he or she can be held civilly liable for false arrest and false imprisonment if the offense or "crime" committed by the subject cannot be proven in a court of law. If the subject wins an acquittal in court, the arrest can be considered groundless and invalid.[1]

With that thought in mind, arrest and detention is examined in some detail in order to expose the security officer to the problems that can arise concerning such actions.

> *False arrest* is defined as the "unlawful restraint of an individual's personal liberty or his freedom of locomotion, . . . consisting of the detention of a person without his or her consent and without lawful authority."
> —*Black's Law Dictionary*.

In essence, it is physically detaining someone without the legal right to do so. False imprisonment may be defined as depriving a person of freedom of movement by holding that person in a confined space, by physical restraint, or by threats.

False arrest is simply another term for *false imprisonment*; they are synonymous in meaning. An arrest without the proper legal authority is a false arrest and because an arrest restrains the liberty of a person, it is also a false imprisonment. An individual may be detained or imprisoned by physical restraint, by a threat of violence, or the threat of a present harm.

So then we can say that false arrest is the unlawful detention of a person contrary to the will of the person detained, whether the arrest was with or without the process of law.[2]

The Elements of False Arrest

1. There Was an Intent to Confine

There is no false imprisonment unless the defendant (the security officer) *intended* to cause some type of confinement without legal process. Because confinement of a person is an "imprisonment," an illegal arrest is an illegal imprisonment. Such confinement or detention can be construed to be in any enclosure such as a store, an office, a restaurant, or in fact, any place of business. Enclosures can also include a fenced-in area, a hotel room, a home, a detention facility, an auto, or a hospital. It may also include the forcible detaining of a person on the public streets.

> The tort of *false imprisonment* is "the nonconsensual, intentional confinement of a person, without lawful privilege, for an appreciable length of time, however short."
> —*Black's Law Dictionary*

In order to show intent to confine, it must be proved that the arrest or imprisonment was caused, authorized, directed, or instigated by the defendant, and that some arrest or detention did in fact occur. Therefore, any physical detention is an imprisonment. However, detaining or detention need not be unlawful. It is determined to be a false imprisonment when the arrest is considered to be an illegal act (a false arrest).

In an effort to show how the courts interpret detention or confinement, the following commentary is drawn from various case law:

- When an employee was *suspected* of theft and was not allowed to leave the premises and subsequently not charged, *false imprisonment was found.*
- When a part-time employee was questioned during her regular work hours in familiar surroundings, was not threatened in any manner, and was free to leave at any time, but feared that she would be arrested or fired if she did leave, *action by the defendant did not constitute the detaining force necessary to establish the confinement required for false imprisonment.*
- When a customer in a restaurant was *suspected* of not paying, and was prevented from leaving, *this constituted intention to confine.*
- The use of force is not a necessary element of false imprisonment, although it may aggravate the damages. Any act by the defendant that restrains the plaintiff is sufficient.
- The restraint of a person's freedom of movement does not have to be induced by force. Threats by conduct or words may be sufficient.

2. There Was an Awareness of Confinement

False imprisonment is considered a dignitary tort (damage to one's personal being; emotions, prestige, or status) and as such, is not suffered unless *the victim knows* of the dignitary violation.

However, although a plaintiff may no longer have any recollection of his or her confinement, it does not mean that he or she was unaware of such confinement at the time. Alcohol or injuries may have confused or clouded the plaintiff's recollection.

Moreover, it appears that adjudication in many states does not require that a child or a mentally incompetent person be aware of his or her own confinement.

3. There Was No Consent to Confinement

A person's consent to confinement does not mean mere compliance or the sort of "voluntary conformity" that occurs when a person is threatened with arrest and volunteers to accompany the police to the stationhouse in the hope of clearing up the matter.

Even though a person seemingly chose to be arrested, it will not constitute consent if that person really had no alternative (police placing the plaintiff in a police car when told by the plaintiff he had nowhere to go). As an analogy, the reader may replace the term *police officer* with *security officer* in order to relate to the above.

Consent to confinement cannot be induced by threats, and the plaintiff's claim cannot be barred when the plaintiff was reasonably put in apprehension and that the use of force would be used against him if he did not consent. As noted, the use of force is not a necessary element of false imprisonment, although it may aggravate the damages.

4. The Confinement Was Not Privileged by Law

Defense to Lawful Detention. Many states, such as New York,[3] have a law that protects the retail mercantile establishment in that it provides a *defense for lawful detention*. These laws may also be known in some states as *merchant's privilege*. The security officer should be unquestionably aware that invoking the merchant's privilege against a possible thief might place the officer in jeopardy of a false arrest unless he or she is completely satisfied that all provisions of the law are complied with.

This and similar laws mandate that retailers have an affirmative defense for any action brought against them for false arrest or false imprisonment, unlawful detention, defamation of character, assault, trespass or invasion of civil rights, brought by a person by reason of having been detained on or in the immediate vicinity of the premises of a retail/mercantile establishment. It is considered to be a lawful defense if the person was detained in a reasonable manner and for a reasonable time for the purpose of investigation or questioning as to the ownership of any merchandise.

Moreover, the statute may further define lawful detention as a defense to an action wherein the person was detained in a reasonable manner and for not more than a reasonable time to permit such investigation or questioning by the owner, the authorized employee, or an agent of a retail mercantile establishment, and that such owner, employee, or agent had reasonable grounds to believe that the person so detained was guilty of criminal possession of an anti-security item or was committing or attempting to commit larceny on such premises of such merchandise.

Under these circumstances "*reasonable grounds*" shall include, but are not limited to, knowledge that a person has concealed possession of unpurchased merchandise of the retail mercantile establishment, or has possession of an item designed for the purpose of overcoming detection of security markings attachments placed on merchandise offered for sale at such an establishment. In addition, "*reasonable time*" shall mean the time necessary to permit the person detained to make a statement or to refuse to make a statement, and the time necessary to examine employees and records of the mercantile establishment relative to the ownership of the merchandise, or possession of such an item or device.

Therefore, those states that offer these laws as a safeguard permit the merchant and/or his agent the right to detain a person if they suspect that person has committed a crime. Remember that the merchant or his agent must have *reasonable grounds to believe* the subject unlawfully possessed an anti-security item, or was committing or attempting to commit a larceny on such premises of such merchandise.

Bear in mind that *reasonable grounds may be equated to probable cause*. It is a conclusion derived upon by an ordinary reasonable person based upon the facts and circumstances of that particular situation. Additionally, reasonable cause to believe that a person has committed an offense exists when evidence or information that appears reliable discloses facts or circumstances, which are collectively of such weight and persuasiveness as to convince a person of ordinary intelligence, judgment, and experience that it is reasonably likely that such offense was committed and that such person committed it. With caution, the security officer may consider such apparent reliable evidence to include or consist of hearsay not alone in itself, but for further inquiry and investigation or in addition to other evidence.

Under this defense of lawful detention, the security officer must act wholly on the basis of facts in which a reasonably prudent, cautious, intelligent person would conclude that a larceny has been committed by a person under observation, and that the suspect intends to take, steal, and carry away property not belonging to the suspect. The retailer's right to make an apprehension under the law and charge the suspect in a court of law is not dependent on guilt or innocence after a court proceeding. If the state in which the security officer is employed is protected by this type of statute, this law will protect the retailer as long as he or his agent acted within the confines of the law. These laws offer a retail merchant a defense, and are enacted to protect merchants from civil litigation even where criminal actions are eventually dismissed. If for some reason, the defendant is found not guilty of the offense, the defendant has no recourse against the retailer for false arrest or imprisonment.

In addition, many of these state statutes protecting merchants in actions of detention in a store may be intended to reach a host of imaginative devices by which merchants are put upon, such as shoplifting, the use of stolen credit cards, issuance of worthless checks or other means, regardless of the device used. The elements that must be present are that a larceny take place in a retail establishment, and that object of the miscreant's activity and desire to steal be merchandise.

Also, when the plaintiff in a civil action attempts to prove a false arrest or unlawful detention, the defendant has under this law the burden of establishing that he had *reasonable grounds* or *probable cause* for the belief that the person detained or arrested was committing or attempting to commit larceny on the store premises. Further, that under the evidence, the detention and arrest of the plaintiff was reasonable and accomplished in a reasonable manner, and that the defendant had reasonable grounds to believe that the plaintiff had committed or attempted to commit the larceny for which he was charged, tried, and acquitted.

It is important to reiterate that whatever the method of larceny, for the security officer to justify a defense for detention, he or she should use caution concerning any criminal act by a finding of probable cause before an apprehension and detention.

THE PRESENCE OF PROBABLE CAUSE

Generally, probable cause is more specific to the police than the private person. However, there has been case law in which decisions have been rendered when probable cause became an issue in favor of the security officer and his or her actions. In essence, the courts have found that if a crime had been committed and that such act was observed and committed in the officer's presence, it therefore constituted probable cause for the officer to make the arrest. Accordingly, at this time, probable cause required for the security officer to act has been broadened somewhat to include other factors that may lead up to probable cause.

The presence of probable cause to act in a given situation must be considered one of the most important determining factors that a security officer or guard must determine before initiating any overt action in an apprehension. It doesn't matter if the occurrence in question is a larceny or any other crime—the facts must be present for probable cause before any response takes place. If the defendant in a criminal action is acquitted at a later time for whatever reason, the security officer's actions concerning the arrest will be under scrutiny. If it is found that the apprehension was made with little or no probable cause, the former defendant may now become a plaintiff in a civil suit against the officer, the retailer, and whoever else was involved in the incident.

In any case of lawful action against a person, there must be probable cause for the security officer to act.

Probable Cause Defined

Probable cause relates to reasonable cause. According to *Black's Law Dictionary*, probable cause is "having more evidence for than against . . . more than mere suspicion."

The terms *reasonable grounds*, *reasonably believes*, and *probable cause* may be considered synonymous.

- Probable cause may be defined as facts and circumstances that would lead a reasonably prudent person in like circumstances to believe the defendant (the perpetrator) is guilty; or
- The existence of such facts and circumstances as would excite belief in a reasonable mind acting on the facts within the knowledge of the prosecutor, that the person charged was guilty of the offense for which he or she was or is being prosecuted; or
- Such a state of facts and circumstances as would lead a person of ordinary questioning and prudence, acting consciously, impartially, reasonably and without prejudice, upon the facts, within his or her knowledge, to believe that the person accused is guilty; or
- As a reasonable ground of suspicion, supported by circumstance sufficiently strong in itself to warn a reasonable prudent person in his or her belief that the person accused is guilty of the offense as charged.

Probable Cause

Probable cause is a conclusion reached by a *reasonable person* after examining all of the facts and circumstances relating to the question at issue, and once determining that an offense did take place and was in fact committed by the perpetrator, an arrest of that perpetrator can take place.

Reasonable Person Defined

A *reasonable person* (in our case, a security officer) may be defined as a person of ordinary intelligence, experience, and judgment (the average citizen) who acts on what he or she reasonably believes to be true.

Reasonable Grounds Defined

As defined by some courts, the retail merchant (as well as employees and agents) have been granted certain privileges (merchant's privilege) when it comes to the apprehension, arrest, and detention of a suspected thief. Under these statutes, *reasonable grounds* may be defined as including, but not limited to, knowledge that a person has possession of unpurchased merchandise concealed on his or her person, which belongs to the retail establishment.

If *merchant's privilege* or *defense to lawful detention* statutes have been enacted in your state, they most probably include the following:

- The merchant has a complete defense to any civil action if there are reasonable grounds for the detention, notwithstanding the outcome of any criminal action, the actual guilt or innocence of the accused, or whether or not a crime was in fact committed.
- The retail merchant has a defense in an action for false arrest and imprisonment for the detention of a suspect shoplifter if the detention was reasonable, even if the criminal action against the accused was dismissed.
- The retail merchant may act upon what appears to be true even though it may turn out to be false, provided the merchant believes it to be true and the appearances are sufficient to justify such a belief.
- Additionally, when merchandise has admittedly been taken with neither payment nor exculpatory explanation (a reasonable excuse for a person's actions), the merchant's statutory defense is established whether or not the accused has the required intent to commit the crime.
- Whether or not the accused is found guilty of the crime he or she was arrested for, the security officer must be conscious that the officer's actions in the arrest and detention was based upon reasonable grounds and reasonable belief according to the law, so that in any event, the officer has the privilege of a defense.

However, no matter whether there was complete justification to make an arrest, jury verdicts can sometimes cause bewilderment. Because facts and circumstances will define how the court or a jury will view a case and render a verdict, some previous decisions described below will cause the security officer to use caution and question his own actions based on reasonable grounds.

In a civil case, whether the defendant (the retailer) had reasonable grounds for detention or not *may* be considered a jury question.

In a criminal case, the defendant's (the arrested perpetrator's) testimony was that after he placed merchandise in a shopping bag without paying for it, was leaving the store and headed for the street, and while holding the inner vestibule door and facing inward was apprehended by a security officer. The defendant immediately admitted he had not paid for the merchandise, but further stated that he was about to pay and then proceeded to the counter, tendered $20.00 but was arrested. Evidence was insufficient to establish that the security officer had probable cause to make the arrest. The defendant was acquitted because the jury questioned whether there was reasonable grounds for the arrest.

If the merchant's privilege or similar law is applicable in your state, a merchant may use it as an affirmative defense action permitting a private individual to detain a subject in a reasonable manner, in which the merchant has probable cause to believe the subject was committing or attempting to commit larceny of merchandise on the premises of a retail mercantile establishment. But it will not be applicable as a defense in an action for false imprisonment when the subject who was detained was accused of stealing cash and not merchandise, and therefore, the retailer could not invoke that part of the law.

In another case, the storekeeper was entitled to invoke such a defense when the plaintiff was not detained on suspicion of shoplifting but on suspicion of passing counterfeit money.

Reasonable Time and Manner Defined

One of the more important points that a litigant's attorney will look for in order to substantiate and bolster his case is to find if his or her client, the plaintiff, was handled in a reasonable time and manner. The attorney will attempt to determine if the plaintiff was subjected to unlawful actions or delaying tactics, overly dragged-out procedures, embarrassing overexposure of the accused to the public, or any other exposure or procedure that had "damaged" his or her client in some way.

Many laws affecting the retailer may define *reasonable time* to mean the time necessary to permit the person detained to make a statement or to refuse to make a statement, the time necessary to examine employees and records of the mercantile establishment relative to the ownership and value of the merchandise, the time required for the compilation of necessary reports, and ordinary arrest procedures prior to turning the defendant over to the police.

The manner in which a suspect is handled would be based on lawful and reasonable custodial and arrest tactics, which may be found in several areas of the various criminal codes and criminal procedures, including the necessary force that may be employed to effectuate an arrest, the protection of the accused and other persons, and detention procedures among others.

Presumptions and the Burden of Proof

Regarding a civil litigation, except as otherwise provided by law, the burden of proof requires proof by *a preponderance of the evidence*. This is the opposite of a criminal action where all the evidence of the crime must be proved by the state *beyond a reasonable doubt.*

To sustain an action for false arrest, the *plaintiff* has the burden of proof in initially establishing specific elements that will constitute his or her claim for a false arrest. Notwithstanding, in any litigation regarding a false arrest case, the *defendant* has the burden of proving legal justification as an affirmative defense.

When the accused becomes the plaintiff in a civil case and establishes what he or she believes to be the elements of a false arrest or an unlawful detention, the defendant has the burden of proving to the court that it had reasonable grounds or probable cause for the belief that the accused committed, was committing, or attempted to commit a larceny on the store's premises. The plaintiff need not prove that the defendant lacked probable cause to make the arrest, but the existence of probable cause is a defense by the defendant that will defeat the action.

Reasonable grounds or probable cause does not depend on the guilt or innocence of the accused or upon whether a crime has in fact been committed or attempted. The merchant or his or her agent (the security officer) may act upon what appears to be true even though it may turn out to be false, provided that the merchant or his or her agent believes it to be true and the appearances are sufficient to justify that such belief is reasonable.

Factors Leading to a Probable Cause Conclusion

Other than concealment and suspicious activity, which may or may not give rise to probable cause, some courts have noted that it would be almost impossible to list all situations indicating theft. However, these courts have listed some factors in their decisions for the security officer in leading to his or her probable cause:

It will be particularly relevant that the defendant (the accused) concealed the goods under clothing or in a container. Such conduct is not generally expected in a self-service store and may in a proper case be deemed an exercise of dominion and control inconsistent with the store's continued rights.

Other furtive or unusual behavior on the part of the defendant should also be weighed. Thus, if the defendant surveys the area while secreting the merchandise, or abandons his or her own property in exchange for the concealed goods, this may evince larcenous rather than innocent behavior.

Relative also, is the customer's proximity to or movement toward one of the store's exits. Certainly, it is highly probative of guilt that the customer, who was in possession of secretive goods, just a few short steps from the door or moving in that direction, passes the last cash register in which he or she has the opportunity to pay for merchandise.

Possession of a known shoplifting device actually used to conceal merchandise, such as a specially designed outer garment or a carrying case with a false bottom, would be all but decisive of intent.

Of course, in a particular case, any one or any combination of these factors may take on special significance. There may be other considerations that should be examined. So long as it bears upon the principal issue—whether the shopper exercised control wholly inconsistent with the owner's continued right—any attending circumstance is relevant and may be taken into account.

In conclusion, when a security officer has *reasonable grounds* to believe that a person is shoplifting merchandise from the store, these defense of lawful detention or merchant's privilege laws give the officer privilege to stop and detain that person for a *reasonable time*, and in a *reasonable manner* for the purpose of further investigation in order to determine if in fact a crime has been committed.

All security officers should research their state's civil and criminal laws, which may make available to the retail merchant and authorized employees any defense to a action for false arrest, false imprisonment, or unlawful detention.

MALICIOUS PROSECUTION

Malicious prosecution is a prosecution that is begun with malice and without probable cause to believe that the charges and such action can be sustained, and finally ends in failure.

> ***Cautionary Note***
> Security officers must be cognizant in how their actions and reasoning for a prima facie case resulting in an arrest will be subject to review by the police. When the police respond at the officer's request, and they determine after their investigation that there is no basis for an arrest and prosecution, they are duty bound to refuse to proceed any further and must release the subject. To do otherwise would place them in jeopardy of malicious prosecution.

If a person is taken into custody by a security officer and it is then determined that the elements for the arrest are not present, it would be more advantageous to "unarrest" and release the subject, rather than continue the act and become involved in an action for false arrest and malicious prosecution. Any course of action to stop and release the suspect with apologies despite the belief that probable cause may have existed at the time of the apprehension will show *good faith* on the part of the security officer or the officer's manager. At that point, when the subject is released from custody, there is a great probability that the subject will hire an attorney for the initiation of a civil action against you and your company. Even if the court acts upon subsequent litigation at a later time regarding false arrest and it is found for the plaintiff, it will never be as serious as it would be if a merchant or security officer continued to proceed on a bad arrest. The motivation here is not to aggravate or escalate the incident, but rather to stop the activity from becoming much more serious.

To reiterate, be aware that a police officer, who has been called to the scene at the request of a security officer for the criminal processing of an accused person, does not have the obligation of entertaining the security officer's complaint. Based upon the facts in the case, the police may refuse to accept custody of the "citizen's arrest" declaring that the elements for the crime and/or the arrest are not present. The police are then obliged to release the accused from custody, but by doing so, they thereby place the security officer in a possible litigious situation.

The Elements of Malicious Prosecution

The elements for a cause of action for malicious prosecution by a plaintiff are as follows:

1. The Commencement or Continuation of a Proceeding

To satisfy this element the proceeding must have commenced or was continued by the defendant against the plaintiff and must be judicial in nature. Commencement of an action could include the serving of a summons, by mail or otherwise. A cause of action for malicious prosecution by the plaintiff does not arise out of a prior civil proceeding *unless* in that previous proceeding there was some interference with the person or property of the plaintiff, such as an arrest, attachment, injunction, receivership, or notice of pendency.

If the other necessary elements noted below are present, a previous criminal or extradition proceeding against the plaintiff will give rise to a cause of action *from* malicious prosecution.

2. The Proceeding Was Terminated in Favor of the Plaintiff

This element will be satisfied by any termination in favor of the plaintiff on the merits as the result of a judicial decision, regardless of the basis of that decision. A favorable termination can also be shown when there is an acquittal. Additionally, there are two other instances when a favorable termination can be found—absent of any evidence of a fraud or compromise, the favorable termination of a previous criminal proceeding may be shown by the fact that the complaint was withdrawn, or that the complaint was dismissed for lack of either prosecution or evidence, or on a motion by the accused. Second, the voluntary discontinuance of a previous civil action by the plaintiff *not* as a result of a compromise, inducement, trick, or device of the defendant is a sufficient favorable termination to support an action for malicious prosecution against the defendant.

Conversely, a favorable termination is not shown where the ending of the previous action appears inconclusive or was affected by a settlement or some fraud, or where the plaintiff's case was dismissed because of the prosecutor's failure to procure a speedy sentencing. Further, there is no favorable termination when there was an "adjournment in contemplation of dismissal," which is neither a conviction or an acquittal, and therefore leaves open the question of guilt, or when the plaintiff's sentence was suspended, which is in fact a conviction. Also, the previous action in which the plaintiff complains must be terminated *totally and not partially* in the plaintiff's favor, in that it is not enough that one cause of action against the plaintiff was dismissed but that a second still awaits adjudication.

3. There Was an Absence of Probable Cause for the Proceeding

Generally, a defendant who had *probable cause* to subject the plaintiff to a reasonable detention has a complete defense to a cause of action for false arrest and imprisonment (see definition of PROBABLE CAUSE on page 21). Therefore, if probable cause does exist for the initial action by the defendant, it will serve to bar any action by the plaintiff for malicious prosecution. However, the plaintiff can initiate an action for malicious prosecution even though the plaintiff has not been falsely arrested, imprisoned, or detained, if the defendant between the time of arrest and detention and the time of prosecution knows some intervening fact exonerating the plaintiff.

- ***Defendant's good faith belief***—The defendant's belief in the guilt of the person he or she charges with a crime is not enough to be exonerated in an action for malicious prosecution; there must also be probable cause for the belief.
- ***Reliance on information from others***—The defendant may show as justification of probable cause that he or she had reasonable reliance on information received from others. This rule has been applied where the defendant relied on a report of a private investigator, and the word of an employee who had been in the defendant's employ for many years and had proved to be honest and reliable. Generally, to rely on this information only would not be enough without some type of corroboration.
- ***Mistaken identification***—One can make a mistake about the identity of another if the party acted reasonably under the circumstances in *good faith*. For example, the liability of a person who mistakenly identifies another as a criminal depends on the good faith and reasonableness of the person's identification, or the good faith on a clearly sound identification by another person.

- ***Extent of investigation by the defendant*** —The defendant has probable cause to file criminal charges against the accused *only* if he or she believes, and a reasonably prudent person in the same position would believe, that he or she has sufficient information and evidence to do so without further investigation.
- ***Plaintiff's possession of stolen property*** —Absent of some reasonable explanation by the accused, possession by the accused of recently stolen property belonging to the defendant is probable cause for the prosecution of the accused with an appropriate charge connected with the larceny, and will avoid liability on the part of the prosecutor for malicious prosecution. See CRIMINAL POSSESSION OF STOLEN PROPERTY on page 85 for details on this crime.

4. The Defendant Was Motivated by Actual Malice

Malice is defined as conscious falsity—a wrongful act done intentionally without just cause or excuse, in that the plaintiff must prove that the defendant commenced the criminal proceedings with actual and not implied malice.

According to *Black's Law Dictionary*, in the law of malicious prosecution, it means that the prosecution was instituted primarily because of a purpose other than that of bringing an offender to justice.

In addition, malice may also be defined as a condition of mind that prompts a person to do a wrongful act willfully, that is, on purpose to the injury of another, or to intentionally do a wrongful act toward another without justification or excuse. Malice in law is not necessarily personal hate or ill will, but it is that state of mind that is reckless of law and of the legal rights of the citizen.

Malice may be inferred in several ways. It will be sufficient to show malice where the defendant commenced the prior proceeding because of a wrong or improper motive, or some intent other than to see that justice was served. Malice can be inferred from a lack of probable cause, the defendant's unnecessary zeal, eagerness and activity, or from the total circumstances of the incident regarding the relationship of the parties and the objects of concern.

Malice may also be inferred by conduct inconsistent with proper motives. It may be presumed from gross or culpable negligence such as the failure to make reasonable inquiries before beginning any proceeding, or from wanton and reckless disregard of rights of others, but not from ordinary negligence.

5. Damage Was Suffered by the Plaintiff

We must be cognizant of the fact that too often the actions by a security officer in any apprehension or confrontation will be subject to intensive review by the defendant and his or her attorney soon after the occurrence. This examination by the attorney is to determine if in fact the arrest and/or imprisonment was justified and legal. Basically the attorney will wish to determine that there was insufficient or no probable cause for the actions by the security officer against his or her client, or if any excessive force or abuses took place. In this way the attorney is able to lay a defense in court for dismissal, and once dismissed, to initiate civil action against all parties concerned. If a civil action is considered, the defendant (criminal) now becomes the plaintiff (civil).

Damages recoverable by the plaintiff could include *compensatory damages* (injury or harm to self or damage to property only) and *punitive damages* (awarded as punishment to the wrongdoer for the wrong he or she did) with responsibility found against the company and/or the employees.

Additional information on compensatory and punitive damages follows.

DAMAGES

In an effort to show how detrimental and costly illegal and wrongful acts can be to the merchant and the security officer, the following concerns are explained in detail.

As we have seen, when the plaintiff feels he or she has suffered a wrong and initiates a lawsuit in civil court for some type of recovery, damages may be awarded to the plaintiff by the court after adjudication.

Damages may be defined as some type of compensation that can be recovered in court by a person (the plaintiff) who has suffered a loss, detriment or injury to person, property, or rights by the unlawful act, breach of some duty, omission, or negligence of another.

The "other" party in the civil case is considered a defendant—the person or persons, company or others, individually or as a group, that allegedly caused the loss, injury, etc.

Those "wrongs" suffered by a plaintiff may include a range of actions committed by another person, and may encompass false arrest, false imprisonment, assault, pain and suffering, and emotional distress among others.

The damages sought are usually in the form of money, and may be *compensatory* or *punitive*. The awarding of these "damages" are disbursed for the actual loss suffered or as punishment for the offensive and/or excessive conduct committed by the defendant, and to deter any future transgression by the defendant or anyone else in similar circumstances. Although money damages are frequently sought, it may not be necessarily so. A plaintiff may seek to change a procedure, process, or practice conducted by a corporation or organization that may affect one or more persons, and as such may sue as an individual or as a class of individuals.

Compensatory Damages

Defined as compensation to the plaintiff for the injury sustained, which includes restitution, harm, personal injury, or property loss. As the name suggests, the intent here is to compensate the injured party for loss or injury.

Generally, the measure of damages for false arrest and detention is a sum of money that will fairly and reasonably compensate an injured person for injuries caused by the defendant's wrongful act. Injuries can include, among others, medical expenses, legal fees, loss of income, and/or loss of future income, which will be awarded under *compensatory damages*.

Damages are defined as compensation to the plaintiff, which the law will award for an injury. The damages for false arrest/false imprisonment under the law will be measured from the time of the actual arrest to the time of arraignment or indictment, whichever occurs first. The reasoning is that an arraignment or indictment involves a separate and independent evaluation of the grounds for the charges against the accused. Therefore, the detention of the accused subsequent to such an evaluation cannot be attributed to the unlawful arrest since there has been an independent determination of probable cause to hold the accused, which thereby terminates the liability for the arrestor at that point.

Punitive Damages

Defined as exemplary or punitive damages, which are awarded to the plaintiff over and above that which barely compensates the plaintiff for money or property loss where the wrong was with violence, oppression, malice, fraud, or wanton, wicked, or reckless conduct by the defendant. The intent is to repay the plaintiff for quality of life after suffering the injury, and to punish the defendant for wrongful behavior and to set an example.

This payment could include those injuries to the plaintiff such as the plaintiff's reputation, standing in the community, shame, disgrace, humiliation, embarrassment, pain, and emotional and mental suffering. Any or all may have been suffered by the plaintiff and are considered under *punitive damages*. Moreover, punitive damages to the plaintiff can be awarded in an action for false imprisonment only where malice has been proved. The record must demonstrate that there was actual malice on the part of the defendant or defendants, or such wantonness or recklessness in their actions as to imply or permit the inference of malice. Therefore, punitive damages may also include and be awarded as a sum of money in an effort to send a message to the defendant that a serious wrongful act did in fact occur and should not have occurred, and severe punishment must be placed against the defendant for such actions.

The defendant may attempt to show "*good faith*" in his or her actions, but good faith will not rectify an otherwise unlawful arrest. But where established, proof of good faith is relevant to mitigation of damages, and may result in nominal damages to the plaintiff.

Compensatory Damages

Those damages awarded as fair and reasonable compensation for pain, injury, humiliation, disability, expenses or some loss suffered by the plaintiff because of actions by the defendant.

Punitive Damages

Awarded in reality to punish the defendant for wrongful actions, and to serve notice as an example to others that such actions will not be tolerated.

The Measurement of Damages Awarded

When the plaintiff establishes that both false imprisonment and malicious prosecution took place, damages for false arrest are measured up to the time of arraignment or indictment, and damages for malicious prosecution are measured from the time of the arraignment or indictment, to the conclusion of the criminal prosecution.

Damages for Malicious Prosecution

An action for damages concerning malicious prosecution may be brought by a person who has been acquitted of a criminal action, or the termination of a civil suit in the person's favor. One who takes an unlawful active part in the initiation, continuation, or procurement of civil or criminal proceedings against another may be liable to that person.

Malicious prosecution actions usually involve "damage or injury" inflicted on the plaintiff's reputation, character, feelings, employment, business opportunities for employment, credit, health, and well-being. In addition, damages may be awarded for imprisonment, the cost of counsel to defend the prior action, mental suffering, and humiliation. A spouse has a cause of action for loss of consortium based upon the false imprisonment of the other spouse. Any other damages or injuries are restricted to the person who suffered the hurt and not the spouse.

Note that although probable cause was present at the time of the arrest, some fact or facts could come to light at a later time that would eliminate that probable cause, and if probable cause no longer was present by the time of arraignment or indictment, and the complainant (the security officer) continued the action, malicious prosecution may then be a fact. Where malicious prosecution was not established, and where a false arrest action was found for the plaintiff, such action would be limited to recovery as damages of legal fees incurred up to and including the arraignment.

Malicious Prosecution and Vicarious Liability

Relevant to malicious prosecution, the security officer must be cognizant of vicarious liability. In tort law, vicarious liability refers to the liability assessed against one party due to the actions of another party. Simply put, the plaintiff may sue for damages against the security officer for the officer's actions, including his or her supervisor, manager, trainer, the retailer, and whoever else can be made a party to the suit. The plaintiff's attorney will attempt to bring as many defendants into the lawsuit as possible in order to increase the monetary award.

The Awarding of Damages

The following examples of court decisions are some indication of why damages may or may not be awarded to the plaintiff:

The retail mercantile establishment has the duty to take appropriate measures to avoid mishandling customers; it has the duty to provide not only a physically safe place, but one in which customers will not come to emotional harm, embarrassment, humiliation, and mental anguish because of a negligent operation of premises with respect to detention of customers who are suspected of shoplifting.

The conduct of security personnel must be wanton or malicious to warrant punitive damages.

An award of punitive damages against a store will most assuredly be upheld in an incident that involves the ridiculing and/or the unnecessary roughness and handcuffing of a mentally retarded or slow-witted customer. Witnesses to these events will actively come forward against the security officer because of what they perceive to be an outrageous act.

Conviction of the criminal offense is viewed as establishing the existence of probable cause for the arrest, and the defendant cannot recover under any circumstances for a false arrest if in fact the defendant was convicted of the offense for which he or she was arrested and charged.

In an action for false arrest, acquittal after trial or other dismissal of the criminal action has no effect on the disposition of a civil suit. The key issue in a civil action is whether the security officer had "*reasonable grounds*" for the detention.

DEFAMATION

When a person is called a thief in public for everyone to hear, he or she may have been defamed. If a person is accused of a crime where other people become aware of this accusation, and when in fact that person is innocent, he or she has been defamed. If a report contains information that contains privileged information and such a report does in fact become public causing embarrassment to someone, that person has also been defamed.

For the security officer, the chances of an action that would include defamation is a possibility, and therefore, the officer should be aware of what he or she says, how and where it is said, and to whom. No matter how minor an incident, comments made in the presence of witnesses or elicited from you by the media may surface at a later time and cause you harm. The security officer must be aware at all times that the officer's professional bearing, comments, and manner of speaking will all reflect upon him or her at, or subsequent to, the incident in question.

The Elements of Defamation

In a case where the plaintiff believes that he or she was defamed, the plaintiff must prove that the defendant used:

1. Defamatory words or written material against the plaintiff that were untrue, and
2. Such words or written material were said with malice, and that
3. Such an act caused special damages.

Regarding libel and slander concerning privileged communications, "malice" involves an evil intent or motive arising from spite or ill will; personal hatred or ill will; or culpable recklessness or a willful and wanton disregard of the rights and interests of the person defamed. Conversely, the person claiming the privilege must have acted in good faith under a sense of duty, with an honest belief that the statements made were true.

Libel and Slander

A person may be defamed in two ways:

1. ***Libel***—A malicious publication in printing, writing, signs, or pictures tending to blacken the reputation of one who is dead, or the reputation of one who is living.
2. ***Slander***—Defamation by words spoken; malicious and defamatory words tending to the damage of another.

Libel is the written word; slander is the spoken word.

See THE MEDIA in Chapter 10 and INVASION OF PRIVACY AND DEFAMATION in Chapter 8 for cautionary behavior by the security officer regarding these issues.

ASSAULT AND BATTERY

The security officer must be cognizant of the fact that in any type of a "stop" where the officer lays his or her hands on the person of another, or the officer's body comes in contact with another in any way, unless such occurrence happens during a lawful action, a plaintiff could lay claim to an assault and battery as part of a civil action. Because of the importance regarding the confrontations and contacts with customers and visitors in the retail environment, whether suspected of a crime or not, it must be considered most important for the security officer to have some knowledge of what constitutes an assault.

Definition of Assault

Assault is any intentional, unlawful offer of corporal injury to another by force, or force unlawfully directed to the person of another, under such circumstances as to create a well-founded fear of imminent peril, coupled with the apparent present ability to effectuate the attempt if not prevented. Assault can be further defined as an attempt or an offer to beat upon another without touching; for example, lifting a fist in a threatening manner at another.

Definition of Battery

The least touching of another's person if done willfully in a violent or insolent manner, or in anger constitutes *battery* or the unlawful beating or touching of the person without that person's consent by another.

- ***There may be an assault without a battery***—An assault may be committed without physical contact. Battery can only be committed by the actual touching or striking the person of another.
- ***Therefore, assault and battery can be defined as***—The unlawful touching of the person of another by the aggressor, or by some substance put in motion by the aggressor (bullet, knife, baseball bat, etc.). If an unlawful attempt to do corporal hurt to another is combined with an actual use of force, there is an assault and battery. The terminology *assault and battery* is not commonly used in criminal complaints today; it is usually referred to in civil actions. For further information on the various degrees or types of assault in which to charge a defendant in a criminal action, refer to your state's criminal laws.

Remember that assault and battery are both a criminal and a civil offense.

The Elements of Assault and Battery

Overt Act

In an effort for the plaintiff to claim an assault, there must be an overt act, or an attempt, or the appearance of an attempt with force and violence to do physical harm or injury to the person of the plaintiff. Words not accompanied by a circumstance that would induce a reasonable apprehension of bodily harm are not sufficient.

In the case of a battery, an unlawful touching of the person of another is sufficient.

Intent

A cause of action for assault requires that a person intends to inflict personal injury on the person assaulted, or to put that person in apprehension of that intent to harm.

In an action for battery, the person must have intended to make contact, and it is not required that the person who made the contact intended to do the injury.

Lack of Consent

A plaintiff cannot recover damages for an assault or battery when that person consented to the assault or the battery. However, the consent cannot be obtained by fraud or deceit, and the assailant cannot exceed the scope of the consent.

Damages

If established, the plaintiff may recover damages for the humiliation, pain, disability, discomfort, and inconvenience caused by the assault and battery. The plaintiff may also recover for mental anguish irrespective of whether or not a physical injury was sustained. Additionally, the plaintiff may recover for loss of earnings, which occurred as a necessary and direct result of the assault and/or battery. The plaintiff's family may not recover for their own mental anguish and humiliation.

False imprisonment necessarily involves the element of an assault in a technical sense, but a battery is not an essential element of false imprisonment.

GENERAL RELEASES

> A release may be defined as the relinquishment, concession, or giving up of a right or claim or privilege by the person to whom it exists.
> —*Black's Law Dictionary*

If after investigation, it were found that the security officer has made a mistake in the apprehension and detaining procedures, it would do well to ask that the subject execute a general release form. In addition, an apology would not be unwarranted. Whether the security officer is in the right but does not wish the process to continue on toward a prosecutorial arrest for whatever reason, or finds that the arrest or the officer's conduct lacks merit and wishes to cease any further course of action as soon as possible, the execution of a release by the subject cannot be demanded as a condition of permitting the subject to leave. If the release is not given knowingly and voluntarily, the courts may set the release aside.

Whatever the circumstances, if the security officer intends to release the subject who has been detained, a request for that person to sign a general release form could be made. Receipt of a release of this type will alleviate or at least mitigate any claim that the subject may have against the store arising out of an unlawful or wrongful arrest and detention. However, such an action could result in repercussions at a later time. If the retailer believes that a signed release be acknowledged prior to any release from confinement, the loss prevention department should have the retailers' attorney draw up a general release form that may be used in cases such as described above.

Payment in Lieu of Release

A retailer or agent (the security officer) who demands payment of the shoplifted merchandise before any release of the suspect is then in jeopardy of possible prosecution for extortion. In many cases, an incident such as this may occur when a juvenile is apprehended, and the retailer or security officer requests payment for the merchandise from the juvenile and/or the juvenile's parents.

In any case, if the request for payment is made or coupled with the threat of possible prosecution, or made in such a way to imply an arrest and prosecution unless payment is made, the retailer or agent can be arrested for extortion.

A retailer or agent, a security officer, can be held guilty of extortion when money is obtained from an alleged shoplifter by threatening the suspect with criminal prosecution unless payment is made, even though the money received was the same as, or less than the amount that the suspect would have paid.

Also, a retailer or agent (manager or security officer) should not "request" a signed statement of incrimination, or a signed release not to initiate any civil action for any "wrongs" that the subject believes may have been committed against the subject. To do so could place the officer and the retailer in civil jeopardy. The implication that would be perceived is that unless a signed instrument was received, no release would be forthcoming. It is not uncommon today that a person at a later time initiates a civil action for false arrest stipulating that at the time of release, he or she was coerced into surrendering a legal right by signing a release form or confession admitting guilt before the actual release was made.

A merchant may not condition a release of a detainee on the execution of an incriminating statement.

As a further example, an interesting case occurred in New York:

The defendant who had been accused of shoplifting a pair of shoes from a department store claimed that he had purchased the shoes earlier in the day but had left the sales receipt at home. He was not believed and he was arrested and charged with larceny. At a subsequent court hearing, the defendant's attorney produced a sales receipt for the shoes on the same day of the larceny charged in the complaint.

The district attorney requested that the charge be dismissed, and the judge agreed but stipulated that the former suspect first agree to waive any rights that he may have in suing the complainant, the store, the city, and the police department. Both the defendant and his attorney agreed, and the charge was dismissed.

A few months later, the former defendant sued the department store for false arrest, false imprisonment, and defamation. The department store based their defense on the waiver and the release. The lower court agreed. However, the Appellate Court disagreed, and held that since the district attorney had concluded that there was an inadequate case for prosecution, it was coercive to require the subject in this case to waive and release any claim as a condition of dismissal.

The waiver and release was set aside,[4] and the former defendant, now the plaintiff, continued his lawsuit without any impediment.

Regarding repayment and/or restitution, see CIVIL RECOVERY in Chapter 14.

ENDNOTES

1. *People v. Horman*, 22 N.Y. 2d, 292 N.Y.S. 2d 874, 239 N.E. 2d 625, 89 S.Ct. 698 (1968).
2. *Jackson v. Police Department, City of New York*, 447, N.Y.S. 2d 320, 86 A.D. 2d 860 (1982).
3. *New York State Business Law*, Article 12-B Mercantile Establishments, § 218-Defense of Lawful Detention.
4. *Dziuma v. Korvettes*, 403 N.Y.S. 2d 269 (1978).

Chapter 3

Criminal and Civil Litigation

This chapter contains an orientation and summary into the criminal justice and court system that most people are unaware of or have had little exposure to. This chapter attempts to familiarize the security officer with the complexity and fractions that make up the criminal justice system, the differences in criminal and civil actions, and the pitfalls and responsibilities he or she will face.

THE CRIMINAL JUSTICE SYSTEM

The most visible person in the criminal justice system is the uniformed patrol officer. Depending on the geographical area of the state and whether the officer is employed by a village, town, city, county, or the state, that officer may be designated a police officer, a state trooper, a sheriff, or a deputy sheriff depending on the municipality or state and the officer's formal duties. All are sworn police officers with full powers of enforcement. These "powers," known as "police powers," are the basis of a multitude of state regulatory statutes, which obligate these officers to preserve the good order, prevent and detect crime, and enforce all laws.

Depending on the local or state government in which they are employed, peace officers and/or constables may also have equal authority with full powers of enforcement as police officers. Generally though, a peace officer is different than a police officer since a peace officer's powers are not as broad. Many states grant the peace officer only specific authority to cite and arrest for certain offenses, and only within the jurisdiction of their employment. Examples might include fire inspectors, corrections officers or jailers, parole and probation officers, court officers, and game wardens, to name a few.

Additionally, federal agents have jurisdiction throughout the country concerning violations within their scope of authority. Some examples would be FBI agents involved in federal statutes, DEA agents concerned with drug violations, and ATF agents concerned with alcohol, tobacco, and firearms offenses. Also, postal inspectors have an interest in enforcing postal regulations, and the Secret Service is obligated to provide executive protection, along with enforcement of laws concerning counterfeiting and credit card fraud.

For the security officer, after an arrest is made, the initial contact with the criminal justice system will be the uniformed police officer. Once the suspect is turned over to and accepted by the police, the suspect will be processed into the criminal justice system.

THE CRIMINAL JUSTICE SYSTEM

The criminal justice system includes the police who investigate and arrest the perpetrators, the district attorney who prosecutes the offenders, the defense attorney who represents the defendant, the court (consisting of the judge, the jury, court officers, and other court officials), parole and probation officers, and finally, the prison, jail, or correctional facility, which will either house the convicted offender, or those held without or in lieu of bail.

From police officer to incarceration as briefly explained above, all are considered part of the criminal justice system.

PRE-LITIGATION

The Court System

The Criminal Court. Before a criminal trial can take place, the subject must be charged by an indictment or a sworn information, which is a formal accusation or allegation that he or she has committed a crime, and that the subject must answer to the indictment or the complaint before a judge.

Minor offenses may be heard and disposed of in the lower courts. Depending on the state, these lower courts include justices of the peace, city magistrates, and district courts. Most arraignments take place in these lower courts. But when there is a grand jury indictment the offense may be brought before a higher court for arraignment, preliminary hearings, and trial. These higher courts will include county courts, and supreme or superior courts.

Grand Jury Action. Some states may differ about the makeup or quorum for a grand jury. But generally, a grand jury is composed of twenty-three citizens but not less than sixteen for a quorum. A quorum is required for the purpose of a finding. They will decide whether or not to indict the suspect after the district attorney (or an assistant district attorney) has presented the state's case (the evidence of the crime). If the grand jurors find a *prima facia* case to believe that the accused person committed the crime, they will return a "true bill"—an indictment. Only felonies and indictable misdemeanors will be presented to the grand jury (again, depending on the state). But upon investigation or inquiries of their own, grand juries may indict for any crime. If the defendant has not already been arrested and charged before the court, the suspect will be arrested and appear for arraignment where the indictment will be presented.

Arrests Prior to Grand Jury Action. Prior to any grand jury action, if any, when a subject is summarily arrested and brought before the court, an *information* is drawn up and presented to that court where the subject is arraigned on the charge. In addition, the *information* may also be sworn to and laid in the lower criminal courts for misdemeanors and felonies prior to any arraignment or grand jury action, and before an arrest takes place. The judge then issues a warrant for arrest of the defendant after accepting the sworn *information*. After a grand jury action where a "true bill" is handed down, the district attorney may request that the person indicted surrender himself or herself for arraignment, or an arrest warrant may be issued by a judge based on the indictment.

An *information* that is sworn to before a judge or a police desk officer is in reality a "bill of particulars," a "complaint" or "affirmation" that contains specific allegations in which the complainant swears that a crime has been committed, that it was committed by the defendant, and that the complainant wishes the defendant to face the charge or charges in court.

If an indictment is sought prior to any court action, the next step after an indictment would be the arraignment, where the suspect, now a defendant, appears at this formal hearing.

At any arraignment, the judge will ask how the defendant pleads to the crime as stated in the indictment or the sworn information. If the defendant pleads guilty, the case is set down for sentencing, but because defendant's rights are such an issue today, rarely is a plea accepted other than a "not guilty" at arraignment. If a plea of not guilty is given, the judge may or may not set bail, may release the defendant on his or her own recognizance, or the judge may remand the defendant to jail. A date for trial is set in either case. If the defendant does not have an attorney, the court must make sure that the defendant has one, usually before any plea is accepted. If the defendant is deemed poor and cannot afford an attorney, the court will provide one.

The Civil Court. A civil case begins when the plaintiff, the person who has been wronged or believes to have been wronged, files a complaint in court containing a statement of his or her claim against the defendant. The wrongs that the plaintiff could seek as redress may include a false arrest, physical injury, loss of income, and harm to his or her reputation. The defendant in a civil case is the person and/or company who is being sued. The defendant, through his or her attorney, then files an answer with the court disputing all charges brought by the plaintiff. Once a case begins, the lawyers prepare for trial, which may take years because of full trial calendars. The lawyers look for witnesses favorable to their case, examine witnesses or evidence that may be used by the other side (discovery, EBTs, depositions), collect evidence, do legal research, hire investigators and expert professionals, and file arguments and motions with the court relating to procedures in the case.

Civil courts are also generally divided by the type of cases they may handle, which usually concerns the amount of loss or the type of offense. Lower courts, such as district courts, may at times also act as small claims courts, and may set a maximum amount of loss or recovery at no more than $5,000. Depending on the state, a lawsuit seeking damages above that amount would be heard in a higher court.

The Trial Process

Fundamentally, the trial process can easily be characterized as two opposing forces doing their best to defeat the other. There are several groups or individuals who are involved in the trial.

In the criminal case, it is the judge, jury, prosecutor, complainant (or police officer), defense attorney, defendant, and witnesses.

In the civil case, it is the judge, jury, the parties (plaintiff and defendant), attorneys for both sides, and witnesses. The plaintiff is the complaining party, and the civil defendant may be private individuals or corporations. The defendant may be an employer, employees, and in some cases a government entity.

In most civil and in all criminal cases, the defendant has a right to a jury trial if they so wish. After trial, the judge will charge the jury by explaining what the law is, and the jury will decide on the facts. In a criminal trial, the jury must decide the fate of a defendant based upon the facts in the case, and if there is a reasonable doubt, the defendant must be acquitted. In a civil trial, the jury will base their finding on a preponderance of the evidence presented by one side over the other. The defendants in both types of actions and the plaintiff or prosecutor have a right to appeal to a higher court. If they feel that they may have an issue of due process or a point of law, or the decision or actions of the judge or jury was prejudicial in some manner, an appeal conceivably can go as far as the United States Supreme Court. The appeals process is based on oral arguments and the record (transcript) of the trial and not on new evidence or testimony.

Preserving Physical Evidence

Depending on the police jurisdiction and local district attorney procedures, stolen property recovered from the defendant may be photographed and returned to stock so that the merchant won't suffer a loss on the sale of outdated merchandise when it is returned after adjudication at a later time. Two sets of photographs should be taken—one set for the police and one set to be attached to and made part of the security officer's incident and/or arrest report. Date, time, case number/s, description of items photographed, and signature or initials of the person taking the pictures should be noted on the rear of the processed photos. So as to give immediate access of photos to the police, a Polaroid camera is adequate and acceptable in most jurisdictions. However, some police administrations require all evidence be invoiced to the police property clerk for future court actions. The security officer will act accordingly. In the case of weapons and/or contraband recovered from the defendant subsequent to the arrest, the security officer will act as directed by the police concerning the preservation of evidence and the identification of these items for trial.

In any event, the security officer will be guided by local police procedures in the handling and safeguarding of evidence and recovered property.

Obtaining Confessions, Admissions, and Witness Statements

If possible, a written and signed confession taken from the defendant without coercion is evidence considered most desirable in admitting guilt. If a written statement cannot be taken, any oral admissions or statements made by the defendant (or a witness for that matter) should be reduced to writing by the security officer as soon as practical. In any case, a witness should be present when the defendant reads and signs a written confession or makes any oral admissions.

Concerning oral admissions or statements made by a suspect after apprehension, any remarks made can be used against the suspect as long as they are related to the incident. Remarks such as "You got me," "I didn't mean to do it," "I'm sorry," "Please, I won't do it again," or "If I pay for it now, can you let me go?" are all considered an admission of guilt, and may be used against the defendant.

Telephone conversations in which the suspect implicates himself or herself can also be used in court. Consider also, if the suspect remains "mute" or refuses to make any statement or say anything at all particularly in self-defense, such may be considered as a sign of guilt. As noted, these admissions, statements, or actions should be reduced to writing and made part of the arrest report by the security officer to whom the remarks were directed, or who overhead such remarks or observed such behavior.

Of serious concern and to be considered grave unethical conduct is a promise given to a person in custody by a security officer that in return for a signed confession the suspect would be released, but in fact once received, the promise is not kept.

This type of behavior should be condemned for any promise made to a suspect or perpetrator in return for something. Beside the validity of the confession, your integrity and veracity is in question.

The *Miranda warning* need not be made part of the statement nor as a warning prior to any questioning since security officers are not police officers. But if a police officer is present, or in the vicinity and has knowledge of the incident, and/or asks the security officer to take a written statement or an oral admission, the security officer is then acting as an agent of the police officer, and must issue the *Miranda warning*. See COLOR OF STATE LAW in Chapter 4 concerning this procedure by a security officer at the request of or in the presence of a police officer.

Regarding witnesses, a written statement should be taken from any person having direct knowledge of pertinent facts concerning the crime or the incident. If a written statement cannot be taken for whatever reason, the witness's identity should be noted for future reference and any oral statements of importance should be reduced to writing, attributed to that person, and made part of the written report.

In any case when the crime is of a serious nature, the police will subsequently interview all witnesses, and the security officer will be of great assistance in identifying to the police all witnesses involved.

Statements and the Written Confession. It should be noted that if the security officer has the ability and is required to take a written confession from a defendant or written statements from witnesses, the security officer should have some training in this regard. The format and what is required to be included in the confession and/or statement is most important so that the writing will be able to stand up in court under scrutiny.

As in any statement taken from a pertinent witness, that witness should be identified by at least name, address, and telephone number prior to the body of the statement.

But for a defendant in particular, it should contain the pedigree of that person—as much identification as possible to identify the person on paper who is giving the written statement. This may include full name, any aliases used, home address and telephone number, date of birth, social security number, whether married or single, number of children if any, occupation, and business address.

All statements and written confessions should begin with the date when the statement is given at the top of the first page. Following that and before the body of the narrative, the statement should bear the title, "Statement of John Doe."

Following the pedigree, the body of the written confession taken from a perpetrator should note certain elements of the crime that was committed. As much as possible of the following particulars should be included:

- The date and the approximate time of the crime.
- The place or location of the crime.
- The intent of the perpetrator; what he or she was going to do, how he or she was to do it, and how he or she did it.
- Did the perpetrator act alone or in concert in committing the crime, or did someone help the perpetrator before or after the crime?
- Describe what was taken (the stolen proceeds) and its value.
- How the perpetrator left the scene or what he or she did after the crime.
- What the perpetrator did with the proceeds of the crime (if applicable).

Some localities require or authorize a defendant to place on paper a confession written in the defendant's own hand with as much information contained therein as noted above, particularly in a police-dominated atmosphere. However, in order to determine that all facts and circumstances are covered and put down on paper in a timely manner (before the defendant changes his or her mindset), it is suggested that the security officer write out the confession for the subject.

The person taking down a written confession would do well to make at least one typographical or spelling error on each page of the confession. By crossing out the mistake, and having the perpetrator place his or her initials above these "errors" at the time he or she reads and signs the confession will indicate to the court, if necessary, that the defendant did in fact read the statement before signing and was conscious of its contents.

Particularly in the case of a written confession taken and put down on paper by a security officer, the writing should be single spaced, and a paragraph should also be contained immediately following the statement indicating the following:

- That the statement is being written for the subject by "James Roe," security officer for XYZ Company (unless given in the subject's own hand),
- That the subject has read the statement and all that is contained in the statement is the truth, and
- That the statement was freely given, without promises or threats of any kind.

Following that, the subject should initial any corrections, sign his or her name, and add his or her address, telephone number, and the date in the subject's own hand.

Moreover, witnesses to the criminal defendant reading and signing the confession should indicate so by their signatures. These signatures must include the person taking the confession and at least one other.

A confession or statement should not be taken or received under threat or duress. If received under these conditions, the court will not allow any statement, oral or written, to be accepted and entered as evidence. The court may also disallow any written instrument received because of a promise made to the giver, whether the promise was granted or not.

Remember that no *Miranda warning* needs to be included in the written confession unless the security officer is operating under the *color of state law*.

If the police are going to become involved because the incident is criminal and serious in nature, it is best to let the police investigate in their capacity and not take confessions or witness statements. On the other hand, if a written confession is in fact taken when the defendant admits to the crime, it will be gladly accepted by the police since they may not have the opportunity to gain such an admission while the subject is in their custody. This because a *Miranda warning* given to a suspect by the police might suppress any admissions that might be received in the interrogation process. Therefore, it should be noted that most police agencies look favorably on confessions taken by security officers prior to their involvement, as long as the security officer has the ability and expertise to do so. But any statement, whoever takes it, becomes part of the case file and is subject to scrutiny by the defense attorney or the prosecutor at discovery or trial. Because of this, some police agencies have procedures that vary with jurisdiction. Regarding criminal prosecution, it would be wise for the security officer to determine what situations should only be handled by the police, and what incidents can and could be handled by security officers.

See the Appendix for an example of a written confession that may be used against a defendant in an arrest for a larceny.

Interview Attempts by Unknown Parties and Damaging Remarks by Others

Security officers must be aware that following any occurrence or incident in which an investigation, litigation, or any type of court action may be forthcoming, that they be conscious of who interviews them or attempts to glean information through an apparent normal conversation. In essence, officers should not answer any questions from anyone unless they are positively sure that the person requesting information is an attorney or investigator representing the security officer, his or her employer, or the company that the officer is contractually assigned to.

Naturally, while in court and under oath, the security officer will be required to answer all questions truthfully, unless upheld on objection by an attorney representing either side.

Most importantly, security officers need to remember that defense or the plaintiff's attorneys are seldom in the pursuit of justice, and more or less are out to protect their defendant, improve their win/loss record, or in the case of a civil action, obtain as much money as possible, all this with little concern for the victim in the case. Private investigators are hired by the defense or the plaintiff's attorney to try and gather evidence or statements that will bolster their case. They will attempt to interview witnesses or complainants before trial for anything that may be helpful for their side. Although they may indicate that they are interested in the truth, their behavior and honesty is self-serving. These attorneys and private investigators will attempt to gain any information that will help them and hurt your case, or damage your credibility, reputation, or testimony.

You have no obligation to talk to any attorney or private investigator, and it is never in your best interests to do so. In fact, the prosecutor, attorney, and/or the insurance carrier representing you and/or your company will not want you to speak with anyone who is or may be representing the other side. This admonition pertains to both criminal and civil cases.

Be mindful also of the presence or imposition of the media for television interviews, comments, or photographs that may place you or your case in a damaging or unjust position at a later time.

If contacted by anyone, as a security officer, you should advise them to talk to your attorney or the attorney representing your company, or in a criminal case, the district attorney. If you feel that you are being harassed or intimidated in any manner, advise your attorney or the district attorney immediately.

Additionally, be alert that any comments or statements, however insignificant, made by you, the security officer, or anyone else at the scene of an arrest, accident, or any incident, may be noted by potential witnesses or the persons involved, and thereby held against you or another at a later time. You should not express any opinion, speculation, action, or response that will place you or your employer in jeopardy or liability. This will include facial expressions such as "rolling of the eyes" or feigning disbelief. Attempt to advise all associates and any employee assisting at the scene, if any, to remain as noncommittal as possible while doing what is required of them.

Reporting the Incident. All incidents and occurrences must be recorded, no matter how minor. Many people who are a party to an incident, particularly an event such as an arrest or serious injury, will ask for a copy of the report. In fact, if there is any criminal or civil litigation, attorneys and insurance investigators representing that party will attempt to procure a copy of any report of the incident. No report should be offered to anyone other than the employer's insurance carrier or legal representative. For further detail on this question, see REPORT WRITING in Chapter 21.

LITIGATION

The Civil Lawsuit

There is nothing more disturbing for a loss prevention or security manager than being served with or receiving a summons and complaint citing a civil action against all and everyone who may have been involved in the incident in question. Vicariously, that could include the initial security officer who made the apprehension or was involved in the incident, any assisting officers or employees, the security officer's supervisor and/or manager, the store or building manager, and the corporation. Furthermore, in some instances, the police department is included for whatever part they may have played in the incident.

Along with noting the date, time, and place of occurrence, the lawsuit will list the wrongs committed by the company personnel, the injuries and/or "wrongs" sustained by the plaintiff and/or others, and the damages demanded. Wrongs could include false arrest, false imprisonment, assault, battery, pain and injuries suffered, medical expenses, slander, libel, civil rights violations, emotional stress, and fear. Also included may be personal embarrassment; injury to reputation; loss of work, wages, or employment; and loss of services to a spouse among others. Some of these "wrongs" do not have to occur only during an arrest or investigation; it could occur at any time, and in any confrontation with a dissatisfied or disgruntled visitor or an injured person not properly protected or attended to.

Service of the Lawsuit or Intent to File Suit. In large stores or companies with the services of a loss prevention or security manager, it is that person who will usually acknowledge and/or accept service regarding all lawsuits, and will be the one to be in direct contact with the store's insurance broker and/or insurance carrier. This is because the security manager and the security department is the depository of all incidents and records of concern, is aware of all insurance coverage, has ongoing contact with insurance investigators and attorneys, and is most familiar with criminal and civil litigation. A senior or lead security officer may be given the responsibility to handle some or all of these tasks along with or in the absence of the security or loss prevention manager.

Furthermore, in the larger retail companies, the importance of a corporate legal affairs department or a risk management department cannot be overstated. Their counsel and guidance in the protection of all assets of the business establishment against all risks can have a significant and reflective effect on the bottom line. All individual loss prevention managers within these large retail corporations must be attentive and responsive to these departments, particularly in the immediate advisement of all litigation matters. Any business that wishes to stay in business has insurance to cover all perils from property damage to obligations, as well as accidental and criminal liability. Because few security personnel are familiar with the processes of a lawsuit, it would do well here to describe and explain it in some detail.

A lawsuit can come to the attention of a business in two ways, and the following scenarios are essentially the accepted procedure to be followed by the loss prevention department:

The Intent to Sue. In the first scenario, a letter of representation from an attorney (with the possible additional notice of intent to sue) requests that the receiver advise their insurance company of such representation so that communication between the two can begin. The attorney usually sends this letter to the store manager, an officer of the corporation, or the loss prevention/security manager. Based on the details noted in the letter, the loss prevention manager will determine first that the occurrence did in fact take place in the store by examining the records. Second, the manager would advise the company's insurance broker, or the insurance carrier directly if that is the working arrangement, of receipt of the attorney's letter. The letter, along with a copy of the incident or accident report, will be sent usually via fax to the broker or the insurance company as soon as possible. If after research, loss prevention can find no reference to the incident, the loss prevention manager should contact the plaintiff's attorney for further details. If such contact still does not produce information that the named plaintiff did or did not in fact suffer a wrong, and no report of any kind was received from anyone on or around the date of occurrence, such information should then be sent to the broker/insurance carrier along with the attorney's letter. A case should be taken at that time and a report compiled noting the receipt of the letter, the subsequent negative investigation into the "incident," and all contacts and advisement's conducted.

The Service of the Lawsuit. In the second scenario, someone of importance, sometimes a receptionist, but usually the store manager, loss prevention/security manager, or another senior manager is personally served with a summons and complaint that details the essence of the lawsuit. A process server usually completes this, but it is not uncommon for an attorney or a plaintiff to serve the defendant. Included will be a cover letter by the attorney requesting that the defendant (the store/company and whoever else is named in the suit) advise the defendant's insurance carrier of such service. A summons and complaint may also be received via certified U.S. mail. Again, the loss prevention manager will conduct an investigation into the incident as described in the complaint. If a report is found, a copy of the summons and complaint, the cover letter, and the report will be sent to the broker/insurance carrier. If no report can be found on the incident, initiate a case/report noting receipt of the service and minimal details as described in the complaint, and send all to the broker/insurance carrier for their investigation.

In both cases, all communications from any attorney, summons and complaints, additional following actions, fax cover sheets, all internal reports and communications, and all subsequent continuation forms should be placed together in a case jacket and maintained in a separate file drawer marked "current litigation." Any photos taken immediately after the incident or taken subsequently should also be contained in the case jacket. If photos or original internal reports and communications are requested by insurance investigators or attorneys representing the company, make certain that copies are made for your case jacket, and note where and who has the originals.

Additionally and if applicable, follow procedures dictated by corporate headquarters in notifying senior managers or administrators who must be apprised of such service and litigation.

DOCUMENTATION

The probability of future litigation demonstrates how important and consequential the taking of a report can be. No matter how minor an incident or how minimal the information gathered for the report, whether an apprehension, a personal injury, lost child, or a disgruntled customer, a specific formal report should be compiled and maintained for future reference.

To reiterate, no matter how insignificant an incident may be, if some action is taken by a security officer, it should be documented in some form.

Other than the possible initial contact with the plaintiff's attorney as described above and for the purpose only to elicit information for a proper investigation of an unreported incident, the security officer should use extreme care in any conversation with anyone unknown to the officer about any incident. This includes any attorney, broker, or investigator not connected with your insurance carrier or company attorney.

The Role of Loss Prevention

Once the security manager or loss prevention manager becomes aware of a civil suit concerning a negligence, products liability, or other liability case, it may fall upon that manager to conduct an investigation in order to determine as much of the facts surrounding the incident as possible.

If the suit details an injury suffered by the plaintiff, the first order of business is to determine based upon the complaint the name of the injured party, date, time, and place of occurrence. Following that, a search of the records should be made, such as a CUSTOMER ACCIDENT REPORT, in order to determine that the incident did in fact occur on the premises and was reported to the loss prevention department, the basic facts are correct, and what action was taken by store or security personnel.

If the suit involves some physical action by an employee such as an alleged false arrest, assault, or some other behavior, conduct, or condition considered an intentional or negligent "wrong" suffered by the plaintiff, a search of the records should be made. This includes any record that may pertain to the incident such as an ACCIDENT REPORT, ARREST/APPREHENSION REPORT or INCIDENT REPORT, again to determine if in fact such an incident took place as described in the complaint.

If the action is a products liability complaint, the loss prevention department should gather as much information as feasible, including the possibility of contacting the plaintiff's attorney for any information not noted in the complaint. Inquiry must include a description of the incident and/or the product to determine if in fact the product was carried and sold by the retailer, and the plaintiff has a record or confirmation of the sale by the retailer. The loss prevention manager should also become aware of the circumstances surrounding the product and how it caused the injury or damage, the damages suffered by the plaintiff, and the present location of the product.

The final determination of how a response to the civil action will be made will fall on the retailer's insurance carrier, since they are commissioned to represent the retailer in these matters.

Discovery

In a criminal case, a form of discovery may be held in criminal court presided by a judge, court reporter, court officer, and other court personnel. It is a formal hearing, in that the defense attorney attempts to determine the legitimacy of admissions, confessions, and evidence that may be used against the attorney's client.

However, in a civil case, discovery is conducted to obtain information through demands for the production of documents, depositions, and interrogatories, and any other evidence. It is where the attorney representing either the defendant or the plaintiff attempts to obtain as much information as possible from the other side prior to trial so that neither party may keep secrets from the other. It may be defined as a hearing or meeting, in order to obtain all facts, witnesses names, statements, evidence, and anything else of importance that the other attorney may need from his or her adversary in order to build a strong defense and/or to present a more informed case.

Most civil lawsuits will never go to trial. If the defendant's attorney finds that the case against the retailer is strong and that going to trial will or might be a lost cause, or that the expense of continuing the civil action may cost more than a possible recompense, the attorney may attempt to request a settlement with an offer to the plaintiff. If a settlement cannot be reached because the plaintiff refuses to accept what is offered, the case will be set for trial. Cases end up in court for trial because the parties disagree to a great extent over the facts in the case so that a judge and/or jury is unavoidable in deciding on the facts. On the other hand, a plaintiff may realize up to and including the trial proceedings that his or her case is weak, and may plead for or accept a settlement from the defendant. In the case of a criminal defendant, this procedure would be called a plea bargain or "copping a plea."

Discovery is a disclosure of facts and may consist of the following procedures:

- ***Depositions***—A deposition is a more formal statement reduced to writing, signed and sworn to before a notary public, such as a stenographer or court reporter who is a notary. A deposition is part of the pretrial discovery process conducted by the attorney for the opposing party. Basically a confession does not differ from a deposition except that no notary public may be involved. When one is deposed, it is a method in which a person is asked under oath about any knowledge of the facts in the case, and reduced to written form. Parties to the action and witnesses are required to answer questions under oath about their knowledge of the dispute. This action may take place in a private room in a courthouse away from the courtroom or at an attorney's office. Attorneys for both sides are present. Even though the security officer may have been previously deposed, the officer may also have to appear at a trial for testimony. If there is a change in testimony from the prior deposition, the written statement may be entered into evidence at trial.
- ***Interrogatories***—This process is also part of pretrial discovery. An interrogatory is a question-and-answer examination in written form, in which one party sends the other party written questions to be answered and notarized under oath, and returned by a certain date. This may also be used to identify the source or validity of documents that may be introduced into evidence at trial. It is similar to a deposition except it is a Q-and-A format in a written presentation.
- ***Admission of facts***—In a civil case, each party is permitted to submit a written list of alleged facts and/or statements, and request the other party to admit or deny whether each is true and correct. Anything not denied may be admitted at trial.
- ***Production of documents***—The production of specified documents, photos, forms, reports, and writings by one party at the request of the other. If necessary or required, the court may issue a *subpoena duces tecum*—a writ or order requiring the attendance of a person at a particular time and place to testify as a witness, and/or commanding that person to attend and produce some book, paper, or document (bring the record).

Testifying at Examinations Before Trial

In essence, discovery in a civil case may include one or more of the above processes and can be conducted as an *examination before trial* (EBT). An EBT is testimony taken under oath, in response to questions asked by the opposing attorney with respect to the facts and circumstances surrounding the incident or occurrence. The hearing can take place in a private room in a courthouse or in either attorney's offices. It will include the attorneys for both sides, a court reporter to transcribe testimony into a formal record, and who as a notary public will swear in all witnesses under oath, including the defendant and the plaintiff. The security officer or any another witness may be subpoenaed to bring all notes, statements, records, forms, or photographs that are particular to the case in question. It is at this point that all in-house reports, previously held as a private business record, must be identified and, if requested, submitted and marked into evidence. There may be more attorneys present, particularly if there is more than one defendant or plaintiff. If a witness refers to any writing in order to refresh one's memory while being examined, those documents may be taken by the opposing attorney for inquiry, exploration, or entry into the record as a court exhibit. Be guided by counsel before giving any testimony.

Testifying at Trial

The average citizen rarely enters a courtroom, and more rarely is called as a witness before the court. Most legal matters never reach the trial stage because they usually get settled for one reason or another. Because civil litigation is becoming more prevalent in our society, the security officer has a greater chance of ending up in court than the typical citizen.

When appearing at any hearing or when testifying in any court, the security officer should have a presentable appearance. The male security officer should wear a clean shirt, tie, and suit or sport jacket. The female security officer should wear a dress or a suit with a skirt or slacks. Jeans or dungarees should not be worn to court by any security officer. If the security officer wears a uniform while on duty, he or she should check with their attorney or prosecutor to determine whether they would have the officer testify in uniform rather than in civilian clothes. Shoes should be appropriate and shined, and generally the officer should be neatly groomed. The court and jury will consider officers as unprofessional and inappropriate if they appear in court wearing jewelry such as eyebrow, lip, tongue, or nose rings, or any other unsuitable adornment.

The officer should also be on time, attentive, and responsive. As a security officer, you should review all reports and statements so as to refresh your memory prior to testifying. Generally, before any proceeding, you will be required to consult with the prosecutor or attorney representing you and/or your employer concerning the case in question, your testimony, and what to expect from both sides. Remember that the judge, jury, and the opposing side are closely watching a witness's demeanor and presence of mind while on the stand.

While on the witness stand, you should speak clearly, and loudly enough to be understood by the judge, the attorneys, and the jury, if any. Your head should be kept high with hands on one's lap, and try not to use hand gestures or become fidgety. You should answer all questions put to you by the prosecutor or any attorney truthfully and as briefly as possible. Do not attempt to clarify or add information not asked. The idea of the opposing attorney is to discredit or destroy your testimony. He or she will try to make you angry and try to confuse you in your testimony; this attorney may become angry, rude, annoying, and question your character, veracity, and integrity. Try to act and speak calmly, and do not become frustrated or angry with the attorney—realize the attorney is just doing his/her job—whether you like it or not. Answer all questions honestly; if you don't know the answer, say so. If you don't understand the question, ask to have it repeated or clarified. Take your time in answering; the prosecutor or your attorney may wish to object to the question. Nothing will rattle an attorney more than a witness who mulls over the question and takes time to give a truthful answer.

Behavior on the Witness Stand. When you as a security officer are to testify in court, whether a criminal or civil case, you should be cognizant of the following:

- ***Never lie.*** Tell the truth. If you perjure yourself, you commit a crime. Never enlarge on an answer even though it is the truth. Provide only the answer to the exact question that is asked. It's all right to say, "I don't remember," or "I don't know."

- ***Listen carefully.*** Pause before answering. Think and understand the question before you answer. Take your time. If you don't understand the question, ask that it be repeated or rephrased.
- ***Never guess.*** If you do not know the answer, state simply that you do not know. Even if you "think" you know, you should only answer that which you *know* to be true. If you don't guess, then no one can make you to appear to be lying.
- ***Never answer too quickly.*** A proficient attorney can fire questions at a very fast pace in an effort to confuse and rush a witness into making an incorrect or improbable statement, or blurting out more than the witness may wish to do. The witness should take time, think every question through thoroughly, answer truthfully but deliberately, factually, and concisely. Moreover, the attorney for the witness may wish to object to a question. If at any time your attorney makes an objection, stop talking immediately.
- ***Keep your answers simple.*** Whenever possible, answer *yes* or *no*. Don't elaborate unless you're asked to clarify your answer. Use understandable language.
- ***Don't exaggerate.*** Give definitive answers. All answers should be well thought out and as short as possible. Don't give the impression that you are a braggart or a show-off.
- ***Never volunteer information.*** A question is asked for a purpose. If the answer is not explicit enough, another question will be asked. Do not try to second-guess or anticipate your attorney or the other attorney. Answer only the question asked and do not elaborate; stop when you have answered. Do not offer your opinion unless it is asked.
- ***Be alert to trick questions.*** Don't let the opposing attorney put words into your mouth. Watch for the same question being asked with different words. Be aware of making comparisons or what you personally believe—"Wouldn't you agree that," "Are you telling me," "Have you spoken with your lawyer before you entered the courtroom" (of course you did), or "Have you ever lied?" (yes, but never under oath). One question that flusters most witnesses is "How much are you being paid for your testimony here today?" You should answer truthfully—"I'm just receiving my regular salary . . . it's my job, and I'm here because I was subpoenaed."
- ***Never argue or lose your temper.*** Proficient attorneys can easily goad or lead a witness into making rash statements, blurting out information helpful to their case, or making the witness look like an emotional idiot. Be patient and keep control of your temper regardless of the tone and content of the questions. Your complete testimony can be ruined if you fall into this trap. Don't become sarcastic, combative, or behave in a "wise-guy" manner. Answer questions from all attorneys in the same courteous manner.
- ***Be aware of your physical actions.*** Be attentive to the seriousness of your testimony. Try not to laugh or smirk, even though it might be a nervous reaction. Do not roll your eyes in a response to an action or a question, or permit a facial expression that may convey your thoughts or attitude to the judge and/or jury. If you are nervous on the stand, place your hands clasped on your lap. In this

manner, you will be less conscious of your nervousness by your hands being somewhat out of sight.

In conclusion, as a security officer you must realize that your knowledge, demeanor, and presence in court will reflect upon any past actions you have taken or prior comments you have made. The more professional you appear, the more favorable weight that the judge and/or jury will give to your testimony and prior actions.

Cautionary Behavior

Be careful about anyone who attempts to gain your confidence and questions you on a particular incident, whether such conversation takes place before or after any known litigation. Be particularly aware that any telephone conversation can be recorded, and unless the other party is unmistakably known, no information or comments should be made on the telephone.

Moreover, you should be aware that during a trial or any hearing, persons will approach you outside the courtroom in an friendly manner to pass the time of day and strike up a conversation. Consider that the inquisitor may be an agent for the other side. You must be conscious of an approach by anyone, particularly during recesses or breaks in court proceedings where court "observers" or "spectators" will begin "friendly" conversations with you in an attempt to glean any information or comments that can be passed on and used by the opposing attorney. This is not an uncommon tactic, when after a court recess the officer is called to the witness stand and is confronted with questions by the opposing attorney regarding comments made by the officer during that recess.

If approached, advise the "sociable" questioner that you cannot divulge any information regarding the case as directed by the prosecutor or your attorney. If the questioner persists, walk away from this person and advise your counsel of the incident as soon as practical.

RULES OF EVIDENCE

There are many different types of evidence that can be used in court against a criminal or civil defendant. Security officers most probably will not become directly involved with the various types of evidence described herein, but knowledge of what may or may not be evidence should be an important part of their training. Therefore, security officers should be aware what constitutes evidence and what can be used in a court of law.

Definition of Evidence

A system of rules and standards by which the admission of proof at a trial or hearing is regulated. In the broad sense it is the means or method by which any disputed or necessary matter of fact is proved or disproved.

For a complete list of the types of evidence and the definition of each, see the GLOSSARY. However, the following definitions are of some importance to the security officer in the collection of evidence.

The Exclusionary Rule

Evidence that is not allowed by the court to be entered as such is excluded. This rule commands that when evidence has been obtained in violation of the privileges guaranteed by the U.S. Constitution, the evidence must be excluded at the trial.

Evidence that is obtained by an unreasonable search and seizure is excluded from evidence at trial under the Fourth Amendment of the U.S. Constitution, and this rule is applicable to all states.[1]

Motion to Suppress Evidence

In a court of law, an attorney may attempt to suppress evidence on a motion based on several factors. This may include an unlawful search, illegal eavesdropping, right to privacy offenses, unlawful confessions, *poisoned tree concept*, and illegal identification.

Reasonable Doubt and the Preponderance of Evidence

In a criminal court, the state (the people) has the burden of proving guilt beyond a reasonable doubt. It does not mean absolute proof of guilt, but it does infer that the possibility of innocence is removed. The defendant does not have to testify, and no inference of guilt can or may be drawn by failure to testify. Under our law, a person is considered innocent until proven guilty.

If a judge or jury finds that there is a reasonable doubt in their mind that the defendant is guilty, then they must acquit. Whereas in civil law, all that is needed for the plaintiff to win his/her case in court is a preponderance of the evidence.

To reiterate, in order to convict the defendant at a criminal trial the burden of proof for the state is that the judge or the jury must find guilt "beyond a reasonable doubt." However, at a civil trial before a judge or jury, the parties on either side (plaintiff or defendant) require only a "preponderance of evidence" (greater weight of evidence) in order to prove their case, and is less demanding than "beyond a reasonable doubt."

ENDNOTE

1. *Mapp v. Ohio*, 367 U.S. 643; 6L.Ed.2nd 1081; 81 S.Ct. 1684 (1961).

Part 2

CRIMINAL LAW AND THE RETAIL LOSS PREVENTION OFFICER

Because a retail establishment serves a vast category of customers, there will be times where the security officer or guard will come across various forms of misconduct or offensive behavior, which may include loud and abusive disgruntled customers. Moreover, particularly in the more cosmopolitan metro areas, customers from many walks of life or different cultures will at times be confused, misunderstand or be unfamiliar with certain procedures and/or policies that a business may have. But more importantly, crimes against persons or property, along with the safety of the individual, is to be considered a greater concern to the security officer. Whatever the occurrence, the officer should be aware of all laws and ordinances of consequence within the scope of his or her employment, which will give the officer the authority to act in a variety of situations. This would include the knowledge of a large array of assorted statutes and laws from minor trespass to a serious crime or business interruption.

As long as security officers act within the authority granted to them by their employer, and within the confines of the law the officer is about to enforce, the courts will look favorably on his or her actions and the business establishment they protect in the event any civil action is subsequently initiated against the officer. Therefore, the security officer must have some foundation in the culpability and interpretation of his or her authority as a citizen and the basic laws with which the officer will be concerned. If the officer doesn't understand the law, and how to apply it to his mental state and to his physical actions, the officer most assuredly will become involved in false arrests and other wrongful acts. Accordingly, we can say that proper training and instruction in the laws and rules that concern the security officer and the attitude and demeanor exhibited, along with the officer's professional attributes and personal appearance will serve the officer well, and will be an asset to his or her employer.

The duties and responsibilities of a security officer may be varied and complex, from routine monotonous tasks to extreme emergencies. This part attempts to cover the more prevalent topics that pertain to the retail establishment. But initially and more importantly, this material is offered so that the security officer may understand the possible risks, how to avoid repercussions by acting other than in a litigious manner, and how to do a better job.

Chapter 4

Legal Powers and Limitations

As a security officer or guard you need to be aware of the following:

1. **Security officers or security guards are not sworn police officers, or peace officers.**
2. **He or she therefore do not possess the power and authority of a law enforcement officer.**
3. **The legal authority of a security officer/guard is very limited.**
4. **The security officer/guard is considered a private citizen.**
5. **As a private citizen, the security officer or guard has a legal right to make a citizen's arrest under restrictive circumstances.**

If an arrest made by a security officer or guard is unlawful, then the officer, his or her supervisor, trainer, and employer (the defendant/s) may be liable (vicarious liability) for damages to the person (the plaintiff) unlawfully arrested and/or unlawfully imprisoned. If the plaintiff is unable to include anyone else into the lawsuit, the security officer or guard will face civil litigation and possibly criminal charges as an individual.

SECURITY AND CIVIL LAW

Depending on the severity of an incident, most security personnel will be placed in some type of a liability situation at some time in their career, when some remedy will be sought by a litigant for some wrong or a perceived wrong committed against them.

Police officers are trained and retrained routinely in the powers of arrest and the seizure of evidence. In-service training is a must because of the ongoing changes in legislation and court interpretations and/or opinions (case law) that will affect how the officer performs what is required. Moreover, if a police officer oversteps his or her bounds, and a citizen suffers a wrong because of an act that may be considered illegal, then or at a later time, the officer usually is protected by the municipality from monetary damages, and may suffer no more loss than censure or termination.

Security officers, as private persons, do not have that privilege of protection, nor do they have the intense initial or ongoing training that a sworn police officer is exposed to.

The laws of arrest and the seizure of evidence or property is complex and many times obscure, even to the police professional. Security officers must be consistently aware of their thought process and actions in this regard, so that they may avoid the hazards conducive to this profession.

Consider the following topics concerning probable cause, arrest, the use of force, and search and seizure as part of the most important functions of your job as a security officer.

THE ARREST

Definition

An *arrest* is defined as the restraining of a person and that person's freedom of movement, and to bring that person into legal custody to answer to the alleged criminal act. The restraint of a person's freedom, and/or the detention of that person, can also be construed as an unlawful imprisonment if the arrest is unlawful. The security officer and the officer's employer may be held liable for that wrongful act.

The security officer must be aware of the varied interpretations of the criminal laws that have been enacted and/or held as case law in the various states. It is incumbent that the officer be well versed of the laws in his or her own state regarding arrest, detention, the use of force, and juvenile custodial procedures among others.

The following is generally accepted as applying to most state criminal codes.

Evidence to Support an Arrest

Other than the perpetrator being caught in the act or shortly thereafter, as in the case of a shoplifter for example (observation of the criminal act), the following evidence can be used to sustain an arrest and/or present a *prima facie* case after an investigation:

- Recovery of stolen property taken from the offender or gathered at a later time.
- Confessions and/or admissions by the perpetrator.
- Witnesses and information given by others concerning the crime.
- Business records, VCR tapes, photographs, fingerprints, or any other physical evidence.

Under no circumstances should a security officer take the word of a store employee, coworker, manager, passerby, or a customer regarding any alleged offense they may or may not have witnessed.

Any information received should be used only as a guide for further inquiry and investigation. If an arrest does take place based on probable cause, such information given by someone else may be used in the form of evidence as given by a witness.

Culpability. It is of some importance that the security officer be aware of the mental state of a person who commits an act that may be considered an offense under the law. In essence, that person must have intent to commit a crime, knows that it is a crime to do so, and has the ability and wherewithal to do the crime. This may be different from that of a person who was required to do something mandated by law or by that person's position, and in omitting or failure to act as required, death, injury, or damage occurred. In either case, each is culpable.

According to *Black's Law Dictionary*, culpable conduct is defined as those actions by a person who is blamable, censurable and may be criminal; one who is at fault.

Perpetrators of crime (criminal defendants) must have one of the following mental states; proof of any one these mental states of being at the time of the criminal act is sufficient:

- ***Intentionally***—by design (or willfully); the presence of will in the act that consummates a crime; they intentionally committed or attempted to commit the crime for their own purpose/s.
- ***Knowingly***—with knowledge; they knew what they were doing and had knowledge that the act was wrongful.
- ***Recklessly***—they recklessly and without concern or without due regard to another of the consequences of their act, did commit the act.
- ***Criminal negligence***—an act committed against another with negligence; doing or omitting to do something required of them, or what people of ordinary prudence would not have done or omitted to do.

For further insight concerning one's mental state, see Chapter 5 the section LARCENY where culpable conduct, unlawful desire, opportunity, and ability are further examined.

Criminal and Civil Culpability by a Security Officer. Other than an act by the criminal defendant, we must also be cognizant of the actions and mental state of a security officer. The security officer, in order to be held criminally and civilly culpable for a particular act, must also display one of the above mental states as part of that act.

This is important enough to be repeated—if the security officer commits an unlawful or litigious act having one of the above mental states, the officer is culpable for that act.

In final analysis, whether criminally or civilly, the court or a jury will determine if the security officer is culpable.

Defenses. The following are defenses by a defendant in a civil court action initiated by the plaintiff:

- ***Warrant***—A warrant is an official judicial order directed to a police officer or a peace officer that a certain act be undertaken, such as an arrest. Unless your state statuary laws define differently, a security officer *will not* be given a warrant of any type to execute.

- ***Probable cause***—The defendant had probable cause to make the arrest—with or without a warrant. In the case of a security officer (without a warrant), the arrest was made with probable cause.
- ***Merchant's detention statute***—If a state has a statute that protects the retail merchant regarding the ability to stop and investigate a possible larceny under probable cause, the retailer *may* have an affirmative defense for the actions based on that statute.

AUTHORITY TO ARREST BY A SECURITY OFFICER

Offenses Defined

Because security officers do not have the power of arrest afforded to a police officer, their actions in this regard are limited. Moreover, because of the restrictions placed on an ordinary citizen, security officers must be aware of those offenses they may or may not act upon.

Security officers should have knowledge of the classification and definition of offenses as prescribed in their state's criminal code. It would benefit security officers to review those definitions.

The following is a basic description of the difference between offenses and what constitutes a crime:

> . . . "offense" is defined as any conduct performed which violates a statutory provision defining the offense, and for which a sentence to a term of imprisonment or to a fine is provided by any law of the state or by any law, local law or ordinance of a political subdivision, or by any order, rule or regulation of any governmental instrumentality authorized by law to adopt the same.

Offenses include infractions, violations, misdemeanors, and felonies.

- ***Infraction***—Infractions are minor offenses such as traffic violations, where a fine can be imposed and are enacted by the state or local authority to control some type of conduct. It is not a crime. (There are some sections of the traffic laws that are not infractions but are classified as crimes—driving while intoxicated, leaving the scene of an accident.) A citation is issued to the offender since rarely is a summary arrest made by a police officer for an infraction.
- ***Violation***—A violation is an offense other than an infraction, where a minimal imprisonment can be proscribed but usually a fine is imposed. These are usually minor offenses prohibited in the state's criminal code or by local ordinances, and can include simple trespass; causing an environmental, health, or physical hazard; or disorderly conduct. A citation to the offender is usual, but an arrest can be made for a violation. It is not a crime.

Most important for the purpose of this book are misdemeanors and felonies, which are crimes because they are considered much more serious offenses. These include laws enacted by the state to incorporate those egregious misdeeds that are contrary to the good order and safety of our society.

- ***Misdemeanor***—A misdemeanor is an offense for which a term of imprisonment may exceed 15 days, but cannot exceed one year if found guilty. The sentence is served in a local or county jail.

  In some states minor offenses such as petit (or petty) larceny (e.g., any property valued at $1000.00 or less, depending on statutory law in your state), simple assault, harassment, and some sections concerning gambling, vice, and disorderly conduct are defined as misdemeanors.
- ***Felony***—A felony is a more serious offense for which a term of imprisonment exceeds one year and/or up to a sentence of life imprisonment or death, if found guilty, and which must be served in a state prison or a state correctional facility. Examples are murder, rape, sodomy, arson, kidnapping, grand larceny, or felonious assault (bodily harm causing serious physical injury or deformity).

Therefore, only *misdemeanors* and *felonies* are crimes, and because security officers are employed to protect the client's interests, not the public interest, they would do well to confine themselves in reacting to only crimes in which they are assigned to enforce within the scope of their employment.

Although a citizen has a right to arrest anyone for any offense committed in their presence, security officers would do well to stay away from any offense that is not a crime or within the purview of their authority and duties. Consequently, the officers should limit activity and response to their specific area of employment, the policy and procedures of their employer, and arrest for crimes only.

Other than some exceptions when officers are employed in areas that include private parking fields where local ordinances cover parking and traffic signs, or security officers hired by some governmental or public agencies, officers would do well to become very familiar with the duties, requirements, and authority the officers may or may not possess, including what protection they may have if they are classified as a public servant.

Consider also security officers who investigate crimes. Depending on the authority given to them, some loss prevention officers have the ability to investigate crimes perpetrated on the premises. Because of the possible legal restrictions or knowledge required concerning case investigation, the retail merchant would do well to give this authorization only to those officers who have had a law enforcement background. In any event, after a proper investigation establishing that a crime has in fact been committed, that the perpetrator has been identified as having committed the crime, and a *prima facie* case exists, an arrest may be made. Following that, the subject must be turned over to the police, along with any confessions, statements, and evidence. In some cases at the conclusion of the investigation, in order to determine that he or she has a *prima facie* case, the security officer may wish to present the matter to the police or the district attorney for a judgment and the issuance of an arrest warrant. Regardless, after initial investigation when it is determined a serious crime has occurred or when more expertise and inquiry is necessary or mandatory, the crime must be reported to the police.

The Security Officer and the "Private Citizen" Concept

Because the law regards security officers or guards as *citizens*, not as sworn police officers or peace officers, they have the basic right as any citizen to arrest a person who has committed a crime under the circumstances enumerated below.

- Security officers may act only for an offense committed in their presence or within their view. The security officer must be a witness to the crime committed, or if the crime was not committed in full view, it must be a crime classified as a felony.
- Security officers may act to prevent the consequence or continuation of a crime. The security officer must witness the crime committed, or about to be committed, and the perpetrator is in view at all times.

If the offense has not been committed within view of the security officer, the crime must be a felony and the security officer must know that the felony has in fact been committed, and that the person the officer is about to arrest is in fact the person who committed the felony crime. This terminology, "has or is in fact," can be described as an act that has occurred within view of the security officer, or that the officer has positive and absolute proof that the act that took place was a felony and the perpetrator about to be arrested is the one who committed it. If a mistake is made on the officer's part in the "arrest and/or detention" of a "suspect" who may have committed the alleged felony and subsequently found innocent or not to be the perpetrator, the security officer is completely liable for any damages that may result from these actions.

Conditions Required for an Arrest. The following conditions must be present for security officers to consummate an arrest:

1. A crime must have been committed and the security officer acts in a lawful manner to make the actual seizure.
2. There must be an actual intention of arrest by the security officer, in that he or she takes a person into custody, depriving that person of his/her movement or liberty—to deny this person of their constitutional right of freedom.
3. The security officer must detain or apprehend the person in question. The use of force may be used if required, but only that force necessary to make the apprehension.
4. The person being arrested must understand that the security guard is arresting and detaining him or her then and there at the scene. The person arrested should be informed of the reason for the arrest if practical. There is no need for the security officer to touch the person arrested to execute an arrest.
5. The security officer has the intent of presenting the person under arrest to a police officer without unnecessary delay so as to answer to the alleged crime.
6. If applicable, a communication by a police officer may be provided to the person arrested about the security guard's intent and purpose.

Police officers are not required to take an arrested person into custody or to take any other action proscribed in the law on behalf of the person requesting the arrest if they have reasonable cause to believe

- that the arrested person did not commit the alleged offense,
- that the circumstances surrounding the incident lack the facts for *prima facie* case, or
- that the arrest was otherwise unlawful or unauthorized.

Prints and Photos. Be aware that security officers should not take fingerprint impressions of a subject in custody, whether that subject is a defendant or not. Other than for a licensing process that may be authorized by the state, fingerprints should be taken only by police officers under sanctioned procedures. Some states restrict police officers to the taking of prints and photos from defendants under strictly controlled circumstances.

Many loss prevention departments take Polaroid photos of persons arrested by their officers for future reference, or viewing by other security officers not present at the time of the arrest. So as not to place themselves in a litigious situation, security officers should check with their own state laws or counsel to determine if there are any restraints pertaining to photographing an arrested subject in legal custody. If the security officer has no legal impediments and is able to do so, photos should be taken prior to the arrival of police, and not in their presence. Also, photos should be contained in a photo album and not displayed in a security office where people other than security personnel can see them.

In Conclusion

The subject arrested by the security officer must have in fact committed the crime. If the crime, felony, or misdemeanor was committed in the officer's presence, an arrest may be made at any hour of the day or night. Any person may arrest another person without a warrant for a felony when the latter has in fact committed such felony, and for any crime when the latter has in fact committed such offense in his or her presence.

Depending on the state in which the security officer is employed, and if the facts are present for a felony arrest, the arrest may be made in any county of the state and at any time of the day. However, if the security officer did not observe the felony crime, he or she must be positive that a felony has in fact been committed, and that the person he or she is about to arrest committed it. If in doubt and rather than place oneself in criminal and/or civil jeopardy, the security officer should advise a police officer to investigate.

A misdemeanor is a less serious crime, and again depending on the state of employment, an arrest may be made only in the county where the misdemeanor crime took place. The arrest may also be made at any hour of the day or night for a misdemeanor committed in his or her presence at the time of the offense or immediately thereafter. If unable to execute an arrest under these conditions because the perpetrator has fled the scene, the proper law enforcement authorities should be advised for further legal action on their part.

In order to effect an arrest, a security officer may use such physical force as is justifiable to consummate that arrest.

The security officer must without *unnecessary delay* deliver or attempt to deliver the person arrested to the custody of an appropriate police officer. The police officer will then process the arrested person as required by law. In some states, unnecessary delay is deemed to mean immediately after paperwork and processing of the defendant is completed by the security officer, that police presence is requested.

THE USE OF FORCE IN EFFECTING AN ARREST

Justification of Physical Force by a Private Citizen

Under certain conditions, *reasonable physical force* may be used to consummate the arrest for larceny or any other crime that takes place in the officer's presence.

> Security officers must remember that they have the same powers of arrest that an ordinary citizen has, including the necessary and reasonable physical force that may be used to consummate that arrest, but no more.
>
> Under *no* circumstances should the use of *deadly physical force* be used in effecting an apprehension and/or arrest of a suspect unless the security officer can show at a later time that the officer's life or someone else's life was in extreme danger or in jeopardy of a serious physical injury.

Once security officers have been granted the authority by their employer to effect arrests during the course of their duties, or to prevent an offense against persons and/or property they are employed to protect, the time will come when *justifiable force* may have to be used to consummate an arrest or deter an unlawful act. Whatever physical force is used, security officers must be prepared to justify their actions to the police once they become involved, or if and when a plaintiff seeks damages in court.

- ***In self-defense***—A person may use only that force that appears to be *reasonably* necessary to prevent the harm. A person may not use force likely to cause death or serious physical injury unless he or she *reasonably believes* that there is danger of serious personal physical injury or death. If more force than necessary is used (force that is excessive), the privilege of self-defense may be lost.
- ***In the defense of another***—When a person commits a forceful act in the defense of another person or persons (protecting a person or persons from deadly force or serious physical injury), the person must believe that such aid is necessary, and that the victim/s have a right to defend themselves. This is a privilege authorized when the security officer or a citizen reasonably believes such force is necessary to prevent the threatened harm to another.

The Use of Force Defined. Remember that whatever type of physical force is used by the security officer, the officer may have to justify his or her actions to the police, district attorney, or a civil court.

In order to have a more thorough understanding and overview of arrests by a private person and the use of force, the security officer is urged to examine the criminal codes that cover justification of the use of force in the state in which he or she is employed. By such inquiry, the officer will determine the exact legal conduct he or she will be required to follow.

Generally, the interpretations that follow may be considered what is found in most, if not all, states in the union.

The use of *physical force* upon another person, which would otherwise constitute an offense, is justifiable and not criminal under any of the following circumstances:

- A person may use *physical force* upon another person in self-defense or in defense of a third person, or in defense of the premises, or in order to prevent larceny of or criminal mischief to property, or in order to effect an arrest or prevent an escape from custody.
- The use of *physical force* upon another person in believing it necessary to defend self or another person is applicable, *unless* the security officer provokes or is the initial aggressor, *but* if the officer then withdraws and communicates such withdrawal but the latter (the other subject) persists to continue and engage in the use or threatened imminent use of unlawful physical force, the security officer is justifiable in the use of *physical force.*
- Security officers (private persons) acting on their own account may use physical force, *other than deadly force*, upon any other person when and to the extent that they reasonably believe such to be necessary to effect an arrest or to prevent the escape from custody of a person whom the officers reasonably believe to have committed an offense and who in fact has committed such offense.
- Security officers *may use deadly physical force* for such purpose when they reasonably believe such to be necessary
  (a) For self-defense or to defend a third person from what the officer reasonably believes to be the use or imminent use of deadly physical force (deadly or serious physical injury); or
  (b) Effect the arrest of a person who has committed murder, manslaughter in the first degree, robbery, forcible rape, or forcible sodomy and who is in immediate flight therefrom. (Again, check the criminal code in your state; security officers must be sure of their actions.)

The use of deadly physical force:

- *Deadly physical force* is generally defined as physical force that, under the circumstances in which it is used, is readily capable of causing death or a serious physical injury. At present, the majority of states hold that deadly physical force may be used when it is reasonably necessary to deter the threat of death or serious physical injury. A few states differ in that they hold that deadly force may only be used when absolutely necessary to preserve *one's own life.*

  But security officers may not use such force if they know they can with complete safety to themselves or to another avoid the necessity to use deadly physical force by retreating. Security officers, as private persons, cannot use deadly physical force if they have the ability to retreat or "back off" safely other than to immediately save their own or someone else's life, and the commission or attempted commission of the serious felonies noted below. (Some states note that a person does not have to "retreat" if in their own dwelling.) A police officer does not have that privilege of withdrawal; the officer must stand fast and act.

- Also, in the case of *deadly physical force*, security officers may do so if they reasonably believe that such person is using or about to use deadly physical force, or that they reasonably believe that such person is committing or attempting to commit a murder, kidnapping, forcible rape, forcible sodomy, robbery, or arson.
- Security officers may use *physical force* upon another when they reasonably believe such is necessary to prevent or terminate the commission or attempted commission of damage to a premise. They may use *deadly physical force* if they reasonably believe such to be necessary to prevent the commission or attempted commission of arson.
- Further, a person in control of any premises, or licensed and privileged to be thereon or therein, may use *physical force other than deadly physical force* upon another person that he or she reasonably believes necessary to prevent or terminate a criminal trespass upon such premises.
- A person may use *physical force other than deadly physical force*, upon another to prevent or terminate the commission or attempted commission of larceny or criminal mischief with respect to property other than premises.

In summary, security officers must be cognizant of the following:

PHYSICAL FORCE

It must be justifiable and it cannot be excessive.

Security officers must believe that the use of physical force is necessary to effect an arrest, or to prevent escape from custody if they reasonably believe such person committed an offense or who in fact did commit such offense.

DEADLY PHYSICAL FORCE

Security officers reasonably believe it necessary to:

Defend self or a third person from what they believe to be the use or imminent use of deadly physical force (imminent fear of death or serious physical injury), or

Effect the arrest of a person who has committed or attempted to commit murder, kidnapping, robbery, forcible rape or forcible sodomy, and arson.

Regarding the security officer's ability to use deadly physical force on a person in immediate flight from certain crimes previously described, security officers would be well advised to use caution and restraint in the pursuit of such behavior. The probability of liability concerning damage or injury to others is great, particularly during the heat of the chase when emotions are intensified. In fact, the U.S. Supreme Court has ruled that a police officer cannot shoot at an unarmed felon who poses no immediate threat to the police or other citizens.[1] This ruling applies only to police officers, but the apparent message from the Court appears to be that no one should shoot at fleeing unarmed felons. Apparently, it will be only a matter of time when a citizen kills some felon under these circumstances and this ruling is tested in the courts.

Security officers should not solicit assistance from anyone whether a passerby, customer, or store employee, other than a police officer or a fellow security officer in the apprehension or pursuit of a suspect.

Both security officers and their employer become liable if the person assisting the security officer suffers an injury or acts wrongly against the suspect, and civil action is initiated because of that person's action.

Aiding a Police Officer

In addition to the justification described above, there may be a section in the criminal code of your state that gives a police officer the authority to direct a private citizen to use the necessary force in assisting him or her in an arrest, preventing the commission of an offense, or in an escape situation.

If during an incident a police officer requests the assistance of a citizen (a security officer), and that person or security officer refuses or in any way does not assist that police officer, that person commits an offense that may be considered a crime (refusing to aid a peace or a police officer).

Consider also, that the security officer should be mindful of any action that may be considered as interfering with a police officer or a public servant in the performance of their duties. See OBSTRUCTING GOVERNMENTAL ADMINISTRATION under POLICE OFFICERS in Chapter 10 for details.

Resisting Arrest

In most criminal codes, a person may not use physical force to resist an arrest, whether authorized or unauthorized, which is being effected or attempted by a police officer when it would reasonably appear that the latter is a police officer.

Note that a defendant may be charged with resisting arrest only when such an act—the resistance—is committed on or against a police officer. Security officers do not have that endowment or authority to charge a person with resisting arrest. If the subject resists the arrest of a security officer, and other than a charge of assault against the officer if applicable, the officer's only recourse is justification in the use of necessary force to make the apprehension as earlier noted.

SEARCH AND SEIZURE

The Search After the Arrest

Once the security officer has probable cause to make an arrest, a search of that person can be made under certain restrictions.

A person who is subjected to an illegal search is protected by the Fourth Amendment.[2]

In general, you must meet the test of reasonableness by:

1. Probable cause, and
2. To prevent general search and undue harshness.

A search can be made on the person and anything within the person's reach or distance (the ability to reach overtly and grab something). The security officer may conduct a search of the person for:

- Weapons (for the protection of the security officer and others),
- Access to items that could aid an escape,
- Property taken by the perpetrator during the commission of the crime and so observed as being secreted,
- Evidence that was used in the commission of the crime (e.g., an anti-security device), or
- Evidence that could be destroyed.

If the defendant possesses any contraband legally seized from the defendant and found to be illegally possessed (weapons, controlled substances), additional charges may be laid against the defendant.

Consider the following case law:

- Searches must be *limited* to the arrestee's "person and the area from within which he might have obtained either a weapon" or "something that could have been used as evidence against him."[3] (". . . a search or seizure without a warrant as incidental to a lawful arrest has always been considered to be a strictly limited right.")[4]
- Unreasonable search and seizures are protected by the Fourth Amendment, and in *Wolf v. Colorado*, the Supreme Court held that evidence obtained in violation of the Fourth Amendment is inadmissible in a criminal prosecution.
- Bear in mind that the courts have held that if an arrest is lawful, a search by a police officer or a private citizen is valid, and that justification existed for a search incidental to the arrest. As an example, if an arrest was legal, and a search was made of the defendant in a legal manner, and a concealed unlicensed loaded weapon was found on the defendant, he or she could additionally be charged with a weapons violation. This will include any contraband possessed in violation of the law.

Remember however, if the arrest was unlawful, then anything procured from that arrest is unlawful. See "*fruit of the poisoned tree*" concept on page 66 for details. This would include admissions, confessions, and any unlawful property or contraband taken or recovered from the subject.

THERE ARE TWO TYPES OF SEARCHES THAT A SECURITY OFFICER AS A PRIVATE PERSON MAY CONDUCT:

1. A search of the person that is *incidental to a lawful arrest*:
   - To prevent harm to the security officer or others by the use of a weapon or instrument possessed by the person arrested,
   - Search for any weapon or implement that will facilitate escape,
   - Search for any item or instrument used in the commission of the crime, and
   - To recover the proceeds of the crime (recovery of property), and to avoid the destruction of evidence.
2. A search with the *consent of the person* being searched, or the consent to search the property owned or under the control of the person who is the subject of the search.

Search of the Person. Generally, concerning search and seizure, when it entails a personal search of a person, private security personnel are not regulated by the same restrictions found in the Fourth Amendment as a law enforcement officer would be. The U.S. Supreme Court held in 1921[5] that search and seizures only applied to law enforcement and not to private persons. Subsequent decisions handed down in several state courts reaffirmed that position. For example, a security officer acting without any probable cause searches a young person's backpack and discovers a controlled substance illegally possessed. That officer could detain the youngster and turn him over to the police as a valid arrest, because a private person conducted the search. So it would seem that a security officer acting in this manner would not be in violation in searching a person or the person's property.

Although it would appear that such an act is legal by a private person, security officers should realize that caution must be used concerning the facts and circumstances surrounding a particular situation. Security officers acting outside of the *scope of their employment,* attempting a search without any reason, or committing some outrageous conduct such as requiring a subject to a strip search would be considered as unreasonable force in the minds of many.

Moreover, the employment of private security officers by a governmental agency raises certain questions. To illustrate this, consider a security officer employed by a public school district. Such employment depending on the municipality's control over the school district and its personnel may place that officer under *the color of state law.* This officer may also be required to act according to the restrictions placed upon law enforcement officers when custody of a subject requires a search and seizure under Fourth Amendment guidelines.

Consent to Search. Consent searches, other than a search of a person incidental to an arrest, have been held to be more reasonable and binding by the courts.

Whether the subject gives consent to search orally or in writing, the consent must have been given freely, intelligently, and without reluctance, fear, or provocation.

If the consent was asked of the subject, and it was given orally, such conversation should be witnessed by at least one other person and so noted in detail on the written report following the occurrence. Written consent is considered more binding, and if used, should be compiled prior to any search. See the Appendix for a sample copy of CONSENT TO SEARCH form.

As noted, a search of the person incidental to an arrest need not require permission to make that search. But if the subject under arrest owns or has possession of a vehicle in the retail establishment's parking lot that may contain stolen property from the officer's employer, consent should be obtained. Whether given orally or in writing, the search should be confined to the incident or investigation at hand. If the subject revokes the consent at any time, the security officer must cease the search.

If the security officer is conducting an internal investigation, and any search of the employees' property on or off the business premises is required, a written consent form must be compiled. The security officer should be aware that some restrictions may apply in a case such as this, and counsel should be sought from the company's attorney. Additionally, if there is a crime involved or the employee may be subject to arrest, authority to conduct an off-premises investigation and search should be given to the police.

Plain-View Doctrine. Consider also, that if security officers have the right to be in a certain place or area, and they happen to observe evidence or contraband in plain view, those items can be seized and will be admissible in court (*the plain-view doctrine*). In other instances, as a security officer you are not an agent of the government, and thereby have the right to search with due notice. For example, if the retailer posts signs noting "All packages are subject to search" as company policy, entry into the store can be denied to a person who refuses to give access to a search of the package. Also, if certain company rules are noted to all newly hired employees as part of their hiring procedures that all packages, bags, etc., are subject to inspection upon leaving the store or at the end of the workday, the search is legal and they must submit or suffer termination.

Regarding a consent search given by a subject, any search and seizure off the premises of the retail establishment should be conducted by the police. As narrated earlier, if the subject has an auto parked in a parking lot adjacent to the store, and gives consent even orally with witnesses present, it will be more binding if the consent is in writing before a search is made.

However, if the arrested person denies permission to a security officer to search an auto used and in possession by that person, and a search is made where stolen property is recovered, such a search and seizure may be considered illegal whether the auto is securely locked or not. The legality of such a seizure might be a question for the court to decide where property in full view is observed through a car window, and where the perpetrator cannot produce a sales slip for that property, and once recovered an additional charge of criminal possession of stolen property was added to the original.

In such a circumstance where property is later considered illegally obtained and therefore may not be used against the defendant, the security officer may have the satisfaction at least of making a recovery of the store's property to which the defendant had no right.

The security officer would do better and be on safer ground if the police become involved in searching the contents of an auto. If a search is not made and the auto is impounded by the police for safekeeping because the perpetrator has been arrested and placed into the custody of the police, an inventory of the auto's contents will be routinely conducted by the police for security purposes. This is standard procedure for police departments so that the perpetrator or the owner of the auto cannot claim at a later time that property or an item is stolen or missing from that auto while in police custody. If property is found not belonging to the defendant, and where the defendant cannot prove ownership but can be identified as belonging to the retailer and is considered part of the proceeds of a crime, such seizure is legal and the crime of criminal possession could be added to the initial charge.

Search issues concerning security officers and the admissibility of evidence seized are routinely brought before the courts. At present, a search of the person by a security officer incidental to a lawful arrest has been held to be proper. The courts have ruled that as long as the arrest was legal, any stolen property or contraband possessed by the subject may be charged against this person.

But there is a growing concern among civil rights activists that such actions by security personnel are encroaching into the areas of law enforcement. As security officers tend to augment and exercise traditional police functions in a escalating manner, and as civil rights issues become more applicable to this question, the courts may one day constrain them, and apply Fourth Amendment restrictions and guidelines to their conduct as well.

"Fruit of the Poisoned Tree" Concept. Remember, that the security officer must have reasonable grounds or probable cause to act, and the action must be "fresh," in that it must relate to an event that is occurring at that time or has occurred a short time prior, which is usually measured in minutes rather than hours.

If the rights of the suspect are violated in any way, such as an improper arrest or false imprisonment, then any evidence arising from that arrest is inadmissible. This would include incriminating oral or written statements made by the suspect, recovery of stolen property, and any other evidence gathered as a result of that arrest will be inadmissible in court, and the case would be dismissed (*"fruit of the poisoned tree" concept*). The retailer and/or the security officer can be sure that civil litigation against them will follow.

Other Issues. The loss prevention officer must also be cognizant that under the Fourth Amendment, "*The right of the people to be secure in their persons, . . . against unreasonable search and seizures . . .* " will include unlawful use of closed circuit television (CCTV). A hidden camera placed in a restroom or other area where a person has an objective *expectation of privacy* and not spied upon would be considered a violation of law. Such action by a loss prevention department would be considered a "search" and subject to the Fourth Amendment's requirement of reasonableness and privacy. The individual who suffers this offense could initiate criminal and civil action.

Employee Searches. Concerning searches conducted on employees, the employee has an expectation of privacy even if on or within the employer's premises. But if the employee has been advised of certain rules and regulations during the hiring process regarding an employee's conduct and what is expected of them, and such notification has been acknowledged by the employee, they must submit as may be required. As an example, an employer may require that all packages, backpacks, knapsacks, valises, and handbags be retained in lockers provided by the company upon beginning the workday. Also, that upon leaving the premises, all employee packages and hand-held items may be subject to inspection. A property removal pass signed by a supervisor or manager will accompany property not belonging to the employee that may be removed from the premises.

In particular, company lockers can be considered one area of specific importance in this regard. If the lockers are provided to the employee, along with a lock or padlock, under certain conditions the locker can be searched at any time. The employer has a master key for entry into that locker, and a search without permission under certain circumstances is legal. If the newly hired employee does not wish to accept the locker under these conditions, the employer may refuse the assignment of a locker to that person. But if employees are permitted to provide their own lock and key, the interior of such lockers could be considered private property by the court, and inspection of the contents of those lockers as privileged.

The contents of an employee's desk will be viewed generally as private property if assigned to that one employee, but if the desk is communal, no protection exists.

CIVIL RIGHTS

A violation of the Civil Rights Act would include any action that can be construed as denying a citizen his or her civil rights as defined in the Articles of the United States Constitution. This would include, but not limited to, cruel and unusual punishment;

freedom of speech, assembly, and movement; freedom from harm, detention, or imprisonment; freedom from unlawful search and seizure; right of privacy; and due process.

A violation under federal law, as noted in the *Civil Rights Act, §1983 Action*, can be charged against a person even though he or she may be charged with a crime for that same act in state court; there is no double jeopardy.

Federal Civil Rights Act—42 USC §1983

Basic Provisions of the Act. Section 1983 of Title 42 provides a broad spectrum of rights to every citizen as found in the Constitution. It denotes the above described protections in addition to the right to sue state officials and others acting under the "*color of state law*" to deprive a plaintiff ". . . any rights, privileges or immunities secured by the Constitution and Laws."[6] Further, it provides that any person, when under the color of state law, subjects another to a deprivation of rights secured by the United States Constitution shall be liable to the injured party. The provisions as defined covers many facets of civil rights, and are of particular importance to security officers in the performance of their duties.

Note that the defendant (violator) may also be subject to this federal law over and above any state actions for unlawful conduct. Double jeopardy does not apply. Activity in this area of law enforcement by the federal courts have become somewhat controversial, and these actions placing a defendant in jeopardy a second time are considered by many to be politically motivated.

To reiterate, double jeopardy does not apply concerning the enforcement of this law. In other words, whether the offender is charged in a state criminal and/or civil court, under this law, that same person can be charged in federal court for the committing the same act. The rationale established by these actions is that the victim was deprived of his civil rights under the United States Constitution and therefore, the federal courts may act.

ENFORCEMENT OF THE CIVIL RIGHTS ACT

The United States attorney may act under Title 42 of the United States Code when a citizen's civil rights have been violated. For example, if a security officer professed and/or identified himself as a police officer in effecting an "arrest" or some custodial action, he could be charged in a state court as impersonating a police officer. A federal action could also be laid against the offender for acting under the "color of state law," whether found guilty or not on the charge in the state court. As a further example, if a defendant is charged in a state court for murder and is found not guilty, the federal government may arrest and charge that same defendant in federal court for *civil rights violations* for the same act because the victim was deprived of life, liberty, etc. By the federal government seeking redress in a second court they satisfy the "public's" concern of accountability, if not in one court, then in the other.

The "Color of State Law"

To be in violation of the part of the law contained in this Civil Rights Act, the violator must have acted under the color of state law. This federal statute prohibits those who act under the color of law from violating a person's rights and privileges. It is intended to protect a citizen from illegal actions by a law enforcement officer or agency—the misuse of lawful authority.

Therefore, under this federal Civil Rights Act it can rarely be satisfied in the case of anyone except a state or government official. However, if a security officer acts *on behalf of*, *in cooperation with*, or *at the request of a law enforcement officer*, his or her actions are subject to the same restrictions as the law assigns to that law enforcement officer.

A §1983 action could lie against the defendants alleged to be police officers who used excessive force, or a citizen who collaborated with a police officer in making an unlawful arrest.

Consequently, we can say that the following occurrences in which a private person (a security officer) can be held accountable under this act are circumstances about which the officer must be aware and cautious:

- When a person's conduct (the security officer) is the direct result of a state agent's encouragement or command. The "state agent" can be a police officer, sheriff, district attorney, or any law enforcement officer in which the security officer acts on that person's behalf.
- When a private person (security officer) undertakes the performance and activities that are ordinarily exclusive to or only within the purview of a governmental entity. This would include a citizen or a security officer who professes and acts as if he or she were a police officer.
- When the private person has been granted certain benefits by the state (or any municipal authority) of such a nature that the individual and the state are inseparably linked. Note that this may include private security officers employed by a municipality or a school district.

The following court holdings refine the law:

- State statutes concerning the defenses accorded a retailer do not transform tortious conduct by a private merchant into an action undertaken by the state or under the color of state law in violation of title 42 USC §1983.[7]
- A case is noted involving a citizen who collaborated with a police officer in making an unlawful arrest.[8] But in another case, the security officer was a SPO (special police officer) appointed by the state pursuant to the New York Administrative Code (certain rights granted by a municipal authority).[9]
- When the plaintiff was stopped in a store by store detectives for stealing a telephone answering machine, he was handcuffed and taken to the security office. He was released a few hours later after issuance of an appearance ticket to appear at a later time to answer to the charge of petit larceny. A year later the plaintiff was acquitted of the charge. The plaintiff brought claim against the store under §1983 of the Civil Rights Act. The store argued that the store detectives were private citizens and, therefore, the store cannot be held vicariously liable.

But the store detective who initially stopped the plaintiff was in fact an SPO appointed by the New York City Police Commissioner pursuant to the New York Administrative Code. Under the code, a SPO possesses all the powers of a regular sworn police officer.[10] The court held that such a "police officer" with the power to arrest is a government official and is subject to §1983 liability. The store was held vicariously liable because the actions of the SPO were for the store's benefit and employees of the store "conspired" with the SPO in his actions.

Further, there was evidence presented that it was the store's unstated policy to arrest more readily minorities such as blacks and Hispanics, so the store could be subject to an independent liability also, along with the plaintiff's wife suing for emotional distress of seeing her husband taken into custody and placed in handcuffs.

- When a private person and the state jointly act to deprive a person of his rights.[11]
- It is not sufficient to make broad and conclusory allegations concerning the existence of an alleged conspiracy between private persons and state officials; the plaintiff must plead the facts with specificity.[12]

SEXUAL HARASSMENT AND PRIVACY RIGHTS

In 1980, regulations were issued by the Equal Employment Opportunities Commission (EEOC) defining sexual harassment as a form of sexual discrimination prohibited by the *Civil Rights Act of 1964*. In addition, the U.S. Supreme Court held that sexual harassment was a form of job discrimination.

Sexual harassment may be defined as any unwanted verbal or physical advance, sexual explicit derogatory statements or written material, or sexually discriminatory remarks made by someone in the workplace, toward the person, male or female, which is offensive or objectionable to the recipient. In addition, it includes when such action may or will cause the recipient discomfort, emotional distress, humiliation or a hostile work environment, and/or interferes with the recipient's job performance.

Sexual harassment violations may be brought before the federal courts by the EEOC, which enforces the law or before the various state courts that have enacted fair employment practice laws.

Sexual Harassment Conduct

The security officer must be cognizant of the fact that different people may consider or perceive certain words, phrases, or actions (inappropriate or unprofessional behavior) as unacceptable, improper, or that which may constitute sexual harassment. Therefore, the security officer must be constantly aware of how he or she interacts with another person, whether a customer or fellow coworker. The officer may also have to investigate a charge of sexual harassment by one coworker against another. In these instances, they will be guided by company policy and procedures, and may have to act in cooperation with the human resources or the personnel department of the company during the investigation and final outcome.

In any event, the officer must be aware of the state labor and criminal laws that define behavior such as this type of provocation, and that a victim of sexual harassment may have recourse in a civil as well as a criminal court.

Conduct that will or may be construed as sexual harassment:

- ***Touching***—The violation of personal space; caressing, patting, pinching, grabbing, kissing, or unnecessary touching or brushing up against of any part of the other person's body.
- ***Verbal***—Lewd comments, sexually explicit jokes, questions about personal life or behavior, whistling, and requests for dates.
- ***Visual***—Posters, magazines, articles, or cartoons that may be considered as lewd to that person. Also staring, ogling, or offensive gestures toward that person.
- ***Written***—The receipt of love letters or poems, particularly obscene letters or poems, and lewd or obscene written material.
- ***Power and threats***—The promise of promotion in return for sexual favors or dates. The demand for sexual favors with the threat of loss of job, bad performance evaluations, or loss of promotion.
- ***Force***—Rape, sexual abuse, sexual misconduct, and physical assault.

All of the above actions would be considered sexual harassment, and whether individually or in conjunction with other inappropriate acts may be considered *contributing factors to a hostile work environment.*

Sexual Harassment and Its Effects

Sexual harassment toward an employee can be the cause of several problems in the workplace. The security officer should become aware by observation, investigation, or inquiry, particularly after being advised by the human resources/personnel department, of possible problems that are or may be affecting some personnel. This would also include any information received from actual or anonymous sources.

Some of the factors that could bring about this perception by a security officer may be considered as follows:

- ***Economic***—when there is a overly noticeable turnover in personnel within one department or business area; when there is a noticeable rise in transfer requests or low productivity or interference with a person's job performance.
- ***Psychological***—where a coworker is visually embarrassed, has loss of self-esteem, has guilt or self-blame; also anger or emotional stress, the fear of the loss of their job, bodily harm, and impressions of their peers.
- ***Physical***—stress-related physical problems such as headaches, ulcers, and rashes; when it affects the recipient and his or her attendance or work performance.

Prevention of Sexual Harassment

Although it is almost impossible for the security officer to control another person's behavior in regard to many illegal acts, he or she should be aware of the elements that constitute sexual aberrant behavior and harassment. There must be an immediate reaction by the two departments of concern, human resources and loss prevention, to any report or indication of sexual harassment, to include investigation, analysis, determination, and consequences if any.

More importantly, the security officer should be an example to other coworkers and employees regarding his or her personal characteristics and proprieties. This would include the following:

- Know and completely accept the company's policy and procedure concerning sexual harassment.
- Report any behavior coming to his or her attention that may be construed as sexual harassment, whether there is a complaint or not. A written incident report should be compiled in any event.
- Perform all duties in a professional and diligent manner.
- Treat everyone fairly and with respect, including customers, visitors, and employees, without regard to gender, race, color, religious, or political affiliation.
- Refrain from making personal or derogatory comments about others, or making jokes to the detriment of someone else.
- Remember that such offensive conduct may be considered illegal if the result of such behavior is perceived as harassment.

Invasion of or the Right to Privacy

The right to privacy can be defined as the right to protection against unreasonable interferences with one's *solitude*, essentially the right to be left alone, the ability to lead a secluded life if it is one's wish, free of unwarranted publicity and without interference on private matters being made public.

Additionally, an invasion of privacy is a violation of one's *personality*, and since it is personal, the wrong committed does not extend to one's family or to a corporation. Among other elements for a *prima facie* case for invasion of privacy, the act must be an intrusion and would be found objectionable to a reasonable person.

There are four kinds of wrongful acts relating to a person's right to privacy:

1. Intrusion upon the plaintiff's affairs or seclusion by the defendant.
2. Appropriation of the plaintiff's picture and name by the defendant.
3. Public disclosures of private facts about the plaintiff by the defendant.
4. Publication by the defendant about the plaintiff of facts that place the plaintiff in a false light.

See also INVASION OF PRIVACY and DEFAMATION in Chapter 8 for further details.

JUVENILE APPREHENSION PROCEDURES

Without a doubt, many larceny offenses and other crimes against property coming to the attention of the security officer will involve a juvenile as the perpetrator. The security officer must be aware that there are different laws and procedures concerning the handling, apprehension, and custody of a juvenile. Various states detail specific actions that must be carried out by police and/or peace officers regarding children. Additionally, these statutes may also note the requirements that must be undertaken by a private citizen (security officer) prior to and after a juvenile is taken into custody.

Juvenile and Delinquency Defined

For the purposes of identifying when a child becomes classified as a delinquent, the following narration is offered.

According to *Black's Law Dictionary*, juvenile delinquency is antisocial behavior by a minor, especially behavior that would be criminally punishable if the actor were an adult.

A *juvenile* is a minor; a person who has not reached legal age; a child. A minor or juvenile may also be considered a person who has not reached the age of legal competence, which may be designated as the age of 18 in most states. Moreover, in some states, a minor may be classified as an infant in civil law.

A *juvenile delinquent* is a classification given to a minor who has committed a criminal wrong, and the offender is usually punished by special laws pertaining to children. Recent definitions of juvenile delinquency note that a delinquent is an infant of not more than a specified age who has violated criminal laws or has engaged in disobedient, indecent, or immoral conduct, and is in need of treatment, rehabilitation, or supervision.[13] Infancy is defined as the physical existence of a person who is under the age of *legal majority*,[14] and depending on the particular state, the age of legal majority may be from 18 to 21 years.[15]

Generally accepted is that the designation "juvenile delinquent" is a child who has engaged in an act that would be a crime if such crime was committed by an adult. Depending on a state's criminal code, juveniles may be classified as such depending on their age at the time of the offense. Some states require a minimum age of 10 or 12 years, and a maximum of 15, 16, or 17 years for a juvenile delinquency specification.[16] However confusing we may view the definition given to a juvenile offender by the various states, we must consider that each year court decisions reevaluate the status of a juvenile. Moreover, a juvenile court is in itself created by statutory law. Therefore, the boundaries of jurisdiction between the juvenile and criminal courts are subject to review and modification.[17]

The Courts

Depending on the individual state, the court that has jurisdiction over children may be called a youth court, a juvenile court, or a family court. These courts have been legislated by the state in favor of a specific jurisdiction of a parental nature, over delinquent, dependent, and neglected children.

The first juvenile court was established in Chicago in 1899 by educators and reformers seeking the causes of juvenile delinquency, and what role society, poverty, social status, and the family had in the performance of mischievous behavior. By 1945, every state had a court established with its own set of laws specifically for juvenile offenders. Most experts in the field of juvenile behavior believe that laws pertaining to children were originally conceived in an effort to place the youth, not the offense, at the forefront. Moreover, critics have noted that there is no uniform juvenile justice system in the United States. Unfortunately, the system today leaves much to be desired. Juvenile courts appear to be incapable of addressing the complex needs of children and families, often causing more harm than good to the child.

Some states make no legal definition or distinction between juveniles and adults when it comes to a crime committed or charged. Other states designate children of a certain age as "delinquent offenders" if they commit an act that would be a crime if committed by an adult. For those minor acts not reaching the status of a crime, such as truancy, runaways, or incorrigible conduct, a child could be classified as a "status offender," which might be described as a *person in need of supervision* (PINS). Each state may differ in the classification and treatment regarding children. Depending on the seriousness of the crime committed by the juvenile, the local prosecutor or district attorney along with the judge sitting in the appropriate court may adjudicate that the juvenile should face the charge in a criminal court and suffer the consequences as an adult.

However, the United States Supreme Court has set certain criteria for states in deciding whether a juvenile should be transferred or waived to a criminal court for trial.[18] The case before the court that brought about this decision concerned a 14-year-old boy named Morris Kent of Washington, D.C., who was arrested for the crime of rape and robbery. Although admitting to the crime, the boy was found by the court to be tried in violation of due process and the court dismissed the case.

It was found that the parents of Morris Kent were not notified of his arrest, that he was interrogated without informing him of his rights to remain silent or representation by an attorney, detention without a probable cause hearing, and the police had matched his fingerprints from previous records on file.[19]

In addition, the U.S. Supreme Court set standards for transferring or waiving a juvenile to a criminal court.[20] These precepts include the following:

- The seriousness of the alleged offense.
- The aggressive, violent, and premeditative nature of the act, whether against a person or property.
- The death or serious nature of personal injury to another.
- Whether the juvenile's associates acting in concert during the crime are adults who will face the charges in criminal court.
- The juvenile's maturity, emotional and social attitude, and the effect of home environment.
- The juvenile's previous criminal or juvenile record, if any.

In some states for the purpose of not designating or "branding" a child a "criminal," the juvenile may be considered a "respondent" and not a "defendant" as an adult would be, and when that juvenile is apprehended, he or she is "custodialized," not arrested.

Exceptions to this rule are some of the very serious felonies in which a child who initially falls under the designation of a juvenile delinquent may be charged as an adult in a criminal court. The age categories may differ in some states but the seriousness of the crime would be the determining factor in a charge against the juvenile as an adult defendant in a criminal court.

The court and the prosecutor acting in the interest of justice will make the determination as to whether the juvenile is to be "charged" as a juvenile delinquent in a juvenile court or as a defendant in a criminal court. Undoubtedly, the public's view of a horrendous or egregious act by the juvenile, particularly upon another child or person, would have some input in that decision. Depending on the state, extremely grievous crimes would include offenses such as murder, rape, sodomy, arson, or kidnap.

JUVENILE CUSTODIAL AND DETENTION PROCEDURES

A private citizen/security guard must advise the juvenile of the cause and purpose of the apprehension and the taking into custody, and require that he or she submit. Thereafter, most states require that without unnecessary delay, the juvenile must be taken to his or her home, before a family/juvenile court judge, or delivered to a police or peace officer.

Other than that proscribed in a particular criminal code, bear in mind that you cannot take a juvenile into custody (which is in fact an arrest) for a noncriminal act. The security officer can only take a juvenile into custody if the act committed by the juvenile was a crime if committed by an adult.

It is important to reiterate this principle: a juvenile can only be custodialized ("arrested") and detained if the crime committed was one that an adult could be arrested for.

But there will be times where a juvenile conducts himself or herself in such a manner to be a nuisance, become disruptive or cause a disturbance, but is not considered serious enough to charge the child with a "crime." Taking a child into custody under these conditions is technically an arrest, and most retailers will require that the child who is taken into custody be immediately turned over to the police for whatever juvenile procedures that they follow. However, it is suggested that for a circumstance in which a juvenile is "custodialized" but will not be charged and no police action will be requested, that the loss prevention manager be guided by the retailer's legal counsel concerning action to be taken. Counsel may feel that under some minor noncriminal circumstances that the parent/s or guardian of the juvenile be advised immediately by telephone of the circumstances surrounding the incident, and that they come to the store's location as soon as practical in order to take the juvenile into their care. If the parent/s or guardian will be delayed or will take an inordinate period of time, the security officer should request police assistance and turn over custody to the police even though there will be no court action. They are required to accept custody if a parent is not responding within a reasonable time. In this situation, the most that will happen will be that a "juvenile" or "juvenile incident" card is compiled by the police detailing the incident and with parental notification following. Remember, be guided by the procedures concerning juvenile apprehension in your state.

If the juvenile is taken into custody and is to be "charged," the police should be notified without delay. It then becomes their duty to advise the parent/s or custodian that the juvenile has been taken into custody, the circumstances surrounding the incident, and that the minor will be charged as a juvenile delinquent.

Custodial and Questioning Procedures

The security officer should also be aware that once detained, there are different procedures for juveniles than those that may apply to adults. The juvenile should be taken from public view as soon as practical, and should not be held in the same room as adult defendants if at all possible. Because a juvenile may become frightened and/or disorientated, the security officer should attempt to act in a calm manner and not aggravate the situation. The use of restraints, such as handcuffs, should not be used on a juvenile *unless* the juvenile is being charged as a juvenile delinquent and becomes unruly, attempts to escape, or acts in such a way that he or she may harm themselves or others. If restraints are used in these situations, and if called upon, the security officer may have to show to the court why it was necessary to do so. In these instances, the security officer should note witnesses to the actions of the juvenile and the necessity of restraints, and make the appropriate notations on the arrest/apprehension report for future reference.

Caution must be considered in the questioning of a juvenile. Other than that mandated in some state statutes, detaining a person for a period of time for questioning because of some suspicion and without probable cause, particularly if the subject believes such detaining is by force or threat, should be considered an unlawful arrest or unlawful imprisonment. However, in the case of juvenile offenders, in reality they cannot be considered able to relinquish their civil rights because of their age. Juveniles may become intimidated by a security officer, and place themselves in jeopardy by making admissions that may later be excluded in court. Nevertheless, a security officer could question and investigate a juvenile's actions if the officer receives voluntary compliance.

Voluntary compliance may be defined as consent by a person to communicate and/or respond to questions put to him or her by another. Juveniles in reality cannot give voluntary compliance if they don't understand what right they are giving up, and the court will definitely rule to that effect. But if a parent or a guardian is requested to accompany or meet the security officer in a security or a private office along with the juvenile and the child is questioned in that parent's presence without any hindrance from that parent, voluntary compliance may be presumed. This presumption is generally accepted in most states, but some restrictions may apply to the questioning of juveniles in the state in which the security officer is employed.

Many young adults and teenagers carry false or altered identification in an effort to prove an older age. When the age of the person detained is doubtful, or cannot be verified, it is recommended, regardless of the person's appearance, size, and maturity, that person should be treated as a juvenile. To reiterate—be cautious—if it is questionable as to the age of the person, treat that person as a juvenile rather than as an adult. There may be sanctions for treating a juvenile as an adult, but none for an adult who is treated as a juvenile prior to police custody.

Parental Notification Regarding a Written Record

The handling of juveniles can place a security officer in various litigious situations, particularly if the parent or guardian feels that the child was treated poorly or unfairly, has a propensity for suing anyone, or realizes that they might have reason to seek a civil action in court. Even though the security officer may request the parent to come to the store in order to release the child into their custody and to advise them of the incident with no further action contemplated, this may not cover a security officer's action or liability where certain procedures must be followed if required by law.

There may be some state laws, such as noted in New York State,[21] where there is a provision that requires a child who is under the age of sixteen, who has committed an act of theft within or directly proximate to a place of business, and whose alleged acts had they been committed by an adult would constitute a *misdemeanor* larceny under the Penal Law, must have the parent or guardian notified by regular mail within 72 hours if an "adverse information file" is compiled.

An *adverse information file* is defined in the law as any written or other communication compiled by a "person" specifying the particulars of an incident that alleges the theft by the child, and which then or at a later time might have an effect upon the child concerning benefits or other various legal eligibility's or abilities as defined in the law. The law does not concern itself with whether an "apprehension report" or an "incident report" is an in-house form or not, or whether such information or legal procedure would be a closed and sealed record for the juvenile. Any information is to be considered adverse whether the child is apprehended or detained in any manner or not, or whether the child is prosecuted as a juvenile delinquent or not. *Person* is defined in the law as any individual, corporation, or employees thereof, who maintains and operates a business, retail or wholesale or otherwise, for the purpose of offering commodities for sale. This law does not specify what action is to be taken or followed if the child commits an act that if an adult committed such act would constitute a felony.

Conclusion

At this point, it is important to reiterate the apprehension and custodial procedures of a juvenile. Generally stated, a security officer may take a child under the age of *legal majority* into custody as a juvenile delinquent for a crime if that crime committed by an adult would in fact be a crime and in which the officer would arrest that adult. The same admonitions apply as to any arrest—informing the child of the cause thereof, and requiring the child to submit unless custody is made immediately after a pursuit. After taking that child into custody, state statutes require that the child be turned over to a parent, magistrate, or police officer without delay. Most importantly, the security officer is responsible for the complete well-being of the juvenile while in the officer's care, and the officer's actions are ultimately guided by federal and state law.

The security officer should be cognizant of the laws and procedures governing the custody and terminology of a child in their particular state of employment.

Remember and be extremely aware, that as legislated in most state statutes, the security officer may take a juvenile into custody only if he or she committed an act that would be a crime if such crime was committed by an adult.

ENDNOTES

1. *Tennessee v. Garner*. 105 S Ct. 1694 (1986).
2. *Wolf v. Colorado*, 338 U.S. 25 (1949); *Mapp v. Ohio*, 367 U.S. 643 (1961); *Chimel v. California*, 395 U.S. 752 (1969).
3. Op. cit., *Chimel v. California.*
4. Reaffirmed position found in *Trupiano v. United States*, 1948, 334 U.S. 699 (1948).
5. *Burdeu v. McDowell*, 41 S.Ct. 574 (1921).
6. Jethro K. Lieberman, *The Evolving Constitution* (New York: Random House, 1992), p. 104.
7. *Newman v. Bloomingdale's*, 543 F. Supp. 1029, SDNY (1982).
8. *Alexnian v. New York State Urban Development Corp.*, 5544, F.2d 15 (2nd Cir.)(1977).
9. *Pratt v. Taylor*, 451 U.S. 427, 101 S.Ct.
10. *Rojas v. Alexander's*, 654 F. Supp. 856 (EDNY) (1986).
    Note: Under The Administrative Code of the City of New York, special patrolmen may be appointed by the police commissioner pursuant to the law and shall possess the same powers, and be subject to the same rules and regulations as regular members of the New York City Police Force; New York City Administrative Code § 14-106.
    However, as detailed in the New York State Criminal Procedure Law, § 2.10, Subd. 27, all special patrolmen appointed by the police commissioner are *peace officers* and have the powers conferred upon peace officers by New York State law. This appears to be in contrast to the NYC administrative code.
11. *Follette v. Vitanza*, 658 F. Supp. 492, modified, 658 F. Supp. 514, vacated in part, 671 F. Supp. 1362 (NDNY) (1987).
12. *Hauptmann v. Wilentz*, 50 F. Supp. 351, (D.C.N.J.) (1983).
13. *Dictionary of Legal Terms* (Dobbs Ferry, NY: Oceana Publications, 1996).
14. Ibid.
15. Margaret C. Jasper, *Juvenile Justice and Children's Law* (Dobbs Ferry, NY: Oceana Publications, 2001) p. 119.
16. Ibid., p. 67.
17. Franklin E. Zimring, *American Youth Violence* (New York: Oxford University Press, 1998) p. 117.
18. *Kent v. U.S.*, 383 U.S. 541 (1966).
19. Ellen Heath Grinney, *Delinquency and Criminal Behavior* (New York: Chelsea House Publishers, 1992) pp. 37, 40.
20. Op. cit., *Kent v. U.S.*
21. New York State Labor Law, Art. 7, §215-b.

Chapter 5

Applicable Laws and Alternative Charges

LARCENY

The most frequently committed crime is larceny, and as we shall see, it is the most frequently committed crime in the retail industry. Whether as a uniformed security guard assigned to a fixed post or as a plainclothes store detective, the most potentially liable situation that can place security officers in jeopardy is their actions, or inactions, concerning the arrest for larceny or the confrontations concerning a larceny investigation. If he or she is trained to make the proper decisions and react correctly in any action, the officer will not be placed in a situation where litigation could follow.

In regards to the theft of merchandise within a retail establishment, "shoplifting" is not a crime; the crime committed by a perpetrator is larceny, and "shoplifting" is a type of larceny.

Depending on the value of the property stolen, the crime may be a misdemeanor (petit larceny) or a felony (grand larceny). Whether the defendant is charged with committing a petit larceny or a grand larceny will depend on the monetary delineation given to the crime in the state in which you are employed.

Central to any "stop" or apprehension, a security officer must have seen the crime of larceny committed. In the case of an officer involved in the area of retail theft, he or she must also keep as close contact as possible until the subject leaves or is about to leave the store so as to be sure that the item stolen is still on the person and not disposed of prior to leaving.

In other words, "when in doubt, let it out."

If you didn't see it, it didn't happen. Accordingly, unless the security officer is *positive* that a larceny did in fact take place, that the subject under observation did in fact commit the larceny, and that this subject still has the stolen item/s on his or her person as he or she is leaving or about to leave the store, the officer should *not* make the "stop" or pursue any confrontation.

Larceny Defined

Larceny may be generally defined as the theft of property, and the property may be money or anything of value. A person who steals property, with intent to deprive another of property or to appropriate the same to himself or herself or to a third person, or wrongfully takes, obtains or withholds such property from an owner thereof, commits a larceny.

Depending on the individual state criminal codes, larceny is delineated into two categories, and within each category, various degrees of criminal liability:

1. ***Felony***—Grand larceny or grand theft
2. ***Misdemeanor***—Petit larceny, petty larceny, or misdemeanor larceny

The difference between the felony and misdemeanor larceny is the value of the property that is stolen. Some states define misdemeanor larceny as anything of value $1,000 or less. With the felony classification of a larceny in the value of over $1,000, the crime is grand larceny, with the more serious degrees depending on the total value of the property stolen.

Grand larceny sections may also include property consisting of a public record, scientific material, a credit or debit card, or regardless of the value of the property, property that is taken from the person of another *without force* (e.g., pickpocket, purse snatch).

Culpable Conduct

Larceny occurs because the offender has the *desire* (intent), *opportunity*, and the *ability* (the means) to commit the act. Security officers should be constantly aware of those opportunities and attempt to correct or guard against them. Desire reflects the mind-set of a person who wishes to commit a criminal act, and this desire cannot be anticipated. It can be controlled or reduced to some extent from a crime occurring within particular retail premises, by the knowledge that if caught the perpetrator will certainly face criminal charges. In this case, fear of apprehension may reduce the desire. The opportunity to commit the crime and the ability for the criminal to complete the act can also be neutralized or diminished by security safeguards such as employee awareness, property protection, and security hardware. The more these factors are in motion and are effectively utilized to complement each other, the criminal will go elsewhere.

Value of Stolen Property

In the case of retail theft, the value of the property stolen and for which the subject could be charged depends on the retail price. For example, if an item of merchandise is marked to be sold at $99.00, then that would be the value of the loss that the retailer would have suffered, because that is what the retailer would have received if it was sold rather than stolen. Caution must be used, however, in situations of "sale prices." If an item were marked down from $1,199.00 to $999.00 for example, the charge would be petit larceny—if the law stated that larceny of $1,000 or less is a misdemeanor—and not a felony. Again because the retailer has placed the value of that item at $999.00, which is what the retailer would have suffered as a loss.

And yet some jurisdictions may consider that the tax on the merchandise should be added and made part of the loss. As an example, if an item is to be sold at $999.00 and the added state tax would bring the total price above $1,000.00, the accused would be charged with a felony, since that is the loss with the tax that the retailer would have suffered if the item was in fact sold.

Some state statutes may relate to how the value of property can be ascertained. Value may be described as the market value of the property at the time and place of the crime. Among other definitions, property that cannot be ascertained pursuant to the standards set forth in the law may have its value deemed to be in the amount less than grand larceny.

Defense By a Criminal Defendant

Claim of Right. In any prosecution for larceny committed by trespassory taking or embezzlement, it is an affirmative defense that the property was appropriated under a *claim of right* made in good faith. The security officer assigned to the retail establishment should be acutely aware of this area of law regarding a person who might fall into this type of predicament.

A good example of an incident where a claim of right may occur could be described as follows:

A person purchases or receives as a gift an expensive coat. He finds that the coat does not fit him or, for whatever reason, wishes to exchange the coat for another of the same value. He enters the store and rather than going through the store's procedure of returning the item and making an exchange, he goes directly to the coat department and selects a coat of equal value to his liking, takes that coat and places the coat he is returning on the rack before leaving. In actuality, his motive was not to steal—there was *no intent* to steal, but he did, at least in a technical sense, exercise control of property belonging to another in which he had no right to do so. If all of the facts in this case are unknown (or not believed), and an arrest is pursued in this case, the subject could produce a defense under the *claim of right* made in good faith. If court action was taken and the reasoning accepted by the court, whatever charge laid against this subject most assuredly would be dismissed.

Anti-Security Item

An anti-security item may be any tool or device designed for the purpose of overcoming detection of security markings, attachments, or devices placed on or around property offered for sale at a retail establishment. Under many state laws, a person who knowingly possessed or used such a device in a retail mercantile establishment may be guilty of this offense.

The subject must have the intent to commit the crime of larceny, and be aware that he or she does in fact possess an anti-security item that can overcome a security system, and a conscious objective to use it in effecting the larceny. If the subject possessed an item that could disable or impair an alarm system or an electronic tag, but possessed it for legitimate reasons, there is no crime. The possession of a simple pair of pliers, if used in the commission of a larceny under these circumstances, would satisfy the intent of the law and the defendant could be charged with an additional crime.

LICENSE AND PRIVILEGE

Retailers confer open and free access to the public for one reason—to do business. The retail enterprise is open for people to purchase and/or browse. They therefore give the public license and privilege to enter their premises.

Customers who enter a retail establishment are generally considered to do so pursuant to a license or privilege. However, retailers can limit license or privilege by imposing lawful conditions.

License and privilege can also be granted by paying a fee for entry to facilities such as a theater, sporting event, or a museum. If a person enters such an establishment without paying the required fee, he or she commits a trespass.

Some conditions also limiting license and privilege might include the following:

- The wearing of shirts and/or foot coverings by customers while in the store, or other restrictions such as no bathing suits to be worn.
- A customer accompanied by any type of animal (unless a "seeing-eye" dog).
- Prohibition of smoking, loitering, congregating, or the taking of photographs within the building.
- Prohibiting access to areas within the building not open to the public (storerooms, mechanical rooms, warehouse areas).
- Posting of signage at the store's entrance regarding the retailer's right to examine all packages carried by a person entering the building, and if refused, entry can be denied. This may include the electronic search of the person prior to entry into a building.

Appropriate signage may be required at the store's entrance or within the building for some of the restrictions noted above so that if enforcement is required, the conditions of denying entry may be pointed out to the offender. Check with local laws.

In particular, license and privilege can also be taken away by removing a person from the premises under certain conditions.

Removal from the premises may include the person who becomes unruly, obnoxious, loud, and boisterous, causes a crowd to collect because of his or her behavior, causes damage, offends other employees and/or customers, causes a business interruption, or has been caught in a criminal act. The retailer or his agent, advising the offending person to leave or never to enter the store again under threat of arrest for trespassing, can give such a person a trespass warning orally or in writing. The threat or warning of an arrest for a trespass effectively takes away that person's license and privilege to enter at any time after being so warned.

No matter in what type of business enterprise a security officer is employed, the value of a trespass warning and the threat of arrest for that trespass against a person who causes any type of business disruption in any manner cannot be overstated.

Trespass Defined

A person may be guilty of trespass when he or she knowingly "*enters or remains unlawfully*" in a building or upon real property.

A person "enters or remains unlawfully" in or upon premises when he or she is not licensed or privileged to do so. This privilege may be taken away from a person with a written or oral warning.

A person who, regardless of intent, enters and remains in or upon premises, which are at the time open to the public, does so with license and privilege unless he or she defies a lawful order not to enter or remain, personally communicated to the person by the owner or agent (security officer) or other authorized person of such premises.

A license or privilege to enter or remain in a building, which is only partly open to the public, is not a license and privilege to enter or remain in that part of the building that is not open to the public. A trespass may occur on property that is clearly marked or posted against trespass by signs or fences. Also, a trespass occurs when a trespasser remains or comes onto a property after being ordered off by a person authorized to do so.

A security officer in control of any premises may use physical force *other than deadly physical force* if believed necessary to prevent or terminate a criminal trespass on such premises.

Privileged Access. Security officers should be aware that certain public officials have a *legally implied consent*, in that they have *license* (a qualified privilege) to enter on and into a property or building for the purpose of an investigation of a crime, fighting a fire, a legal inspection, or other type of official conduct. These public officials would include police officers, firefighters, fire inspectors, fire marshals, building inspectors, and tax assessors, among others. If access is denied, or clearly slow in granting access, it is possible that the person denying access to the public official could be charged with obstructing governmental administration.

Burglary Defined

A person is guilty of burglary when he or she knowingly *enters or remains unlawfully in a building with intent to commit a crime therein.*

The crime committed within the building may be a misdemeanor or a felony, and the crime may be against a person or property. There are several degrees of burglary, depending whether the building is a dwelling or not. If it is a dwelling, occupied or not, whether the subject is armed, with an accomplice and whether the crime takes place during the day or night will determine the seriousness or degree of the burglary.

Because a retail mercantile establishment functions as a business in a building, open for business or not, it is not a dwelling and therefore is considered the least serious of the burglary classifications. However, we must remember that all degrees of burglary are felonies.

Burglary vs. Trespass. Be mindful that when a business establishment is closed and secured for the night, in effect closed to the public for business, license and privilege to enter has been taken away. If a person breaks into or enters upon a closed premises, he or she enters and remains unlawfully therein. If this person commits a crime within the building, he or she will be charged with a burglary *and* whatever crime he or she committed. But if a homeless person enters unlawfully for the purpose of keeping warm on a cold night, he or she commits a trespass, not a burglary. There was no intent to commit a crime therein, but the person was there unlawfully. If this homeless person had to break into the building where damage occurred, he or she may also be charged with criminal mischief. A burglar need not commit a *break and entry* to perpetrate a burglary. A burglar may enter through an open window, or an open or unlocked door. He or she may also hide within the building until after the store is closed, commit the crime intended, and "*break out*" or leave through a door that he or she may unlock from within. The elements to remember for a crime to be considered a burglary is that a person comes aboard *unlawfully with intent to commit a crime within* the premises. Consequently the perpetrator has committed the crime of burglary, in addition to the crime committed within.

A burglar enters a building by whatever means for the purpose of breaking into a money safe. On the way to the room where the safe is contained, he observes a woman working late that particular night. He accosts her and commits a rape. After restraining her with the use of rope, he directs his attention to the safe. After a few hours of working on the safe, he realizes that he is unable to enter the safe and leaves the premises.

A few days later, the police arrest the perpetrator after an investigation and charge him with burglary, rape, and attempted larceny. If he had gotten into the safe and removed the money from therein, he would have been charged with larceny, the degree (misdemeanor or felony), depending on the amount (value) of money stolen.

The Advantage of the Trespass Warning Particular to Larceny Offenses. Retailers or security officers may use the trespass and burglary sections in their state's criminal code to their advantage as long as it can be applicable and legally applied. You are advised to check with your local police department or district attorney in order to determine whether the following course of action is acceptable.

The charge of burglary can be a very useful tool in the reduction of repeat shoplifting offenders, or in passing the "word on the street" to other possible shoplifters. In order for a shoplifter to be charged with the additional crime of burglary, he or she must have been previously warned. If a shoplifter is apprehended, whether he or she is charged with the crime or not, the security officer as part of routine processing should issue a "trespass warning" to the subject. The warning may be verbal or in writing, but the written warning would have more validity.

The trespass written warning should be read to the subject and then asked if he or she understands the warning just read. This person should then be asked to sign the written warning with the security officer and one other person witnessing the acknowledgment. If the subject refuses to sign the document, the security officer should read the complete warning as written, and in the place reserved for the subject's signature make note by writing in that the subject "*refused to sign,*" and place his or her signature along with one other as witness in the appropriate place. An incident report should specify the circumstances surrounding the occurrence along with the offering of the trespass warning, and the refusal of the subject to acknowledge with his or her signature. A copy of this trespass warning should be attached to and made part of that incident report.

(See the Appendix for a sample TRESPASS WARNING form.)

Subsequently, if a person is charged with trespass because he or she violated the directive not to or never to enter, the prior oral warning would be substantiated by the recording of that prior incident, if only in an incident report. It would be more advantageous, however, to issue a written warning signed and acknowledged by the subject, and witnessed by one or more persons; the retailer or security officer/s. In any event, a trespass warning compiled correctly and maintained for future reference can be used if the same subject enters the store at a later time for whatever reason, particularly if he or she commits or attempts to commit a crime.

A person "enters or remains unlawfully" in or upon the premises when he or she is not licensed or privileged to do so since a trespass warning takes away that privilege. A person who, regardless of intent, enters or remains in or upon premises, which are at the time open to the public, does so with license and privilege unless he or she defies a lawful order not to enter or remain, personally communicated to the person by the owner or agent of such premises. By defying such lawful order not to enter or remain, a person may be charged for violation of the trespass sections of said criminal code.

Accordingly, after having been so directed by an owner or authorized person not to enter the premises in question, if a person thereafter and knowingly enters therein with intent to commit a crime, and in fact does commit a crime, such person may be charged with *trespass and burglary*. Of importance in this regard is that any person who may commit any type of crime, attempted or not, on a premises for which he or she has been warned never to enter may be charged with committing three crimes—trespass, burglary, and the crime attempted or committed.

Additionally, if the subject were in possession of an anti-security device at the time of apprehension (which could be considered a burglar tool under the law) or any other contraband (illegal weapon, drugs), he or she could be additionally charged. As an example, see ANTI-SECURITY ITEM on page 80.

ATTEMPT TO COMMIT A CRIME

A person is guilty of an attempt to commit a crime when, with intent to commit a crime, he or she engages in conduct that tends to effect the commission of such crime.

The security officer must realize that the intended conduct of the subject must lend itself to the commission of the crime. The act if completed must be a crime, a felony or a misdemeanor to be classified as an attempt. The subject must initiate the crime, so that if completed, a crime in fact would have taken place. Planning or thinking of committing a crime is not a violation of law. But if the subject completes certain actions or elements of the crime, and because of circumstances does not complete the act, he or she can be charged with this offense.

Consider the following incidents:

1. A perpetrator decides to commit a burglary at ABC Hardware Co. He has the intent to break in and steal certain merchandise. At 3 A.M. one morning, he breaks the window at this establishment with the use of a tire iron and is about to enter therein when an audible burglar alarm sounds and scares him away. He is apprehended by the police a short distance from the store in possession of the tire iron.
2. Based upon observations by security personnel, a shoplifter carries away certain merchandise with apparent intent to steal. She passes several cash registers

without offering to pay for the merchandise. She is about to pass through the exit doors of the store when she is stopped and apprehended. She never exited the building. She explains to the security officer/s that she was going to pay for the merchandise but wanted to step outside for a cigarette, then reenter, and continue shopping before going to a register to check out.

3. A shoplifter goes throughout the store taking merchandise, and is about to exit the store when he realizes that store detectives are closing in and about to apprehend him. He drops the merchandise at the exit and runs from the store. He is apprehended a block away.

In example number one above the perpetrator could be charged and convicted of attempted burglary. And in both the number two and three instances above, an appropriate charge would be attempt to commit a larceny, and depending on the value of the merchandise the perpetrator attempted to steal and was recovered, the crime could either be a misdemeanor or a felony. Because we can assume in both cases that there was intent to commit a larceny (the intent to take, steal, and carry away property belonging to another) but the merchandise never left the store, attempt to commit the crime can be presumed with such intent under probable cause.

However, caution should be used in case number two above. The "smoker" noted may use her "excuse" as a defense to the charge in that she had no intent to commit a crime, is addicted to nicotine, and had to have a cigarette at the time she was apprehended. If the court accepts the explanation, she could receive a dismissal. Therefore, whether charged with the attempt to commit a crime or criminal possession of stolen property, the security officer/s should make note of their probable cause in detail. This would include the subject's actions and movements as he or she progressed through the store, his or her selection of the most expensive items in each category, his or her apparent constant observation and location of cameras and sales persons, etc. Moreover, any actions by the subject that led to suspicious activity or actual theft captured on tape would add to the justification for the stop. In other words, the security officer should "build probable cause" to justify the officer's later actions, and destroy any defense offered by the defendant.

CRIMINAL POSSESSION OF STOLEN PROPERTY

Additionally, there may be another section of the criminal code that can be used to the advantage of the mercantile retailer or the security officer. Criminal possession of stolen property may be considered when a subject cannot be charged with the larceny or another crime but did possess property not belonging to him or her and had no right to, and a presumption exists that such property was stolen.

A person may be considered guilty of criminal possession when he or she *knowingly possesses stolen property* with intent to benefit himself or herself, or a person other than the owner thereof, or to impede the recovery of said property by an owner. Depending on the value of the property, the crime of criminal possession of stolen property may be a misdemeanor or a felony.

Therefore, if the facts are not present for a charge of larceny, where the actual "taking" of the property was not witnessed by the security guard, and subsequent investigation based upon probable cause found that the "thief" has possession of property that has been stolen, the charge of criminal possession could be used. Moreover, the thief may be charged with "possession" whether the stolen property is on the thief's person or in an auto under his or her control.

It may be considered a *presumption* that a person who knowingly possesses stolen property is presumed to possess it with intent to benefit himself or herself or a person other than the owner. Further, there is no defense for the defendant in whom he or she had no participation in the theft, or the actual person who committed the larceny has not been identified, apprehended, or convicted.

We can see then, that there is much more latitude given to the retailer and/or agent, the security officer, in the applicable use of the criminal possession statutes rather than the larceny statutes.

THEFT OF SERVICES

For those retail establishments that offer restaurant or cafe services to their customers, there inevitably will be incidents when a customer will refuse to pay for the food. Whether it is a cup of coffee or a full-course dinner, failure to pay is considered a crime in many states. If the management wishes to pursue it, legal action can be taken against the offender.

Again, depending on the state in which the offense may occur, if a person with intent to avoid payment for restaurant services rendered, avoids or attempts to avoid such payment by unjustifiable failure or refusal to pay, by stealth, or by any misrepresentation of fact he or she knows to be false, he or she is presumed to have intended to avoid payment. A person who fails or refuses to pay for such services may be arrested and charged with "theft of services."

If the security officer did not witness the service (the serving of the food) and did not witness the refusal to pay, he or she cannot make the arrest for the crime. The officer can, however, assist another employee who witnessed the offering and refusal in making the apprehension and requesting police assistance. The employee in this case must act as the complainant; the security officer is only assisting in the arrest.

Note also that if a person makes use of a stolen credit card or debit card for a service, that person commits a crime (possession/use of a stolen credit/debit card, larceny, *and/or* theft of services). Additionally, if a person makes use of a credit card legally possessed and used, and subsequently refuses to pay for that service, he or she may also have committed a crime. Remember that in this case there must be intent by the perpetrator to refuse to pay for this service.

See also the next section on CREDIT CARDS and DEBIT CARDS and THEFT OF SERVICES BY AN EMPLOYEE in Chapter 13.

CREDIT CARDS AND DEBIT CARDS

Without doubt, credit card fraud has become excessive in the past few years with retailers and banks suffering great monetary losses. The experienced security officer will find that the card issuers, with banks in particular, generally fail to respond to inquiries or investigations by limiting information to a great degree. It has been acknowledged that with the finance charges and yearly subscriber fees paid by the cardholder and the fees charged to the merchant for the use of the service, the losses suffered by fraud is minimal compared by the exceptional income generated, and more than satisfies these losses. Accordingly, other than the more serious cases of fraud and larceny do banks and issuers of cards rarely investigate and prosecute.

Unless the security officer has a good working relationship with the credit card investigators of a particular issuer, cooperation will be almost nonexistent in any type of inquiry or investigation you may conduct. Rarely will credit card investigators be in contact or conduct an inquiry via a retailer unless the offense involves a loss of some consequence to their institution, and is in their interest.

According to the 2001 National Retail Security Survey published in 2002, the least serious source of financial loss for the retailer was credit card chargebacks, accounting for .014% of annual sales of the participating retailers. This was a significant reduction in credit card loss compared to the NRSS total of .23% for the year 2000.[1]

So then, in reality, retail establishments should not become involved in extensive investigations that involve credit card fraud and/or larceny. Other than the local police agency that has jurisdiction, the U.S. Secret Service has the mandate to investigate these crimes, and the individual card companies or banks have their own investigative services that may become involved. Security officers should restrain themselves to an inquiry or a current illegal act that would be taking place immediately at a point of sale. This would entail the investigation of a perpetrator at the point of sale who offers a stolen or fraudulent credit card for the purchase of merchandise or a service, and once confirmed, the arrest of that perpetrator for the crime attempted and the criminal possession of the stolen or fraudulent card.

The following *may* be included in the criminal legislation of the various individual states concerning the use or misuse of credit cards:

- Many states now include a *public benefit* card in their statutes along with credit and debit cards.
- It is generally considered *unlawful use* of a credit card, debit card, or public benefit card when in the course of obtaining or attempting to obtain property or a service, a person uses or displays such a card that he or she knows to be stolen, revoked, or canceled.
- Further, a person is guilty of criminal possession of stolen property when he or she knowingly possesses stolen property with the intent to benefit self or a person other than the owner thereof, or to impede the recovery by an owner thereof, and when the property consists of a credit card, debit card, or public benefit card.
- Generally a person who possesses two or more stolen credit cards, debit cards, or public benefit cards is presumed to know that such cards were stolen, and is guilty of criminal possession. Possession of two or more stolen credit cards, debit cards, or public benefit cards is criminal possession as a felony in many states. When used in the course of obtaining or attempting to obtain property, the perpetrator may also be additionally charged with the second crime (larceny, unlawful use, etc.).
- If a person obtains or attempts to obtain a service, or induces or attempts to induce the supplier of a rendered service to agree to a payment thereof on a credit basis, by the use of a credit card or debit card that he or she knows to be stolen, such act may be considered a theft of service, in which the perpetrator may be charged with a separate crime.

- Regarding the merchant's "defense of lawful detention," some states give the retailer and agent a defense into the investigation of a possible crime in cases where a credit card or debit card was used unlawfully within the retail establishment.

Confiscation of Cards

Relative to the unauthorized or improper use of credit cards or debit cards reported lost or stolen by a cardholder or the issuer of the card, the security officer should determine distinct facts before any action the officer may be about to take when confronted with a possible credit or debit card fraud. This should encompass only those cards contractually accepted by the retailer, and following the particular requirements and certain procedures that the card issuer demands prior to the completion of the transaction. These procedures most certainly will include the following:

- The monetary limit of the sale required for approval, after which the card must be swiped or telephone inquiry made for an approval code.
- The inspection of the card for fraudulent impressions or markings, effective and expiration dates, and if necessary, comparison of signatures.
- The acceptance of the card by the retailer from only the person named on the card.

Any violation of these procedures required of the retailer and/or if the card was misused by the cardholder in some manner, the retailer will suffer a "chargeback," in that the retailer will suffer the monetary loss and not the issuer.

Consider also that upon a clerk attempting an approval on a sale, the credit card issuer fails to approve the sale and requests confiscation of the card from the holder for various reasons other than criminal, the retailer under contract with the issuer is bound to take custody of the card. However, an action of this type usually causes some type of confrontation with the customer, and in many cases, letting the cardholder retain custody with another choice of payment might be the better way to calm the situation.

On the other hand, many banks offer an incentive of $50.00 or more to the cashier or salesclerk for the seizure of a canceled, reported stolen, or fraudulent credit card. Such an enticement could cause the situation to escalate into a physical encounter. In an effort to control any confrontation, a security officer should respond to the location of the incident and be present at the time of the seizure.

All employees who handle credit card transactions should be instructed that if the bank or company that issued the credit card requests that the card be confiscated for whatever reason from the person offering such card, discretion and prudence must be carefully considered. Rather than becoming involved in an argument or a physical confrontation over the custody of the card, the employee should relinquish the card and request another form of payment.

ENDNOTES

1. Richard C. Hollinger and Jason L. Davis, *2001 National Retail Security Survey—Final Report.* A Security Research Project, University of Florida, Gainesville, 2002.

The Fundamental Elements of Retail Security and Safety

Part 3

THE RETAIL LOSS PREVENTION OFFICER

A security force exists is for one purpose only—to protect the assets of the employer, or the client to whom that force is contracted to safeguard. These assets include, but are not limited to, customers, employees, merchandise, stock, equipment, money, proprietary information, and the facility itself. The primary components within that security force are the security guard and the security officer.

The most important attribute that security guards or officers can have in a retail environment is the confidence and reliance placed in them by their superiors and fellow coworkers. The managers and employees must have the assurance that their security personnel have the ability, levelheadedness, and knowledge to handle any situation or emergency in a professional manner. Whether they are uniformed security guards stationed at a fixed post or plainclothes security officers, the guards or officers must have the wherewithal to accomplish the tasks and functions of that particular position. And they must possess the expertise, confidence, and initiative to perform these functions when supervisors are not present.

In addition, this would include the officer's demeanor—how calm and professional an officer acts in a given situation, particularly a volatile situation where an incident could escalate into a serious altercation. The individual's dress, bearing, attitude, speech, personal and business ethics all play a large role in how he or she is received by superiors, other employees, and the general public. Knowledge of company policy and regulations, the laws that officers must enforce, how they must act in enforcing those laws, and the consequences of any unlawful acts on their part are essential components of the officer's general expertise.

Perception by all who view security personnel is a most important aspect in this field of endeavor. A uniformed security guard's job isn't the most stimulating activity in the business world. Assigned to a fixed post, they can easily fall into a rut, become bored or apathetic, and lose enthusiasm for the work they do. However, the uniformed security guard is the visitor's or customer's first impression of the company the guard represents. If the guard's dress is sloppy and their demeanor is below par, they hurt their image and the company that employs them. The uniformed guard is part of the business community and the personification of the company he or she works for whether their employment for that company is contractual or proprietary in nature.

Remember that private security, like the police, is a fluid field. Laws change, court rulings can affect your actions, technologies are advancing rapidly, and techniques are constantly improving. If you study, seek training, develop professional skills, and conduct yourself professionally, your attitude and behavior will be reflected in your job performance and how the public perceives you. In addition, the retailer and employees must have the assurance that their security guards and officers have the ability, prudence, sensibility, and knowledge to handle any given situation or emergency in a professional manner.

However, and to the detriment of the profession, many businesses are not staffed with trained security/loss prevention officers to investigate suspected and existent retail theft issues, in addition to safety and liability concerns. The trained retail investigator can be an asset identifying and correcting the problem quickly, assist in the recovery of property and currency, and minimize associated liability exposures. It is hoped that the intent and analysis advanced and clarified in this book concerning retail loss prevention will add to the body of knowledge of the profession and the expertise of the retail loss prevention officer.

Chapter 6
Loss Prevention

Until recently, safety and security were often viewed as unrelated disciplines. Because of the investigative, detection, and protection functions of security, some security professionals and corporate management regarded "security" as strictly a preventative and punitive function.

Security was the terminology attributed to security guards or officers who worked in a business or retail environment. Their tasks were fundamental to catching thieves and recovering the property that they stole—basically crime prevention. Because deterrence is difficult to define, how and if security contributed to the bottom line could hardly be determined on how many apprehensions and/or recoveries were made during a particular period. If shrinkage problems increased, or at least remained the same even though thieves were caught, there had to be other attainments where theft and fraud losses could be reduced. Hopefully, we will cover those areas in this book.

Safety, on the other hand, was usually associated with customer and employee injuries, worker's compensation, fire and building safety, and claims investigations among others. Safety was a secondary issue with security officers, and was usually left to management with only some of the investigative and reporting elements as part of the security officer's job.

Because many of the goals and objectives of security and safety are identical in nature, both disciplines will have an effect on the business enterprise, in addition to employee production, morale and integrity; in reality, job satisfaction and their commitment in protecting the company's assets. As the loss prevention philosophy developed to cover all risk areas, more businesses, particularly retailers, combined the responsibilities of both disciplines into one department.

The terminology and designation used most often today is *loss prevention*, which entails the coverage of all risks—security and safety, and consequently takes on a much broader definition and a larger range of responsibilities. No matter whether the security officer is employed in a public agency, institution, hotel, or a retail establishment, loss prevention will entail a variety of duties and accountabilities.

RETAIL LOSS PREVENTION

There are various areas or fields that retail loss prevention officers will come across in some manner, which have or will be reviewed here in some detail. Whether they are empowered to investigate some or all of the criminal acts described, or the ability to conduct other responsibilities noted below would depend on their expertise, their employer, and the authority granted them.

Therefore, as we shall see in the following pages, loss prevention may be considered an all-encompassing designation that includes the responsibility, authority, ability, and control over the following:

Internal Audits

Safety inspections and audits
Fire inspections
Inventory audits
Safe/cash room audits
Access control

Accident Investigation

Customers/visitors
Employees
Auto and property damage

Professional Interaction

Law enforcement and police agencies
Attorneys
Insurance /bank investigators
Customer service

Internal Investigation

Shrinkage
- Paper loss
- Employee theft
- Intentional damage
- Unintentional damage

Employee larceny and fraud
Criminal mischief
Computer fraud, loss, damage, malicious interference
Theft of services
Cashier shortages
On-site drug use
Hazardous occurrences
Sexual harassment
Employment and civil rights violations
Misappropriation of property

External Investigation

Larceny; shoplifting
Check/credit card fraud
Theft of services
Property damage
Product liability
Sabotage, espionage, and terrorism
Business disruption—power loss, electric or gas, and telephone
Vender fraud and larceny
Bomb threats
Extortion

Computer Crime

Sabotage and espionage of business records, programs, and theft of services

Other Concerns for Loss Prevention

In addition to the myriad of duties noted above that may be assigned to retail loss prevention officers, the following incidents and/or obligations are to be considered most important in the safety and security of the facility, its personnel, and its visitors:

- Fire, burglary, alarm response, and the control, operation, and maintenance of fire and burglary alarm systems
- Building, personal, and workplace safety; employee training in safety and security
- Disgruntled customers/employees; strikes, pickets, unruly crowds; crowd and traffic control
- Disaster planning and response
- Workplace violence
- Cash, check, and credit card controls; money escort

Additionally, security officers must be aware and concerned with the present and ever-changing laws and ordinances, and that of their employer's and/or client's policy, procedures, rules, and regulations, all of which will have an effect on the officer's conduct and duties.

Defining the Security Officer

It should be understood that in the retail environment, there are two distinct security officers—the uniformed guard and the plainclothes store detective. Although the terminology *security guard* is somewhat outdated, and the title of *security officer* is becoming the norm, there is still a variance of tasks between the two as used within the retail security industry.

For the purposes of this book, the loss prevention officer, security officer, and the store detective will be synonymous in meaning. When referring to a security guard, it will mean those uniformed officers who basically stand a fixed post. However, depending on the retailer, these guards may have some or many of the duties assigned to a loss prevention (security) officer, but will be hindered in many instances because of the uniform worn by the guard.

Security Guard. This officer usually is assigned to a fixed post such as the entrance and/or exit to a retail establishment, and is the most conspicuous deterrent to shoplifting. Guards may or may not inspect purchases or packages depending on the desires of the store proprietor. Guards may also be assigned to a warehouse receiving dock or a customer pickup area, or to act as a receptionist for access control. Their mere presence at doors will usually reduce loss by shoplifters to a manageable level. Moreover, security guards assigned to a shipping or receiving dock is a definite deterrence to a great degree concerning internal and vender larceny. The presence of uniformed guards in any event helps to ensure security protection in most people's minds. They may wear a variety of uniform styles. It may be a police-type uniform (the hard look) or be attired in a blazer jacket, white shirt, and tie (the soft look). The type of uniform will depend on the image that the retailer wishes to project. In most high-priced showrooms or business establishments outside of urban areas, retailers are adverse to the use of uniformed guards, for fear of the image that is projected or perceived by the customer. But in recent years, the trend appears to be changing as business losses escalate.

Security Officer/Store Detective. This security officer works in plainclothes, because he or she wishes to blend in with the type of clientele served by the retailer. In the recent past, the plainclothes detective was the employee principally charged with the apprehension of a shoplifter or any other person who committed a criminal act on premises. This officer is the one most knowledgeable regarding the laws of arrest, seizure of persons and property, use of force and detention, and civil rights violations among others. Although the shoplifter may know all the tricks of the trade, hiding from closed circuit TVs, or circumventing electronic devices, store detectives are their greatest threat, because the person near or next to the shoplifter could be watching his or her every move.

At present, *loss prevention officer* is the job title most often assigned to this employee, although generally he or she is referred to as a *security officer*.

Today, retail loss prevention officers (security officers) have been assigned tasks and functions within their job description that will include a multitude of duties other than the reduction of loss by shoplifting or other larcenies. These duties and responsibilities are noted throughout this book.

THE ESSENTIAL QUALITY OF A SECURITY FORCE

The efficiency and effectiveness of a security force equates to the qualities of good security officers. These qualities can be measured by:

1. The care and effort taken by the employer in the selection process
2. The care and effort in the training of all security personnel
3. The effective supervision of the daily functions, tasks, and other performance of all security personnel

In addition, the loss prevention manager must utilize the personnel and resources given by the retailer as *efficiently*, *effectively*, and *economically* as possible in an effort to provide as much protection to the company's assets as practicable.

The Security Officer's Role in Security and Safety

Basic Responsibilities. The employer defines the role of the security officer. A good loss prevention manager helps the company to define that role properly. The basic duties and responsibilities are the following:

- The prevention of injury, loss, or damage to people and property

The protection of persons and property from harm or loss is the security officer's primary responsibility.

- The prevention of criminal activity on the property of the employer or client
- The enforcement of the policy and procedures, and the rules and regulations of the company the officer serves
- Control of access to areas not open to the public
- Prevention of trespass for those persons denied access or who wish to commit a crime
- Control of people and/or traffic
- The compilation and maintenance of reports and records for the purpose of control, inquiry, research, criminal and civil contentions, statistical review and critique, and governmental regulations
- Assistance to the employer or client in acting as their agent as directed by company policy and procedures
- Assistance to customers, visitors, and employees

In essence, the role of the security officer is to provide order, safety, and security.

Additionally, the retail security officer should consider the following in order to become a successful member of the security team:

- The employer or client always comes first.
- Safety and security means protection and detection, not acting or reacting as a police officer.
- There are criminal and civil laws covering the security officer's actions, as well as his or her employer's policy and procedures. The officers should be aware of their limitations concerning any of their actions.
- Security officers should consider themselves as professionals, and act within the standard required for their behavior, which is higher than the standard set for the average employee. Because security officers have been given more authority, access, and freedom to move about than any other employee, they will always be open to scrutiny by managers and coworkers. Therefore, their professional and ethical conduct should be a model for other employees of the company.
- Security officers have the responsibility to report all inappropriate or illegal behavior by employees, which includes damage to property, theft of property, theft of services, and failure to adhere to the policy and procedures set by the company.

The Functions of a Security Officer. To reiterate, security officers are hired to protect life and/or property from all harm and loss, and from any unlawful activity occurring on the property to which the have been assigned.

The following *functions* of *detect*, *deter,* and *report* would apply in most cases to all security officers and guards, but are of particular importance to retail security officers:

1. ***Detect***—the retail security officer should:
   - Be alert, observe, perceive, *and*
   - Discover—by the use of investigation, inquiry, inspection, informants, and loose talk.
   - Conduct routine and diligent patrol or rounds throughout the facility—internal and external.
   - Be cognizant of the indicators of theft, drug or alcohol abuse, and equally as important, safety problems or violations.
   - Make use of his or her five senses and be aware of "gut feelings," which come with experience and expertise.

As part of this process, security officers should be aware that employees know what is occurring or what has occurred in their store, office, or warehouse. They are aware of who steals, uses drugs, violates safety and loss prevention policies, of potential violent situations in the workplace, or those guilty of civil rights and/or sexual harassment violations. Most employees wish to eliminate those situations that have a negative impact on the workplace. In order to accomplish this, a system must be placed in effect where the employee who comes forward with information is granted complete anonymity. Without the employee remaining anonymous, the fear of retaliation in some manner will cancel the flow of information that security officers should have and rely upon in their investigations.

Statistics have shown that most apprehensions of shoplifters and dishonest employees are the result of information received or reported by other company employees. In an effort to reinforce messages to employees on how losses affect them and the bottom line of the company they work for, the loss prevention manager should institute an ongoing awareness training program for all employees with all assigned security officers assisting in this training. This can be accomplished by visual aids, postings on bulletin boards, company newsletters, and actual training classes. A most effective means of eliciting information would be a reward system, where the informant would receive a monetary reward if a positive conclusion were accomplished as a result of the information received. See INFORMANTS on page 115 for further details.

2. ***Deter***—there are three elements required for a perpetrator to commit a crime:

   Intent—the desire to commit the act.

   The opportunity—the chance to perform, and if possible, to complete the act.

   The means—the perpetrator has the tools, the ability, or the assistance to complete the act.

The security officer has no control over the intent that a person may have, other than close surveillance where the subject is aware of being watched. But by removing one of the two other elements noted above, the crime has little or no chance of being completed. The retailer can remove the opportunity and means by various types of deterrents. Some of these are:

- Visible closed circuit TV cameras and monitoring
- Locks, secured areas, gates, alarms, and signage
- Visibility of uniformed security guards at entrances and exits
- Mirrors covering secluded areas
- Salespersons being actively conscious of all movement, and all that occurs within their department. This includes acknowledging a customer's presence with a nod or greeting with immediate assistance, or advising that the customer will be helped shortly.

See also DETERRENCE AS A FACTOR IN CRIME CONTROL in Chapter 7 for further details.

CULPABILITY

In order to understand the elements or conditions that are necessary to execute and consummate the criminal act, we must also understand culpability. The perpetrator of the crime must have one of the following mental states (culpability), in that the perpetrator did:

- Intentionally commit the crime, or
- Knowingly committed the crime, or
- Recklessly committed the crime, or his act was one of
- Criminal negligence.

3. ***Report***— document all occurrences.

All incidents that come to the attention of the security officer, during or after an incident or occurrence, no matter how minor, should be reported in writing and filed by category. Each report should be separate by designation and may be titled as one of the following:

- "Incident report," or "case report" (This may include reports of damage to company property, products liability concerns, or any other report that should be documented.)
- "Apprehension/arrest report"
- "Customer accident report" (customers/visitors—statistical and insurance purposes)
- "Employee accident report" (worker's compensation—statistical and insurance purposes)
- "Bomb report" or "bomb threat checklist"
- "Property recovery report," *and* any other report that the retailer may require

Document every incident or encounter; if it is not documented, it did not happen.

The reports should be numerical and/or chronological within each year, so that easy research can produce an individual report if needed at a later time. In larger loss prevention departments, the loss prevention manager might wish to have a separate type of report for different incidents.

The purpose for a report is to maintain records for future reference that may be required by law, insurance and liability purposes, or company policy, and if filed and maintained within categories or type of incident numerically, they can be easily researched. Any incident such as accidents, injuries, and criminal occurrences can create problems beyond the immediate impact of that incident, particularly if these incidents are not reported immediately and accurately. These incidents include, but are not limited to, any unusual occurrence, criminal activity, accident, loss, and all safety and security concerns, conditions, and/or circumstances.

For further information on report writing, the contents of reports, the importance of a report, and problems that can arise from poorly written reports, see Chapter 21 REPORT WRITING and recordkeeping under that same title.

Security vs. Safety Considerations. In conclusion, although the above three functions appear to relate to criminal and security occurrences, the terms *detect*, *deter*, and *report* may also be applied in the area of safety.

A security officer while on routine patrol may detect some type of safety problem. As an example, it may be the detection of the smell of smoke or gas, where through further inquiry and investigation the officer determines that a fire or gas leak is in fact taking place. If it is a fire, the officer must now deter that fire by controlling and putting it out and/or by calling for the fire department. Deterring the gas leak can be made by shutting down the gas flow, or if unable to do so requesting emergency response from the gas company. In either occurrence the security officer would further deter harm and injury by an evacuation of all customers and employees. And finally, the officer's written report would contain all the particulars regarding the occurrence.

Remember that *detection* and *deterrence* may not only occur in an emergency situation. Routine inspection and auditing procedures can uncover safety and security violations that may require immediate correction or further study.

THE SECURITY OFFICER AND THE EMPLOYEE

In many retail establishments, the security officer is very often requested at the scene of minor arguments or confrontations so that the occurrence does not escalate into a more serious situation. Moreover, many managers will solicit ideas, viewpoints, or concurrence on various issues solely because security officers gather expertise as they become involved in a variety of problem-solving incidents on a routine basis.

Therefore, being aware and considerate that the position of security officers is a step above the ordinary store employee because of their duties and assigned responsibilities, loss prevention personnel should be encouraged to make use of the following hints as a guide in their daily contact with other employees and supervisors during their routine duties:

1. Ensure that all employees are trained, and retrained, in what to look for and how to respond to a possible shoplifting, tag switching, or other confrontations in a manner that will not cause them to fear such a challenge or legal involvement.
2. Ensure that as part of their security and safety training, that all employees are aware of what will happen—not *can* happen—what *will* happen if they are caught stealing.
3. As security officers pass through all areas of the store during their routine patrol, they should give employees feedback on their performance, particularly positive feedback and praise and let them know that their input is appreciated.
4. Make sure that all controls, systems, and procedures concerning security and safety are user-friendly.
5. Make it easy for employees to request the assistance of a security officer by various means and for various reasons. When an employee requests immediate assistance, stop whatever you are doing, and respond quickly.
6. If the situation is minor or unfounded, try not to criticize the employee in public for being overcautious or overzealous. Take the employee aside when convenient and discuss the occurrence and your response in detail. Avoid peer and public embarrassment so those employees will not be encouraged to circumvent the system or procedure in the future.
7. Although it may appear that the most important person that concerns the retailer is the customer and the business the customer brings to the store, never treat a customer better than an employee, and never belittle an employee in the presence of anyone.
8. Set an example for employees in all things, since management holds the security officer above reproach and has been given more authority than other employees.

9. By being friendly, and making yourself accessible to employees and encouraging a close working relationship, you gain friends and information. However, be aware that close fraternization or socializing with other store employees, particularly during working hours, could compromise the officer's perspective or actions in the performance of his or her duties.
10. Most important of all, treat all employees and superiors with respect and consideration.

THE USE OF WEAPONS, DEVICES, AND CONTROLS

The security officer is not a police officer and normally does not have the authority or training to use the following weapons or devices described here. Whether defensive or restrictive in nature, the retailer and the loss prevention manager must realize that no device should be used by a security officer without the necessary training and the legal use of that device. Improper or illegal use will most assuredly result in criminal action against the officer, and civil action against the officer and the retailer.

Possession and Use of Firearms

An armed security officer in a retail establishment, uniformed or not, can produce a serious threat to personal injury and customer relations. The image that a uniformed armed guard presents to the customer is not the impression that the retailer wishes to project. As generally perceived and accepted by security professionals, the police, and the public, the use of armed security personnel should not be considered even in locations or establishments where the probability of robbery is high. The chance of serious harm or death to customers, employees, and passersby is too great a threat. Regular department, market, or discount stores really have no need for an armed officer, and unless a specific retail establishment such as a high-priced jewelry showroom warrants that their security officers are to be armed, the retailer should not have their officers carry a weapon. If it becomes necessary to carry a firearm, many states require licensing. In addition, some require training and certification over and above that of an ordinary citizen who may be licensed to carry a firearm, concealed or not.

The reason for these restrictions and the required training is that the use of a firearm can be devastating and final in a life-threatening situation. The chance of death and/or injury to customers, visitors, passersby, and employees is elevated to a greater degree for misfortune with weapons on the premises, notwithstanding the associated criminal or civil liability that will occur. Therefore, in general, an armed security guard on retail premises should not be employed.

Handcuffs

Handcuffs are used only to restrict the movement or prevent the escape of a defendant, or to protect the defendant or others from harm. Handcuffs are never to be considered as a weapon to be used to pummel or punish a suspect or defendant. All security officers who carry and have the need to use handcuffs must be trained in their use, and should maintain the necessary documentation for future reference in order to negate any possible civil or criminal liability actions.

Generally, any person placed under arrest may be secured with handcuffs. However, juveniles (children under the age of sixteen, or who may appear to be under that age) should not be handcuffed for any reason other than if the juvenile becomes so combative, unruly, or disturbed so as to hurt self or others, he or she must be restrained. See JUVENILE APPREHENSION PROCEDURES in Chapter 4 for further information on this subject.

Although handcuffs are considered a restraint and are to be used in that manner only, some business establishments require that their officers not possess or make use of handcuffs or any other type of restraint. Notwithstanding local or state laws that may permit or govern the use of restraints, the security officer must abide by the rules and regulations of the retailer that requires compliance.

Batons and Jacks

Batons, known generally as "nightsticks," are carried by all police officers. They are carried on all tours of duty, and not only during the night tours as were common many years ago. It is an impact weapon, and can be harshly effective in pain compliance. As with the firearm, the baton hanging from an officer's belt can also be intimidating to the general public.

Without the specific training and the legal and correct use of this device, many law enforcement agencies frown upon security guards carrying and using batons under any circumstance. However, because the baton can be perceived by the courts and the general public as an offensive weapon, there are some states, cities, and towns throughout the country that have ordinances or laws against possession of this device.

Blackjacks, saps, slapjacks, and billy clubs are concealed weapons and are against the law to carry. Generally, any pain compliance weapon or instrument that can be concealed on the person, or any other device that may be described as an offensive weapon are not to be possessed, carried, or used by a security officer. Security personnel cannot justify their use in any way.

Chemical Sprays and Electronic Devices

Simply stated, a chemical spray may be defined as a "noxious material" and may include any container that conveys any drug or other substance capable of generating offensive, noxious, or suffocating fumes, gases, or vapors, or is capable of immobilizing a person. Possession of chemical devices containing a noxious substance such as "mace" or "pepper spray" may be considered against the law depending on the state in which the security officer is employed.

However, there are some states where a *self-defense spray device* is not prohibited. It may be described as a pocket-sized spray device that contains and releases a chemical or organic substance, and is intended to produce temporary physical discomfort or disability through being vaporized or otherwise dispensed in the air. Possession and use of a self-defense spray device may be defined as the protection of a person or property, under circumstances that would justify the use of "physical force."

Although the use of this device could be perceived by the public as excessive, security officers should be guided by state or local law and their employer's policy in regard to possession of such a self-defense device.

Regarding electronic dart and stun guns, other than the exceptions noted in the various state statutes for police and other law enforcement officers, electronic dart guns and electronic stun guns are also against the law and are never to be possessed or used by security personnel. Moreover, the use of this type of weapon could cause serious cardiac injury, is generally frowned upon by the public even when used legally, and can be a serious liability issue.

Radios and Public Address Systems

Radios—A handheld two-way radio can be one of the most useful tools employed by security personnel. It is a link to headquarters or point of dispatch, and between other security officers. When used properly, the radio has been considered the one tool that has saved many a life. Immediate transmissions during emergencies save time and more serious consequences. As with the police, many security groups use the familiar "10 code" system for transmitting and receiving. This or a similar type of code serves two purposes. When used in this manner it conveys the brevity or precise meaning of a message. It is also an attempt to communicate a cryptic message so that other passersby or customers will not have the knowledge of some activity taking place.

All security officers and guards in a retail environment should carry a two-way handheld radio. Because they may require some type of help or immediate assistance from another security officer, or may be first aid responders and/or part of the emergency response team, an immediate contact via radio is vital. The Federal Communications Commission (FCC) regulates and routinely monitors all radio frequencies, in that the use of obscenities and improper transmissions are forbidden. Moreover, improper and unprofessional transmissions could place the security officer in an embarrassing position if overheard by another person.

Public Address Systems—The public address system is usually used to make sales or other business announcements throughout the store on a routine basis. It also can be a very useful tool for loss prevention. During a fire or bomb threat, a coded message may be used to alert certain or all store personnel and in any event, a subsequent evacuation if necessary. It can also be of great use in lost or found children, or when used to direct security personnel to a particular area without anyone suspecting their response.

One effective use may be the public announcement "security to area 30, please." Although having no meaning whatsoever, an announcement such as this several times during the workday, with assorted "area" numbers, will cause some discomfort to the shoplifter or someone intent on some larcenous intent since they will not know if they are in "area 30" and if security is responding to this location. It is important that only members of the loss prevention department are informed of this tactic, and its use limited to those days when the store is busy and overly crowded. If all store employees are aware of the rationale, they may make the public conscious of it and its use will become valueless. When used discreetly, the public address system can be put to good use.

Chapter 7

Risk Analysis and Threat Potential

IDENTIFICATION OF THE AREAS OF LOSS

The retail merchant has the responsibility to eliminate or reduce as much risk potential as possible as best reflects his operational needs and financial capabilities. Therefore, the retailer may consider the nature of his or her business in "risk-taking" terms. Other than those risks that the merchant takes with potential profit in mind such as business location, purchasing popular and seasonable merchandise in advance or granting customer credit, the retailer must consider the risks that his or her business is exposed to just because it exists.

Because the greatest loss that a merchant suffers is from internal and external theft, the overall objective of risk management is to use a systematic approach that would afford the retailer the highest level of protection (lowest risk) against criminal acts at the lowest cost in terms of security investments. Those investments could include an able security force, security hardware, and awareness training. In reality, proactive measures such as these will produce a reduction of criminal opportunity.

Risk analysis is a complete and thorough assessment of the perils and hazards that a business may face.

Loss Prevention Surveys

A loss prevention survey may be defined as an in-depth on-site examination of a physical facility and its surrounding property for the purpose of determining its security and safety status. This will include identifying all forms of deficiencies that may be found in a retail establishment, and defining and recommending the protection and/or corrections needed. A cost-benefit relationship should be included in the final report so that the retailer may be apprised of the cost of options offered, if any, to alleviate the problem.

Corporate loss prevention departments or internal auditing departments of large retailers should be able to conduct routine inspection and auditing functions at various stores or sites within their company. At some on-site loss prevention departments, loss prevention personnel may have the expertise to investigate in-depth procedural problems and can do so effectively, but because of other duties, may not be able to extend themselves to finding and/or correcting the problem. Whether it becomes a corporate internal audit function or not, there are times when an outside audit or advisor might be helpful in seeing things differently or offer a different viewpoint. In these instances and if necessary, the retailer should have the resourcefulness to look for the services of a security or safety consultant.

There are a limited number of private security or safety firms and consultants that have the capability to conduct loss prevention surveys for retail businesses. Their intent is to focus on prevention rather than a specific loss. With the help of management and the on-site loss prevention department, it is their goal to determine where the losses are occurring, and devise methods and systems to correct and/or control the issue. Success of these consultants will depend on their or their firm's expertise and knowledge in their field of endeavor—both security, safety, and the business in question.

Finally, the retailer must institute and/or carefully consider those controls identified and brought to the retailer's attention, which will be necessary to bring about changes in policy, procedures, employee actions, and attitudes.

A loss prevention survey may be defined as an in-depth on-site examination of a physical facility and its surrounding property for the purpose of determining its security and safety status. This will include identifying all forms of deficiencies that may be found in a retail establishment, and defining and recommending the protection and/or corrections needed. A cost-benefit relationship should be included in the final report so that the retailer may be apprised of the cost or offered options, if any, to alleviate or control the problem.

Examination and Inquiry. Regarding inquiries into retail shrinkage, a prominent and reputable national survey and report has been conducted and published annually by the University of Florida. Because these security research projects are important in identifying sources of loss, prevention strategies, and asset control policies and procedures, we should consider in some detail what the authors offer the loss prevention professional.

These surveys have identified the issues of loss and provided accurate information for loss prevention departments to make best use of systems, prevention, and use of manpower. The latest survey completed in 2001 was the tenth of an annual series, and its focus was strictly on retail loss prevention and retail store security activities. Retailers responding to the survey represented twenty different retail markets. This included a spectrum of the entire retail industry other than restaurants, bars, auto dealers and service stations, and catalog and Internet retailers.[1]

It has been noted that shrinkage can be defined as the financial losses due to several factors that include employee theft, shoplifting, vender fraud, and administrative errors.[2]

According to the National Retail Security Surveys conducted by the University of Florida over the past decade, an analysis of losses and strategies that affect the bottom line would include the following:

A THREAT ANALYSIS OF LOSSES AND STRATEGIES FOR THE LOSS PREVENTION MANAGER

Sources of shrinkage—employee theft, shoplifting, vender fraud, and administrative errors (poor stock control, paper loss, pricing and cashier errors).

Other losses due to crimes—bad checks and credit cards, fraud, vandalism.

Loss prevention strategies—employee screening measures, loss prevention awareness programs, asset control policies and procedures.

Corporate commitment ($) to loss prevention—loss prevention systems, hardware and personnel.

Average dollar loss per incident

The retailers responding to the 2001 survey questionnaire experienced an average shrinkage rate equal to 1.80% of the total 2001 sales. This figure was greater than the 1.69% reported in the year 2000. The survey also notes that with the retail base of $1.845 trillion in annual sales for the retailers involved in the study, the annual loss due to inventory shrinkage was approximately $33.21 billion.[3]

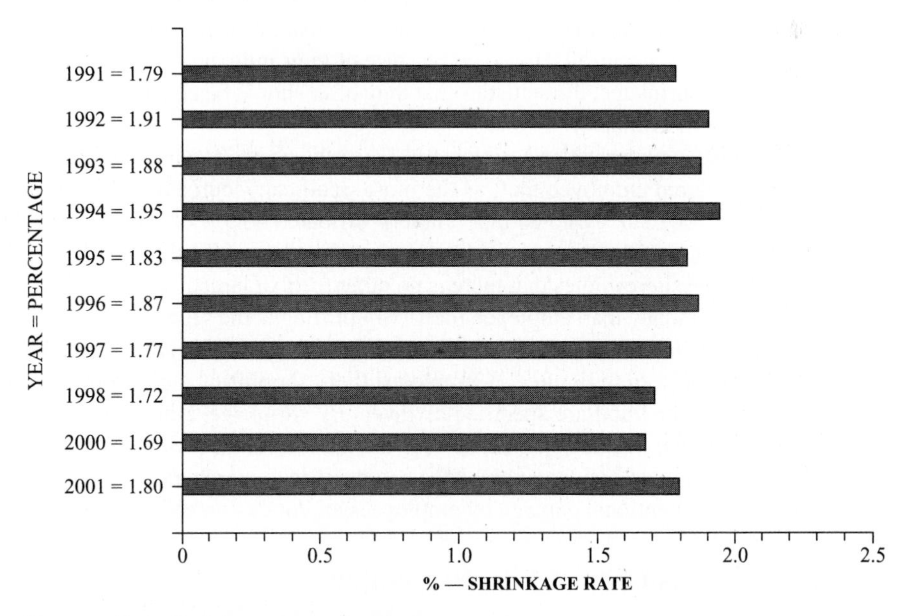

Figure 7-1 Shrinkage Rates by Year

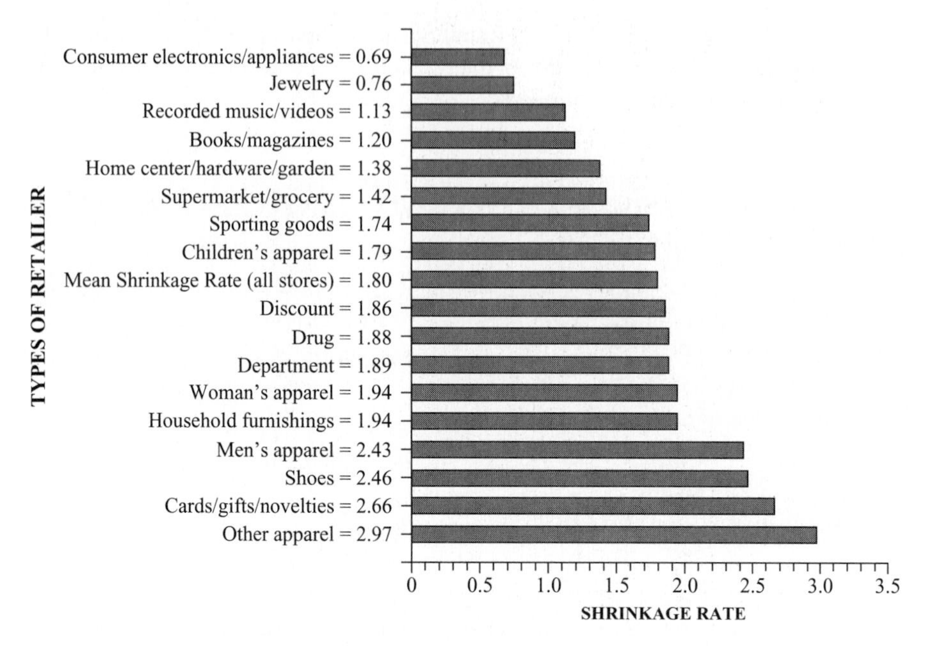

Figure 7-2 Shrinkage Rates by Retail Market

The authors of this study caution that the perceived sources of inventory shortage identified by loss prevention executives is not exact because of an indefinite audit trail in most cases, so that these executives must estimate or make educated guesses about how their losses occurred. However, because of their intimate knowledge regarding the problems of shrinkage, the statistics that they offer should be considered the best source of information available.[4]

Consistent with retail security surveys over the past ten years, loss prevention managers considered employee theft as the most significant source of inventory shrinkage. In fact, the 2001 survey noted that retailers attributed 45.9% of loss to employee theft, which was in fact the highest yet observed in the ten-year history of these surveys. In particular, the survey notes that there is no other form of larceny that costs the American public more money than employee theft.[5] Shoplifting is the second most important area of shrinkage, and retailers attributed 30.8% of their loss to this type of larceny.[6]

As can be seen in Figure 7.3, employee theft, shoplifting, administrative and paper loss, and vender fraud are specified as inventory shrinkage. But there are a few other areas of loss that must also be addressed, and also affect the profitability of a company. This would include accidental breakage and damage to merchandise and not written off as such, and intentional damage by employees and/or customers.

The Responsibility of Loss Prevention

The loss prevention manager is responsible for the ongoing appraisal and analysis of all the possible risks, threats, and assorted hazards that may or will occur within the retail

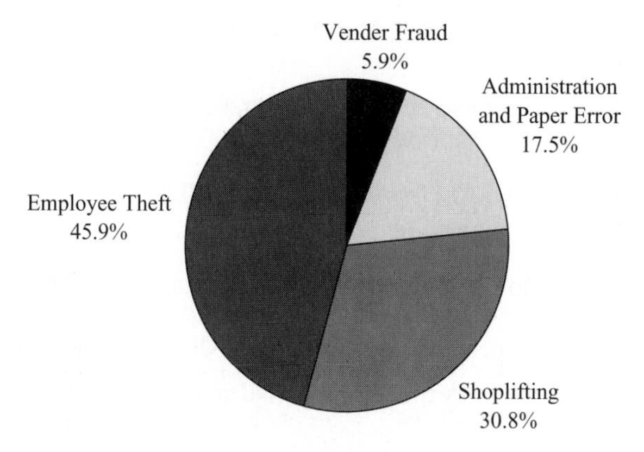

Figure 7-3 Sources of Inventory Shrinkage

establishment. This would include not only loss by criminal activity, but by civil litigation and unintentional losses.

This is a continuing examination that must be achieved so that the loss prevention manager may adjust the level of security, safety, and personnel to meet the threat. Procedures are set for a purpose and are required to be followed, but circumstances change, and it can be said that facts and circumstances can alter any situation. But realize also, that most deterrents or deterrent issues cannot be measured, and though various factors contribute to shrinkage, some can also never be measured.

Although it is the responsibility of the loss prevention manager to be aware of all threats and risks and to act accordingly, security officers should be attentive to the immediate and/or imminent security and safety problems. Officers should advise their supervisor or manager of their observations, thoughts, possible changes or corrections that might be made, or any situation that should come to the attention of the manager. In this way, old procedures can be corrected or amended to fit the new threat or risk. The contributions and feedback from security officers to management is of utmost importance in the security and safety of the facility, and in the creation of prevention strategies and/or solutions.

Before a loss prevention manager can begin to search for solutions, he or she must first make a systematic approach to safety and anticrime procedures:

Initially—

- Clearly identify the problem.
- Determine how significant are the losses or safety concerns.
- Determine what and where are the major losses or safety problems.
- Conduct a survey of present anticrime procedures and systems. Look at present safety procedures.
- Determine how can they be prevented, or at least reduced to an acceptable level.

- Determine how the new procedures or systems will affect the present business operation.
- Determine how management and employees will receive these new procedures or systems.
- Determine if the present security personnel are proficient and properly trained in safety *and* security.

Second—Once the problem area/s is discovered, research the following:

- Analyze employee theft—where, what type of merchandise, areas of largest losses.
- Analyze business vulnerabilities to major external sources—shoplifting, credit cards, bad checks.
- Analyze injuries to customers and employees—type, location, severity, and reoccurrence.
- Plan a program.
- Determine the resources that will be required.
- Determine how the resources will be implemented and maintained.
- Hire good, effective, and dedicated security officers, train them, and retrain them periodically.
- Train all new employees in security and safety procedures soon after the hiring process, and retrain periodically.

Deterrence As a Factor in Crime Control

Whether the crime is robbery, burglary, or larceny, criminals want to commit the crime as fast as possible before their presence has alerted the police, security, or anyone who may be able to capture or identify them then or at a later time. The longer it takes to get to their goal because of security impediments, the chance of apprehension is increased. Other than that, if criminals have the desire to commit a crime and have the time, the expertise, and the tools to complete the act, it can be done. Remember that nothing is safe as long as criminals have time, stealth, and criminal experience on their side.

Effectiveness of a Deterrent. Notwithstanding that, most security professionals are aware that the problem with any deterrent or most security procedures is that as a value of measurement it is intangible. How can we measure a crime that has not been committed, and substantiate that the reason the crime was not completed was because of some deterrent? In regard to the "bottom line" (the profitability of the business), if a deterrent cannot be measured, the question will arise—was the use of that deterrent worth the time and cost? However, a comparison can be made to some satisfaction. If the losses suffered by one retailer are much lower than that of another similar retailer located geographically nearby, and does not use the same preventive measures as the first retailer, we can assume that the deterrents are functional and of some use.

A DETERRENT CAN BE DESCRIBED AS TWO DISTINCT FACTORS:

Barriers—Anything that will deter or increase the time it takes for the criminal to commit the crime. Barriers include locked doors, extra locks, bars, chains, padlocks, sophisticated alarm systems and traps, more secure and stronger safes and cabinets, security guard and watchman rounds (particularly if not routine), and any other type of obstacle that would stop or at least slow down the perpetrator. This would include uniformed security guards posted at entrances and exits for the deterrent effect.

Exposure—Anything that is likely to enhance the possibility of the criminal's identity being exposed or identified. For example, this would include windows where the interior of a business is exposed, good lighting, mirrors, still cameras, and CCTV. This would also encompass the plainclothes loss prevention officer observing suspicious persons or activity.

Reactive vs. Proactive

There are times when the administration of a retail business may feel that the loss prevention department is reactive rather than proactive—reactive in the sense that security will respond only to occurrences, and does not take a proactive stance in the control of these incidents before they occur. If management is not directly involved in some manner with the overall operation of the loss prevention department, they may not be aware of the legalities or liabilities in the use of certain security systems or procedures. Consider also the constant problem in many cases of the department attempting to acquire the funds for security because of the expense that may be required, and/or the long period of time that may be necessary for a system or a control to be up and running.

Security is preventive in nature, not reactive. It is a continuous state that must have the complete backing of company management to be successful.

Unless the administration and management is inclined to finance a practical loss prevention department and program, and the requisite tools for that department and its personnel, security and safety will suffer.

So how does a loss prevention department become efficient and effective, and thereby create a proactive stance in the control of theft or the loss of any nature? First, the administration must be dedicated to the idea that a good loss prevention department can have a great effect on the bottom line. Second, administrative management must be prepared to place enough revenue and resources toward that end. Finally, the administrators and all department managers must be part of the security team, committed to active participation in the reduction of theft and the safety of all.

Toward that end, the following controls can be put into effect:

- Establish or sharpen present security and safety control systems and procedures.
- Review all management and supervisory techniques, policies, and procedures. Managers or supervisors should act and have command of the position they are assigned to.

- Rout out the dishonest or disruptive employee.
- Invest in capable security officers and investigators with experience.
- Redefine the selection process in hiring for all employees and managers.

ENDNOTES

1. 2001 National Retail Security Survey; Final Report, by Richard C. Hollinger, PhD., Director, and Jason L. Davis, Graduate Research Associate, p. 3; Security Research Project, Department of Sociology and the Center for Studies in Criminology and Law. ©2002 University of Florida, Gainesville, FL 32611-7330. (www.soc.ufl.edu/srp.htm).
2. Ibid., p. 4.
3. Ibid., p. 3. Graphs reprinted with permission.
4. Ibid., p. 4.
5. Ibid., p. 5.
6. Ibid., p. 5. Graph reprinted with permission.

Chapter 8

Investigative Techniques

INVESTIGATION OF LOSS, THEFT, AND SHRINKAGE

For our purposes, *loss* is described as the loss or possible loss of anything of value by known or unknown means. Initially and in actuality, there may have been no determination that the loss was due to some factor such as theft, damage, or a paper loss.

Theft may be described as property stolen from someone, in that the thief did take, steal, and carry away property belonging to another. The stolen property can belong to the retail establishment, an employee, or a customer. If it is taken from the store, the theft can be internal (by an employee), or external (by a person who shoplifts or commits other theft or fraud).

Shrinkage can be caused by several means. It includes internal and external theft, pilferage, intentional and unintentional damage, paper loss, poor recordkeeping, and inadequate stock control.

The investigation should be directed toward a particular goal depending on the specific circumstances and conditions. There are two types of methods for the investigation of any type of loss regarding an internal inquiry:

1. ***Overt***—An overt investigation is sometimes unavoidable because the occurrence may be widely known by the workforce even before loss prevention has become aware of the problem. Some advantages to this are that the employees, once loss prevention is informed, will know that loss prevention officers are on top of the situation and are immediately involved in an investigation. Another is that because of this close scrutiny, the thefts will cease.

   On the other hand, any perpetrators might be very cautious and lay low for a period, and then resume their activity at a later time.

2. ***Covert***—A covert investigation of an incident or suspected incident of a theft, whatever type, consists of conducting the investigation as secretly and as discreetly as possible, with as little people aware of such an investigation. It may involve background investigations of the employees who *could* be involved, undercover operations, various surveillance methods in varying degrees, and prudent interviews in an attempt to gain information or evidence. The advantage of a covert operation is that the person or the perpetrators under investigation are unaware that they are under suspicion and will continue to commit their activities. In this way, if nothing else, the possibility exists that they will be

caught in the act. Also, another advantage is that little reaction and attention will be perceived, and the investigation will not disrupt normal operations or the morale of the workforce.

Although an investigation is performed for a particular purpose, there may be other unintended benefits that management may find useful. This could include internal intelligence that would include information about conditions in the workplace or with various job positions, dislikes or problems with managers and supervisors, emotions and morale among the personnel, and performance and conditions that could be corrected.

CONDUCTING AN INTERNAL INVESTIGATION

An investigation begins when the loss prevention department receives information that concerns a crime or other improper behavior, and is then required to determine what type of crime has been committed, what business practice was violated, how and by whom. The basis of this information can be from informants, business records and paper trails, violations of company policy and procedures, and observation and inquiry by security officers, to name a few.

The police will conduct an investigation only when a crime has been reported to them, and they will usually be assisted and guided by loss prevention personnel in their inquiry. The reason for this would be that loss prevention would be more familiar with the facility, the operations of various processes, and the employees. And of course, the "crime" should be serious enough to warrant the attention of the prosecutor and the courts. The police would look upon overtime abuse as minor and not worth the time and effort to process through the criminal justice system, even though the crime of "theft of services" had been committed. Because most investigations that occur within a business establishment involves employees and not hardened criminals, and who have little or no criminal history, it is rare that businesses endeavor to prosecute an employee. Most often the business would rather get rid of the rotten apple and minimize losses by termination.

The loss prevention manager will be the person who will determine if in fact that a *prima facie* case exists, if an investigation is warranted, and how the investigation will be conducted. Agreement by an administrative manager may be required, but the final decision must be left to the loss prevention manager. This should be considered an important factor because he is the manager most familiar with the law and legalities, particularly determining when an employee has certain rights and specific cautionary factors must be considered.

Once the decision is made to initiate an investigation, documentary and/or physical evidence is collected first. The second step would be the detailed observation by loss prevention personnel zeroing in on the problem and/or the people involved. Surveillance would be part of this process if required. Hopefully, this can be completed before any detailed interviews of employees take place. In any event, it is considered that the most important skill that an investigator could have is the ability to gain as much information as possible during the interview process. Most investigators learn this ability through experience rather than by formal training. Following that, the next most important skill would be making use of the information gathered during interviews and applying that information in the interrogation process. By knowing all the pertinent facts and being in command of them, the investigator is able to confront the suspect in a more confident manner, and ultimately, has complete control of the interaction.

Depending on the specific case, an overt investigation could include the following procedures:

1. Determine the loss—the type, amount, and the total value.
2. Determine the place of occurrence or where the loss took place.
3. Determine the time period of the loss as close as can be discovered.
4. Determine if persons other than employees could be involved in the loss. This would include truckers/helpers, as well as delivery and repair personnel.
5. Evaluate all of the available information surrounding the loss and physical area of the loss.
6. If it has been established that the loss was a theft, then a crime has been committed and loss prevention may want to advise the police.
7. If loss prevention wishes to conduct an investigation before any police involvement, there should be extensive interviews with all personnel who had or may have had access to the stolen property. Formal interview and interrogation procedures are to be followed at this point. Consider that word of the loss and investigation will spread rapidly from here on.
8. Evaluate all notes and statements received from employee interviews and interrogations.
9. Follow up with interviews and interrogations as needed to clarify questionable facts and information.
10. Follow up with investigations of possible or apparent suspects based on interviews, interrogations, surveillance, and information received.
11. Investigate the possibility that the stolen items may still be on the premises or at some other private location. If a recovery of the stolen property is made, attempt to trace back the item/s to the perpetrator/s.
12. Be observant of an employee's increase in "wealth," spending habits, material goods, boasting, and flaunting.
13. Be observant for a motive—problems with drugs, gambling, family finances, etc.
14. Consider the use of a polygraph examination of *all* the suspects.
15. The final evaluation in which investigators conclude their report to management regarding their findings should include whether the case is still active and the investigation continues, or whether the investigation has concluded with an arrest, recovery, and/or a prosecution of the persons involved.

Reports must be compiled and submitted by each security officer involved in any part of the investigation. All written statements are to be attached to and made part of the report. All evidence must be marked, maintained in their original condition, properly safeguarded, and identified in the report. It is important for the security officer to remember that all evidence and any surveillance information or material must be legally obtained.

CONCLUDING THE INVESTIGATIVE PROCESS

Unless the suspect or suspects are caught in the act prior to or during the investigation and immediate action must be taken by loss prevention, the interrogation process will take place as follows:

1. After completing the initial phases of the investigation, if it has been decided that all interviews and evidence have been obtained that can reasonably be obtained, loss prevention personnel should begin the interrogation of the suspect or suspects. This will be the culmination of the investigative process, in that it is calculated to elicit a statement of admission—a confession that will be legal and binding.
2. The definitive confession would be a written statement admitting to guilt, signed by the suspect, with such signature witnessed by at least two people.

   If a written statement cannot be obtained or is unavailable, all oral statements made by the suspect should be taken down, reduced to writing, and made part of the report. Particularly note anyone who was present and witnessed an oral admission made by the subject. If possible, have that witness place in writing what he or she heard concerning an oral confession or statements. Oral statements include the suspect admitting his guilt, describing his actions (how he did it), and his past or present mental state concerning the incident/s (why he did it). In effect any statement made by the suspect that places himself in jeopardy. In actuality, this writing is sort of a deposition in which a conversation took place between the officer questioning the suspect and what was spoken by both.
3. The inference of guilt can take several forms. Even if the suspect does not actually admit to any wrongdoing, information can be obtained that can incriminate him, reduce his credibility, and destroy any defense he may raise in the future. If asked why the suspect committed the crime—why he did it—the subject may just shrug his shoulders. He may refuse to cooperate by directing his attention elsewhere when questioned, or attempt to disrupt the interrogation by his actions. Consider also, that if the suspect refuses to answer or participate in the questioning, basically not saying a word, he "stands mute," and this can be considered in a court of law as possible guilt, because an innocent person would deny guilt if he was in fact guiltless.

Threats or promises should never be made to a witness or suspect, otherwise any evidence or statements given may not be admissible in court. In any situation where voluntary consent is required (as in a search), the security officer would be wise in obtaining written authorization first. If the case is later presented at trial, the defendant's lawyer will certainly attempt to have any statement or evidence dismissed because of coercion, intimidation, promises, or illegal search and seizure. Don't place yourself in a position of losing a case in court because of sloppy or illegal procedures.

For further information on the investigative process, see SEARCH AND SEIZURE in Chapter 4, and INTERVIEWS AND INTERROGATIONS on page 125, and DISCLOSURE OF CONFIDENTIAL INFORMATION on page 120.

Informants

Whether in the criminal, civil, or private sector, the use of an informant is a valuable tool in any investigation. An informant may be cultivated surreptitiously or the informant may be voluntary. In either case, the reason for informing on another includes recognition, monetary reward, personal morality and ethics, or a desire to "get even."

A significant program for loss prevention is the "hot line" where, if the informant wishes, information can be reported to the security office's telephone and recorded on voice mail anonymously or not. If possible and the security officer has the authority and permission of his or her superior, the officer should attempt to meet with the informant at a particular location off premises so that a more complete interview may take place privately and secretly.

Substantial cash incentives for information given by a known or an anonymous employee leading to the termination or arrest of a dishonest employee should also be in effect and widely publicized as corporate policy. This policy should note the details of the monetary reward and the procedure that the employee should follow. The identity of the informer should only be known to a select few, and particularly never revealed to anyone outside of the loss prevention department, whether an employee or supervisor.

Some retailers operate a "silent witness" program where an anonymous person reveals pertinent information concerning a crime on the premises by leaving the message on voice mail. Recorded instructions will advise the informant with the procedure to follow, and if the information is fruitful, the informant will be rewarded surreptitiously with his or her identity never known to anyone.

Closed Circuit Television

At present, one of the most important tools that a loss prevention department may employ is the closed circuit television camera (CCTV). The means of surreptitious observation and detection in real-time or time-lapse recordings can be a most effective tool in the reduction of loss in all sectors of concern. There have been studies that indicate that CCTV is an excellent deterrent to business crimes such as robbery, shoplifting, employee theft, and insurance liability claims. This has been determined by valid comparisons of similar businesses located in the same geographical area, with the only variable being whether the business in question used CCTV or not.

Some businesses feel that the presence of a TV camera may inhibit shopping, and/or make the legitimate customer feel uneasy. One way to alleviate this potential problem is to house the camera in an opaque plastic half sphere attached to the overhead. Legitimate customers are seldom aware of this type of contraption, with many not knowing what it is. But shoplifters and others with larcenous intent are fully aware of them, so they can serve as a great deterrent because the shoplifter cannot see if the camera is zooming or turning in their direction.

In contrast, the visible cameras located throughout the store in both public and employee areas give notice that all behavior, suspicious or not, is being observed and/or recorded. These cameras would necessarily be used in those areas of recurrent loss or areas that are highly sensitive to loss, particularly for those "spur-of-the-moment" thieves who will have second thoughts upon observing these cameras. Additionally, the use of systems connected to the point of sale for visual observation and recording reduces sloppy work habits, reinforces correct procedures, and identifies any collusive larcenous conduct between friends, relatives, and the cashier.

The technology of covert cameras and lenses has advanced so that the innocent-looking motion detector or smoke detector attached to an overhead is in actuality a unit containing a camera, with the cost of this equipment the only limiting factor for its use. In a covert surveillance system, there is little doubt that ethical and legal issues will arise. The security officer must be aware that there are certain states where covert cameras are not allowed without proper notification, particularly in customer or employee dressing rooms. As far as the use of visible or covert cameras in public and employee rest rooms and locker rooms, it should be considered highly improper and illegal. Common sense would dictate that the privacy of a customer or an employee should be held in the highest regard. Note also, if a covert camera is discovered by an employee under observation or a department under surveillance, it could provide ramifications such as union involvement, contractual violations, civil rights violations, and privacy issues.

Notwithstanding these problems, once discovered and the word gets out throughout the store, it could be a devastating effect on morale, and the quality and quantity of work. The loss prevention manager would do well to contact the company's attorney to review the need and potential risks involved in the use of covert systems concerning employees.

The Use of CCTV. When or when not to record will depend on whether the TV monitors are constantly manned or not. Many loss prevention departments will record continuously in real time or in a time-lapse mode. Others may only record suspicious activity on tape when observed. In an effort to cut expenses and monitoring equipment, several cameras may be replaced by one *pan-tilt-zoom* camera. This camera has the ability to pan 360 degrees, and when required, the capability to tilt and zoom in closely on a subject or circumstance.

The use of CCTV in loss prevention is a proven factor, and the loss prevention manager would do well to make full use of this type of surveillance. If not already in use, inquiry into various types of equipment should be initiated, along with the allocated capital and a determination of where these cameras would be most useful.

Covert Surveillance

There will come a time when certain issues will arise concerning closed circuit television, two-way mirrors, coops, listening devices, or other types of surveillance or inspections that some people may consider an invasion of their privacy.

Basically, CCTV cameras in such public areas as passageways and storage rooms can be used in the legal sense, in that employees and/or customers cannot expect the same right to privacy as they would have within their own homes. Certain rights of privacy are given up upon entering a public building or someone else's property. A customer may be considered a guest in the place of business, and the merchant or retailer may make use and justify the use of cameras, two-way mirrors or other types of surveillance based on the nature of work (for the employee), and the necessity for measures in combating and/or reducing theft of merchandise, property, and services.

However, certain restrictions must be considered for the sake of propriety and decency when the use of cameras and/or one-way glass is contemplated. A valid case can be made by a person concerning their right to privacy when there has been an invasion of such privacy in certain areas of a public building. This would include the observation of people in lavatories, rest rooms, locker rooms, or dressing areas, whether male or female, customer or employee. A person using a public rest room has an *expectation of privacy* and any installation of a hidden TV camera might well be considered a "search" or a privacy issue under the Fourth Amendment requirements of search and seizure.

No matter how serious a problem may be and the retailer's attempt to correct that problem, the possibility of some civil action or litigation, because of a invasion of privacy or the perceived notion of such invasion, is not worth the risk. Moreover, some state statutes note that if a person enters a dressing or fitting room and is subject to being observed, the merchant or retailer must post such written notice outside of the dressing room. In this way, the person may then have the choice to enter or refuse the use of the room. Of course, the retailer who has this policy does harm to his or her business and good will, if nothing else. Therefore, it would be most prudent not to have any cameras or one-way mirrors in any dressing room for any purpose. Other procedures may be instituted to control theft when a dressing room is used to facilitate the crime. One procedure used in many retail establishments is an assigned employee making use of numbered tags for each garment taken into the dressing or fitting room by a customer, and the return of the same number of tags to garments upon leaving.

AREAS OF CONCERN FOR THE PLACEMENT OF CCTV CAMERAS

- Those areas conducive to loss, or of proven losses
- Coverage of areas containing high-end merchandise
- Receiving and shipping docks
- Warehouse and storage areas
- Elevators and escalators
- Garbage/trash disposal areas
- Entrances and exits (crowd control)
- High traffic areas
- Highly sensitive areas (cash offices or rooms, computer rooms, records storage, electric/telephone rooms, etc.)
- Sensitive exterior areas
- Parking garages and fields
- Those areas subject to surreptitious internal investigation

WIRETAPS AND THE RECORDING OF TELEPHONE CONVERSATIONS

Eavesdropping Defined

Generally, most states have defined the use of a "wiretap" or the recording under clandestine circumstances as *eavesdropping* when one unlawfully engages in wiretapping, mechanical overhearing of a conversation, or intercepting or accessing an electronic communication.

Moreover, the possession of eavesdropping devices when, under circumstances evincing an intent to use, or permit the same to be used in violation of law, a person possesses any instrument, device, or equipment designed for, adapted to, or commonly used in wiretapping or mechanical overhearing of a conversation is a crime.

Wiretaps

Wiretaps on company telephones could violate federal and state laws depending how the procedure is set up and conducted. Although it may be said that the employees right to privacy may be balanced against the needs of the employer, consider this a no-win situation. If the loss prevention department believes that a crime is being or has been committed, and believes that one way to gain evidence would be through a wiretap, let the police do it. Once the crime is reported to the police department, loss prevention could advise that a wiretap might be useful. The police will determine the benefits and legalities, and obtain the necessary court order to set up the tap.

A security officer who sets up, condones, or is part of an illegal or improper tap is subject to criminal arrest and civil litigation.

Many companies have a recording for incoming business calls that advises the caller that all conversations may be recorded for business or quality control purposes. This is considered legal as long as the announcement is made before a conversation takes place.

This is not to say that a security officer cannot record a telephone conversation surreptitiously *as long as he or she is a party to that conversation*. Such a recording by a security officer where identification of the other person can be established, and where certain admissions are made by the other party may be considered of great use as evidence at a later time. But be aware that there may be some restrictions in some states concerning the legalities of a recorded conversation that you are part of. Check with your state law, your company attorney and company policy, on any situation where any recording of a telephonic conversation is to be conducted.

EMPLOYEE SEARCHES

The retailer may also have a policy concerning certain restrictions on employees, and as long as these policies are enforced equally, there is no loss of privacy. An example would be that all female employees must secure their pocketbooks in their lockers, and if they wish, make use of a clear plastic bag for the carrying of personal contents into the work area. This would include the restriction of all bags, valises, knapsacks, backpacks, and so forth of all employees. Another example would be that all employees are subject to a bag check upon leaving the premises or work for the day. In this case, all employees leaving or leaving at a given time must be examined. However the security officer may not act in a random manner or subject one employee to the examination and not another. This cannot be considered an unreasonable search and seizure under the Fourth Amendment of the U.S. Constitution, because it is not an action by a government employee—such as a law enforcement officer, but by a private person—a security officer, as per the employer's written policy and procedures.

Examination by a security officer into a private office, private desk, or opening an employee's mail can be regarded as an invasion of privacy because people have an expectation that these areas are private. Moreover, there is a greater risk of civil action if the security officer is working with or in cooperation with the police, because this will involve the issue of search and seizure and/or the color of state law, and therefore, criminal liability. A search of the contents of a desk may be made if the desk is communal or shared by more than one employee. If only one employee has use of a desk, that employee has an expectation of privacy.

Concerning employees' lockers, the employee must give access to that locker if he or she has read and acknowledged written company policy that his or her locker is subject to inspection at any time. The employee may refuse such access and no search of the locker can legally be conducted, unless there is a serious public safety issue. However, the employee can then be subject to termination of employment in this circumstance. Regarding employee searches and privacy rights also see SEARCH AND SEIZURE in Chapter 4.

INVASION OF PRIVACY AND DEFAMATION

Defamation

The issue of defamation must also be of concern to security officers and investigators because it may be the basis of a civil action or part of the litigation along with invasion of privacy. During any internal investigation, security officers may open themselves to an accusation of having defamed a person's reputation or character. When accusations or comments are made that are later proved to be wrong, and those accusations or comments are made outside of the *closed circle*—those protected by privilege—then the person who has been accused has been defamed—if in fact that person did not commit the act.

We must be mindful that defamation may include two wrongful acts:

- ***Slander***—the spoken word
- ***Libel***—the written word, including pictorial or posted matter

An employee who is the subject of an investigation cannot initiate a slander or any form of a defamation action, when during an interrogation the security officer accuses the subject of a crime or some other offense, whether or not the subject is charged or punished in some way.

However, if such accusation is made to the detriment of *privacy or privilege*, the subject may be considered to have suffered some type of damage, in that defamation is defined as a civil "wrong." In order to clarify this point, bear in mind that no form of slander occurs when such accusations occur "privately" within the presence of only those people of concern. These people may include security officers, police officers, and the subject's manager who are *privileged* to hear and be present if and when an accusation may be made. Additionally, the presence of a union representative at the request of the subject may be considered as *privileged*, and can be a party to the occurrence without any fault or wrong attributed to the security officer.

The terms *privacy, privilege* and *legitimate interest* are further defined below:

PRIVILEGE AND PRIVACY

Privilege—The term *privilege* relates to those persons who have an intrinsic interest in, are privy to, and have an interest in the investigation or its final results. This may be called "the closed circle," those protected by privilege, and might include loss prevention personnel, select administrators, or managers of concern.

Privacy—Basically a non-public individual has the right to be free of public scrutiny, from public disclosure of embarrassing private information, intrusion of one's solitude or private affairs, or publicity which puts him or her in a false light to the public.

LEGITIMATE INTEREST

The term *legitimate interest* can be defined as the total set of circumstances that would lead a reasonable, prudent, and professionally trained person to believe that an offense has occurred, is occurring, or will occur, and has the authority to investigate such offense. Basically, this could be less than probable cause but more than mere suspicion.

Disclosure of Confidential Information

For retail security officers, the area that they may become involved would be in the case of an investigation of some criminal act, and where the employee in question may be subject to public disclosures of *private* facts or information, or the publication by the officer (defendant) of facts that place the employee (now a plaintiff) in a false light. A publication may be considered any written report where the plaintiff is identified publicly. Truth is no defense regarding an action for invasion of privacy.

It is for this reason that all investigations, based upon fact or hearsay, should be confidential in all aspects. The loss prevention manager should be cognizant that any written report or conversation regarding the subject in question must be held strictly confidential to only those personnel who may have business or a right to that information. This includes any activity or action prior to or after the conclusion of the investigation. If information about the subject is exposed in some manner and becomes public knowledge, and the subject becomes aware of it and believes or perceives that a wrong has been committed, civil litigation may become a reality.

Privilege and Invasion of Privacy Defined

There is no doubt that an investigation can cause some emotional stress to both the guilty and the innocent. But for the plaintiff to engage in an emotional distress lawsuit, he or she must prove that the investigator engaged in some extreme or outrageous conduct that in fact caused severe emotional distress and/or embarrassment resulting in physical symptoms, bodily harm, or personal embarrassment. So then, the investigator should be cognizant of possible civil action alleging an invasion of privacy whether the officer is involved in an investigation of a person's pre-employment, violation of company policy, or the report of a crime.

Publicity of private facts (invasion of privacy) can occur when an investigator makes a statement about an employee to another person not protected by privilege. The employee may also believe that some intrusion takes place when an investigator looks into the private matters of that person without having legitimate interest. In other words, the investigator publicizes facts regarding another that are highly offensive to a reasonable person in which the investigator does not have a legitimate interest or passed on such information to one not protected by privilege.

Conclusion

Procedures, expertise, and talent vary with different investigators, as well as the type or seriousness of the investigation and how it is to be carried out. Therefore, the investigator should follow some simple rules in conducting a professional investigation:

1. Although the security officer may have the authority to initiate an inquiry or investigation into any process, procedure, possible or apparent loss, suspicious activity, or circumstances, the officer should have a *legitimate reason* to conduct an investigation on or into another person.
2. The security officer should respect the privacy and other rights of the people involved in the investigation.
3. The security officer should refrain from making any unnecessary comments or opinions to anyone whether they are part of the investigation or not. This is not to say that security officers and their supervisors should not discuss among themselves feelings, thoughts, opinions, the direction, or target of a suspect in the investigation, evidence gained or to be gathered, or the complete process of the investigation.

THE INVESTIGATION AT A SCENE OF OCCURRENCE

The Scene

Investigation is an important part of the job description of loss prevention and the duties assigned to that department. Whether the place of occurrence is an accident or crime scene, certain precautions must take place, depending on the situation or the seriousness of the occurrence. Once the emergency situation is under control, such as the fire being extinguished or the injured person being attended to and removed from the scene, security officers should then attempt to preserve the scene as much as it was when the occurrence took place. Because a scene of importance needs to be controlled as much as possible, security officers may not be able to do all that needs to be done without some help. If other security officers are not present to assist, a responsible employee or manager can be put to use in helping protect the scene.

Security officers should identify the complainant (if any), and all persons who were present during the occurrence, whether they witnessed anything of concern or not. If possible, attempt to separate witnesses so that any discussion between them will not be controlled or distorted by one over the other. If necessary and before taking any written statements that may be required, make sure the identification includes the name, address, age, date of birth, home and business telephone number, and a very brief recounting of what they observed and where they were when the incident took place. Such notations should be made in the officer's field notebook and should be maintained for future reference.

Anytime there is any remote possibility of subsequent civil litigation because of an accidental injury to a customer, or because of the severity of the occurrence or injury, photos of the scene should be taken. In the case of an injured employee, photos may be helpful to that employee or to the company, depending on the occurrence. And in the case of a crime scene, photos taken before police arrival may be of some importance because a scene may inadvertently change or become contaminated because of people standing around and handling objects. If necessary, a diagram may be drawn of the scene with measurements noting windows, doors, and important objects. Security officers should note everything of importance upon arrival at the scene and while they are there. The officers should describe the conditions upon arrival, and note if certain things or objects were out of place, or appeared to be placed in position to accommodate a prepared scenario. The area of the scene should be searched thoroughly for any evidence that would pertain to the incident, no matter how insignificant the officers may believe it to be.

The Collection and Preservation of Evidence

Photographs of the scene are considered evidence because they can show what and how the scene appeared at the time of the occurrence, and therefore of great importance if required at a later time. A scene can change, particularly in a retail environment where renovations are routinely commonplace and will not appear it is was at the time of the occurrence. By the time the need to describe a scene takes place, many changes can occur—hence the need for photos, and if necessary, hand-drawn diagrams noting measurements and distances. In addition, physical evidence collected at the scene may be defined as any material that will aid in identifying the problem, the people involved, the cause of the accident, or how the crime was committed. If the scene is of a serious criminal nature, the police will make use of a forensic team to search for clues and evidence. The security officer is not expected or prepared to lift fingerprints, collect hair samples, or body fluids for example. Some evidence may be so microscopic that only trained crime scene search investigators or fire marshals may be able to gather, preserve, identify, and present in court. See EVIDENCE defined as to type in the Glossary.

If the police are not involved in the investigation, the security officer must then decide if the case is serious enough to warrant the search and collection of evidence for possible future inquiries or court action. Everything that may be considered evidence must be tagged, labeled, distinctively marked (with the initials of the finder), or identified with the case or incident report number assigned to the occurrence. Once collected and labeled, it should be placed in a secure area protected from any other employee. Only loss prevention personnel should enter into this secured area, because the continuity of evidence (the chain of custody) must be established to a certainty for a possible court hearing. The evidence must be identified as to where and when it was found, by whom and how secured, with all this information carefully noted in the report. Anytime the evidence is handled, removed, and returned to the secured evidence area, it must be noted in subsequent entries to the report. Reasoning for this is to show that the chain of custody hasn't been broken, and the evidence hasn't been tampered, altered, contaminated, or changed in any manner. Evidence protected in a secure area by loss prevention would usually be saved for those instances that might include subsequent civil litigation. Evidence collected and preserved for any future criminal prosecution will be tagged, labeled, marked, removed, and secured by the police according to their procedures. Although the chain of custody or evidence is not legally as applicable to the security officer as in the case of law enforcement, the security officer should follow the same guidelines as close as possible as an indication of a professional approach toward case management.

On some crimes such as sexual harassment, money loss, or embezzlement, the security officer may discover a document that will require professional examination in an effort to make a determination about a suspect. Unless management wishes to keep the investigation in-house, loss prevention might consider reporting the incident to the police and let their forensic detectives examine the document as part of their investigation. But if the incident is not be reported to the police and the investigation is kept in-house, the loss prevention department should have a qualified document examiner available for situations such as this.

ACCIDENT INVESTIGATION AND INSURANCE FRAUD

Cons, Scams, and Flim-Flams

Because many of the small insurance claims filed against a retail business may only be a few thousand dollars individually, in total they add up considerably. Although the retailer will have to absorb these petty losses because of the deductible on their insurance coverage, the intervention of loss prevention and the insurance investigator can identify fraudulent claims in many instances.

Slip and falls are usually staged at major retail and restaurant chains, with these "con artists" preying upon supermarket/grocery and department stores most often. These claims of injury appear to be the most common type of insurance fraud because it requires little time or effort to set the stage. The injured party does not have to provide premium money for an insurance policy, as he or she might need in other frauds, and the alleged fall is most often without witnesses and difficult to disprove. Additionally, there is often a delay in reporting the injury and claim. Because of this delay, the investigation is hindered by no witnesses, the alleged accident scene has changed or has been renovated, and the subject has had time to set up doctor's examinations, hospital stays, and bills. Many times this scam artist is the so-called "upstanding citizen" who finds that by staging a phony slip and fall, or by building upon a minor fall into a major injury, this person can wait out the insurance company all the way to a civil trial. His claim is usually exorbitant and feels even if he settles just before trial he will come out ahead. This subject most often has representation by an attorney and the services of a doctor, both of whom may be as shady as the subject. Again, many times the report of the alleged injury is made at a later time after the alleged date of occurrence.

The dollar amount of the claim is usually under $5,000.00, and most of these incidents are set up by a group of people known as "gypsies."[1] Because of the overwhelming volume of these types of claims by this group, the insurance industry finds that they are a tremendous problem to deal with. These gypsies are a mobile group and change names and addresses frequently as they move from town to town. The changing of names and other identification makes matching of these claims difficult for the insurance industry's Property Insurance Loss Register (PILR). The existence and furtherance of the gypsy lifestyle and identification of their scams depends on secrecy. The gypsy claimant does not wish the scrutiny or publicity that a courtroom will bring. The other scam artist also does not wish publicity and usually will not involve an attorney. Therefore, both will want to settle rather than go to court. These types of cases are referred to in the insurance industry as "nuisance cases."

Note also that gypsies are also involved in stolen or bogus credit card and bad check scams and flim-flams at cash registers and returns counters. Bear in mind that a larceny committed by trick or false pretenses is still a crime.

Caution should be taken, however, concerning the honest customer who has in fact sustained an injury through no fault or little fault of their own. In any event, in aiding an injured person and the subsequent accident investigation, all cases should be handled with equal consideration and appropriate professional conduct. Whatever you may believe concerning the facts, respond as though the incident is a bona fide accident. Make no personal comments or overt actions that might be litigious at a later time. Also, this admonition is to be applied to any coworker present or assisting at the scene, because one never knows who may be listening.

Early detection and thorough investigation of claims having involvement by certain groups such as gypsies have proven to be the best defenses in defeating fraudulent and nonmeritorious claims. Once an accident and injury has been reported, loss prevention should examine the scene immediately for witnesses, inconsistencies between the "injured person's" statements, and physical evidence observed at the scene. Photographs and measurements should be taken of the accident scene. Comments by the subject, however minimal, vague, or inconsistent, should be noted and written down as soon as practical. Complete identification should be gathered from the subject, particularly from photo ID of an official nature such as an operator's license. Include the social security number, business address, and if possible, the previous home address. Note if any of the corroborating and "overly cooperating" witnesses present are friends or relatives of the subject, and properly identify them and all witnesses for future reference. If the security officer has any suspicions of a possible fraud, the officer should advise the insurance representative or assigned investigator upon submission of the accident report.

Make sure that all required information is taken so that an accident report may be completed soon after the incident. Many times the injured party or a relative at the scene of the accident, or a legal representative at a later time, requests a copy of your "official" accident report. Respectfully deny that request. You could offer them any pertinent information, names of witnesses, and the name of the retailer's insurance company, but no company or insurance company accident form should ever be supplied to anyone. Advise them that only the retailer's insurance company representative or attorney representing the retailer will have that right of disclosure. The retailer and agent have the legal right to deny a request or demand of any written formal report. In fact, the only time a copy of an accident report or any other writing relevant to the case will be offered is on demand by the plaintiff's attorney at a discovery hearing or at trial. See example of a customer accident form in the Appendix.

INTERVIEWS AND INTERROGATIONS

Every security supervisor and officer should have some knowledge of the questioning process. The officer who knows how, when, and what to ask an individual regarding any inquiry or investigation can be greatly informative. Consider the following to be of some significance for the influence and proficiency that can only add to the loss prevention officer's performance.

There are two distinct differences concerning the use of interviews and interrogations[2] conducted during an investigation:

1. ***The interview*** is the first step in the investigative process in that it is not accusatory in nature. It is a way of ascertaining facts, witnesses, and evidence, and whether any liability exists or if the incident is criminal or not in nature. Every security officer who has controlled or assisted at any type of occurrence, if it is a disturbance, an accident scene, or a report of a crime, has conducted an interview of a participant or witness to determine what happened, when it happened, and who is or may be involved. In essence, this will include the six basic questions—what, when, where, why, who, and how.
2. ***Interrogation*** is accusatory and is considered "an art whereby through the use of questioning and observation the truth is elicited from a suspect by sound reasoning and understanding without the use of threats or promises."[3]

The intricacies of an interrogation compared to an interview are far more complex. No two human beings are alike, and how they think and react in various situations will differ widely. Some people will give information willingly, whereas others may be reluctant do so under any circumstances. Most people become intimidated when questioned, particularly by a skilled investigator or a police officer. People who are unsophisticated or uneducated are more likely to become intimidated and/or answer questions truthfully and completely. Others who have had prior contact with authority figures such as the police or the courts, or who have prior criminal convictions will be the toughest to elicit information from. Where one person will listen to reason, another might not be approached in any manner. But when the interrogator is organized, persistent, focused, and coherent, the subject will be unable to evade or hide his or her comments in irrelevant answers. Moreover, one must remember the principle that no one can successfully lie consistently to a good interrogator. Security officers who master the techniques of investigation, including how to elicit information from witnesses and suspects, will be an asset to their profession.

Routine Investigations

Interviews

- An interview of a person or persons in order to determine basic or particular facts in a case is not accusatory in nature.
- A security officer will conduct interviews throughout the workday as part of the officer's normal tasks.

- However, the more important interviews will be for the purpose of gathering information for insurance purposes and possible future civil litigation, and the investigation of internal crime.
- In the case of the personal injury of a customer or employee, damage to company or personal property, product liability, and apprehensions and arrests, to name a few, certain inquiries and actions by the security officer, now investigator, must take place.
- Information is to be gathered for forms and reports that must be compiled and maintained, and photographs if applicable must be taken. In addition, witness statements must be obtained and reduced to writing, and if not, at least identified and made part of the report/s.

Criminal Investigations

Interviews

- Not accusatory—it is basically a conversation between the interviewer and the interviewee in order to determine the facts.
- The investigator may have little or no evidence at this point.
- There are no formal charges against the suspect, and there are no overt indications that any suspicions are being formulated.
- The investigator takes notes for future reference, and begins to form a strategy.

Interrogations

- The investigator now dominates the conversation, and the tone of the interaction becomes accusatory.
- The guilt of the suspect is reasonably certain in the mind of the investigator.
- Evidence against the suspect is known or insinuated (the interrogator may have or lead the subject to believe the officer has independent sources of information).
- The interrogation of the suspect must be private with no interruptions or distractions of any kind.
- The investigator takes no notes during the interrogation so as not to give the suspect time to think or become wary that information is being put down in writing.

Because of the importance of the interrogation process, the following is offered as a method of acceptable procedure:

THE REID NINE STEPS OF INTERROGATION[4]

1. ***Direct positive confrontation***—Advise the subject that he is in fact considered the guilty party, based upon the facts and/or evidence.
2. ***Theme development***—*The most important of the nine steps.* Once the interrogator identifies the theme, the *psychological* blame for the crime will be placed elsewhere. He will give social and moral justification to the subject that gave cause or led to the crime.
3. ***Handling denials***—The interrogator should limit the amount of interruptions

during the session, so as to cut down on denials.

4. ***Overcoming objections***—Attempt to develop a theme out of the subject's excuses or objections. Turn and use against the subject.

5. ***Procurement and retention of the subject's attention***—Direct the subject's attention towards you, the interrogator. Move closer to the subject. Touch the subject lightly physically, on the arm or the hand. Show sincerity, compassion, some agreement or understanding of how the "act" could have occurred.

6. ***Handling the subject's passive mood***—The interrogator should recognize the subject has reached a point and is ready to "give up"—ready to confess.

7. ***Presenting an alternative question***—Attempt to obtain an admission. Offer a "face saving" solution—an alternative that is not as self-incriminating in the subject's eyes.

8. ***Have the suspect relate various details of the offense***—The interrogator should now gather all the specifics of the offense.

9. ***Converting an oral confession into a written confession***—The reduction of the oral admissions to a written statement, signed and witnessed.

THE MIRANDA WARNING AND OTHER ISSUES

The *Miranda warning* is basically a warning given to a suspect of a crime in which the suspect is advised that he or she has certain constitutional rights, in that the suspect has the right not to self incriminate (as provided in the Fifth Amendment). This requirement of advising a subject of his or her rights applies only to law enforcement officers or those persons acting under the *Color of State Law*. The warning is obligatory as defined by the Supreme Court, and must be given orally to the suspect of a crime *before any questioning by a police officer,*[5] *and under certain conditions by a security officer as noted below*. In the case of a written confession given by the suspect or defendant in police custody, any statements or admissions must be preceded by the Miranda warning in writing. A written confession taken by a security officer need not have the Miranda warning contained therein.

Any admissions or confessions obtained from a person in police custody in violation of the required Miranda warning or unlawfully taken under the *Color of State Law*, will be considered "*fruit of the poisoned tree*," and not admissible in court.

The police officer has some restrictions regarding interviewing and interrogation that the security officer, a private person, does not have to abide with. After interviewing or gathering the facts, once the police officer determines or establishes that the subject in question is a *suspect*, the Miranda warning must be issued, and the interview now becomes an interrogation.

The requirement that a *Miranda warning* be given to a suspect is *binding only on police officers* or other law enforcement personnel concerning a person they wish to question, and who is then considered a suspect or whom they have in custody. *It does not apply to security officers, security guards, store detectives, loss prevention officers, or private investigators,* even if the suspect to be questioned is in custody and under arrest.[6]

If the security officer is requested by a police officer to conduct an "interview" or any type of questioning, or the police officer is present during that interview or questioning, the security officer has now become an agent of the police and the *Miranda warning* must be issued. Otherwise, any admissions or statements made by the defendant will not be admissible in court because the security officer acted on behalf of the police officer, and the warning was not given.

Be also aware that if the person under arrest and questioned by a security officer is in a "police-dominated atmosphere" (in a police car or at a police station, or where police officers are congregating or milling about in the vicinity of the accused), the courts may tend to agree with the defendant that he or she was intimidated, and any statements made by the defendant were coerced by such presence of the police. Note that the federal courts may view this "atmosphere" as a violation of the federal Civil Rights Act (see COLOR OF STATE LAW in Chapter 4).

Remember that the security officer need not give the *Miranda warning* to a suspect unless the officer is questioning the suspect at the direction of a police officer, with the police officer present during such questioning, or in any way acting under the *color of state law.*

Juveniles

As a general rule, the interrogation of juveniles is best left to the police and at their discretion. Excuses such as the parent not being present when the child was questioned, or that the child is too young to understand the nature of surrendering his or her rights, would most assuredly come up when the child or the child's family obtains legal representation and an attorney enters the case.

Unions

For those security officers employed in a business that is unionized and the suspect employee is also a union member, a restriction might apply in the interrogation process. If the outcome of the investigation will result in disciplinary action such as termination and/or possible arrest, the union employee has the right to request union representation or another member of the union to be present.[7]

The security officer is not obligated to advise the union employee of any right of representation by a union delegate. It is up to that employee or the union to make the request.[8]

As noted, the union representative or another union member may be present during the investigation and/or interrogation of the suspect employee. They may not, however, act on behalf of or in an adversary manner as an attorney would if the employee were a client, nor can they interrupt the process other than to make suggestions, clarify facts, or offer other information on other employees.[9]

Conclusion

There are many personal aspects in the making of a good interviewer and interrogator. Most investigators will agree that the most important part of an investigation is their skills in the course of the interview in which most of the information they will gather will be in this process. In this regard, the art of interviewing is learned through experience rather than through formal training. To be successful, the interviewer must rely on the cooperation, and in many instances, the collaboration of the person interviewed. Because the officer doesn't have the ability to compel information or testimony from the person as a police officer might (withholding information, obstruction of governmental administration, etc.), the investigator in the private sector must stress those methods that will elicit as much information as possible.

In summation, there are many other techniques that will govern positive results from an interrogation. These will include the close observation of the suspect's behavior, attitude, physical changes, body postures, facial expressions, gestures, tics, and eye movements among others (body language). Unless the security officer has previous experience in law enforcement and has had some training in this area, it is suggested that attendance and formal training be had from a reputable firm that conducts specialized training and seminars in this field.

ENDNOTES

1. The author wishes to note that the word *Gypsy* when used herein does not refer to a particular ethnic group, but rather it refers to a criminal lifestyle, and is not intended to include the law-abiding members of the Romani people or their culture. See glossary for the definition of *Gypsy* and *Romany*.
2. *The Reid Technique® of Interviewing and Interrogation*, © 1993; John E. Reid & Associates, Inc., 250 South Wacker Drive, Suite 1100, Chicago, Illinois 60606.
3. Ibid., p. 3.
4. Ibid. *The Reid Nine Steps of Interrogation*, pp. 60–105. Reprinted with permission.
5. *Miranda v. Arizona*, 384 U.S. 436 (1966).
6. *People v. Deborah C.*, 177 Cal.Rptr. 852, 635 P.2d 446, (1981), and *People v. Ray*, 65 N.Y. 2d 282, 480 N.E. 2d 1065 (1985).
7. *NLRB v. Weingarten*, 420 U.S. 251 (1975).
8. *Pacific Telephone v. NLRB*, 711 F.2d 134 (1983).
9. *Southwestern Bell v. NLRB*, 667 F.2d 470, 5th cir. (1982), and *NLRB v. Southwestern Bell,* 730 F.2d 166, 5th cir. (1984).

Chapter 9

Loss Prevention Contractual Services

Specific practices or services may be necessary in order to get to a root of a problem or an issue in question. However, at times some of those practices employed by a retailer may affect public, employee and/or union relations. Because of the sensitivity of the issues in the use of these types of operations or services, some mention must be made in this narrative.

UNDERCOVER DETECTIVES AND OPERATIONS

The Role of the Undercover Detective

When there is no other apparent way to determine who, what, when, and where merchandise or stock is being stolen, the use of an undercover detective or undercover operative (hereafter designated as UC) becomes a reality. Similar to a regular store detective, who mingles with and pretends to be a customer in order to observe criminal activity, the UC is an unknown, hired to work in a specific position or a particular area in the store and to act as a regular newly hired employee. Both positions require skills and training distinctive to the job, and both are directed to observe criminal behavior. The differences between the two are that the store detective can leave the selling floor at will and commingle with other store coworkers professionally and socially. The UC, however, must never escape his or her "role," and because of this the UC basically becomes a loner. The UC must act the part as a regular employee and a regular member of the "team." Whatever position the UC is assigned, he or she must be accepted by the others as a member of that work group; if not, he or she will be considered an outsider. The UC therefore must gain the confidence and camaraderie of fellow coworkers. As soon as the UC becomes aware of illegal activity, his or her goal is to be "let in on the action." Once the method of operation and corroborating facts becomes known, the UC can then advise the security supervisor that enough documentation and evidence has been obtained to close down the operation. Such information may include the type and extent of stock or merchandise that is taken, how it is disposed of and to whom, and some type of validation to confirm the UC's subsequent testimony. Evidence can include CCTV recordings, paper trails, recovered stolen property, corroborating witnesses, and cooperating co-conspirators.

Whether a supermarket, discount store, or a department store, almost 31% of losses can be attributed to external losses,[1] mostly because of exposed merchandise or poor controls. The average shoplifter could be involved in a theft of a two-dollar item from a supermarket to a theft of several hundred dollars in merchandise from a department store. But the most vulnerable and primary area of concern for a security officer is that almost 46% of a store's theft and loss is committed internally.[2] Recent surveys have shown that in comparison to past years, shoplifting losses have gone down and internal theft has risen. Agreeably, it can be said that security devices, controls, and human resources should be directed more into this area of loss.

The Use and Operation of the Undercover Detective

There may be some qualms by retail management regarding the use of undercover operatives (UCs). They may feel that it's "unethical" or that "spying" on an employee is counterproductive if discovered. Naturally, the operation must be carefully controlled with specific guidelines about what is to be investigated. If company objectives, rules, and procedures are being violated, the company has the right to correct and/or control any departure that affects the company negatively. "Fair play" does not enter into the picture because the investigation is directed toward the dishonest, unethical, and immoral employee. Honest employees should have no fear of such a program. Management has the right to ferret out dishonest employees as well as to seek out dishonest customers.

Additionally, retailers may flinch at the cost of an undercover operation. A good UC agent may cost more in salary than the present on-site store detective, but if the operation is completed with recoveries and/or terminations of dishonest employee/s, the investment can be worth hundreds of thousands of dollars. In many instances, the cost of employing the UC is trivial compared to what can be saved or recovered in a single case.

The experience and expertise of the UC operative, and the UC's ability to convey deception in a relevant manner is most important in the selection process. Moreover, whether the person hired as the undercover operative is a male or female, they should receive some attention or exposure to the business goals, rules, and regulations of the company they will be assigned to as an undercover. There is some validity in using an undercover operative who is employed elsewhere or in another store within the retail chain or company because he or she will be familiar with the operation/s. How, when, and where a UC operative can be used is limited only by one's imagination and the restrictions of the law.

Some of the reasons for the use of an undercover operation are:

- To detect thefts that cannot be discovered under present or normal security controls or procedures.
- To detect thefts in a nonselling area such as the warehouse, receiving or shipping docks or holding areas, merchandise handout areas, and refund/exchange areas.
- To uncover thefts or any wrongdoing after business hours, where there is the cover of darkness and few observers, and usually less supervision.
- To uncover methods of operation and loopholes in security systems that allow employees to steal.
- To probe and attempt to uncover reasons for high shortage areas that cannot be explained.
- To clear and/or resolve the problem concerning a "suspected" employee.

In almost all cases, the placement of an undercover operative should be *unknown to all managers, supervisors, and employees.* Extreme care must be used if certain administrative personnel, no matter how minimal, are to be advised.

Depending on the seriousness of the case, this may have to include loss prevention personnel being completely unaware of the operation, with only the loss prevention manager and store manager having knowledge.

Receiving and shipping areas can be most vulnerable to larceny. The operation can be confusing and appear to be haphazard, with conditions made worse by poor supervision, housekeeping, and received goods or goods to be shipped located indiscriminately or haphazardly all over the docking area. The receiving, shipping, and warehouse areas are usually isolated from management, both physically and mentally. They may neglect the operations in these areas as they become more and more concerned with the retail or selling operations of the business. Because all incoming goods and merchandise pass through the receiving and warehouse areas, these areas are conducive for theft by individuals and alliances. During peak activity in these areas, systematic confusion and the rush to move goods and merchandise can increase larcenies more easily and covertly. We must also consider that if the retail business is not unionized, particularly in the warehouse and receiving/shipping departments, management may do as much as possible legally to keep the union out, which includes loose controls and little security intrusion, all for the purpose of keeping people happy.

Concerning groups of employees involved in larcenous acts, note that not all employee theft rings operate in nonselling areas of the store. Checkers, price markers, and cashiers, to name a few, acting in collusion with other employees or friends and relatives, are uncovered daily throughout the country. In recent years, security professionals have seen a shift from the individual thief who operates alone to the thief acting within a group who has become more flagrant in their behavior.

SUPPLEMENTARY AND BENEFICIAL CONSEQUENCES

As a consequence to an undercover operation, a positive result that can also be gained by a UC is information concerning a variety of issues. This could include the discovery of failure of security controls or the need of more stringent security procedures. In addition, the disclosure of poor management and supervision, employee morale, problems in employee and union relations, the falsification of company records, sources of production slowdowns, vandalism, sabotage, or undesirable activities or groups that may or may not be part of the problem the undercover operative is there to investigate.

HONESTY SHOPPERS

Honesty shoppers (also known as integrity shoppers) are a proven method of undercover investigation, and an effective way to determine if store employees are working in the company's interest. This type of operation originally began and was used by retailers to determine customer service, attitude, courtesy, efficiency, and that correct procedures were followed particularly regarding checks and credit cards. In recent years, retailers have added the factor of "honesty shopping," which primarily is an examination of honesty concerning sales and cashier personnel. Posing as customers and making cash purchases for merchandise, the shopper will target a suspected dishonest employee. The random purchase and selection of an employee will not be as productive nor cost beneficial, as it would be if a particular employee or groups of employees were targeted.

In respect to the selection of a shopping service, they should be hired via a signed contract, which will describe the terms of the operation and service. It will include the fee for the service (which is not governed on the recovery of money or merchandise), length of the contract, the number of times and time of day they are to be engaged in their duties, areas or employees to be tested, and the nature of training required to acclimate the "shopper" to the client's operation. It will also include the type and number of reports to be submitted, subsequent tests on suspected employees if required to confirm prior acts, and the possibility of a second shopper to assist close by in observing the test sale and the actions of the employee after the initial associate leaves the area.

The two basic types of testing techniques are the following:

1. On a purchase, the "customer" hands over to the cashier or salesperson the exact amount, including tax. The "customer" then acts and states that she is in a hurry, places the purchase in her handbag, and leaves without waiting for the purchase to be rung up, or to be given a receipt or a bag.
2. On a purchase, the "customer" hands over uneven money for the merchandise plus tax so that change is returned (for example: hands over a twenty and a ten [$30] for the total purchase amounting to $23.98). The "customer" obtains her change, and a sales receipt. If the sales receipt does not contain the cashiers' identity code, date, and time of the sale (in actuality, the correct sales slip for the transaction), the "customer" will make note of it. If no receipt is given, intentionally or not, a follow-up investigation will also be required.

In many situations, a second undercover honesty shopper assisting the other may be in the area of the sale, and will remain to observe the salesperson's actions after the transaction. In any event, both register tapes in each of the instances noted above will be examined at the end of the day or at a later time in order to determine if the purchase in question has been rung up and is so noted on the register tape.

Rather than identify all of the types of testing techniques in determining the integrity, credibility, and other factors of employee transactions with customers that is of interest to an employer, the security officer should investigate and be aware of the types of services that can obtained for the officer's particular retail operation.

COMPLEMENTARY CONTRACTUAL SERVICES

Watchclock Systems

There are two types of watchclock procedures or patrol management systems that may be in use in the retail environment. The facility that is protected by a watchman during nonbusiness hours when the store is closed will usually have a watchclock that is carried to various points in the store to show when and where the watchman's appointed rounds were made and recorded as required by the employer. This watchman is usually a contracted security guard, but the larger retail establishments may use an in-house guard. In any event, the duties are generally the same. In addition, unless a computer controls various functions within the facility, heating, air conditioning, and lighting systems may have to be manually shut down for the night by the watchman.

There is one problem with night watchmen who are required to commit themselves to precisely timed rounds. If the guard is bound to a routine timed interval between key stations, it can be helpful to a criminal who may have that guard under observation and be aware of the guard's specific location at a given time.

The other system most often used is upon the closing procedures of the store, when the security officer is conducting a "sweep" of the floors making sure that lingering customers make their way to the exits, determining that would-be burglars are not hiding in the store, and that no hazardous conditions exist prior to securing the premises. A watchclock is also used in this procedure because it will show that the security officer did complete the rounds as required, and indicate for insurance purposes, if required, that the procedure was in fact completed.

In both systems the use of a Detex® or a Detex-type mechanical clock is utilized where there is a series of "key stations" located at strategic points throughout the building in sensitive or high-risk areas that must be inspected, either routinely throughout the guard's tour as in the case of the night watchman, or just before closing by the security officer. These areas may include the kitchen and cafeteria, smoking rooms, boiler, sprinkler and machinery rooms, truck receiving areas, and perimeter doors, to name a few. The procedure followed was that the security officer or watchman would insert a key that is attached to the particular station into a portable watchclock. This key, which is embossed with a number of the station, will be impressed on a pressure-sensitive tape contained within the watchclock. This impression will record the station number, time, and date. As the watchman proceeds along the rounds, he or she will stop and insert the key into the watchclock at each station. The clock is tamperproof so that a true accounting of the required patrol would be forthcoming. Although antiquated, these systems are highly effective and still in use today.

Today, watchclock systems have become more sophisticated and advanced electronically. Although still required to physically walk the facility, the key and watchclock have been replaced with various systems and equipment that use magnetics, barcodes, or chip technology to collect data. Examples of this new technology are Data Acquisition Units (DAU), which are handheld electronic systems that contain its own power pack. The unit is passed over or scans a data strip (checkpoint) and the officer will receive a visual and audible confirmation that the information has been recorded in the unit. At the end of the watchman's tour of duty, the unit can be linked and downloaded into a computer-based system and provide an evaluation of the stored data and/or hard copy for future reference.

In conclusion, there are several reasons for the use of the watchclock. The first is to make sure that the security officer or watchman is doing the job as required. The second is that when closing the store for the night, the security officer is confident that by using his or her five senses during the sweep, no hazards were present or left unattended. The third reason is that some insurance companies require that the premises be checked before closing for fire, water leaks, burglars, etc., with the watchclock tape or hard copy as documentation. Some insurance companies will give reduced rates to those retailers who conduct these procedures. All documentation should be retained for review and verification as may be necessary by management or the insurance company.

Armored Car Services

The safest procedure for money to enter and leave any retail premises is by armored car, particularly so if large sums of money are involved. Contractual services will include currency and coin drops and money deposit pickups. Strict safety procedures set up and conducted by armored car personnel will negate almost any robbery attempt within the store. The expense for this service is well worth the safety features offered the employee, and the control and management of money.

Polygraph Services

Most polygraph examinations that are conducted today are by police departments and other law enforcement agencies. This will also include federal and state agencies in order to determine falsehoods in other public safety or national security matters. Nevertheless, because so many restrictions are placed on the polygrapher and the rights granted to the examinee in the private sector, testing in this area is usually confined to certain investigations.

The polygraph can be useful in the investigation of a crime or the probing for details of employee dishonesty after a crime has been discovered. Polygraphs are used to narrow the list of suspects in a civil matter or a criminal investigation. Although restricted to certain controlling factors, including employee theft, sexual harassment, workplace disputes, civil disputes, drug use, and pre-employment verification (of information received, qualifications, and criminal and drug histories). In other instances, a business may need to replace a key employee almost immediately, but a detailed investigation into the applicant's background can be expensive and time-consuming. Within certain restrictions, the utilization of a polygraph may be a more affordable solution with immediate analysis. Generally, no employer is permitted to have a prospective or present employee submit to a polygraph test as a condition of employment or of continued employment. The employee, once tested and believing that an error has been made in the testing procedure, has certain rights. The employee may request a second test, retain a second polygrapher for a second opinion (at the employee's own expense), or file complaints with the state licensing board and the Department of Labor under the Employee Polygraph Protection Act (EPPA).

The results of the examination can be released to only authorized persons. These include the examinee, anyone designated in writing by the examinee, the employer, firm, corporation or government agency that requested the examination, and under due process of law. Federal governmental agencies are basically exempt under the law concerning employees, present and prospective. On the state level, except for some very specific governmental or sensitive positions, some states have banned polygraph exams as part of the hiring process because many people feel that it is an invasion of privacy.

A polygraph examination cannot be forced upon anyone; it must be voluntary in that the subject must willingly submit to the exam. This restriction is applicable whether the examination is for an employment position or an inquiry as part of a criminal investigation. In any case, written consent must be obtained. If the examiner finds "deception" and in effect the subject fails the examination, it cannot be used against a defendant in a court of law, even if the subject voluntarily did submit. Conversely, if the subject passed the examination and was found to be truthful (no deception found), the defendant may attempt (with the judge's permission) to introduce the results on his or her behalf to show innocence. Controversial issues have arisen over polygraph test results and their admissibility in a court of law. Some states and/or jurisdictions have a complete ban on the admission of the results of a polygraph test, although some state and federal district courts do allow such admission. Many appeals on the admissibility of polygraph tests are presently before the appellate courts throughout the country.

A private employer can legally test or question an employee with the use of a polygraph under two circumstances.[3]

1. ***Pre-employment verification.*** Restricted to certain occupational duties including security officers or guards, or personnel who will be handling large sums of money or confidential information.
2. ***Suspicion of theft.*** There must be an "economic loss" (a monetary or property loss). Restricted as to how the employee will fall under the law as an examinee, for example, access alone is insufficient to provide "reasonable suspicion" for the required test. The employer must have "reasonable suspicion" that the employee was involved in the incident under investigation. No subsequent action is to be taken against the employee unless there is additional supporting evidence of involvement or misconduct in addition to the results of the polygraph test.

The security officer must bear in mind that an employee cannot be forced to take a polygraph test.

Because the use or attempted use of polygraph examinations can be the cause of controversy and civil litigation, we will cover what a "lie detector" test is and what it is not. Simply put, the polygraph also known as a "lie detector" really doesn't detect lies, but in fact is based on the idea that a lie or lying leads to emotional conflict that can cause fear and anxiety. These emotions are then reflected as physical changes in the subject's body. The polygraph will record four physical features—heart rate, blood pressure, respiration, and perspiration. Although considered to be very accurate, polygraph results can be affected by varied conditions such as illness, pain, excessive coughing, mental or physical fatigue, heart conditions, breathing problems, tranquilizers and depressants, nervousness, and/or the emotional or physical state of the examinee. Also, body movements and the use of drugs can affect the test, but an experienced examiner will pick up on these deceptions and can either correct or reschedule the test for another time.

According to the American Polygraph Association, the accuracy of polygraph testing over the last twenty-five years is estimated to be 85% to 95% for specific issue investigations. It has been found that the new computerized systems produce results closer to 100% accuracy. However, errors do occur and are usually caused by the lack of training and experience of the examiner, poor pretesting and the wording of test questions, misinterpretation of chart results, equipment malfunction, and improper testing techniques. Accuracy and verifiable results will depend on the expertise of the examiner. The loss prevention department should use caution in hiring a polygrapher. The polygrapher should be a true professional—trained, educated, certified, and accepted as a member by the American Polygraph Association (APA), and a person who will follow all the guidelines found in the law and provide all the required forms for the employer.

Polygraph examinations can be expensive, particularly if a large group of employees need to be examined regarding a crime. Loss prevention should consider the cost and the possible benefit in the use of this instrument. Depending on the serious nature and extent of the crime, and the amount of possible suspect/s involved, the expense may be the least of the problem. If the crime was committed within the jurisdiction of a police department and was reported to them, and that department has a reliable polygraph examiner on staff, the loss prevention manager should to let the police handle the case completely.

Insurance and Fidelity Bonding

Responsible businesspeople and retailers procure and maintain insurance to cover all risks—fire, natural and manufactured disasters and accidents, products liability, criminal and civil liability, shrinkage, auto, and business interruption, to name a few. To keep down the cost of insurance premiums, the company may have a deductible of $50,000 or $100,000, for example, with each area of risk having varying deductibles. A large deductible along with effective loss prevention programs will surely induce lower insurance premium costs to the retailer. Therefore, the premium paid by the retailer will be reflected in the dollar amount of the deductible noted in the policy, with the insurance carrier covering any loss over that deductible.

Traditional liability insurance may be coverage that the retailer may suffer for incidents such as fire, smoke, water damage, property damage, customer, visitor and employee accidents, and crimes that may occur against, within, or around the facility. The retailer may also face liability in various incidents such as products liability, food poisoning, loss of goods in transit, and dishonest employees in key positions, to name a few.

In reality, retailers should not rely solely on insurance coverage as their only recourse against losses. However, it should be considered an essential part of a comprehensive loss prevention program, where security and safety policy and procedures, along with appropriate services and devices are the primary standards with insurance as the final alternative. The cost of insurance is a considerable but necessary expenditure. Insurance coverage for all areas of risk should be routinely examined for an increase in coverage or a cutback as may be required.

When an inventory shortage occurs, the possibility of insurance recovery will depend on how the loss occurred. Employee dishonesty will be covered, but if the shrinkage is found on inventory, the insurance company most probably will not entertain the loss. In these situations and unless shown otherwise, it will be unknown if the shrinkage is due to bookkeeping errors, inaccurate physical counts, inadequate records, or sloppy procedures, breakage, or thefts caused by someone other than a company employee. Proving that dishonest employees committed the loss will most likely be placed on the efforts of the loss prevention department. If a retailer doesn't have a loss prevention department or the department is inadequate for the task, and a claim is sought, the insurance company will require that a police report be made. The police, along with insurance investigators, will attempt to determine if a crime has been committed, and if so, how and by whom. If it can be determined that the loss was caused by a dishonest employee, the insurance company will cover the loss over and above the deductible set in the company's insurance policy.

Fidelity Bonding. The retailer may consider fidelity bonding of certain key employees as a cost and part of their inventory and theft control systems. In many cases, it may be considered a psychological deterrent for those employees who might be tempted to steal. Fidelity bonding can also be called dishonesty insurance. Some companies carry "blanket bonds" that cover all theft by employees in a class or group. If available, some companies may also carry a "schedule bond" on a particular employee, and may require the completion of an individual fidelity application for new employees who will fill certain designated sensitive positions. These positions could include company accountants, bookkeepers, payroll managers, and cash room managers.

The security officer should be aware that if an applicant is involved in the hiring process, and the insurance underwriter refuses to bond that person and is not hired because bonding is required to be part of that position, the applicant might seek civil recourse. The insurance company may feel based upon information received, that the applicant should not be entrusted in a sensitive position, and may request that such person be refused or excluded from other employees covered under the bond. Because the information or its source contained in the insurance company's risk files is privileged, a reason for denial will not be forthcoming.[4] The insurance company has a legal right to not issue a bond if they deem it so, and the retailer has the right in the hiring process to require bonding for the position sought, with acceptance by the underwriter before hire.

But a possible litigious situation could arise if a present employee is denied bonding and loses out on a promotion or transfer with potential advancement, or is downgraded and/or transferred because of it. The employee *may* have a justifiable case for a civil action against the insurance company and retailer; however it can effectively be defended because the insurance company and the retailer have certain rights as described above.

Moreover, if a newly hired employee had a background of theft and/or embezzlement prior to hire, or during employment a present employee had been discovered as dishonest, a problem could arise. If the employer has knowledge of this criminal act or background, and it is overlooked by the employer in any manner for any reason, prior to hiring or while employed, the insurance company will not cover any subsequent loss by that employee. The employer, by concealing or not revealing such information or incidents, gives reason to the insurance company to cancel that employee's bond. Also, be aware that if a promissory note is accepted from an employee who had been bonded and is terminated for any type of larceny, the retailer is placed at risk. If the former employee subsequently disappears after making a few payments, the bonding company is usually relieved of any liability to make up the remainder owed by the thief.

Workers' Compensation. A company carries workers' compensation insurance for employees injured in and/or during the course of their employment. It is a safeguard for companies in that it protects them against any type of lawsuit for an action by an employee, and also preserves the employees' rights for some recompense from the employer who otherwise may not be able to provide. The cost of insurance coverage provided by an insurance company will probably be a liberal expense, but this is an area where loss prevention can have a great impact on savings. Consider that injury claims not only include medical expenses, payment of wages and benefits, and probably a costly settlement, but also lost workdays and productivity for the absent employee.

An insurance company is in business to make money, and if not, they will raise premiums or drop the account. So in actuality, it is your company's money that is spent for medical expenses and lost wages due to disabilities, rehabilitation, or death. As part of the premiums paid by the company, the insurance company will provide certain services in an attempt to control and manage the account. In particular, this will include the following:

- *Insurance company loss control representative:* This person helps develop effective safety controls and programs; offers advise on compliance to safety codes, laws, codes, and regulations; and often provides safety training material, bulletins, posters, and so on.
- *Insurance company claims representative:* This person stays in contact with doctors, physical therapists, and other medical care providers; and investigates claims to determine compensatory coverage, evaluate medical information, assist in legal counsel, settle claims, and attend hearings, settlements, and so on.

All loss prevention managers and safety managers have experienced employees who feign or at least embellish a minor injury into a serious disability. Fraud is not uncommon in the area of employee injuries. The new hire must be made aware that not only does the offender commits a theft of services, but also the more serious crime of insurance fraud and that any injured employee will be constantly monitored.

In that regard, the retailer should set up a *Claims Review Committee* to meet routinely in order to determine outstanding claims, how much money has been paid out for each claim and totally for all claims to date, and amounts of monetary reserves held by the insurance company for any future expenses. Moreover, discussion should include prognosis of injuries, contact with the injured employee, and the possibility of a modified work assignment based on medical evaluation. This committee should include the insurance agent or broker, insurance claims representative, the loss prevention manager, and the human resources manager.

Finally, accident investigation of all employee injuries must be a major component of the duties required of the loss prevention department. Whether the initial employee accident report is compiled by the injured person's supervisor or by a security officer, the report must be timely and complete with a conclusive investigation by the loss prevention manager.

OTHER ESSENTIAL SERVICES

Rather than be caught unprepared when an incident occurs and the loss prevention department requires the immediate services of an outside security, investigative, or safety service, loss prevention should maintain a close relationship and availability of certain occupations and undertakings that may be helpful in the future and when needed.

The following list is in addition to those services noted prior in this section:

- ***Document or handwriting examiner:*** internal examination of fraudulent documents or other suspected papers.
- ***Private investigator:*** when a confidential, surreptitious in-depth investigation of a particular subject or other inquiry may be required.

- ***Computer consultant:*** when expert computer experience and inquiry is required.
- ***Safety engineer:*** available for consultation, surveys, training aids, and so on, regarding safety in the workplace (often offered by the retailer's insurance carrier).
- ***Fire safety consultant:*** to assist the loss prevention department with professional counsel and instruction regarding effective fire safety audits.
- ***Fire equipment services:*** provides routine inspection and/or replacement as required by law, usually contractually, of all fire hardware within the facility, such as fire extinguishers, fire hoses, gas suppression systems, etc.
- ***Watchguard services:*** for internal/external patrol during a failure of alarm systems such as burglar or fire reporting system during hours when the store is closed.
- ***Uniformed security guards:*** to supplement the store security when large crowds are expected during special sales or holiday events.
- ***Emergency services:*** outside firms that may be contracted during emergencies include heating and air conditioning repair; glass replacement; municipal water supply; water damage control; damage repair and property preservation; telephone, electric, and alarm repair; and contractual guard service. All of these services should be noted in the *Emergency Procedure Plan* by type of service, firm, and day and evening emergency telephone numbers.

Note that professional analysis or investigation by any of the above described consultants may be used in any court or hearing at a later time if need be, whether in conjunction with a police investigation or not.

ENDNOTES

1. Op. cit., *2001 National Retail Security Survey—Final Report*, p. 4.
2. Ibid., p. 4.
3. *Employee Polygraph Protection Act of 1998*, Title 29, USC § 2001 et seq.
4. Subject to the provisions mandated in *Consumer Credit Reform Act.*, op. cit.

Chapter 10

Other Responsibilities and Considerations

EXTERIOR PATROLS

The elements of patrol, whether internal or external, are observation and protection—in other words, to detect and to deter. All patrol should be random in nature so that the officer cannot be timed and regulated by a person who may be inclined to commit a crime. The officer should alternate time and routes, changing or backtracking without reason or design.

It is always advisable to routinely patrol the exterior of the facility during all work shifts in an effort to detect any potential problems. These problems could be security or safety in nature. Some examples of the conditions that may be found while on exterior patrol are:

- Blocked emergency exits
- Vandalism/criminal mischief, graffiti
- Arson attempts
- Theft of personal and company property
- Trash, trash bins or large dumpster fires
- Light outages
- King Pin Lock infractions, and missing transport containers
- Suspicious persons or persons loitering
- Injured or intoxicated individuals
- Trash accumulation
- Parking field patrol, safety, and security

Parking Fields

A very important area of loss and liability is the parking field adjacent to or part of the building structure. Parking facilities that are poorly patrolled, improperly lighted, containing blind spots or other hiding places can cause not only harm or loss to a customer or visitor, but trepidation by the public. When these fears cause a reduction of commerce because of customers refusing to shop at that location, the business will suffer.

Customers, visitors, and employees who walk through or use the parking lots for their vehicles are subject to robbery, larceny, assault, and rape. Moreover, these lots are prone to auto accidents and personal injuries, which along with criminal acts may place the retailer in civil jeopardy.

There are two types of parking facilities:

1. Open lots that may be remote or adjacent to the business establishment
2. The multi-level or tier parking structure that may be adjacent to or part of the business establishment

The controlling factor here for the loss prevention department is to determine if the parking field is owned, leased, controlled, or maintained in any manner by the retail store that it serves. If not and the field is owned, controlled, or maintained by a mall ownership, or another owner or operator, that entity will have civil responsibility for any occurrence taking place on that property. In this case, the retailer must have no legal authority in the control of the parking field or parking areas, other than the cooperation of the property owner or mall operator in providing a parking service for the retailer's customers. For the owner/operator, this includes the maintenance and sweeping of the roadways and parking areas, snow and ice removal, and the security and safety of everything in those parking fields. Loss prevention should determine the building property lines in an effort to resolve which business or entity is responsible for what property or area. If lease agreements or deeds cannot determine property lines, a surveyor may be required to ascertain responsibility. A timely and accurate delineation of property lines must be known prior to any civil litigation that may arise in order to determine responsibility.

Responsibility regarding control and/or ownership of property is an important liability issue.
If the retailer owns, operates, or controls the parking field in any manner, liability for any accident or incident that occurs on or in that parking field will be the retailer's responsibility.

The property lines are most significant, and it doesn't matter whether the retailer's building is owned, leased, or rented. If all or parts of the sidewalks, parking areas, or any area in question are within the property lines, or are part of the retailer's lease agreement/s, then the retailer can be held responsible for all injuries, and any other occurrence in those areas within the retailer's control. If so, the security officer should routinely examine and report all conditions and circumstances that could place the retailer at civil risk. Whether it is a report of an accident or a crime, the security department that protects the parking field will be responsible to investigate, report, and advise the appropriate insurance carrier and/or law enforcement agency.

Threat Assessment. If it is determined that the parking fields are the responsibility of the retailer, then loss prevention must make an assessment of the vulnerabilities. This should include the following:

- Crimes against the person—larceny, robbery, carjacking, assault (rape, mugging, personal injury)

- Crimes against property—vehicle theft, criminal mischief/vandalism, larceny from vehicles (packages, cell phones, other items in view), and any terrorist act (placing a bomb device, particularly within a multi-level structure)
- Safety issues—proper maintenance of roadways and passageways (potholes, ice and snow), and damage to the structure itself so as to prevent auto accidents or personal injuries to those people who use the parking areas

Prevention Measures. The following responses may be considered based on loss prevention's assessment of the extent and seriousness of the threat:

- ***Building design:*** This includes blind spots, nooks and crannies, enclosed stairways and elevators (as opposed to open or glass enclosed), and poor lines of sight must be eliminated in the construction of a parking area, whether open or multi-level. If the facility already exists, care must be taken to eliminate the threat as much as possible.
- ***Proper lighting:*** We cannot overlook the effect that lighting has on security, but also equally important, the safety of the occupants, customers, and visitors in and around the business facility. As an excellent deterrent to crime, good lighting provides a sense of safety for the persons who use the parking areas. Care must be taken that the sectors with the highest threat potential must be well lighted. If the area is underground or poorly lit even during daytime hours, adequate lighting must be available.
- ***CCTV:*** Although expensive to purchase and maintain, adequate CCTV coverage with appropriate monitoring by loss prevention personnel can ascertain any criminal activity or anyone in distress. Over a period of time, that in itself can provide a cost-benefit ratio that can surely be considered as a positive technique. This type of coverage is particularly useful in large open areas particularly if remote from the business establishment it serves. Some problems can occur in that low overhead in underground or multi-level parking fields can limit a camera's view, whereas the higher a camera can be placed, the better the coverage. Additional coverage should be considered for all stairways and elevators. Moreover, if there are many hidden or blind spots, multiple cameras may have to be used, thereby elevating the cost of operation. One way to eliminate multiple cameras in many areas is the use of a pan-tilt-zoom type camera. A single camera of this type can cover a much larger area if it can provide a 360-degree view and the ability to zoom in on a subject or suspicious activity.
- ***Call boxes/panic alarms:*** Strategically placed and available throughout the parking areas, these devices offer the public the ability to request help in an emergency. It provides the means of immediate response, and along with the use of a horn, bell, and/or flashing light, can deter a would-be assailant.
- ***Radio motor patrol:*** Marked vehicles manned by security officers on constant patrol and as visible as possible are a deterrent to criminal activity. Motor patrol offers an officer wider coverage of patrol and faster response to an occurrence.
- ***Raised platform or booth:*** A security booth manned by a security officer using binoculars can effectively cover large open parking areas if the elevation is high

enough. Some business establishments may use a security officer on the roof of the facility protected and hidden by a structure that also may serve the same purpose. The officer should be equipped with a portable radio for contact with a central location or other officers.

- ***Awareness training:*** Employees should be made aware of the dangers that may occur in a parking field that they may use while at work. The seriousness of the problem will depend on various factors such as the parking area, garage or structure, the local demographics and crime statistics, and the time of day when the employees will be present.

  This training could include the following precautions:

  Having car keys out and ready when entering the parking field.

  Checking under the vehicle when approaching it.

  Not to park against a truck or van where an assailant may be hidden within.

  Attempt to enter and leave the parking area only when other people are around.

  Make use of a security escort during night hours and/or when there is little pedestrian and vehicle traffic.

  Avoid leaving packages or other items in full view where they are visible from outside the vehicle. Use the trunk.

  Always locking the vehicle when leaving.

  If possible, try to avoid making the vehicle stand out from the norm by not using certain decals, bumper stickers, license plate frames, or license plates.

- ***Public notification:*** Public awareness signs such as "Lock your vehicle," "Do not leave personal property visible in your vehicle," and "These premises under camera surveillance and security patrol," will only provide as much of a deterrent to criminal intent as can be determined by the observable and actual use of cameras and patrol.

SAFES

The retailer and the loss prevention manager must realize that safes are an important part of asset protection, and consideration should be made during construction or renovation of interior spaces about where a safe will be located, particularly a money safe. The more valuables or money that the thief may believe is contained in a safe, the more of a target it will be. The security officer should give special attention to the types and classes of safes and their significance to crime prevention. There are basically two types of business safes:

The Fire Safe. Used principally for its heat-resistant qualities, fire resistant safes are normally made with a hollow metal or steel wall filled with various types and amounts of insulation. These safes or cabinets are used to store business records, tax and bookkeeping books and records, computer records on tape or discs, and other important papers. The objective of this type of safe is to ensure that after a fire that may have consumed everything around it, its contents will still be usable. A loss or damage by fire could cause a business to suffer greatly if their important records were not protected.

The type and amount of insulation used in a fire safe will determine the degree of protection afforded to the contents. Degree of protection is calculated by Fahrenheit temperature (°F). Because temperatures well above 350°F are quite common during a fire, most fire safes will be designed and classified to keep the interiors below this level. Higher classes of protection are available. Classes of protection are certified by Underwriters Laboratory Inc. (UL) and so noted on each safe.

Unlawful entry is easily made into a safe of this type with little effort. Because of the possibility of loss by theft or by an extreme fire, backup copies of important records should be made and located elsewhere.

The Money Safe. These safes are used principally to safeguard valuables and money, and are constructed to resist forced entry by a burglar. The money safe may have only minimal fire-resistant protection. Construction may be of very thick steel, thick hollow steel walls filled with cement, steel laminate sheets, or a combination of one or more. A good safe is designed to resist attacks by exceptional tools, torches, or explosion. The National Bureau of Casualty Underwriters (NBCU) sets classifications and specifications of the various safes equipped with at least one combination lock. Underwriters Laboratory Inc. also classifies those safes that are secured with a keyed lock.

NBCU designates several classes of safes—Class B, C, E, F, H, and I. The class will designate the construction of the safe, and the length of time to withstand an attack by various means. At this time, Class I is the most secure. Additionally, within these classes, safes come in different sizes and assorted shapes. The most secure safe is considered to be the safe with a round door for entry rather than a rectangular or square door. Many large rectangular safes have an interior safe with a round door also containing a combination lock.

As previously noted, the location of a money safe within an office or other space is most important. If possible, the safe should be contained in its own separate room. Detection equipment such as magnetic sensors, motion detectors, electronic beams, and pressure sensitive pads in front of or around the safe should be installed. Activation of these sensors should be controlled by and assigned as points to the burglar alarm system.

Some businesses have a procedure with their central station that just prior to opening the safe for the day, or when the safe is closed for the night, a telephone call is made to the central station advising them of the opening or closing of the safe along with a code. In this way, the central station is aware that a certain course of action is taking place in an authorized manner, and not under duress.

Safe Access and Security

In addition, certain procedures must be promulgated and strictly enforced for all cash office personnel concerning access to the safe and its contents. This will also include the following:

- Lightweight safes (such as those used for petty cash) should be secured so as to prevent easy removal.
- Cash on hand should be kept at a minimum, with frequent deposits and pickups.
- Armored car personnel should be easily identified by CCTV before entry into the cash room for money pickups. They should also be known by sight. Armored car carriers routinely provide personnel sheets containing photos and

descriptions of all their drivers and helpers in case personnel replacements are made by the company.

- Combinations to safes should not be left where they can be found. The combination should be known only to those employees who have been granted access to the safe and memorized—never written down. See CASHIERS AND CASH ROOMS in Chapter 15 for further information on combinations.
- The safe must be locked securely by turning the combination dial several times before leaving the premises for the night.
- If the safe and/or cash room is alarmed, proper procedure for setting the alarm must be conducted prior to closing. Burglar alarm points assigned to these areas should not be bypassed.
- Loss prevention personnel should conduct routine testing of holdup alarms.

DRUGS ON PREMISES

There is little doubt that the consumption of drugs by employees in any business can cause safety and security problems. It really doesn't matter whether the drugs are possessed and used before coming to work or while on the job, the effect upon employees and their actions is the same. Drugs can cause physical and psychological dependence. Many times addicts suffer both afflictions. It can be said that alcohol also falls into a substance abuse and dependence habit. Whether drugs or alcohol, addicted employees become obsessed with feeding this predisposition, and will do anything to satisfy their need. If the opportunity exists for drug users to steal, they will commit themselves to any method to reach that goal of satisfaction. This is particularly so for persons who are long-time users and the need for the drug becomes more and more excessive. Nothing will stand in their way. Whether employees are heavy users or use drugs only intermittently or socially, loss prevention personnel should be aware of the problems they can cause.

Drug Testing

Questions may arise concerning drug testing, such as *if, when, and the right to do so* by a company. There are two conditions under which companies may test—at preemployment or randomly. Some companies have preemployment physicals as a standard procedure for employment in their company, but most do not.

However, in other circumstances a demand to test an employee would have to be based on the terminology "fitness for duty," where the opportunity to test a particular employee for specific reasons could be held. Such reasoning could include if the workplace has been made unsafe for him or other employees, or that his work habits are contrary to the safety of his person or others, and that he is suspect in the use of a drug or other intoxicant. This reasoning may be based on the employee's appearance and behavior (actions and demeanor), in addition to physical evidence or information and belief from a trustworthy employee or employees. Ongoing written documentation of such activity or behavior would indicate the potential need for such testing and negate the possibility of mistreatment or illegality. But also consider that an incident of a serious nature, which has come to the attention of management, might require an employee agreement to an immediate drug test before returning to work.

As for random drug testing, whether individually or within the whole group of employees where everyone may be randomly subject to a drug test, there are many restrictions. Union contractual agreements, prior or present hiring agreements, personal civil rights, probable cause, the type and procedures for the test, whether such a test is applicable to retail employment, and other considerations are open to close scrutiny by the legal profession. It is suggested, before a test of this type is seriously considered and contemplated, that legal counsel be sought prior to any action.

Drug counselors generally acknowledge that the following statistics are fair and accurate:

- Drug users are 33% to 50% less productive on the job.
- Drug users are 3 to 4 times more likely to have accidents or injuries on the job.
- Medical claims for drug users are 300% to 400% more costly than nonusers.
- Drug users are absent or late for work 3 times more often than nonusers.
- The estimated loss to a company due to internal theft by drug users is greater than 50%.

Controlled substances are against the law to possess unless a person has medical authorization. Some substances are not legally obtainable and cannot legally be prescribed. Some of these controlled substances include the following:

- ***Narcotics:*** such as morphine, cocaine, and heroin. Indicators of a user include "tracks" or needle marks on the arms, pinhole pupils, frequent scratching, and loss of appetite. A user may appear drowsy after a "fix," or restless with watery eyes and sniffles before the "fix." A user may constantly have a "runny nose."
- ***Depressants:*** such as barbiturates can cause behavior similar to alcohol intoxication, but without the odor of alcohol on the person. Will appear to be sluggish, have difficulty concentrating and poor judgment. A user will also have slurred speech, and impaired motor skills and fall asleep on the job.
- ***Stimulants:*** such as amphetamines. The effects include hyperactivity, exhilaration, repetitive behavior usually without purpose, dilated pupils, and runny noses.
- ***Hallucinogens:*** such as LSD, mescaline, and peyote. This drug is the cause of very wide shifts in behavior and moods, and a person may appear to be in a trancelike state or terrified. They may experience sweats, chills, trembling, nausea, and irregular breathing.
- ***Cannabis:*** includes marijuana and hashish. The use of this common and easily obtained drug causes intoxication, lethargy, impaired motor skills, and a distorted sense of time and distance.

The security officer should be aware of the implements used by the drug user. Depending on the drug of choice and how it is administered, they will include a needle and syringe, a small or bent spoon, small metal or clear plastic bottles, glassine bags or tinfoil packets, mirrors, razor blades, and a straw or a tightly rolled currency bill. Realize that a needle and syringe may not pertain to a drug user, but to a diabetic. Possession of tablets or capsules may have been legally prescribed and sniffles may also be caused by hay fever.

Caution must be used by the security officer regarding the search and seizure of drugs and/or drug paraphernalia. The security officer should not act alone if he or she suspects illegal drug use. If the use of drugs is widespread, it can be assumed that the sale and distribution of drugs are also taking place on premises. The loss prevention manager may wish to involve the local police or narcotics squad once evidence comes to light that the use of drugs is prevalent. The possibility may also exist where the retailer may not wish the publicity regarding the arrest or arrests of drug users and dealers caught on the premises, and therefore may make use of an undercover operative. The retailer may wish to identify these employees and terminate them for cause quickly and as quietly as possible. The actions of loss prevention will be guided by company administration.

Caution

Care should also be used in the personal search of *any* person arrested. While searching subjects, the possibility of a needle stick with attendant infection or exposure to bloodborne pathogens cannot be overstated. The security officer should make the initial search with a "pat down," followed by cautiously having subjects empty their own pockets onto a table or desk with a watchful eye, then following up with a "frisk" of the subjects.

LOST AND FOUND CHILDREN

Lost or Missing Child

One of the most stressful and anxiety-filled situations that can occur in a retail store for a parent is the report by that parent or guardian of a missing child.

The security officer must consider the report of a lost or missing child as a possible abduction or a custodial interference situation.

As with other emergency situations, the retailer should have a procedure that would go into effect once a report of a lost or missing child is made. This procedure should be written, and the responsibility carried out by the loss prevention department to conduct and control the occurrence and the actions of employees involved.

The *minimal* suggestions for the procedure to be followed upon a report of a lost or missing child should be as follows:

1. The first security officer or manager at the scene of the report should gather a full description of the child including name, age, race, complexion, hair and eye color, approximate weight and height, language spoken, and a complete description of clothing worn (type, color, etc.).
2. Make sure that all of the above information is given to loss prevention personnel and employees involved in the search. Radio communication is invaluable in these circumstances.
3. The loss prevention manager, or if unavailable, a security officer or a responsible manager should be in charge of coordinating the search activity and assigning employees to various parts of the store.

4. One employee should remain with the parent/guardian, preferably with a portable handheld radio. This is in case the child is found by the parent, the search can be canceled, or so that the found child can be returned to the parents location.
5. As soon as possible, assign an employee or employees, also preferably with a radio, at the entrance/s and exit/s, in order to view the persons leaving the premises.
6. A search should be made of all rest rooms, unlocked closets and mechanical rooms, fire exits and stairwells, and any obstructed or hidden areas, paying particular attention to evidence of child's clothing that may have been discarded.
7. If the child has been located or found, the child should be returned to the parent or guardian who made the initial report. Once positive recovery is made, loss prevention should advise all employees involved in the incident of the recovery so that they may return to their routine duties.
8. If the child is not found within a reasonable period of time (10 to 15 minutes), loss prevention should request the police to be notified and advised that the store has a report of a missing child and store personnel have been unable to locate the child.
9. If a child is observed leaving the premises and matches the description, that child should be stopped. If an adult is with the child, the store employee should advise the adult of the situation and the apparent matching description of the child, and request that they remain until loss prevention or the parent respond to their location. Generally, the person stopped will understand, sympathize, and cooperate. If the adult is not cooperative and is intent on leaving with the child, delaying procedures should be employed, and an attempt should be made to communicate with the child in an effort to determine if any force or coercion is being used.
10. Unless the employee is *reasonably certain* that the child leaving the premises is the reported missing child, no stop should be made. However, a description of the adult should be noted, along with any car used, the registration plate number, and the direction of leaving.

Consider that the term *reasonably certain* will take into account the physical description of the child, the clothing that matches as reported, the demeanor of the child, and the actions and attitude of the adult accompanying the child. These factors will all contribute to what a reasonable person (the employee under these conditions) would consider sufficient for a stop and further inquiry.

Security officers and employees must be conscious that the only way that a person may legally be detained is if it is *known* that an *abduction* (a felony crime) is in progress and in their presence. Physically detaining a person later found to be innocent might result in civil litigation against the employee and the retailer.

Nonetheless, if the security officer or employee is reasonably certain based on the facts known, and bases his or her belief on these and other facts taking place at the time (probable cause) that the child leaving the store is the missing child, and the officer acts reasonably under these circumstances to make the stop, one wonders if anyone would find fault with the officer's actions.

If it were found later that a error had been made, and the adult who was stopped initiates civil litigation, it would be expected that the court would look favorably on the defendant if in fact he or she acted in a reasonable and professional manner. In essence, did the officer act in a prudent, rational, and sensible manner under the circumstances?

In a *custodial interference* occurrence, the security officer would have no immediate knowledge that the parent who now has possession of the child does not have the right to such custody. The security officer should not restrain that parent from leaving the area unless the officer has reason to believe that the child is or will be in danger. Generally, most if not all states consider a routine custodial interference a misdemeanor crime. If the other parent is present and demands custody from the other, the security officer could act on behalf of that complainant and restrain the second party who has control of the child until the police arrive and take charge of the situation.

Found Child

If it comes to the attention of an employee that a child has been found who is lost or separated from its parent or guardian, the following action is suggested:

1. The employee should take immediate custody of the child and advise loss prevention. Security officer/s will attempt to locate the parent/guardian in the vicinity where the child was found. Usually the parent/guardian will not be too far away. If not, the child will be taken to an office area, such as the security office or switchboard/receptionist area.
2. An announcement may be made over the public address system advising the occupants of the store that a child has been found. A minimal description should be given without naming the child. If the parent/guardian has not made some inquiry to store employees or cannot be located within a reasonable time, the local police department should be notified and advised of the found child, and that the store is unable to locate the parent or guardian.

As always with any occurrence, an incident report must be compiled and maintained on any reported lost or found child. The report must contain details of the actual incident, if and when the police were called, their presence if any, whether the child was placed in the custody of the police or their actions concerning the incident, or whether the child was claimed by a parent or guardian on or off premises. Proper identification of that person should be conducted prior to the child leaving the custody of loss prevention. If the child is turned over to the parent or guardian, note the complete identification of that person on the report. If the security officer has any doubt or misgivings on conferring custody of the child to another person, let the police make the transfer. As a precaution, no food, candy, or liquids should be given to a child while in the custody of loss prevention for fear that if the child has a medical condition where a possible physical reaction could occur, the child may be placed in some danger.

LOST AND FOUND PROPERTY

During the normal course of a business day, customers and visitors lose or misplace everything from sunglasses to cell phones, and wallets to checkbooks. The item found should ultimately come under the custody of loss prevention, whether it was turned over to an employee or a security officer. All items of this nature should be placed in a centralized location so that if an inquiry is made, and the property identified, the owner may retrieve the item. Any item of value, such as a wallet or pocketbook containing currency and/or credit cards, jewelry, cell phones, should be noted as to when and where it was found on a "Found Property Report."

The property should be safely secured. When properly identified and returned to the owner, the report should be signed as received by the owner. These reports will be filed and maintained for future reference. If the property is of great value, such as jewelry or a considerable amount of currency and not claimed within a reasonable time (approximately one week), it should be turned over to the police. See the Appendix for a copy of a FOUND PROPERTY REPORT.

POLICE OFFICERS

Obstructing Governmental Administration

Regarding police officers, the security officer should be mindful that any conduct considered as interference with a public servant may be unlawful.

> All states have a law similar in content, which mandates that a person is considered guilty of obstructing governmental administration when he or she intentionally obstructs, impairs, or perverts the administration of law or other governmental function, or prevents or attempts to prevent a public servant from performing an official function, by means of intimidation, physical force, or interference.
>
> It may also include any independently unlawful act, or any interference, whether or not physical force is involved.

Although the security officer may be loyal and responsible to his or her employer, there will be times when the police may come on board in order to conduct an investigation that the officer or employer may or may not be privy to. If the police are present on official business, they must be given free access. This will include other law enforcement agencies for a legal or mandated inspection of premises, safety equipment, and records, among others. The obstruction described herein could also include the hindrance of official duties by fire inspectors and building inspectors. These official duties are considered governmental business, and any obstruction, prevention, or delaying tactics by a security officer regarding the duties of the government agent or failure to cooperate as requested can place the officer in a position in which he or she may be charged with a crime.

Police Cooperation

A most important aspect of loss prevention is the ability to work well with the local police department. When the police officers who are assigned in the vicinity of your store become confident in your ability to make lawful and appropriate apprehensions and arrests, handle evidence and statements correctly, and not request police assistance until all of your own procedures are completed, their cooperation will be gladly given.

As to other incidents where they are called for assistance, they are required and will respond to keep the peace, try to mitigate or correct the situation, and if not, make a lawful arrest, or if possible, to refer the participant/s to court.

However, if the police have to respond to unlawful and/or sloppy procedures, or are requested for minor or frivolous incidents that should have been taken care of by the security officer, they will soon become disenchanted with your loss prevention department. Their job regarding an arrest is to respond and give assistance, make sure that the law is followed and enforced, take custody and transport the suspect to a stationhouse or holding facility for further processing, and return to patrol as soon as possible. They should not have to respond to unnecessary actions. In other words, if you cry wolf too often, police response may become slower and slower until the message becomes clear to the security officer. The ideal is to have a good working relationship with the police because you may need them when least expected and in a great hurry.

The police are employed to keep the peace, prevent crime, and arrest the offender.

They are not enforcers of private rights, where the security officer is employed and acts within the scope of his or her employment.

They should not be called to a scene to take care of a situation that should have been taken care of by the security officer.

Other than to assist in completing the arrest processing procedure, an emergency or public safety situation, keeping the peace or for defining legal actions, there is no need for a police presence.

Police Officers Hired as Security Officers

In recent years, the use of sworn police officers hired as part-time security officers and guards has become very popular among many businesses nationally. As crime tends to increase, many retailers feel that in hiring a police officer, they will have a well-trained responsible individual who will serve them well in the area of security and safety. But also note the use of police officers as part-time security officers may complicate the "*color of law*" issue by the introduction of new problems. See COLOR OF STATE LAW in Chapter 4 concerning a possible civil rights violation under the federal statute.

The reason that most retailers hire police officers is that they are already trained in the law, have experience in crisis intervention, make very few mistakes, require less supervision, and presumably know what they are doing. In addition, employees who have a propensity to steal will generally resist any nefarious thoughts when a police officer moonlighting as a security officer is on duty.

However, there are drawbacks to the above statement. In actuality, trained off-duty police officers often forget that they are off duty. In most instances, particularly complex and stressful situations, they will act as a police officer with all the legal powers with which they are empowered. The retailer's business philosophy may differ from that of a police officer, in that his or her training, duties, and perception differ somewhat from that of a security officer. The police officer routinely becomes involved in assorted violations and crimes in varying degrees and varying circumstances. The police officer is concerned with lawful investigations to determine if in fact a crime has been committed, that the person apprehended is presumed guilty based upon probable cause, and that the person should be brought before a court of law for punishment (law enforcement through lawful punishment). The active police officer has a "mind-set" that is difficult to change. A security officer might appear to have similar duties but has a different end-view. The security officer's mission is not primarily to apprehend, arrest, and prosecute—it is the protection of the company's assets. Moreover, in the area of apprehensions, detainment, and arrest, the police officer's viewpoint and actions may conflict with that of the retailer. The police officer's powers of arrest, questioning and interrogation techniques, search procedures, and the production of evidence are different from that of a security officer. In addition, the possibility of a "police-dominated atmosphere" could be a liability in the prosecution of a defendant and subsequent litigation. Many police departments prohibit their personnel from "moonlighting" as security officers because of the possibility of a conflict in duties, obligations, and liability.

As a matter of policy, the loss prevention manager should use extreme caution in hiring and the use of active police officers employed within the loss prevention department.

THE MEDIA

The loss prevention department must be aware that there will be incidents or occurrences in which some or all segments of the media may wish to come in contact with the company for some information. It is assumed that the retailer will have a manager or spokesperson according to company policy who will be the person, and the only person, who will make any public comment regarding any incident or occurrence.

Because loss prevention personnel are usually involved in some manner in an incident that may become sensationalized by the media, they will seek out the security officer for any information, insight, or comment that they can use. Remember, as with attorneys, members of the media are self-serving and are looking for information and the opportunity that will embellish or sensationalize their story. Many times, comments and interviews are cropped or edited to suit their viewpoint or time slot, not caring whether the subject of the interview is placed in an embarrassing position or made to look foolish in some way. Also, many times the final story presented by the media may not be what the company wishes to present, at least not without their side being presented to the public, and which may not be provided by the reporter.

If approached for any information or comment by a newsprint or television reporter, politely and professionally advise them that you have no comment to make, and that you will refer their presence or their questions to the appropriate company spokesperson.

Consider also that any time a group of reporters or a television crew comes aboard your business establishment, people will gravitate to a scene or their location thereby causing a crowd to collect. Remember that the retailer, and you as his or her agent, have control over your business premises, and any disruption of your business should not be tolerated. The retailer has the right to require reporters and TV crews to relocate or move to an office or secluded area out of public view. If they refuse to do so, security officers may demand that they remove themselves from the business premises under the threat of criminal trespass, if necessary. Although they may accuse the retailer of suppressing their constitutional First Amendment rights (freedom of the press), they are fully aware of how far they can proceed before a businessperson may suffer some loss because their presence has caused a business disruption.

- Do not answer any question or make any comments to anyone from the media.
- Do not place yourself or your company in an embarrassing position or in jeopardy of being misquoted.

Part 4

EXTERNAL AND INTERNAL RETAIL THEFT

Loss from Theft and Fraud

THE SHOPLIFTER AND THE DISHONEST EMPLOYEE

The retail establishment suffers more loss from internal theft and damage by employees than by shoplifters and scam and con artists. It is impossible to state a true percentage of internal loss as opposed to external loss because many retailers don't always publicly report their losses. When a dishonest employee is discovered, rather than go through the time and effort involved in a prosecution, the retailer would more willingly terminate and cut their losses in many instances. If some type of restitution can be made, that would be a plus.

As previously noted on page 106 regarding the *2001 National Retail Security Survey* (NRSS) conducted by the University of Florida, those retailers responding to the survey produced a figure of 30.8% loss by theft to shoplifting and 45.9% loss attributed to internal theft. Associated loss of 23.4% was attributed to administrative paper loss and vender fraud. With a reported total shrinkage for that year at $33.21 billion, this would translate into $15.24 billion attributed to internal theft and $10.23 billion attributed to shoplifting losses. In fact, the loss attributed to internal (employee) theft was the highest observed in the ten-year history of the NRSS.[1]

Employee dishonesty can occur in various forms from pocketing a small inconsequential item before leaving work to embezzlement and computer fraud. High-risk items such as jewelry, furs, cameras, guns, all types of electronics, and expensive small appliances need to be as secure as possible from external as well as internal theft. This type of merchandise is highly regarded by the thief because of its higher value and its easy disposal.

Retail stores operate on a tight profit margin, and any significant loss can place that business in jeopardy. Bear in mind that there have been prior instances in which a company has fallen into bankruptcy because of shrinkage.

We can identify the problem of shrinkage as having several basic causes:

- Internal theft and fraud by employee/s
- External loss by shoplifting
- Other losses due to external fraud and theft
- Damage, misappropriation, and misuse of property
- Inventory, paperwork, and computer errors

There is some agreement among retailers and security professionals that total shrinkage losses of 2% or less based on annual gross sales is acceptable, with closer to 1% or less as exceptional.

The University of Florida has been conducting the National Retail Security Survey since 1991. Although there has been some fluctuation in the reported figures, the overall average (mean) shrinkage percentage has remained relatively stable over the past decade as we can see in Figure 7.1 on page 105.[2] For the year of 2001, the national average for inventory shrinkage was 1.80% based on reporting retailers.[3]

INVENTORY LOSS

Inventory loss or shrinkage occurs in several ways, both internally and externally. It can occur at the receiving dock when merchandise is delivered, and where improper procedures are used to accept what is actually delivered against the manifest. There could be collusion between the receiver and the trucker regarding the theft of merchandise. When truckers know that a store has sloppy procedures in checking in the contents of a delivery, they are prone to try to conduct a shortage in their favor. If caught, the excuse is "someone must have made a mistake." It also could occur in the shipping area, where unordered or unpaid merchandise is added to the truck for sale on the street or some other purpose known only to the thieves. It can occur when an employee hands unpaid merchandise out the back door to an accomplice, or when that same employee walks out of the store with merchandise he or she never paid for. Also, it can occur at the cash register when a cashier fails to correctly identify an item via a bar code, and punches in another code in order to speed up the process, causing not only a problem of probably shortchanging the company, but also with stock control. Also at the cash register, the collusion between a cashier and a friend or relative can occur in short-ringing or not ringing up an item.

Finally, we must consider fraud and shoplifting as other major causes of shrinkage, which can be committed by children, the ordinary housewife, the proverbial little old lady, or the professional. Figure 7.3 on page 107 shows the various sources of inventory shrinkage as identified by retail loss prevention managers in the year 2001.[4]

The author wishes to acknowledge another viewpoint regarding the term *acclaimed apportioning of external vs. internal losses*, which is used in the industry. Because it is accepted that shoplifter losses are less than one-third of total shrinkage and employee theft is the greater part of all losses, there might be some disagreement in these figures, and the "facts" may be subjective. It is much easier to make rules and enforce policy and procedures for the employee, as opposed to the customer who is catered to and considered much higher in the natural hierarchy as far as the businessperson is concerned. The dishonest employee can be detected more easily because of security systems, devices, and safeguards. It may be argued that controlling a smaller group (employees) is easier than controlling a larger group (customers).

There is no doubt that larger retail or chain stores are staffed with a loss prevention department that will employ trained and experienced security officers, as opposed to smaller business that must rely on sales or floor employees only. If the large retailer has a commitment to security and safety, the retailer is able to direct capital to that undertaking, whereas a smaller business may not afford to do so. Moreover, when apprehension, arrest, and security systems fail to measure up, the larger store is able to absorb losses from theft more easily than the small business that can't afford to allocate funding in that direction. Financially, the smaller business can be hurt more substantially without the advantages of the larger business.

THE RELATION OF COST, BENEFIT, AND VALUE TO THE RETAILER

The cost of customer and employee theft and fraud affects not only the bottom line of the business, but insurance rates, cost of security services and equipment, and loss of money and merchandise, all leading to higher prices for the merchandise offered to the public. Increased costs equate to increased prices. Therefore, a business can ultimately be affected in two ways—the retailer's prices become so high that the prices are no longer competitive, or the retailer absorbs the losses until—in both cases—the retailer closes shop and is out of business. Shrinkage can also include poor stock control and recordkeeping, and damage to stock and merchandise intentional or not. These are meaningful factors in shrinkage, but the shoplifter and the retailer's employees will cause the retailer's greatest monetary loss.

The indirect costs from all types of theft would be the cutting back or the curtailment of raises, benefits, and possibly work hours, thereby causing dissatisfaction and low morale among employees. Subsequently, low morale affects productivity, product quality, customer service, and the loss of goodwill and business image. The loss of goodwill and the image that the retailer wishes to project to the public is the retailer's most important asset. The worth of a business is associated to a great extent to goodwill.

The application of those security devices and procedures described in this book can cause a great deal of cost and time to be expended for the retailer and his or her employees. This includes the personnel who install, maintain, and control these devices, and the arrest and prosecution of the offender.

Consider the customer who must put up with the same inconveniences that the shoplifter must contend with. The appearance of an unpleasant atmosphere within the store and the inconvenience of anti-shoplifting measures are a great concern to the retailer. Ultimately, the shoplifter steals the pleasure of the shopping process. For the consumer, there is little joy in the time-consuming process of removing EAS tags (electronic article surveillance), unlocking glass cases or cabinets, unchaining merchandise, stapling bags closed, having guards stationed at all doors scrutinizing shoppers as they come and go, and being self-conscious in carrying a large handbag or shopping bag and to feel strange eyes peering and prying while walking through the store. This is not only a cost to the retailer in goodwill, productivity, hardware and materials, but also to the good customer who is "taxed" for the store's losses by adding to the price of goods.

A business is in business for one reason only—to make a profit. In order to stay in business and to receive that profit, the retailer must pass on to the consumer the costs of conducting that business. Among others, this includes manufacturing, transportation, warehousing, advertising, wages, taxes, security measures, and losses attributed to theft. The retailer must decide if the various security items and procedures available are appropriate for his or her business and the clientele that the retailer wishes to reach, and whether the cost to purchase and maintain these devices, systems, and programs is justified and necessary. The retailer therefore must achieve a happy medium in how to protect the establishment from loss and the price to the consumer so that the retailer can remain in business.

ENDNOTES

1. Op. cit., *2001 National Retail Security Survey—Final Report*, pp. 4, 5.
2. Ibid., p. 3.
3. Ibid., p. 4.
4. Ibid., p. 4.

Chapter 11
The Shoplifter

CLASSIFICATION

Shoplifters are generally classified into three groups:

1. ***Spur of the moment:*** This person seizes a perceived opportunity to steal for personal use and acts alone with usually no premeditation, but performance may be habitual. This includes the regular customer who may be the primary shopper in the family, the psychologically impaired (kleptomania, a classification of illness that is considered very rare), and individuals who act on impulse and feel that they can get away with it. It is common knowledge that in recent years more senior citizens have become part of this group of shoplifters due to the decrease in their personal income.
2. ***The "shopping" shoplifter:*** This person usually acts in small groups and steals specific products. This group includes the child or teenager whose act is premeditated only in general, motivated by peer pressure in attempting to steal an item that they cannot afford. If a good opportunity does not exist in a particular retail store, this shoplifter will go elsewhere. Many security professionals consider the "posse" or "gang attack" on a store to be part of this group.
3. ***The professional shoplifter:*** This is the smallest of the three groups—with approximately one in five shoplifters being a professional. This group derives all or much of their income from this type of theft. This person knows what he or she wants to steal and creates the opportunity to do so. Members of this group are considered good actors, and dress and act the part as legitimate shoppers. This person may use various devices to defeat security systems—foil-lined shopping bags, cable-cutters, pliers to pull off EAS tags, etc. This shoplifter may work alone, with other adults or juvenile accomplices, or in collusion with store employees. This professional also looks for the more expensive merchandise with high resale value, particularly high-ticket small items that can be secreted readily and can easily be sold on the street or "fenced." Rarely does this person seek products for personal use, and is attracted to stores with liberal cash return policies. This group includes drug addicts who steal to support their habit.

SOCIAL ISSUES

In recent years, the problem of shoplifting in mercantile establishments has become so intrusive and widely spread that the security industry has greatly expanded to serve the needs of the retailer. Because a retailer cannot absorb the losses and remain in business due to shrinkage, no matter what type, the retailer must pass the cost of these losses and the required methods of containment or prevention on to the customer. Consider this a *shoplifting tax*, because it is in fact a form of taxation added to the final cost of the merchandise because of the wrongs committed by the few. Unless we change our social behavior, then the retailer must pass on the cost and rely on improved technology and related security systems.

Contributing to a rise of this type of larceny are the following demographics and social attitudes:

- Ghettos or poor neighborhoods, or those with no jobs—"crossing over the tracks" to the more affluent areas
- The role of the drug addict and the addict's need to supply his or her habit
- Deviance (desire to steal) going down in age groups—thieves are becoming younger
- The ability to sell stolen merchandise on the street with ease, and the acceptance of the public to knowingly purchase such items
- The compliance of unethical merchants purchasing and reselling stolen property
- Young people are becoming increasingly violent, becoming isolated, and seeing little or nothing wrong with shoplifting (i.e., stealing from the establishment)

Some stores, or groups of stores that may be located in a particular area such as a mall, become involved in various community campaigns or community action programs in an effort to combat some of the causes of petty theft. This could include family services and counseling, career stimulation, job counseling, jobs or work study programs, and anti-crime programs. All programs are set up in an effort to assist in the correction of social ills, attitudes, and the demeanor of the community. The retailer, along with other institutions such as churches, schools, government programs, police, and social welfare agencies can affect criminal activity and antisocial behavior to a great extent. Unfortunately, concern and coordination by these institutions usually doesn't become prevalent until the problem becomes serious enough to affect not only the business community, but also the community itself.

Profiling the Offender. *Profiling* refers to the controversial practice of targeting or "racially profiling" a disproportionate number of Blacks and Hispanics by the police. In reality the term *racial profiling* originally referred to the police stopping minorities in traffic stops on highways and roadways. In recent years, however, profiling has evolved to include almost any type of discrimination toward a minority with heated discussions about the issue, both social and political in nature. Nevertheless, to profile a suspect as a possible criminal because of that person's race, dress, or social status is not only wrong, but can be construed as a civil rights violation.

There are two types of profiling that can occur with the police:

1. Where the minority person is stopped, questioned, and frisked only because of race, color, or ethnic origin (illegal).
2. Where there are several factors—besides race, color, or ethnicity—that would make the officer suspicious enough to investigate and make the stop (legal).

Regard the following scenes of a *police officer* on patrol at three o'clock in the morning:

- Driving through a White neighborhood, the officer observes a young Black male walking alone down the street.
- Driving through a Black neighborhood, the officer observes a young White male walking alone down the street.

In each instance, the officer's suspicions have risen because of their presence in a particular place, which appears "odd," and stops each person for questioning. No matter how cordial the police officer acts and how the questioning proceeds, that person has been "profiled." If the officer had not stopped the Black man and a house burglary was reported on the same street he was observed later that morning, would that have been good police work? If the officer had not stopped the White man and a drug dealer was found in the bushes on the same street murdered later that morning, would the officer kick himself for not checking that person out?

But if the officer based his stop on more than the racial factor, it most probably would not be considered racial profiling. These other factors would include the character of the neighborhood, the hour of the night, the subject walking with no visible transportation in the area, and previous reports of night burglaries in the area. In the case of the White man, in addition to that above, there might have been considerable reports of criminal assaults and drug activity in that neighborhood. Under these circumstances, stopping and questioning the subject might produce further suspicious factors.

Now consider the following scenarios concerning a *security officer* employed in a retail premises:

- A man enters a high-end jewelry salon who appears to be poorly dressed and in need of a shave. He does not fit in with the usual clientele.
- A group of six Black teenagers are observed entering a large retail store in a hurried fashion; they immediately split up and wander throughout the store.
- A person carrying a large box enters the store and appears to wander aimlessly throughout the store.
- A person enters a store wearing heavy and loose-fitting clothing not in keeping with the weather or temperature of the day.
- A woman enters a dressing room to try on clothing and when leaving appears to have gained considerable weight.
- A woman enters a store and immediately begins to look about, apparently for CCTV cameras, mirrors, and anyone suspiciously following her throughout the building.

Can we deny that the red flag would not have gone up in those instances, and that in fact in each of these instances, the person or persons have been profiled to some extent? No matter how we attempt to turn away from that conception, no one can deny that profiling, in some manner or other, does in fact occur. But to make use of racial or cultural profiling as the only cause for a stop is wrong, unethical, and unlawful.

Nonetheless, in order to justify any stop by a retail security officer for a larceny offense, and to negate any belief that racial profiling took place, the application and justification of *probable cause* must be the final determination for the stop.

THE PROFILE OF A SHOPLIFTER

The security officer must be aware that the effectiveness of any security measure in confronting external loss will vary depending on the type of criminal that the retail store attracts. The shoplifter may be male or female, young or old, rich or poor. The person's appearance is most probably the worst indicator of a potential thief. However, there are exceptions where an experienced store security officer can pick up on in identifying a possible shoplifter. As soon as the shoplifter enters the store and begins to walk through, it is basically the demeanor of that person that will give the shoplifter away.

The first indicator is that as soon as shoplifters enter the store, they will focus on store personnel and security systems rather than a product to purchase. These actions will be much more noticeable than that of honest shoppers. Another indicator is that shoplifters will pick up merchandise, hold it as if to examine it, in reality failing to look at that item while looking elsewhere. They may return that item, pick up another and repeat their obvious mannerisms. In actuality, shoplifters are focusing on the store personnel around them—who is paying attention and who is not. They may go to a particular department or area of the store in order to select an item of interest. They determine the size, the price, and anything else in making the decision in taking the item they wish to steal. They leave the area, walk throughout the store, or may even leave the store. Subsequently, they return to the same area, always checking as to who and what is in the area that may cause a problem for them. If somewhat skittish, they may return a third time.

Shoplifters may remove price tags, store labels, and logos. They may conceal the item on their person. They may also pull out a shopping bag used by the store, picked up earlier, which had been secreted on their person, place the item in the bag and attempt to leave. If stopped, their excuse for not producing a sales receipt is that they must have lost it when they went back into the store. Their reason might be that they went back because when they paid for the merchandise, they realized that they had forgotten something and wished to purchase that item too. Unfortunately, they couldn't find exactly what they were looking for and were stopped as they were leaving. Naturally the shoplifters will become offended that they have been stopped with the implication of being a thief. Offensively they will claim that not everyone holds onto receipts.

For example, in this case the security officer must build a probable cause scenario on this suspect. Was she first observed entering the store empty-handed? Was she observed picking up a store's bag or shopping bag and hiding it on her person? When stopped, was the bag creased as if it had been folded and secreted on the suspect? If the security officer did not have total observation on this suspect, consider it a no-win situation.

The security officer should be conscious concerning the retailer who sets a monetary limit or other factors regarding a shoplifter before or after an arrest and turning the subject over to the police for prosecution. Ideally, the retailer may find it more desirable in the probability of recovered property, a signed statement admitting remorse to the crime, and a "promise" never to return. Add to that the possibility of no lost time and effort in the prosecution process by the security staff and the retailer may feel safe in the assumption that shoplifting apprehensions will curtail any losses—until the word spreads and external theft begins to rise.

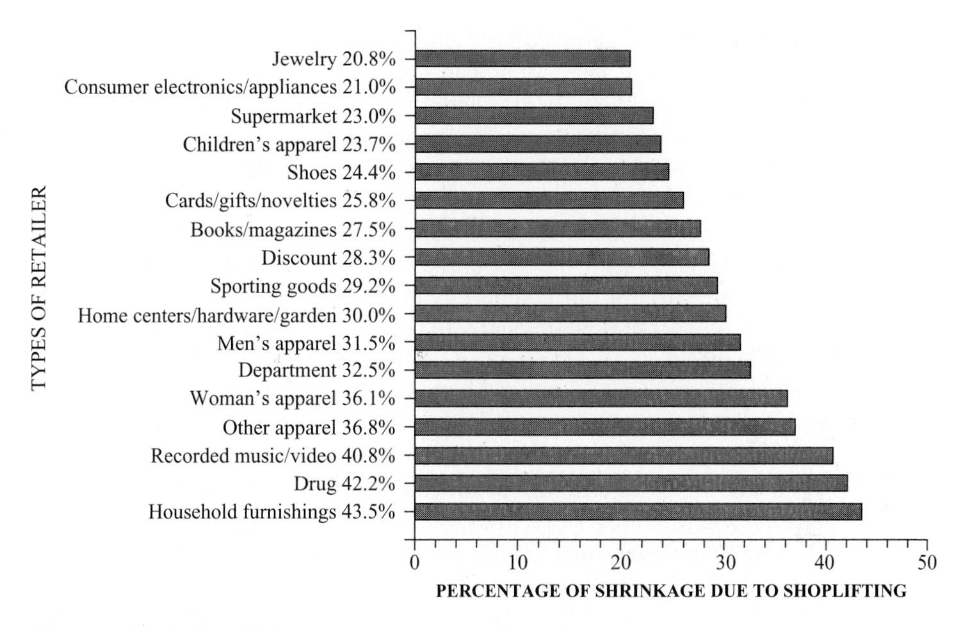

Figure 11-1 Shoplifting percentage by retail market.

We must remember that "shoplifting" is not a crime. It is a type of larceny—larceny of property from a retail establishment. We don't charge the offender with the crime of "shoplifting," he or she is charged for the crime of larceny, as a misdemeanor or as a felony.

Finally, shoplifters will target certain businesses of their choosing (wish list), or the opportunity of easiness in committing their act. In that regard the NRSS has indicated the preferred loss by market segment as shown in Figure 11.1:[1]

The Art of Shoplifting

Handbags and the type of clothing worn or carried are still the most common tools for the shoplifter. An open handbag held close and below the edge of the counter is an easy receptacle for small items, especially jewelry, brushed off the counter. Stores that staple a bag holding paid merchandise find that the shoplifter will carry a staple machine on their person in order to reseal a bag after adding stolen merchandise to merchandise already paid for. In supermarkets, small items can be concealed in the inner rolls of paper towels or toilet tissue, liquid containers with large openings, or boxed food such as cereals or macaroni.

Various scams and smoke screens are set up by shoplifters to shield themselves from observation and apprehension. As an example, consider two women who enter a store carrying the same handbag and wearing similar clothing. One commits the larceny with the other as the lookout. Before leaving, the handbags are switched, with the stolen merchandise now in possession of the "lookout." In another case, a shoplifter will make his actions obvious and before leaving, drop or secrete the "stolen" merchandise somewhere in the store. In either case, when stopped, the "suspect" has no unpaid merchandise on their person. Unless observed very closely, scenarios such as these can be a cause of great embarrassment, and most probably result in a monetary settlement by the retailer.

Juvenile shoplifters usually shoplift with one or more friends, as opposed to the nonprofessional adult who typically shoplifts alone. Juveniles are more prone to communicate to other friends when a store is an "easy mark," particularly if juveniles are not prosecuted when caught. Certain factors and conditions that may or may not be in effect influence all shoplifters. That includes the professional shoplifter who also relies on the "grapevine" about the ease of theft and likelihood of prosecution.

In some parts of our country, a couple of trends are becoming pervasive and alarming, and occur predominently in the inner cities. In some instances, there is no longer an effort to conceal merchandise that is being stolen. In these cases, the thief merely walks into a store, takes what he wishes, and then walks past clerks and cash registers and out the door, all the while giving a "stare of intimidation" or presenting a threatening and menacing manner to anyone approaching him. Another concern is known as "swarming," in which a group of young adults, sometimes called a "posse," will run into a store, grab what they wish, and exit as fast as they can, overwhelming employees and customers as they pass through. This type of behavior usually leads to violence and injury, and is hard to stop even with uniformed guards.

Other than these two intimidating groups of thieves, who have no apparent thought of the consequences of their act, shoplifters don't want to get caught. It follows that shoplifters should not get the feeling of safety or being at ease from detection in the store. Shoplifters prefer to be left alone and not approached by a salesperson so as to remain as inconspicuous as possible. If caught, they don't want to be arrested and prosecuted. Therefore, the retailer must set a given standard about how far the retailer wishes security officers to react in a larceny incident, and how severe the retailer wishes to punish the violator.

Because there will always be thieves who will try new ways to circumvent security systems, shoplifting will never be completely eradicated, but a sound security program, along with physical security devices can detect many thefts and scams, and reduce the loss caused by shoplifting to a great degree.

The Characteristics of a Shoplifter

Although not all inclusive, the following are characteristics or behavior that can be attributed to a shoplifter. The security officer must be constantly attentive to these indicators:

1. The subject enters the store or department and touches and inspects everything, but does not appear to purchase. She shows no interest in items or articles that she inquires about. She may pick up and put down a variety of items while pretending to act confused or undecided.
2. She will attempt to avoid dialogue with salespeople as much as possible; she does not want to be remembered or even noticed. She may be seen walking around apparently aimlessly, while "waiting for a friend to shop."
3. She is viewed as a "swivelhead," in that she is always turning her head looking around in an effort to see if she's being watched or followed. She keeps looking at customers, salespersons, mirrors, and CCTV cameras. She keeps looking over counters or displays and at everyone in the vicinity.

4. She may reach into a display counter, or walk behind a sales counter. She may palm small articles, particularly those openly displayed. She may appear nervous and/or perspiring in a room with normal temperature.
5. The subject walks in an unusual manner, pulls on sleeves, or adjusts socks. She may wear baggy or bulky garments and/or a large heavy coat or clothes that are out of season. She may wear garments with an elastic waistband or may have a slit in pocket of outer clothing. The subject constantly keeps one hand in an outer garment pocket. In this way, items may be carried in her hand under the garment, or she may have hooks under clothes to carry items out of the store.
6. The subject tries on garments, puts on an outer coat over unpaid merchandise, and leaves wearing stolen clothing. A woman may enter the store with very loose clothing and become "pregnant" before leaving, particularly upon entering and exiting dressing rooms. She may be observed wearing no jewelry upon entry into the store, but leaves wearing jewelry.
7. A subject may carry an umbrella, large bags, or boxes to conceal merchandise. It may be a "booster box," a large box or bag with a false bottom or concealed compartments. She may carry a bag lined with silver duct tape in order to defeat an EAS-type alarm.
8. The subject will enter with a baby or child in a carriage or stroller, and place a stolen item under a blanket, the mattress, or the baby. If stopped, the excuse will be that the child must have taken the item by mistake—who would want to prosecute a child?
9. The person leaves the area hastily after casually strolling about. The subject frequents the restrooms. She may enter an unattended section or an area near an outer door, and then she may steal items and leave quickly.
10. The subject may posses a set of pliers or other anti-security device to cut or pull off EAS devices.
11. The subject has an accomplice, who will distract the employee while the subject steals merchandise, or creates a scene so as to distract employees and/or other customers while a partner commits the act.

ACTIONS THAT ENCOURAGE SHOPLIFTERS

Because most shoplifters are nonprofessional adults, the following common factors or conditions may actually invite the criminal into the store, or an individual may possibly attempt a theft not thought of prior to entering.

- When employees appear to be disinterested or too busy to pay attention to customers
- When customers are not acknowledged or serviced by an employee, and can remain inconspicuous.
- When there is no evidence of security cameras or personnel who may be watching.
- When there are no security devices such as EAS, chains, or alarms attached to desirable items.

- When there is an abundance of high-ticket merchandise not tagged with EAS devices, even though it is obvious that an EAS alarm system is observed in place.
- Where there are secluded corners, rest rooms, or dark corners where concealment or breaking into packages and removing the contents is made easy.
- Where employees fail to react or are disinterested to activated alarms.
- When a security guard is assigned at the doors and appears to not be alert, is not checking receipts when it is the guard's routine to do so, and does not appear to be a threat in any way.
- When employees do not take an interest in returned merchandise, and fail to consider each return as a customer service or quality problem.
- When an employee fails to follow correct procedures in the returns process, particularly returns without receipts, or does not check the legitimacy of a store receipt offered for a refund.

All shoplifters are affected by or act upon the factors or conditions noted above, including the professional. Although any shoplifter who is determined to steal from a store may be able to do so, few shoplifters want any unnecessary hassle. Most are unwilling to risk detection when employees are attentive as opposed to disinterested, when security measures are evident, and when they know that the store will prosecute. By routinely using a combination of different security measures that help to cause the shoplifter to be uncomfortable about stealing in a particular store, this type of larceny can be discouraged to a great extent.

ACTIONS THAT DISCOURAGE SHOPLIFTERS

Discouraging the shoplifter is the first step in external loss control. Various ways that the loss prevention department should consider as part of the prevention procedure are as follows:

Protective Devices and Systems

Protective devices and/or systems serve two purposes—to discourage the ordinary shoplifter, and to trap the brazen or professional shoplifter. Protective devices include the following:

- Closed circuit television (CCTV), particularly a pan/tilt/zoom type that the viewer can operate by panning a 360-degree area and zooming in or out on a subject or object
- Wide-angle convex mirrors in specific areas to cover hidden corners or alcoves
- Enclosed booths (coops) or any location where the selling floor can be viewed via a two-way mirror by the security officer
- EAS tags that may be attached on small merchandise. These are particularly effective when inserted within the packaging so that the shoplifter cannot get to the device unless the package is ripped open and a search made.
- Bar coding, which is only as effective as the cashier or person checking out the merchandise at the point of sale (POS) by knowledge of the item or merchandise corresponding to the bar code

- Secured interior doors and those perimeter fire exits with noise alarms that will sound off upon opening the door for emergency egress. Burglar alarm daytime annunciation and activation can also be used on unlocked (or locked) perimeter or interior doors.
- Maintain a surplus of padlocks, chains, mortise cylinders, cylinder cores, and keys.
- Glass cases that contain small expensive items should have locking devices.
- If applicable, block off all checkout lanes that are not in use.
- Keep displays low so that salespeople are able to look over them and see everyone in their department.
- Assignment of an employee or salesperson to fitting/dressing rooms, who counts the number of items that a customer takes in, and gives an applicable tag with the corresponding number.
- Two-way mirrors or CCTV in fitting/dressing rooms. This may be considered an extreme measure that smacks on voyeurism and most probably will be considered an invasion of privacy. Some states have enacted some type of legislation asserting that two-way mirrors are legal if signs are posted outside of the dressing rooms stating that the room/s contain two-way mirrors and/or CCTV, and that customers may be under surveillance at any time. But the use of this type of observation by a retailer may lose more trade than what the retailer may expect to prevent in losses. This action is a violation of decency and cannot be tolerated as an accepted procedure.

Moreover, we must also consider that in the use of the various protection procedures such as alert employees, effective devices and systems, and acceptable management policy regarding arrest, prosecution, and publicity, that the "word" spreads, particularly among the teenagers and professionals who would rather go elsewhere less threatening. But it must also be understood that these various devices and procedures are of little use or become ineffective if store personnel are untrained or unaware of the device or system, or become disinterested or careless in their use.

Control of Ticket Switching

"Ticket switching" may be defined as the switching of price labels or product identification from one article of merchandise to another, or the placing of a higher priced article into another package or similar packaged article for the purpose of paying a lesser amount than the original price.

Although never completely eradicated, thefts of this type can be controlled somewhat by the following:

- Tickets or price tags should be machine imprinted rather than handwritten.
- Tamperproof gummed labels that tear apart when removed should be used.
- Two price tags should be used on expensive items—one in the usual location and the second within or in a hidden location.
- Hard-to-break plastic string should be used that can only be removed by cutting. If a package or box has had the plastic string cut or removed, examination should be made at the point of sale to determine that the contents match the appropriate package and/or ticket.

It is also important to do the following:

- Train employees to recognize and/or know their merchandise, and the packaging that is offered for purchase and rung up at the register (an important deterrent).
- Use anti-shoplifting signage. See ANTI-SHOPLIFTING SIGNAGE in Chapter 15 for details.
- At various times, particularly when the store is busy, the use of the public address system to make a cryptic announcement such as "Code 99, security to area 36," when in fact no code or area exists, but alerts the would-be shoplifter that he or she may be under surveillance.

Additional Support in Theft Control

Other than that noted above, the most important support that a loss prevention department could have is a well-trained security force, and the necessary equipment and controls, which include the following:

- Uniformed or identifiably dressed guards to check merchandise leaving the facility.
- Plainclothes store detectives observing and apprehending offenders, identifying and correcting security problems.
- Employees trained to observe and react correctly to security situations. The security officer must consider that all employees properly trained are to be considered as part of the security team.
- A practical CCTV system—only as good as the equipment and how it is used.
- The use of handheld portable two-way radios for instant and surreptitious communication between security officers.
- The use of and proper alarm response to EAS (electronic article surveillance) tags.
- The proper use of bar codes scanned at the cash registers—for product identification and inventory control.
- Well-trained sales force and cashiers regarding knowledge of merchandise carried by the establishment, in order to become aware of "ticket switches," price irregularities, and unsealed cartons.
- Various integrated systems and procedures to control theft at the point-of-sale, return and exchange area, receiving and trucking, and stock control.
- Correct architectural planning in renovation or construction. Upper management should consider input from security personnel concerning secure areas, security problems, and incorporation of security systems.

ENDNOTE

1. Op. cit., *2001 National Retail Security Survey—Final Report*, pp. 4, 5. Figure 11.1 graph reprinted with permission.

Chapter 12

The Primary Rules in Determining Probable Cause in a Shoplifting Arrest

WITNESSING THE CRIME

The following is to be considered very important in determining how a security officer should act in observing and responding to a presumed theft.

The security officer must be able to answer *yes* to the following questions prior to stopping a larceny suspect:

1. Did the security officer see the suspect take the store's merchandise?
2. Did the security officer see the suspect conceal or attempt to conceal the merchandise?
3. Did the security officer observe or have the suspect in view at *all* times?
4. Did the security officer observe the suspect attempt to leave the store going around or passing checkout points or registers without paying for the merchandise?
5. Does the security officer know where the suspect has the merchandise?

If the security officer cannot answer yes to all of the questions above, he or she should consider that the occurrence never happened.

The legal costs of making an improper stop can be very high, and as a matter of business if nothing else, the above rules must be followed. But, as in all law, facts and circumstances alter all situations. There could be exceptions to the above rule, and therefore, the security guard should use not only his or her powers of observation, expertise, and intellect, but also common sense.

If a customer does take merchandise but makes no effort at concealment, and the security officer can answer "yes" to all other questions, a stop can be made legally. Caution must be practiced in a situation of this type, because the customer may have innocently forgotten to pay for the item. In addition, if the security officer had lost sight of the suspect, even momentarily (walking behind a display, for instance), again caution must be achieved. If a stop was made in this instance, but no stolen merchandise was found on the suspect, a case can be made if the security officer returns to the display where the officer lost sight of the suspect, and finds the merchandise that the suspect "ditched." Consequently, whether or not the security officer makes an apprehension for an attempted larceny would depend on the immediate circumstances, value of the merchandise, type of suspect, and company policy.

A security officer must never accept or act upon the word of an employee, customer, or passerby concerning information given on a possible suspect.

Any information received from *anyone* regarding a theft or any reported crime should be used *only for further inquiry and investigation* by the security officer, and *never for a stop or apprehension.*

Therefore, the security officer must not rely on information from another employee to make an apprehension, whether a trusted and experienced salesperson or not. If that employee is at a managerial level and insists that an apprehension should be made, the security officer should use prudence and alert that manager to the perils that will exist if the elements required for an arrest do not exist. If the manager insists, then the apprehension, detention, and/or arrest is made by that manager with the security officer assisting only. Be aware though, that if the facts against the suspect fail to warrant or prove probable cause for the arrest, the security officer could also become involved as a party to any subsequent litigation along with the manager. The security officer should advise the loss prevention manager or the security supervisor as soon as possible, whether on or off the premises, so as to apprise them of the situation.

Consider an actual situation:

A floor manager in charge of the jewelry department of a large retail store observed what he believed to be a larceny of an expensive ring. The manager called for a security officer who arrived soon after at the scene. Pointing out the "perpetrator" who was still in the store, the manager demanded that the security officer arrest the suspect. Advising the manager that the security officer cannot be a complainant since he did not see the crime take place, and could not swear to any information before a judge without perjuring himself, the manager stated that he would be the complainant, and again demanded the arrest take place. The suspect was taken into custody and the ring, valued at $250.00, was recovered.

The police were called and upon their arrival, determined that a *prima facie* case existed and asked the manager, as the complainant, to sign and swear to the written complaint so that the suspect can be removed from the premises and further processed.

The manager begins to falter and now wishes to retract his demand for an arrest. He states to the police that the ring was of "minimal" value and was in fact recovered with no loss to the company. Additionally, he states that he doesn't have the time to appear in court and wishes not to become involved any further in the arrest. The security officer cautions him privately that an arrest was made and to release the suspect would place the officer, the manager, and the company in civil liability. The manager is adamant, and because the police have no complainant for this misdemeanor larceny, they release the suspect and leave the scene.

Two weeks later the company is served with a summons and complaint for a false arrest. The lawsuit includes the manager and the security officer. The company places no fault on the security officer, determining that he had acted correctly within the scope of his employment. At an *examination before trial,* the company settled with the plaintiff for an undisclosed amount.

THE STOP

If the security officer can answer "yes" to the five fundamental questions noted on page 169, a stop could be made. At the time of the approach and stop, the officer should have the assistance of another security officer for good reason. One is the safety factor in case of a physical confrontation, and second, as a corroborating witness. It is preferable that the person who approaches and makes the stop be the person who has answered the preceding five questions.

Cautionary Note

Never ask or request that a customer, passerby, or another untrained employee assist you in the apprehension of a suspected shoplifter. Their actions against the suspect or any aid or assistance in the arrest or imprisonment of a suspect could place you and your employer in civil jeopardy. Moreover, the person assisting could suffer a personal injury, which could also subject the store to a monetary loss. If need be, request the assistance *only* of another security officer or a police officer.

However, if someone voluntarily steps in to assist you during an arrest procedure, no matter how extreme that procedure is, that person places *himself* or *herself* in jeopardy if that person is injured or commits a litigious act.

At the time of the stop, the security officer should identify himself or herself as a security officer. The officer should act calmly and politely, but firmly in an attempt to get the subject's voluntary cooperation. The use of menacing gestures, words, or tone of voice can backfire at a later time, particularly if the subject is released after investigation. The most important asset the security officer can have is an attitude that conveys confidence and self-assurance. Any doubt or indecision on the part of the officer will be sensed by the shoplifter, who will no doubt seek to exploit it. Do not strike the suspect unless defending oneself. If the shoplifting suspect refuses to be directed to the security office for further investigation and the suspect has been placed under arrest, necessary but minimal force may be used. Remember that striking a suspected shoplifter or anyone else without cause is an assault. It is also a civil wrong called battery for which punitive damages can be awarded.

The possibility also exists that an elderly person or a juvenile may absently or honestly have forgotten to pay for an item, or that a shoplifter is "setting up" the officer. Or that the shoplifter may create a commotion loud enough to gather a crowd for the purpose of the officer backing down and letting the suspect leave. Whether an aggrieved customer or provocative shoplifter, the security officer should attempt to remain calm and tactful. In this way a potentially hazardous situation can be diffused swiftly and safely. Avoid angry confrontations. If the security officer loses his or her temper and it becomes obvious that a loud argument or shouting match is taking place, a crowd will collect. This will consist of passersby, but mostly customers, who most probably won't be aware of all the facts, and who generally will side with the subject rather than the store detective. Whether a crime has been committed or not, right or wrong, loyal customers may become disenchanted with how they perceive store policy or with the actions of an employee. The loss of goodwill to the retailer and the image that the store wishes to project can suffer to a great extent because of a situation that has gotten out of control.

If possible, attempt to direct the suspect (or a legitimate, possibly disgruntled customer) aside and away from public view. Remember, do not become involved in a shouting match. Not only will it cause a crowd to collect but it also may escalate into a physical confrontation. Never accuse someone in public where a third person or more can overhear accusations, such as "You stole a ________," "You didn't pay for ________," "You're a thief," or "You know what you did." Courts have found such accusations to be slanderous, and could be grounds for a civil action if the subject is later released or acquitted of the charge. Those states that empower the security officer with the *merchant's privilege* to stop and investigate under reasonable grounds provide plenty of time to determine if in fact a crime has been committed before any accusations are made.

An equally important issue is the use of derogatory remarks regarding race, color, ethnic origin, accent, mental retardation, religious persuasion, sexual innuendoes, or one's dress. These types of remarks are to be avoided under any circumstance, *whether in private or in public.* Not only can it provoke or escalate an incident into violence, but the federal government and most if not all states have civil rights legislation that prohibits discrimination or defamation of this type, and in which if used, security officers may place themselves in criminal and/or civil liability.

DETAINING AND DETENTION

Security officers can stop and detain a suspect only if the stolen merchandise is from their own store. In receiving a warning, a tip, or convincing information from employees of another cooperating store regarding a larceny from that other store, and you observe the suspect in your store, resist the temptation to make an apprehension. The "*merchant's privilege*" (if applicable) gives the right to stop and detain only if the merchandise was shoplifted from your own store, not someone else's. Remember the five questions listed on page 169 and act accordingly.

Other than to notify to the other store's security officers of the suspect's presence, you should keep the suspect under close surveillance. Be aware that any confrontation on your premises, legal or not, by a security officer from another business establishment, could place you and your employer in civil jeopardy whether you physically assist those security officers or not. Unless the police are involved, it would be more advisable to have these other security officers make the apprehension off your premises.

Concerning a crime that takes place on your premises, detain the suspect only. Unless the suspect acted in concert with others and the security officer has probable cause that these others are principals in the crime, do not apprehend. Do not detain friends and/or relatives who may be accompanying the suspect and may not have had a part in the crime. Relatives may accompany the suspect to the security office (within reason and with caution), but the security officer cannot and should not require it. If the subject is a juvenile and is accompanied by an adult or a more mature person, such as a parent, guardian, relative, or friend, you should urge that person to accompany you and the juvenile to the office. In any event, whether a parent, guardian, or friend is present or not when a juvenile is apprehended, attempt to segregate the child away from any adult accomplices. Although not required to do so (as the police are so required), place the juvenile in a separate room or office if practical.

Use caution if the detained suspect is a female. The male security officer must ensure that when a female suspect is taken from public view and into an office or other secluded area, that a female security officer or other female employee is present with the suspect at all times until released or turned over to the police. Although a female employee may have to be taken off the sales floor or from her desk for this purpose, the security officer must provide this protection concerning the apprehension and detention of any female. The purpose of this second witness being of the same gender will diminish or dissuade the suspect of claiming any type of sexual misconduct against her while in custody or accusations of other improper behavior. Make the appropriate notations regarding the time the female subject was taken out of public view, the name of the female witness and the time present with the subject, and any other notations required in an incident and/or apprehension report.

The Time Record. A most important task for the security officer soon after a stop is made is to note the following time entries in or attached to the arrest or apprehension report. A time record is very important for the purpose of determining the circumstances surrounding the detainment (imprisonment) of the subject (particularly a female) or a very serious occurrence if needed at a later time:

- Time of apprehension
- Time that the subject was placed in the security office
- Time that the police were called and requested
- Time of the arrival of the police at the security office, including names and shield numbers
- Time that the police left with the subject

For further details see the material about the time record in Chapter 21 on REPORT WRITING regarding this and other issues.

Accomplices

Concerning accomplices whom the security officer may believe assisted the suspect in the crime—do not detain if in doubt. But if the second person does aid and abet another to commit the crime (acting in concert), no matter how minimal, that person is just as guilty and may be charged as an equal (see the accepted definition of accomplice in the GLOSSARY).

There may be certain scenarios that the security officer may come across during a shoplifting incident. As an example, three suspicious individuals enter your store and split up going their various ways. Only one commits a larceny. The others, as far as you can determine, are not involved, and should not be apprehended. Another situation could be where three individuals enter your store and two of these persons start a fight, drawing attention to the commotion and causing a crowd to collect. While everyone's attention is drawn to the fight, the third subject commits a larceny and leaves the store. Whether the perpetrator is apprehended or not, unless the security officer can prove that the two "brawlers" acted in concert with the thief, the officer cannot conclude they were involved without any basis and should not include them.

If an accomplice is taken into custody along with the accused suspect, the security officer must be positive and certain that he or she can prove that the accomplice participated or provided aid in the commission of the crime.

Identifying the Suspect. After the suspect is contained in the security office and is questioned in an attempt to establish identification, many times the suspect will give false information or identification. After the police arrive and question the suspect, rather than give false identification where in some states it is a crime, the true identity becomes known.

But there will be situations in minor offenses when a suspect is given an appearance ticket by the police with information based upon false documentation, and will disappear and never appear in court even after a warrant is issued. The security officer should not make erasures or throw out the form with the false information, whether completely filled out or not. Save this form and attach it to the case for further use as evidence. Also, any alias can be placed in security databases for further reference or comparison at a later time if the suspect is picked up again. If correctly identified before release by the police or the court, redo a new form with the amended information, but keep the original report containing the false information for future reference. It will show that the defendant attempted to deceive, and made a conscious attempt to avoid guilt by giving false identification.

THE ROLE OF LOSS PREVENTION AND SELECTIVE PROSECUTION

The objective of loss prevention concerning loss by a shoplifter can be simplified to two basic approaches—apprehension (arrest) and prosecution, and deterrence (prevention).

The apprehension approach emphasizes the capture of the thief (the shoplifter), the recovery of the merchandise (the stolen property), and seeking to punish the thief for his or her behavior (prosecution). Although they may be well trained, overzealous security officers may unintentionally stop a good customer thereby causing an unfortunate and most probably an embarrassing incident. Even though the officer's actions until that point may be covered under the some state's business laws (defense of lawful detention statutes) and all safeguards were followed, the possible loss of the customer and goodwill toward the establishment cannot be overstated.

Additionally, there is the concern of the cost factor—that of the personnel involved in processing the arrest, appearance at the police station or court to swear to the court information, and most probably, one or more court appearances. This overemphasis of the punishment process of the shoplifter may, at times, not be worth the effort. Unless the defendant is charged with a felony larceny and/or has a prior criminal record, most offenders will suffer little or no monetary loss or jail time for the consequences of their act. Therefore, some may say that arrest and prosecution is not a great deterrent. But an argument can be made that if there is a failure to arrest and prosecute, it will only invite more theft once the word spreads on the street that your store is an "easy mark."

Likewise, we cannot overlook the attitude of the store employee. Because our first line of defense regarding the shoplifter is the salesperson, he or she is the employee who will most probably resist or attempt to avoid actions that will cause the apprehension of a thief. This is particularly so if the employee realizes that he or she could possibly become a participant in a civil action, or has to appear in criminal court as a witness. Many employees, as with the general public, don't wish to get "involved." Therefore, the employee is more likely to cooperate in a crime prevention program rather than actively participate in the apprehension of shoplifters.

Finally, studies have shown that a store, which is selective in their prosecution, and with most of its security officers and resources geared toward deterrence, will realize a more significant reduction of shoplifting losses. Accordingly, we can describe *selective prosecution* in the sense that there must be some controlling factor or a loss limit where it would not be worth the time and effort to pursue prosecution.

Cautionary Arrest and Release Procedures

There will be times after an investigation that there is no basis for an arrest or detainment, or because of circumstances, the retail establishment does not wish to continue any further and the subject is to be released. If the arrest is without foundation, and is carried through onto prosecution and the "defendant" is acquitted of the charge/s, we can assume civil litigation will follow. In essence, if the "bad" arrest is continued, it places the officer and likely the company in a possible action for false arrest and/or a malicious prosecution. It is better to release the subject rather than continue and place oneself in criminal and civil jeopardy.

A general release form should be offered to the subject requesting his or her signature if possible. Hopefully it will be accepted and acknowledged, but the subject's freedom must not be predicated on signing such a release. Nevertheless in any event, properly handled and warranted, an apology with an honest explanation should not be viewed by the officer as an embarrassment or a defeat, but as good customer relations and a reduction of liability. Courts and juries realize that ordinary people do make mistakes, and if the security officer can show that the apprehension was handled fairly, and that he or she attempted to correct that mistake and release the subject from custody, a reasonable consideration will be shown in their deliberations. So even if civil litigation does occur, the damages awarded will never be as great as they would be if the "arrest" process was consummated with subsequent prosecution.

For further information and cautionary procedures on this topic, see the section on GENERAL RELEASES in Chapter 2.

The Dilemma of Compassion vs. Prosecution. Be forewarned, however, in the case where the accused did in fact commit a crime, and all the elements of the act and the crime are present for an arrest, and that while in custody it is determined that the accused is a person with some status in the community. The subject may be a lawyer, doctor, cleric, or civil servant. Realizing that an arrest and subsequent public knowledge could cause adverse publicity for the retailer and affect the accused more seriously personally and professionally than an ordinary citizen, the security officer or the retailer may wish to drop the charge and release the subject. The subject may be relieved and very thankful that he or she is to be released without anything other than an admonition.

In an effort to protect yourself and your employer under these circumstances, you may require the accused to sign a release and/or a statement acknowledging the criminal act. Even though this release may be considered an in-house form with no public disclosure, others may perceive that such a statement admitting guilt or a release of any liability was offered as a condition for discharge from custody, whether expressed by you or not. In doing so, you could be placing yourself in civil jeopardy.

In any event and for whatever reason, whether a person has some status or is an ordinary citizen, be aware that there have been instances where the accused was released under these circumstances and subsequently denied any accusations made against him or her, including the allegation that he or she was "forced" to sign a release in exchange for freedom, and thereafter initiated civil action against the retailer and the security officer.

Tread carefully in this area. The retailer or officer may be accused of leniency or placating the "privileged few." Although such a course of action may be rare and appear unconscionable, such occurrences are not exceptional by retail management and security personnel, realizing the possible adverse publicity to all concerned as noted earlier. Before any release of this nature, the loss prevention manager should be contacted for direction. If a release is to be made, whether a signed release is obtained or not from the subject, a detailed account of the incident, along with any admissions, statements, evidence, witnesses, etc., should be contained in the incident and arrest/apprehension reports, along with the reason for the release from custody. The accumulation of this type of evidence will negate or at least diminish any action contemplated by the person released.

Selective Prosecution? Assuredly, some security officers and managers believe if a person commits a criminal act, that person should face the consequences, no matter what the particulars may be. It is their contention that, extenuating circumstances or not, if the arrest is valid, prosecution must be initiated. However, for those who may believe that "giving a break" or affording a leniency to someone who has a position of some importance in the community is contrary to their personal convictions, a similar course of action could also apply to those offenders found in the poorer neighborhoods or the lower levels of society.

A criminal offense may be minor or contain mitigating circumstances. Would justice be served in an arrest and prosecution? Truly, of course it would. But in some instances justice could be tempered with mercy. If released with a stern warning, would the offender commit a similar crime in the future? Hopefully not, but this may be all that was needed to frighten that person from committing this type of act in the future.

The point here is that facts and circumstances will alter all situations, and whether one is a police officer, a security officer, or a retail store manager, judgment and compassion should, at times, be a consideration when handling offenders, no matter where they fit into the social strata.

Accordingly, decisions concerning whether or not to prosecute must be considered carefully based on the particular circumstances and on a case-by-case scenario. Unless handled very carefully, repercussions could follow. The security officer must have the approval of the loss prevention manager or the store manager before any action is taken for a release.

THE ROLE OF THE EMPLOYEE

Retail security begins with the salesclerk, continues with the security officer, and ends with the cashier. All play an important role in helping to hold shrinkage to a minimum. Due to the salesperson and the cashier being in constant contact with the customer, it can be said that they are the backbone of the store's security. Because of this, it is most important that these employees be given special instruction immediately or soon after hire as part of their indoctrination and orientation in the company.

An alert salesperson is the best deterrent to a shoplifter. All customers coming into the salesperson's department should be approached or at least acknowledged. Even when busy with other customers, the salesperson should recognize other customers with a nod or by advising them that they will be taken care of as soon as possible. In other words, salespeople should be aware of all customers in their department, and in this way, the shoplifter is aware that his or her presence has been observed.

The retailer, as the employer, can reasonably expect cooperation from not only full-time employees, but also part-time employees when it concerns safety and security. For the employer to expect this cooperation, the employee must possess or project the following:

- Have high morale and be alert.
- Be trained on a routine basis.
- Be treated fairly and equally—no double standards.
- Create the proper customer service—overt friendly contact with all customers as they enter the employee's department or area. Individual contact is the most important single effort one can make in deterring shoplifting.
- Have the proper employee scheduling to cover the busiest hours—holiday and sale periods.

Employee Training

Salespeople. Regarding conduct and procedures, salespeople should do the following:

- Acknowledge all customers who enter the department. Serve all customers as quickly as possible.
- Acknowledge the presence of other customers with the phrase, "I'll be with you in a moment."
- Keep an eye on all customers who are just wandering around the store.
- Pay attention to everything that goes on in their department—the shoplifter will be aware how well they do so.
- Never leave their area or department unattended, but be mobile by moving around the department so that a shoplifter cannot predict their moves.
- Never allow a customer to enter a stockroom or walk behind counters.
- Remove empty hangers off racks—keep an even number of items on racks so that an instant inventory can be made.
- If possible, secure high-end merchandise in some manner so that it is alarmed or unable to be removed.
- Keep the area clean of discarded sales slips so that the shoplifter cannot use them as a receipt of purchase.
- Remove empty boxes or cartons from the selling floor.

- Keep the displays in order and as neat as possible. Don't place merchandise so high that one cannot see over it.
- If the salesperson believes that a "customer" fits the profile of a shoplifter, they should keep calm, keep eye contact, don't look away, and advise the loss prevention department as soon as you are able to do so.
- If a shoplifter is observed in the act of taking merchandise, the salesperson may wish to approach the suspect and ask "Can I be of service?" or "Can I wrap your purchase?" In most cases the shoplifter will buy the item, return it, or get rid of it. In any event, advise the loss prevention department.

Experience will guide the salesperson about how to act in a challenging situation or in detecting a suspicious person.

Cashiers. A cashier is the last person a shopper will see before leaving the department or the store. Therefore, it is important that all cashiers be trained in the following:

- Don't allow yourself to be distracted during a transaction at the cash register. Pay attention, never look away from the cash drawer, and close the register immediately upon completion of the transaction.
- When away from the cash register, make sure it is left locked.
- Make sure that you know how to remove or deactivate EAS tags.
- You need to know how to spot a tag switch, or how to inspect a box or package for a swapped or substituted item.
- You must be trained on cash register procedures, check cashing and credit card procedures, counterfeit money, scams, and confidence acts.

Cash register locations should be near or next to the exit rather than the interior of the store. This places a deterrent for the nonprofessional shoplifter, and also places any shoplifter attempting to leave in the position of "passing a cash register" without paying. In other instances, it will also increase the employee-customer contact upon leaving.

At the point-of-sale or checkout, one of the most important actions immediately after ringing up the merchandise is to ask a most significant question: "Is there anything else?" The question has two purposes:

1. The customer who had forgotten, just remembered, or couldn't find an item might say "Do you have item X?" Therefore, another sale may be made.
2. On the other hand, if the subject is a shoplifter and feels guilty or anxious about capture, the suspect may become apprehensive that the cashier might know or have been told of a concealed item, and may produce it for payment.

This question, when asked in a straightforward, helpful manner could not be considered a disservice, and may produce unexpected results.

> As part of the training process, emphasize that all employees are cautioned to never, ever accuse anyone of theft—*never.*

Chapter 13

The Dishonest Employee

EMPLOYEE THEFT

The employer has the responsibility to the company, stockholders, and customers to maintain the lowest prices with the highest profit possible. If the company is a family-owned and not a public company, the employer still must maintain low prices and the highest profit possible, particularly if it is a smaller company competing with the "big boys." As described earlier, shrinkage losses caused by internal theft of merchandise, property, or money affect the bottom line more than shoplifting. If the employer cannot compete with other identical companies, and if profits are reduced, the final effect will be felt by honest employees in compensation, benefits, and possible job loss. Long-term theft of any type can be devastating to a company unless caught or controlled in time. This is particularly so for a small business. The profitability of a company can be significantly impacted upon by the honesty and integrity of each employee, from the CEO down to the teenage part-timer.

> The retailer suffers more loss from theft by employees than by external forces.

The National Retail Security Survey (NRSS) for 2001 found that the greatest area for loss by employees was supermarket/grocery, shoes, consumer electronics and appliances, discount, and men's, children's, and women's apparel (Figure 13.1). These eight market segments experienced the highest levels of loss by employees, much above the retail-wide industry average.[1]

As we shall see in the following pages, dishonesty can occur in various forms. We will never know the true reported loss caused by internal or external theft because of various factors. The most substantial example would be those losses by employees that are rarely, if ever, reported as a true figure by employers. These conditions occur because when discovered, they would preferably terminate the thief and cut their loss, rather then spend time and effort on an arrest and prosecution. Because surveys have shown, depending on the type of retail business, that approximately 46% of business loss can be attributed to internal theft, it must be considered the most critical issue to examine. This is particularly so when most security professionals personally believe the actual internal loss figure is as high as 65% to 70%.

During the hiring process, testing new applicants for a position in a company is legal as long as a professionally developed employment test is administered according to its intended use. According to the EEOC these initial tests could include personality, aptitude, and integrity evaluation as long as they are "professionally developed" by a competent testing service that is well qualified in employee-testing procedures. In fact,

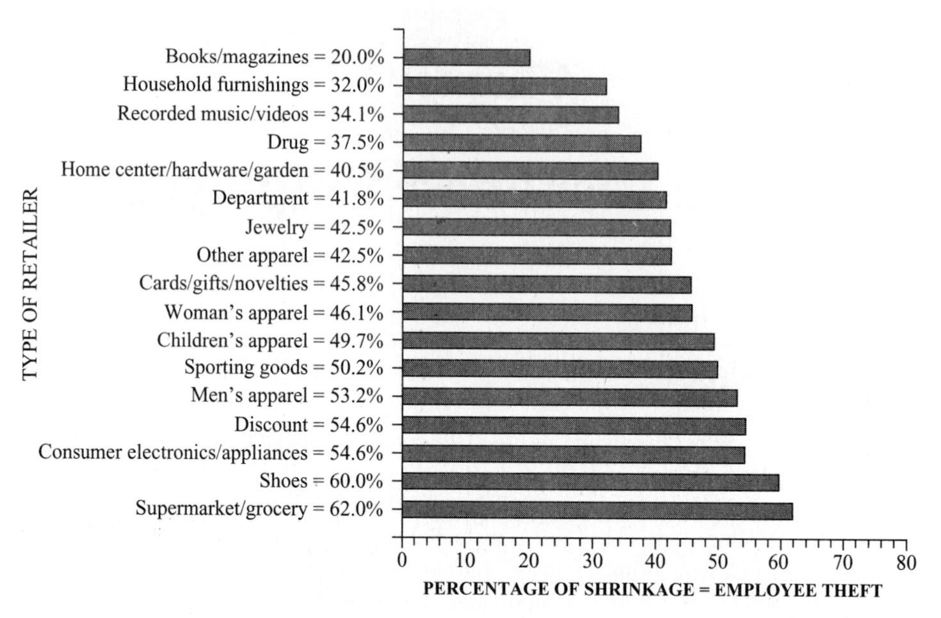

Figure 13-1 Employee theft by retail market.

in an effort by an employer to determine honesty, the EEOC and state agencies have determined that integrity testing in particular does not have a "discriminatory impact" on applicants or present employees.

When an employee has been newly hired, we can assume that the greatest majority has no thought of ever stealing from their company. However, over a period of time, many do become thieves—some minor and some greater. These employees usually come across the possibility of committing a crime by accident. The employee may have discovered another employee stealing, may have observed criminal behavior or received information from another coworker, and wonder if he or she can also get away with it. One of the more important aspects by an employee during idle time is observation and/or determination of weaknesses in security control systems. Although employees may steal, they usually have a different attitude when observing or confronted by a shoplifter. This may be considered a peculiarity of character, but most probably these actions are brought about to throw off blame and show management how "honest" they are.

So then, whatever the true figure, according to studies and asset protection professionals in this country, far more money, merchandise, inventory, and company property is taken by employees than by shoplifters. Generally accepted, information about theft by employees in the retail environment are noted below:

EMPLOYEE THEFT

25% are honest and will never steal.

25% are dishonest and will steal given the opportunity.

50% are as honest as the controls that govern them and their personal motivation dictates. The employees who fall into this group will go either way depending on the need or the situation.

Other than the actual loss in profits from internal theft, additional effects will be felt and will most probably include the following:

- The loss of the terminated trained employee
- The cost of hiring, replacing, and training a new employee
- Lower morale among honest employees when suspicion is directed toward a group or department
- Possible contamination of other employees aware of the losses, leading to other problems
- Possible unfavorable publicity for the retailer
- The possibility of lost, stolen, or altered records and files

The question most often asked is "Why would anyone risk jail and/or termination from a job for theft?" Some personnel who engage in this type of conduct may be long-time employees who feel that they are above reproach. They may have more responsibilities, more freedom of movement within the company, and less supervision because of their status, and therefore, the greater opportunity to steal. At times, they may feel that some reimbursement is in order for the failure to receive a deserved and expected pay raise, or for some incident or out-of-pocket expenditure. At other times, the necessity is so great that they begin to take chances. So theft occurs because of three factors—desire, need, and opportunity. In most larceny cases, thieves never believe that they are going to get caught. In other words, it has been found that the greater the chance of getting caught, the less the chance of theft. This is true not only for the dishonest employee, but for the shoplifter as well.

It must be understood that the retailer or the company hierarchy must have an established positive commitment and a written policy statement regarding the reduction of losses and the subsequent punishment of identified wrongdoers. This must be conveyed and understood by all employees and reinforced periodically. They must believe that they have a responsibility to their employer, and that improper and illegal conduct by an employee or a customer will not be tolerated. Moreover, all employees should understand that loyalty to the company directly affects their job security, pay raises, and benefits. It is in their best interests to discourage thefts by other employees.

The following are three approaches that the retailer can employ in an attempt to create an effective and honest employee group:

1. ***The hiring processes:*** Attempt to hire dependable, honest, and stable employees.
2. ***Security controls and procedures:*** To ensure those new employees stay honest and maintain their integrity.
3. ***Training and retraining:*** In order to affirm the ways that the retailer relies on the employee to assist in security and safety, and the reduction of shrinkage.

But in reality, the honesty and integrity of the great portion of employees on board may be based on wages, benefits, rewards, promotion potential, management's treatment and concept toward an employee, and examples of good character, integrity, and veracity set by management—in other words—*job satisfaction.*

THE EMPLOYEE AS A SECURITY RISK

Employees steal when conditions permit them to steal.

Therefore, the most trusted employee, manager or subordinate are more likely to take advantage of their position becaue they usually have the ability to circumvent security systems, have freedom of movement, or will be overlooked because of their position.

The employees who are most likely to steal are the after-hours staff, which includes the stockers and janitorial/housekeeping crew. These workers usually have little or no supervision and are left on their own most of the time. In the case of janitorial crews, they are usually contractually hired through an outside service and are paid minimum wage in most cases. Because these workers are hired by the cleaning company that employs them and not by the retailer, it is impossible to truly determine what type of hiring procedure and background investigation was conducted. Workers employed by these service companies usually seek this type of employment because they are marginally employable to begin with. Many have frequent arrests, drinking or drug habits, excessive absences and lack many skills. Because of these traits, the conditions they work under, and without any loyalty to their employer, they are prime candidates for committing ongoing larcenies. Security-wise, loss prevention should keep a wary eye on these contractual employees.

Part-timers and young employees are also high on the list of potential thieves. Typically and statistically, teenagers are a very high security risk employee group. Teenagers should work when there is the most supervisory coverage, rather than during after hours when supervision is minimal. Teenagers and part-timers usually have no personal ties to the company, are less likely to have career considerations, and are less concerned with the permanency of their position. In addition, teenagers don't handle frustration or corrective behavior as well as an adult. Consequently, emotional release most often swings toward antisocial behavior. The teenager is considered to be the largest larcenous group in the theft classification of "pilferage." Usually, they start small but as nonexposure and time passes, the thefts grow in magnitude. Motivations vary for this group. It usually is caused by peer pressure, excitement, or "because everyone's doing it," with stealing "on an impulse" low on the list.

Repair workers, mechanics, painters, or construction crews on premises after working hours, with or without store employees working in the building at the time, should be considered a prime example of "the fox left alone in the henhouse." Unless some type of security personnel has these workers under observation, and their tool and lunch boxes are examined when leaving, the practice of outside evening workers should never occur.

Employees who associate with undesirable characters off premises should also be a concern for the security officer. These undesirables have great influence on an individual's actions, and in order to maintain status within the group, the employee will defer to their control. The employee may appear to be the opposite of the undesirables—neat and clean-cut in appearance as opposed to "friends" who visit or socialize.

Thefts that have been committed by employees are usually discovered sooner or later by their coworkers under various circumstances. They may discover a theft by accident or over a period of time by observation or information from another coworker. Other discovery by employees may be by observation and/or the determination of weaknesses in security control systems or procedures. The trick here is to convince the honest employee of the repercussions he or she will suffer because of this act; how the theft affects the company, the customer, and ultimately all employees; and why such acts must be reported.

Why They Steal

Some common factors that can be attributed to or are characteristic of certain employees who may have a inclination to steal are the following:

- ***Substance abuse:*** Alcohol or drugs—alcoholics and drug addicts are honesty risks. Their expense becomes greater as time goes by, therefore the need for cash to satisfy the habit. Their moral judgment becomes blurred, and any latent tendencies toward crime will arise. Count on problems to occur on the job—lateness, workdays lost, poor work habits, and of course, theft.
- ***Gambling:*** Particularly the chronic gambler. Gambling is as much of a disease as alcohol and drugs, with the same abuses, problems, and tendencies. Caution must be used if gambling is discovered on premises. It can cause morale problems, reduction of productivity, changes of attitudes, and possible other illegal activity and unsavory characters.
- ***Family problems:*** Illness or death in a family can cause unexpected or long-term hardship. People do many things that they wouldn't do under normal circumstances. Divorce, alimony, childcare, maintaining a second marriage and family, bankruptcy, family budget issues, family health or legal problems, and addictions can lead a troubled employee to become vulnerable to theft as expenses roll in and become overwhelming.
- ***The long-term employee:*** Whose honesty is taken for granted. These employees have more authority, freedom of movement, and ability to conduct business with little or no supervision. They are sometimes hostile and tell people to "butt out." They get annoyed, particularly when questioned or examined concerning monetary rewards (a telltale sign for the auditor to inspect more closely). They also may appear to maintain a higher standard of living.
- ***The actor:*** Plays up to the boss or any superior. This employee becomes overly friendly with members of the security staff, and will do personal favors for anyone in order to curry favoritism. Basically this employee sets up smoke screens for himself or herself.
- ***The rule violator:*** Leaves early and comes to work late; takes long breaks; makes personal use of telephones, computers, and copy machines. This employee smokes where not permitted, may use unauthorized exits when directed otherwise, and fails to live by the rules and shows lack of responsibility in handling money and merchandise.

- ***The "high-roller":*** Living high or beyond one's means. While maintaining that status, these employees may claim that they are a recipient of an inheritance or an estate. In order to meet their needs, they turn to ways in which they can satisfy their habits or lifestyle.
- ***The spendthrift:*** Can't handle money, and is always in debt. This person always borrows from fellow coworkers and company plans or benefits (i.e., 401K, company credit union). This person is an impulse buyer and creditors keep calling or inquiring at his or her place of business.
- ***The disgruntled employee:*** Makes up by stealing for what they believe should rightfully be theirs, such as failure to get a wage increase or benefits. This employee may commit thefts, damage, or disruption of business in order to "get even" with the boss or the company for some wrong or imagined wrong.
- ***The "joiner":*** The employee who succumbs to peer group pressure, or goes along with the group so as to be accepted.
- ***The chronic liar:*** Lies under pressure or to protect another. This employee is afraid of punishment, is maladjusted, and lies frequently and without reason to do so.
- ***The mentally unstable:*** Those individuals who may be unstable and/or have guilt feelings and want to get caught, or are looking for attention.

The security officer who becomes aware of problems such as these or any leading indicator of wrongdoing among employees should consider close observation and management involvement. Any change in deportment or work habits could be a sign of potential vulnerability. Controls should include routine testing by honesty shoppers, methodical checking of employees' packages upon leaving the store, but most of all, an active investigation, conducted surreptitiously, into any employee who appears to fall into the above categories. We must consider that most employees are honest, and that only some will affect the store's shrinkage and other security problems. Accordingly, each case or incident must be based on its own merits.

Where They Steal

The following are areas that are most vulnerable to theft:

- Receiving and shipping departments
- Cash and credit card sales
- Merchandise returns or exchanges
- Employee sales
- Customer sales (sweethearting)
- Accounts payable and accounts receivable
- General accounting and recordkeeping
- Payroll funds and records
- Inventory records
- Small high-end merchandise taken from stock or display, easily available and concealable

The areas of loss noted above will depend on demographics and the type of retail establishment, and are not listed necessarily by importance.

How They Steal

In order for a crime to be committed, one requires the intent, opportunity, and ability. Consequently, because intent and ability are indefinable components, only opportunity can be considered to be the controlling factor in crime deterrence by a loss prevention department. By setting up controls particular to an operation or function conducted by an employee, the opportunity to complete the act is diminished if not entirely eliminated. How well those controls are in place will depend on the reported and anticipated loss, the vulnerability of the operation or function, the appropriate resources and measures that are applied, and the management of those constraints.

Each criminal act committed by an employee will be specific to the function under his or her control or influence. Therefore, the security officer must be familiar with the procedures, tasks, and functions of all of the operations and/or departments noted here so that the officer may be aware of the shortcomings, the potential for misdeed, and those controls that may be needed.

The following areas are considered vulnerable to some type of theft or misdeed, and must have some type of restraint for employees to adhere to and make them accountable for any job performance that might be subject to inquiry:

- Cash register theft or cash manipulation
- Alterations of cash register tapes or records
- Cashiers giving free merchandise, or the creation of false markdowns or discounts for self, friends, or relatives
- Employees creating situations for easy theft by friends or relatives
- Cashiers not accounting and ringing up all merchandise for friends or relatives (short-ringing/sweethearting)
- Merchandise taken out the "back door" by employees, merchandise taken upon leaving for the day and counting on no bag inspection, or expensive merchandise easily concealed on the person
- Collusion between receiving or shipping clerks and truckers
- Collusion between employees from different departments
- False refunds or exchanges
- Credit card theft or fraudulent use—false business records entries
- Check forgery or fraudulent issuance of checks
- Embezzlement
- Various types of thefts by night employees, and theft by day or night housekeeping crews
- Manipulation of computers and systems—pricing, stock control, or other business information

- Theft of computer time, information, or programs
- Theft of services—telephone, fax machine, copy machine, work time, etc.
- Workers' compensation fraud
- Unauthorized access via keys or duplication of keys for larcenous purposes

See also the section on ASSET CONTROL in Chapter 15 for additional information on policy and procedure.

Some Indicators of Employee Theft

The following instances may indicate possible theft by an employee or the probability that theft has or may occur:

- Inventory shortages
- During close observation of all employees during regular rounds or inspection, the security officer notices sudden movements, over-friendliness or whispering by employees
- Constant complaints by an employee about the company, compensation, the administration, or favoritism
- Bragging to fellow coworkers about gambling winnings and/or losses
- Visual signs of alcohol or drug abuse
- An employee becomes emotionally unstable, erratic in behavior, and unpredictable. Or an employee who had been well adjusted becomes unstable, abusive, sarcastic, sullen, or withdrawn without any immediate apparent or known cause
- Apparent signs of an employee living beyond his/her means—expensive clothes, new cars, new home, infidelity, excessive alimony and/or child support, garnishment, or bragging about lifestyle
- Accusing another coworker of suspicious behavior or theft

Covert Actions in Curtailing Internal Theft

The following equipment or procedures will discourage or curtail employee theft:

- Surreptitious CCTV surveillance (e.g., hidden pinhole or miniature cameras)
- Point-of-sale CCTV monitoring
- Honesty shoppers
- Undercover detectives or operatives
- The rewarding of informants
- Internal auditing procedures
- Selective observation, inquiry, and investigation by security personnel

TYPES OF INTERNAL THEFT

Embezzlement

For our purposes, embezzlement may be defined as the fraudulent appropriation of property by someone who had been entrusted with its care or possession. Basically, it is the taking of property from another, where the offender took or acquired possession of that property legally (had come lawfully into one's hands) by way of employment or trust, and then took or misappropriated that property for personal use.

This method of fraud may happen in three ways, and because the offender is generally a trusted employee, the theft usually occurs over a long period of time where it becomes an ongoing or continuing crime:

1. Theft of money
2. Theft of inventory
3. Manipulation of accounts

Embezzlement is a rather tough case to investigate. The investigator must have some knowledge of the company's procedures, practices, rules and regulations, and possibly bookkeeping processes in order to pursue basically what is to be considered a paper trail. It can be time consuming. If the establishment has sloppy business practices or nonexistent records, and little supervisory oversights, the investigation becomes much more difficult.

Embezzlement is considered a "white-collar crime." The offender doesn't look or act "like a crook." This person could be your friendly next door neighbor or a well-trusted long-term employee. When an embezzler is caught, juries tend to be much more tolerant than if the crime had been committed against a person. Based upon the defense's argument, juries may view the defendant as a working slob taking something due from the "large tyrannical and filthy rich corporation," or that the company had poor bookkeeping practices or oversights to begin with. So then, it is understandable that in crimes against the person (robbery, assault, etc.) convictions usually result in incarceration, whereas crimes against property usually result in restitution with little or no jail time.

In the crime of embezzlement, we must consider the role of the model executive, because it is this employee who usually is involved in a long-term and excessive amount of money loss. The crime is easily hidden because of his position and apparent forthright and honest demeanor. He may gamble to some excess at places like Las Vegas or Atlantic City, but only for a couple of days at a time. He never takes a regular vacation, taking only a day here and a day there. He may drink excessively, frequenting bars and nightclubs. He may have an association with undesirable characters. Usually he is critical of others, and visibly displays a dislike of thieves. He may be a religious fanatic—or appear to be. He may give the impression that he has many "contacts" or friends who give him great deals on cars, jewelry, gifts, etc. He borrows money from other coworkers and pays back late. He borrows from the company's petty cash box, and the IOUs are rarely paid off in a timely manner. He asks that his personal checks be cashed post-dated or "held" for a time before cashing. He often works overtime regularly, needs coaxing to give up records, and is usually fastidious and excessively neat in the maintenance of his records. And when questioned about his recordkeeping or pertaining to a particular point about a record, he may become argumentative, arrogant, and abusive.

Although the executive may exhibit some or most of the above traits, it doesn't prove that this person is a thief; the executive may possess only personality or character flaws. However, the security officer should consider all of the above as indicators of possible wrongful conduct. Moreover, other than the executive position, we must bear in mind that other long-term, well-respected, and responsible employees with similar access to money and other accounts may also commit this type of crime.

Most cases of embezzlement are never discovered or linked to a particular employee. Many are never reported to the police, mostly for fear of publicity. The company may be quick to fire, but slow to prosecute. Long-term employment might offer an excuse for the employee's act in stealing. They may have needed the money to cover some financial hardship and although they hoped to pay it back, never did so. The thief may fall on the excuse that family hardship or sickness caused them to steal. The company may feel sorry for the employee and attempt to recover as much of their loss as possible, let the employee go, and forget the incident.

Although a felony is a crime against the state (the people), and in theory cannot be compromised, anyone can do so for a misdemeanor. However, unless it is a very serious case, felony or not, loss prevention managers and retailers would rather not spend the effort and time involved in a complicated and long and drawn-out case, along with the possibility of having to proceed with further court action for recovery after conviction. Consequently, the procedure of "cutting one's losses," the recovery of as much money or value of the property stolen as possible, and the termination of the employee is not uncommon in the business community.

Theft of Services by an Employee

Theft of services is a crime where one uses the services and/or equipment belonging to another for personal use. This could also include the solicitation of a service and failing to compensate the other party for that service. In respect to a company employee it includes the personal use of a business computer, a business telephone (other than for an emergency or with permission), and the use of a copy machine. Today, the copy machine has become the favorite instrument for the professional and nonprofessional thief to copy and steal records and files without removing the originals from the premises. Unless caught in the act of copying, no one will ever know that sensitive or confidential information has been compromised. In large business establishments, most machines are located in various locations throughout the premises. Many are separate and apart, out of general view, or in discreet recesses. Some controls on copy machine use could include the maintenance of logs at each machine that would include date, name, department, and number of copies made. Keeping tabs on the counter tracking the number of copies made at a particular machine is most important. If a serious problem exists, CCTV coverage on a machine might be necessary for control. Bear in mind that even though a theft of service has been committed in the use of the copy machine, a second crime is also committed in the theft of business records or files.

The theft of time is also a serious offense and includes the improper extension of meal periods or break time, constant lateness for work, and leaving work early. By requesting that a friend punch the offender in or out on the time clock, a theft of services has been committed. Consider also the improper extension of overtime hours for extra pay, or where excessive absences and improper use of sick leave may prove to be unlawful. Some of these offenses could be classified as a crime under various state laws as a *theft of services*, but usually the retailer will terminate the offender for a second offense after a prior warning.

Theft of services is usually a misdemeanor, and the company's reaction to these types of crimes depends on how serious the company administration views it, and how far or in what way they are willing to punish the offender.

Insurance Fraud by an Employee

One area of dishonesty committed by an employee is insurance fraud concerning injuries on the job. A common occurrence would be to fake an injury or exaggerate the pain of a minor injury into a major or permanent impairment. The loss prevention manager must be conscious that pains, aches, and agony can be feigned or imagined, and that he or she must be constantly observant about employee injuries.

The newly hired employee must be made aware at orientation that falsifying an injury and accepting the benefits of workers' compensation commits the crime of insurance fraud. Additionally, all employees must be informed of the required and thorough investigation into all injuries, the safeguards in place, and the company's zero tolerance toward a crime of this type.

The loss of workdays, payment of lost wages, and cost of medical and rehabilitation among other services is a substantial loss to the company. Insurance premiums are paid to cover this loss, but insurance companies are not in business to lose money. If losses are high, premiums will increase or insurance coverage will cease.

Cashier Theft

Unless the cashier is under observation, one of the easiest ways to steal from the retailer is by a friend or relative making a "sweetheart" purchase of merchandise at the register. In this procedure, the cashier will either ring up a much smaller amount for the item or items, or will pass over and not charge the "customer" for one or more of the items.

There is no doubt that shortringing a sale for family and friends takes place more often than one may believe. It has been estimated based upon retail loss surveys nationwide that retail stores with checkout registers at the exit similar to supermarkets and discount houses note that one-third of all cashiers will steal in this manner. This includes full- and part-time employees. Further, of those cashiers who do steal (33% of the total cashiers), 40% will steal at least every week (25% daily and 15% weekly). The remaining 60% of the dishonest cashiers will steal only occasionally. Based upon these surveys, thefts of this type can account for 10% to 20% of reported internal shrinkage. The surveys also found that close supervision of cashiers directly influenced and reduced the amount of shortringing by cashiers.

Any cashier who is observed committing the following behavior or "errors" should be an obvious candidate for close observation and/or investigation:

- Excessive voids, no sales rings, or over-rings
- Money shortages or overages
- Blank spots or loss of continuity of transaction numbers on register tapes

- Observation by supervisors noting odd prices being rung up that are not common for merchandise carried by the store
- Observation of certain "customers" always frequenting the same cashier
- Failure to use the bar code scanner

The use of a hidden camera secreted for the purpose of observing a suspected cashier is useful for short periods, but care must be utilized and the camera must be removed as soon as the operation is complete. The reasoning is so that hopefully other cashiers will not discover the camera.

Some of the ways to reduce or stop theft or dishonest behavior is by the use of the bar code system, in which every item must be swiped past a magnetic reader. If it appears that "the reader cannot read the bar code," and the item must be entered manually by SKU or bar code number, excessive transactions such as these noted on the register tape should be cause for concern.

Another tactic is the use of visible CCTV systems at the point of sale in which the actions of the cashier and the item scanned or rung up is viewed and/or recorded on a monitor simultaneously. The cashier is always aware that his or her conduct is or may be monitored. This is certainly a conspicuous deterrent, because the cashier may never know when he or she is under observation. In addition, this system can be used in conjunction with other point-of-sale features, one of which is the information and control of stock. This security system is usually used in supermarkets, discount stores, or other retail operations where large banks of cash lanes and registers are located in one area and in use most of the time. As part of the training of cashiers, the central monitor control of this system should be shown and explained so that they are familiar with the security procedures covering their position. The psychological effect created by the possibility of constant observation is a great deterrent. It has been shown that retail loss prevention departments that have employed this type of CCTV system have recouped the cost of the equipment in recovery alone in very short periods.

Pilferage

Pilferage is the term that some security professionals may apply to internal theft, and in effect, inventory loss. In actuality, the word "*pilferage*" has the meaning of a theft minor in nature, and therefore should be relegated to minor internal theft.

Pilferage can be described as the theft from the company of small objects that can easily be concealed on the person. They can include pens and pencils, paper and envelopes, small hand tools, or a "damaged" can of tuna. But not all pilferage is taken off the premises. It can also include the theft of food and/or beverages to be consumed on the premises. The usual excuse for this type of theft is that the employee deserves it and the company will never miss the loss.

Pilferage cannot be tolerated. To overlook these minor offenses tends to cause the offender to view his or her actions as insignificant or of little consequence by the employer. If perceived as such, subsequent behavior may lead the employee to consider a more serious criminal act. Consider also that employees who see the employer as overlooking petty theft of this type will cause further thievery as a general rule.

Damage

There are two types of damage that can cause a shortfall in inventory—intentional and unintentional.

Intentional damage by anyone, employee or customer, cannot be tolerated. If a customer is identified and it is a serious intentional loss of considerable value, the customer should be held accountable for that damage and suffer the consequences. If it is an employee, who is identified as intentionally damaging property or merchandise of any value, this employee should also be held accountable and suffer termination at the least, so that all employees are aware that the retailer will not tolerate behavior of this type.

Unintentional damage is any damage that includes the usual breakage that happens or is caused during the normal course of the business day. This damage should be reported, usually on a stock control form, so that the damaged or broken item can be written off by stock control and not be credited at a later time as an inventory loss. Unfortunately, many employees would more readily kick a damaged item under a counter or overlook it completely, rather than fill out a damaged goods form.

In any event, the security officer during general rounds of inspection should be aware and conscious of any damage observed or found, and that the employee in the department where the damaged item is found becomes responsible in completing the required reporting procedures.

Graffiti. Markings or defacement of this type are becoming extensive in our society, particularly on public infrastructure. However, graffiti has also invaded the business establishment, with the greater percentage of damage committed by employees.

Any employee found to have committed damage of this type in whatever manner the graffiti was applied, especially if the markings include racist or hateful messages, sketches or designs, should be dealt with severely. Depending on the seriousness of the act, punishment should include arrest and prosecution, as well as termination.

Computer Theft and Sabotage

Computers are being used more and more over the last two decades and have become an integral part of every retail business. Today's computers are used for management and operational functions, stock control, financial and payroll records, and all types of business records, plans, and projections.

However, this information can be exposed to internal and external observation, espionage, sabotage, and even theft. Files and information can be taken out easily via small floppy disks, or they can be sent electronically to another computer outside the company easily and within seconds. Proper programming instructions must be used to protect information in the computer, otherwise access or loss may never be detected. This includes intrusion from outside computers to elicit information or to create problems that can sabotage the business.

Some problems that can arise are additional programming instructions entered by an employee to destroy data in order to hide a crime, issue false payroll checks to nonexistent employees, issue checks to fictitious invoices, or cause downtime by creating errors. More common is the unauthorized use of computer time to play games or to conduct personal business on the company computer system.

Most computer crimes can be avoided by proper planning tailored to a business prior to the installation of the computer system. If a company is not large enough to have a competent computer expert or programmer on board, as some retail chains do, then one should be hired who will provide the security and safeguards needed with guaranteed protection.

Security Precautions. Any business computer open to electronic commerce or connected via outside communications is vulnerable to intrusion, whether perpetrated by a "cracker," "hacker," or just someone bent on causing sabotage or espionage. We must also consider the probability that it may also be an internal problem such as a disgruntled or larcenous employee, or an ordinary "system crash." The business establishment should recognize that there is a need for quick response to computer security incidents or major system crashes in an effort to protect, or at least save as much computer information as possible.

In that regard, large businesses should have a group of computer knowledgeable people on-site or at corporate headquarters who are able to respond to any computer emergency. They must have complementary skills and able to work independently, particularly in high-pressure incidents. This "team" concept has been termed as the *computer incident response team* (CIRT), and to have complete authority in incidents of this type they must have the adequate funding and complete support of the corporation. Moreover, outside professional consultants may also be made associates to the team, and called upon as needed. In any event, some members of the team may not necessarily require computer expertise, but if criminal intent is found, or an employee is identified as the culprit, the loss prevention manager, human resource manager, and a company attorney may be a necessary part of that team.

If the team operates out of corporate headquarters servicing various sites elsewhere, their duties will usually be complementary to computers such as programming, upgrading, developing policy and security, monitoring and enforcement, and correcting ongoing minor problems. A team that operates in-house may have other duties not necessarily wholly connected with computer operations. In any event, if a serious computer problem or incident does occur, members of either type of team must be able to stop whatever they are doing and direct their full attention to assisting in system protection and recovery.

COMPUTER EMERGENCIES

A response plan should be drafted to include those required notifications to senior management, clients, other business partners, and the assigned members of the computer incident response team. These response procedures should be made part of the *emergency procedure plan.*

Additionally, some or all of the following precautions, which may be related to a retail operation regarding computer security, should be initiated:

- All managers and employees, who are to have access to computer files, particularly sensitive business files and records, should be thoroughly interviewed and investigated during the hiring process.
- Repair personnel must be screened prior to working on any company computer or peripheral equipment. This should also include internal telephone equipment and lines.

- Sensitive computer operations should be placed in a secured or isolated area with only those employees who are permitted into these areas granted access.
- Some type of security should accompany any repairperson or visitor to this secured area.
- Backup files and records must be kept in case of system crashes. They should also be secured in a locked fireproof safe or cabinet.
- Distribution of printout sheets and disks should be available only to certain authorized people, and so recorded.
- Loss prevention audits should include routine inspections in these areas.

State and the federal governments are of the opinion that computer fraud, theft, and damage is so serious a threat to business, the consumer and to national security, that legislation has been drafted in recent years to cover this ever-increasing problem. Because the retail establishment makes use of the computer in many areas (business plans, financial, purchasing, stock control, etc.), the retail loss prevention officer must be aware of the probabilities that may occur in varied situations.

In that regard, state criminal codes may define offenses involving computers in various terms. This may include a person who may be considered guilty of a crime when he knowingly uses or causes to be used a computer or computer service without authorization, and the computer utilized is equipped or programmed with a device or coding system, a function of which is to prevent the unauthorized use of said computer or computer system.

In addition, the various classes or types of computer crime could include trespass, tampering, duplication and possession of computer-related material and may be considered a misdemeanor or a felony depending on the state law in which the security officer is employed. The security officer may wish to review those sections of the state's criminal code for future reference.

Consider also that computer fraud and related activity in connection with computers covers the entry and access of a computer without authorization, which is determined by the U.S. government to be or is protected from disclosure. And that if a person obtains any information and/or causes the transmission of such information or a code to a computer or computer system, and/or causes damage to any information contained therein, this person commits a crime.[2]

In conclusion, all computers should have individual password protection, no matter what type of access or programs that are available. A click of the "on" switch without further safeguards offers no protection whatsoever. According to many professionals in the computer security field, an employee's password can be found on that employee's desk. If not the actual password, then there should be various clues as to how the password was derived. A picture of a wife or girlfriend could mean a password was created from a name, nickname, or birth date. A pet's name, a sports banner or paraphernalia on a desk may also provide clues to a password. Remember that computers logged on and left unattended can cause a person to compromise an entire network, or information derived and placed on a disk can be easily taken from the facility in a shirt pocket.

Finally, bear in mind that any information stored on the computer's hard drive is vulnerable to compromise, destruction, or modification. Although any information can be encrypted to prevent some of these problems, the information can still be destroyed maliciously. One reason that a company might wish to leave information on the hard drive is so that if connected to a network system of computers, others on the network can access this information. And therein lies the problem—the whole network is then vulnerable. The only way to prevent this is to reduce the risk by placing data on CDs or disks off-line as backup copies, and then placing these records or files safely in a secure storage from destruction, fire, and theft.

THE DISHONEST SECURITY PROFESSIONAL

This is an area that can be fraught with danger for loss prevention management. The accusation or apprehension of a security officer initially invested with all the professional authority his or her position entails is almost unconscionable, and at the very least unethical.

How does one secure the services of an honest security officer? And once hired, how can we maintain that honesty and integrity at the highest level possible? Will constant supervision and the use of routine integrity testing of a security force promote an honest crew? Some high-level executives may believe this to be true. But from the viewpoint of the low-level manager and supervisor, we must consider that to install and rigorously enforce integrity testing on the personnel in whom the company expects to have the most trust can cause severe morale problems within that group.

The most generally accepted answer would be the application of intense preemployment investigation prior to hiring any security officer. This may include multiple interviews; criminal history, driving record, financial, credit and personal reference checks; drug screening; and work and education verification. The eligibility or prerequisite of certification as a bonded employee would also involve an investigation by other individuals. Because of the nature of the position regarding the applicant inquiry, the hiring and application process should be considered more intense than that for any other job seeker. Following that, ongoing close supervision of all members in the loss prevention department should be considered an obligation by security management.

Integrity Testing. The primary use of integrity testing is to ensure the quality of honesty in the workforce. However, the possible use of routine random integrity testing of an individual security officer or the security force as a group may be considered a much more serious matter.

Testing an officer's honesty could include the following circumstances:

- The use of an "honesty shopper" turning over a "found" wallet or handbag containing a sum of money but no identification to a security officer in order to determine if the found property will be subsequently reported
- The placement of money or a valuable object in a location where the security officer would easily come across or observe the rigged event, in an effort to determine if the "found" money or object is reported as required
- The close scrutiny of an officer's written reports and personal follow-up in order to determine any falsification or malfeasance

Although some businesses and police departments conduct customary testing of this type, it may be considered one of the most distinct factors in the development of low employee morale. No one wishes to be questioned or examined in any way about his or her character, integrity, or veracity after they have been employed for a period of time. Procedural testing of this type can cause a debilitating consequence on a group of security officers where cohesiveness, camaraderie, and productivity can be affected. This will be particularly so for the long-time employee who is or has been considered an excellent officer in all ways. Once an employee has been surreptitiously tested and then finds out that he or she was the subject of such a test, the attitude and loyalty of that employee toward the company may be completely destroyed. No matter how the process is handled by management, the erosion of that loyalty may occur immediately, or over a period of time for the group if the process becomes a standard practice. Make no mistake about it—morale will decline sooner or later. This may be considered the reason most loss prevention managers will not become involved in testing the honesty of their subordinates unless they have reason to do so.

Nevertheless, it would be unwise to believe that a security officer or any employee would never commit a dishonest act. Depending on circumstances, the use of some type of testing may have to be considered in order to determine the guilt or innocence of the person under scrutiny. If integrity testing is to be conducted within a business establishment, legal counsel should be obtained in order to determine that the reason and type of test might be considered judicious and legal.

Some opponents question the use of integrity testing believing that it may be a form of entrapment. Simply put, entrapment may be defined as a method used to obtain evidence by creating a substantial risk that the offense would be committed by a person not otherwise disposed to commit it, but that the subject was induced or encouraged to engage in such an act that would place him or her in jeopardy. The inducement and/or encouragement must be active in nature. Conduct merely affording a person an opportunity to commit an offense does not constitute entrapment. In other words, setting a trap to catch a criminal in the act may be said to be proper. However, inducing or encouraging someone to commit the act is illegal.

A study that included 69 law enforcement departments from across the United States showed that the use of personality tests in the hiring and application process has some validity in identifying those important relationships that may or are linked to corruption.[3] The study was representative and broad enough that the results attained could easily be attributed to security officers.

According to this analysis, in addition to the identification of personality traits, there are some factors or indicators that should be considered during the hiring process. This would include the following:[4]

- Tolerance of others
- Willing and able to maintain long-term relationships
- Being achievement oriented
- Willing to accept responsibility and blame
- More likely to be controlled by guilt and/or remorse

A business relies on their security force to be their eyes and ears in all aspects of security and safety, and that they expect officers employed by them to be above reproach. Therefore, there can be no doubt that such close inquiry of police candidates can be related to the same type of investigation for security officer applicants. Personality testing, along with close attention of an applicant's personal background and work history would increase the probability of hiring an honest officer. How intense and essential the process may be would depend on the level of security expected and the requisite credentials of the applicant.

Once hired, there should be a probationary period that will include exposure to the company's policies and procedures, asset control policies, and the necessary training for the position. Within this period in particular, the officer's immediate supervisor must offer ongoing adequate and effective training and close supervision.

Whether it presents itself during the probationary period of the security officer or subsequently thereafter, the supervisor must be cognizant of the following:[5]

- On-the-job misconduct (found to be the number one predictor of corruption). This would include violations of company policy, fraud, misappropriation of property, unlawful confiscation, pilferage, extortion, sexual misconduct, favoritism, and/or preferential treatment to name a few. No matter how trivial the transgression, a loss prevention supervisor must be constantly observant and react immediately to any misbehavior by a subordinate.
- Difficulty getting along with others.
- Indications of immaturity, irresponsibility, and unreliability.

Once the security officer has been hired and accepted as an honest and viable candidate in protecting the assets of the company, how do we maintain the same attributes we originally observed in the officer? The answer is simply effective supervision.

A good supervisor must be constantly aware of the conduct and work habits of subordinates. Their level of expertise, levelheadedness, honest reasoning, attitude, tenacity, leadership ability, and demeanor with others is important. But so too is the officer's complete acceptance of the department's mission, ability to work with little or no supervision when necessary, and the aptitude for the required compilation and maintenance of records. Values such as these may be considered good characteristics of professionalism, competence, and confidence.

But the supervisor must also have the necessary attributes for a faithful and reliable reaction from his or her subordinate. The supervisor must have leadership qualities, be truthful, act with fairness in all dealings with personnel, promote excellence, praise good conduct and work, be able to admonish and correct when necessary, seek innovation, and most importantly, possess high ethical standards.

However, there may come a time when an officer commits an act of dishonesty. If so, and if a determination of guilt is made, termination of employment must be the accepted norm. In other words, "zero tolerance," and depending on the seriousness of the offense and company policy, arrest, and prosecution may be mandatory. Other than that, if suspicion of unauthorized or illegal activity becomes known, the possibility of an integrity test or a sting operation may be required to resolve the question.

Conclusion. Notwithstanding a valid suspicion or determination of a dishonest officer, the use of integrity testing as a routine policy and procedure within a loss prevention department should be avoided so as not to diminish or destroy the morale of the group. A cohesive security force may be considered a clique in that they may believe that their status is above that of the ordinary employee of the company. This may be so, because they do have much more ability to enforce the policy and procedures of the company, have free access throughout the facility, and react to any safety and security violations without delay and with some control. Their authority is derived from company management, but if that management resorts to the testing of honesty and morality relative to security officers as a routine or random procedure, loyalty and job satisfaction will suffer.

ENDNOTES

1. Op. cit., *2001 National Retail Security Survey—Final Report*, pp. 4, 5. Figure 13.1 graph reprinted with permission.
2. *Title 18 USC § 1030*—Computer Fraud and Abuse Act of 1966.
3. *Policy Integrity: Use of Personality Measures to Identify Corruption-prone Officers*, Summary of a Research Study by Jennifer O'Connor, Callie Chandler, and Howard Timm. Published by community Policing Exchange, Phase V, # 19, March/April 1998; Police Ethics/Standards, Integrity/Trust. Included as part of various studies and surveys published by Community Policing Consortium, Office of Community Oriented Policing Services (COPS), National Institute of Justice. (http://www.communitypolicing.org/publications/exchange).
4. Ibid.
5. Ibid.

Chapter 14

External Crimes and Frauds Affecting the Retail Establishment

BURGLARY

Burglary Defined. A retail establishment is a business structure and not a dwelling. There are different elements and degrees of burglary when the building in question is a dwelling. However, burglary is a crime against property and can be committed only when a "building" is the primary element of the crime. The unauthorized or unlawful entry of a closed and/or secured building for the purpose of committing a larceny or any crime within is considered a burglary. Nevertheless, the term *break and entry* need not apply, because a burglar may enter through an unlocked or open door or window, take, steal, and carry away property (as in the case of a larceny), and still commit the crime of burglary. In addition, a perpetrator may also commit a burglary by hiding within the store, waiting until the store is closed down and after everyone leaves, committing the crime (larceny or otherwise), and then "breaking" out. Because the perpetrator hides within and is present "unlawfully"—without license and privilege—and then commits a crime therein, a burglary has also taken place.

> The general definition for burglary is when a person *knowingly enters* and/or *remains unlawfully* in a building *with intent to commit a crime therein.*

The "crime committed therein" may be a larceny, rape, assault, or murder, for example, and the perpetrator will be charged with that second crime along with the burglary. Unless other factors are present such as the building in question is a *dwelling*, such that the perpetrator being armed causes physical injury to a person within the building, or other conditions prevail as described in a particular state law, the crime will usually be classified as the lowest degree of burglary, no matter if day or night, as long as the building is closed and not a dwelling. However, no matter what degree of burglary, it is always a felony.

Nevertheless, if a person has been given a trespass warning, in that he or she is never to enter the retail premises at any time (license and privilege has been taken away), and when during business hours enters for the purpose of committing any crime therein, this person also commits a burglary. In this case besides the crime of burglary, the perpetrator will also be charged with the crime he or she has or is about to commit. For further details regarding the use and importance of a trespass warning and how it can be applied to a burglary situation, see the explanation of the advantage of a trespass warning in Chapter 5. Security officers should check with the trespass statutes in their state to determine if a perpetrator may be also charged with burglary under these circumstances if the facts are present.

Note that some states specify that other than a dwelling, a boat, motor home, or a vehicle ordinarily used for overnight lodging of persons, an unlawful entry into an enclosed motor truck or enclosed motor truck trailer may also be covered under the burglary statutes. A larceny from a locked truck or trailer loaded with merchandise and parked in a truck-receiving bay may constitute a burglary under their state law.

The Protection of the Facility and its Assets

Basically, there are two types of business burglars. One is the professional who has the skill to enter a well-protected building, disarm the alarm system, and break into a safe or a secure area containing property of high enough value that will be worth the burglar's effort and vulnerability. This person will leave little clues behind, and most often operates alone. The second is the person who commits a burglary because of need or desire, and the opportunity presents itself. This person is not a true professional, lacking the skills of the more experienced and master burglar. This person leaves many clues behind, and is usually the one who is easily caught sooner or later by the police.

There are various ways to protect the integrity of closed business premises from a burglary, or assorted approaches that will help to reduce a loss by burglary. Consider first of all that if a burglar wishes to gain entry, he or she will do so, one way or another. The trick, therefore, is to make it long and hard for the burglar to succeed. Some of these obstacles may be described as follows:

1. Reduce the time that a burglar can work without being observed or caught. Generally speaking, burglars don't wish to linger. They want to get in, grab the loot, and flee the scene as soon as possible. Doorways and windows should be well lighted so that police or security patrols and passersby may be able to see suspicious activity. Effective alarm systems that will be activated, even if tampered with, reduce the time the burglar must spend on the premises before some response to that alarm takes place. A good "safe man" can open any safe with time, and these burglars have their own particular methods to gain entry into a safe. Ultimately, a strong and well-built safe will take a long period of time to "crack," placing the burglar that much more in danger of apprehension.
2. Reduce the amount of available "loot" or valuables in the event that the burglar makes a successful entry. Professional burglars who will attempt to crack a safe will do so only if they believe that the time and effort is well worth it, and that they have some assurance that the safe will contain a considerable amount of cash or valuables. Therefore, large sums of money should not be kept in the safe overnight, keeping only enough to open and operate the business the following day. Armored car pickups or bank drops should be made on a daily basis. If management consistently maintains a reduction of money or valuables available, this fact will become known to the professional sooner or later while "casing" the premises. If contractual employees such as janitors, other workers, and in particular the professional criminal maintain an observation on cashroom employees and their money procedures, and it appears that they violate money drops, pickup strategies or are sloppy in their operation, this will become known to those with larcenous intent.

Remember, the reduction of cash and valuables on premises, and effective protection procedures of your premises from persons with criminal intent are applicable to the robber as well as the burglar.

3. Make it physically difficult or almost impossible for a burglar to make entry into the building, so that the burglar must go to great lengths to make a successful penetration. Perimeter protection might include fences or walls, night lighting covering the outside of the building, heavy metal doors, and the protection of windows, air vents, skylights, and other openings. The use of certain devices protecting these areas will discourage, slow down, or at least activate a police response.

   Some security devices that can be used to slow down or thwart a burglar include outside mortise cylinders on perimeter doors without an exposed shoulder where a burglar can grip and pull or strip off the cylinder with the use of a tool. "Cylinder pulling" is one of the favorites for burglars. Another is springing an outside door with the use of a pry bar. This is particularly easy for double doors if the deadlock bolt is too short. A laminated steel pivoted bolt with a "hooked" tip that will grab the frame of the other door with approximately a 1½-inch throw bolt can stop or slow down entry through this type of door. One method of getting around a deadlock bolt that is of sufficient length is the "jamb peeling" method—a pry bar is used to tear away enough of the doorframe to expose the dead bolt so that the door will swing free. A heavy steel frame or an armored strike plate can deter this type of entry. All roof hatches should be secured from within by padlock and by an alarm. If possible, all outside perimeter doors should be secured with a steel bar across the door from within. If door hinges are exposed, some type of protected hinge pins should be utilized.

   All windows, skylights, fans, or vents that are required to remain open for ventilation should be protected by the use of gates or "wire traps." These traps are fence alarms containing a wire mesh in various configurations that will activate an alarm if disturbed or penetrated in any manner. On large showcase windows or glass doors where entry can be made by throwing an object through the glass, the use of glass breakage sensors will activate an alarm as soon as the glass is shattered.

These are only a few methods used to protect a building. Further methods and devices are covered in the section BURGLAR ALARMS in Chapter 19 and in the section INTERNAL AND EXTERNAL THEFT CONTROL in Chapter 15.

Remember that all burglaries are felonies and must be reported to the police for investigation and insurance purposes. The security officer should have some knowledge of protecting the crime scene and not disturbing or handling any evidence until the police arrive and secure the scene.

ROBBERY

Robbery Defined. Robbery is forcible stealing—it is a crime against the person. Briefly, it is the unlawful taking of property from the person or in the presence of another, against his or her will by means of *force* or *fear* of injury. The generally accepted definition of robbery is when a person *forcibly steals property, from another* or when in the course of committing a larceny, a person *uses or threatens the immediate use of physical force* upon another person for the purpose of:

1. Preventing or overcoming resistance to the taking of the property or to the retention thereof immediately after the taking, *or*
2. Compelling the owner of such property or another person to deliver up the property or to engage in other conduct that aids in the commission of the larceny.

Because many people link the terms burglary and robbery as one crime, we must define the difference between the two. To put it simply, burglary is unlawfully entering upon or within someone's property such as a building, dwelling, boat, etc., in order to commit a crime therein. It includes the taking and carrying away property belonging to someone other than the thief, or other criminal acts within the structure such as criminal mischief, murder, or rape, where no larceny need be committed. Along with the crime of burglary, the perpetrator will also be charged with any crime that person committed within the building. If the perpetrator is unable to complete the act, an attempt to commit any crime therein will show intent. Burglary, as with larceny, is considered a crime against "property."

Robbery, however, is considered a crime against the "person," because it is the taking of property from another by *force* or *fear*—the use of threats of bodily harm, use of a weapon, or by brute force. The potential for danger is greater in most cases, because there is a face-to-face confrontation between the victim and the thief. Crimes such as a mugging, strong-arm robbery, and threats of bodily harm (either immediate or at a later time and with or without a weapon) is considered a robbery as long as the victim is in fear of death or physical harm.

A robber points a pistol (or a knife) at a person and demands that he turn over his wallet and jewelry. The robber is using force by threatening to use a gun or a knife, and the victim is in fear that he will be shot (or knifed), so he gives up his property willingly.

It doesn't matter if the gun wasn't loaded or that the perpetrator had no thoughts of ever harming the victim, the crime of robbery did in fact occur because force was used and the victim was in fear of death or serious physical injury.

An example of a robbery without force could be described in the following illustration that has often occurred in various situations:

A man enters a bank, determines the location of the bank manager's desk, walks up to this desk and softly states that his partner is at the manager's home holding his wife and two children hostage. He also indicates that if the manager does not open the bank vault and quietly let the perpetrator take as much money from the vault as he can carry and leave without any alarm, the perpetrator's partner will kill his family.

The manager is convinced, particularly after his home address is shared by the perpetrator, so he complies with the robber's demand. The robber now enters the vault freely, and shortly thereafter, leaves the bank unhurried without any hindrance, and with a large amount of cash.

No weapon or overt force was used, but the bank manager was in *fear* that his family was at risk so he granted the perpetrator free access to the bank's money, and acted as he was told.

Whether or not a seizure of the family took place a robbery was in fact committed.

Anti-Robbery Procedures

As far as security and safety is concerned in regard to a possible robbery on or off premises, the following points should be carefully considered when setting up anti-robbery procedures:

- Train those employees who would be most susceptible to a robbery because of their position or status within the company. Training should include those procedures noted below.
- The most important factor is employee safety; so make sure that the actions and comments by employees during a robbery in progress does not place them in danger of harm.
- Minimize loss as much as possible.
- Interview employees and other witnesses immediately after the robbery, so that the possibility of identifying and apprehension of the thief is greater.
- Cooperate with the police in an effort to assist in the apprehension, arrest, and prosecution of the thief, and the recovery of money or other property.

Whenever valuables such as money, expensive merchandise, or other important or valuable items are stored or transferred, there is the possibility of robbery. In most cases, the perpetrator in the crime uses a gun, knife, or other weapon in an effort to intimidate and frighten the victim. The retailer has an obligation to inform, prepare, and protect employees as much as possible if they are confronted with this type of situation. Cashiers, cash office personnel, or anyone who handles money, including company truckers who have custody of company merchandise, must be made aware of how to act and what not to do when involved with this type of confrontation. Employees, managers, or security officers making a bank drop at a bank safe depository are also considered easy targets.

The professional "stick-up man" considers a number of details prior to committing the act. This will include how much resistance might occur, how fast the police will arrive at the scene, the monetary amount involved, whether it is possible to get away without harming anyone, and lastly, plans for a safe escape route. Depending on the pros and cons, the crime may or may not be consummated. Contrary to that, the inexperienced robber is not always motivated by logic and may act on impulse in many cases. Today, many thieves who commit robbery are very desperate, and may be on drugs or coming down off drugs. There is no way for anyone to know how the robber will react to any movement or comment by the victim, and therefore, this robber is the most dangerous.

Invariably, businesses that are open after normal business hours are the targets of opportunity for the robbery perpetrator. Bars, service stations, motels, and twenty-four-hour supermarkets, among others, are most vulnerable to robbery. As for the retail establishment, the robber's interest will gravitate toward the cash registers, safes, counting rooms, cash offices, or the bank drop.

Employee Procedures in the Event of a Robbery

All employees who work in areas of the retail establishment where they may be at risk of a robbery attempt should have in-depth training of procedures and actions to be followed in the event of a robbery.

> The primary objective for the security officer during a robbery is the safety and prevention of injury for all employees, customers, visitors, and passersby.

The following procedures should be part of the training program for all employees who may be exposed to a robbery attempt:

1. ***Remain calm.*** A robbery is a traumatic experience for those who have suffered through one. Try to be as calm as possible; think about what is going on around you. Do not look or concentrate on the robber's gun or weapon. Treat it as an inanimate object and as if it doesn't exist. Gain your composure and assess the situation as much as possible. If you do not remain as calm as possible, the perpetrator will become overly agitated and may act irrationally. Also, you will be unable to give a good description of the robber, and you will make a poor witness.
2. ***Obey commands.*** Attempt to comply strictly with the robber's commands. Do not make any sudden movements. If you wish to move or make some type of movement, tell the robber what you are going to do so that the robber is aware of your actions. If you act contrary to the robber's orders, you will certainly alarm him and increase the danger.
3. ***During the course of the robbery, try to analyze the robber.*** An excellent procedure that may be used in remembering as much as possible of the perpetrator's description is the *Three Portion Analysis Method*:

"THREE PORTION ANALYSIS METHOD"[1]

1. Take a brief glance at the robber's ***upper portion of his body***—head and neck. Make a mental note of his hair, type and color, hat, complexion, color of eyes, glasses if any, scars observed, mustache and/or beard, and any jewelry. Note his height—try to compare against your height or a stationary object.
2. Next make a note of the ***middle portion of his body***—shoulder to waist. Make note of his coat or jacket if any, shirt, color and type, tie if any, and weight. Compare his weight against yours or a coworker you know.
3. As the robber departs, observe the ***lower portion of his body***—waist to feet. Make note of his trousers, color and type, skirt or dress (if female), type and color of shoes or sneakers.

4. ***Sound the alarm.*** Activate the holdup alarm when it is safe to do so, or immediately after the perpetrators leave. This alarm should be silent. Activation will only advise the alarm company's central station that a holdup is in progress and they will notify the police. If the business has no central station holdup activation, the employee should notify the switchboard or other central location for police notification. In the case of a cash register robbery, the cashier should advise a supervisor or cash office by telephone as soon as possible after the act.
5. ***Secure the crime scene.*** Employees and loss prevention personnel should secure the crime scene immediately or as soon as possible after the commission of the crime. Try not to touch or move any item in the vicinity of the crime scene. Fingerprints and other forensic evidence might be contaminated or destroyed. Terminate all normal business at the crime scene or move it to another location.

Responding to a Robbery Report. Security officers most probably will be advised of the incident via radio. If not, a prearranged code via the public address system should be used. A code known only to loss prevention and key employees such as "supervisor 10 to register 3, please" or "signal 30 to area 10" might be very useful.

Regardless of how the on-site security officers are notified, the officers should respond to the robbery location with caution, observing all subjects leaving the area. Unless the security officers are positive that the robbery suspects have left the scene, they should not enter the cash office for fear of interfering with the course of the robbery. Instead they should wait and observe the subjects leaving the cash office, or wait for police response. Security officers should designate a responsible employee to meet the police at an entrance in order to direct them to the crime scene. Of course, if security officers have been advised that the robbers have left the scene they may enter the cash office, particularly if someone has been injured and immediate assistance must be rendered.

Unarmed security officers should not under any circumstances attempt to make an apprehension, whether they have knowledge that the perpetrators are armed or not. Officers should gather as much information as possible—descriptions of the perpetrator, auto used if any, as well as type, color, plate number, escape route, etc. If security officers are armed, and authorized to use deadly physical force as mandated by the law and authorized by their employer, they should be aware that customers and passersby may be injured or killed in any gunplay. For the armed security officers, this type of situation will be the most serious and life-threatening for all concerned—employees, customers, passersby, and security officers. Today, it is generally accepted that armed security officers are not needed on any retail premises. To do so places the retailer in an exceptional vulnerable position in many areas of liability.

Loss prevention officers may wish to interview employees who witnessed the crime in order to obtain the description of the perpetrator. If able to and if available, the employees who were subjected to the robbery may complete a robbery checklist form, answering description questions while still fresh in their mind. Try to keep employees involved in the robbery separated from each other so as not to have one employee impose personal observations or views upon another. Upon arrival, the police will control the scene, and will question employees in their own way. Attempt to keep out of their way, and assist only when asked or required to do so.

Bank Drops. In the case of bank drops, employees should never place themselves in a position where a suspect can approach undetected. Drops should *not* be made in a routine manner, otherwise the robber will have your procedure and time of drop minutely detailed. Whether security officers accompany the employees or not, they should be unpredictable about the method and time of transporting funds. Vary the routes, time of day, and methods of concealment (briefcases, paper bags, store bags—anything but a canvas bank bag in public view). Avoid routes such as elevators, quiet streets or any obstacle that will slow you down or prevent immediate access to the depository or to a safe area. Because routine depository drops conducted on a daily basis, particularly soon after a store closing, are conducive to a robbery attempt, loss prevention may wish to entertain the services of an armored car company.

In the event of a robbery of this type, whether a weapon is shown or not, employees should cooperate completely with the instructions of the robber. Do not attempt to cause the offender to become angry, anxious, or overly nervous.

LARCENY FROM THE PERSON WITHOUT FORCE

In addition, be aware that when property, whatever value or type, is taken from the person of another without force or fear it is *grand larceny*, not a robbery. An example would be a pickpocket who lifts a wallet from a person without their knowledge and leaves the scene. No force was used and therefore only a felony larceny took place. But if the thief is discovered in the act, and the victim attempts to keep his or her property with the thief ripping the wallet from the person, force was used and a robbery took place.

Another example could be as follows: A woman is walking along the street or an aisle in a retail store when a thief grabs the woman's pocketbook and begins to run with it. This is commonly described as a "purse snatch" and it is a larceny, but also as a felony, because the pocketbook was taken from the person. In another scenario, the woman has the strap of the pocketbook around her shoulder and as the thief attempts to take it, she holds on to the bag in an effort to keep it. The thief pulls the pocketbook forcefully enough to rip it from her shoulder and hands, causing the woman to fall to the ground as the thief runs off with her property. This is a robbery because the bag was forcefully taken. It makes no difference whether the woman's handbag contained a penny, a thousand dollars, or something else of value. As with burglary, all degrees of robbery are felonies. Be aware also that causing a physical injury or the use of a weapon in the commission of the robbery will raise the severity of the crime.

To reiterate, if there was no fear of injury or death to the victim and no force was used in the case of the taking of the woman's pocketbook, then the appropriate crime committed and charged would be grand larceny. Under these circumstances a person is guilty of grand larceny when the thief steals the property, and when the property regardless of its nature and value, is taken from the person of another without force or fear.

SCHEMES AND SCAMS

Returns and Refunds

The security officer must be aware that in any retail business there will be "customers" who will attempt to scheme to their benefit when it comes to something of value. This does not necessarily mean that this customer is a criminal at heart, but in many instances will "try to get all they can get." And whether it is truly a thief or a customer out to take some advantage, it all affects the bottom line.

There are many examples of unlawful or unwarranted returns or refunds.

A "customer" approaches the refund counter in order to "return" an item for a refund, which, in fact, was stolen earlier. He doesn't have a receipt, and may have found a store bag discarded outside of the store.

The "customer" may spend an inordinate amount of time during a store's busy period at the returns counter in order to confuse the return transaction, cause delay, cause a commotion, and frustrate the store employee.

A "customer" returns a patio set of a table and chairs two months after purchase, stating that the quality was inferior, didn't fit in with her décor, or some other excuse for requesting a refund. If she receives a full refund, she had free use of the patio set for the summer. If she receives only a partial refund, she "rented" the set, saved money, and still had full use for the summer. Most probably she will be back next year and do the same. A situation such as this also occurs with expensive rugs (e.g., orientals), where the rug is used for a party or to impress someone, and is returned soon after.

A "customer," possessing a stolen item, wishes to make a "return" because of wrong color or wrong size, but has no receipt. An even exchange is granted but the customer asks for a receipt on the exchange. If granted, the subject will return at a later time with that receipt and the exchanged item offering some excuse and demanding a refund.

In an effort to reduce losses in the "returns process," the most effective method is the store's refund policy and the trained employee. In many states retail stores are required to have the refund policy posted and/or noted legibly on the legitimate sales receipt at the time of the purchase. Whether required or not by law, the retailer should adhere to a conspicuously posted refund policy, and require employees to strictly abide by that policy during the return or refund process. To do otherwise would place the retailer in an unwanted position when the "customer" wishes to make a return at a later time.

The store should specifically note—no receipt = no refund.

The "returns" employee should note on the customer's original receipt the fact of the return or exchange, including the date. The employee should examine the receipt carefully for date of sale, that the item returned is the same noted on the receipt, or originally purchased from another store in the chain in another state where the sales tax may be different. Also the employee should check if the receipt is not a counterfeit or that the item/s originally purchased were not "as-is" or clearance merchandise. If so, these items are usually not returnable. If the employee asks enough questions in an attempt to verify a questionable return, he or she may eventually cause a "customer" to leave in a huff, vowing of course, never to return.

Concern must be taken in not setting a double standard or in making exceptions on returns. Customers will never forget, and upon a return to the store will hold the retailer to any prior agreement. Customer service managers, other managers, and loss prevention personnel must enforce the return policy to the letter and without contradiction. The security officer should also remember that confrontations and various predicaments will occur, where there will be mistakes and employees will err. Some of the thieves will get away with their scams; the idea is to keep it under control and within an acceptable limit.

No Sales Receipt? As could be expected in the progression of our present computer systems, some retailers have instituted a new method in tracking the sale of purchased items. The entry of customer and other information at the point of sale, and the storage of this data concerning customer purchases, exchanges, returns, and repairs negates the need for the customer to retain a sales receipt once they have left the store. Upon returning to the store for whatever the problem, customers need only to properly identify themselves at the returns or customer service desk with the purchased item, and if the service required falls within the parameters set at the time of the sale, the store can accommodate the customer. The employment of data systems such as this would be "user friendly" in reducing confrontations with customers over "lost" or misplaced receipts, and the thief who steals merchandise and subsequently attempts to make a "return."

Till Taps and Scams

Cash Drawer Drains. Routinely during the business day, "cash drains" are made from cash register drawers in order to keep the amount of money as minimal as possible in the drawer in case of theft. If pneumatic tubes for the transfer of cash are not available, then of course the cash must be transported by hand from the cashier to the cash room. In these cases, employees transporting the cash or a cash drawer should use the same precautions as noted for employees making a bank drop. They must be aware of all that is going on around them.

Till Taps. In this type of larceny, the thieves will work in pairs. One will be in the process of a purchase at the cash register. When the register cash drawer is open, the purchaser will do or commit an act to take the cashier's attention away momentarily from the transaction. The "customer" might drop something that will cause a loud noise such as breaking glass, or might feign a fainting spell causing great commotion. While the cashier's attention is turned elsewhere, the second thief reaches into the cash drawer and takes out all or most of the large denomination bills. If this occurrence is committed by a professional scam artist, the cashier will never know of a loss until reconciling the drawer at a later time.

Register Scams. Register scams are usually accomplished when the cashier is very busy. The subject will offer a large bill for a small purchase and while the cashier is making change, the subject states that she has a smaller bill and requests that the larger bill be returned. As money is passed back and forth from hand to hand, and the subject confuses the cashier more and more, ultimately the thief will leave with not only the purchase, but with more money than originally possessed.

BAD CHECKS AND CREDIT CARD FRAUD

Along with cash loss noted earlier, bad check and credit card losses can cause an almost immediate financial drain on a business. The 2001 NRSS report notes that retailers reported check losses for that year totaling .08% of annual sales (see Figure 14.1). Cash loss was listed second with a total of .07% of annual sales. The least serious financial loss was credit card chargebacks, which accounted to .014% of annual sales.[2]

It has been determined that 90% of business volume in the United States is accomplished by checks. In addition, more than half of all retail transactions is conducted with credit cards. The potential for loss is so great due to the misuse of checks and credit cards that it presents a serious problem to any business. Other than to stop accepting payment in the form of checks or credit cards, and in order to reduce losses in this area as much as possible and still maintain a profitable business, the retailer must establish a business policy controlling these types of transactions for payment.

It is a crime to utter a check or to unlawfully possess or use a credit card or debit card with criminal intent. Note that in addition to a bad check or fraudulent use of a credit card or debit card that is used to gain money or property illegally, the crime of larceny has also been committed. Also, if a service has been purchased with a bad check or the fraudulent use of a credit card/debit card, the additional crime would be "theft of services."

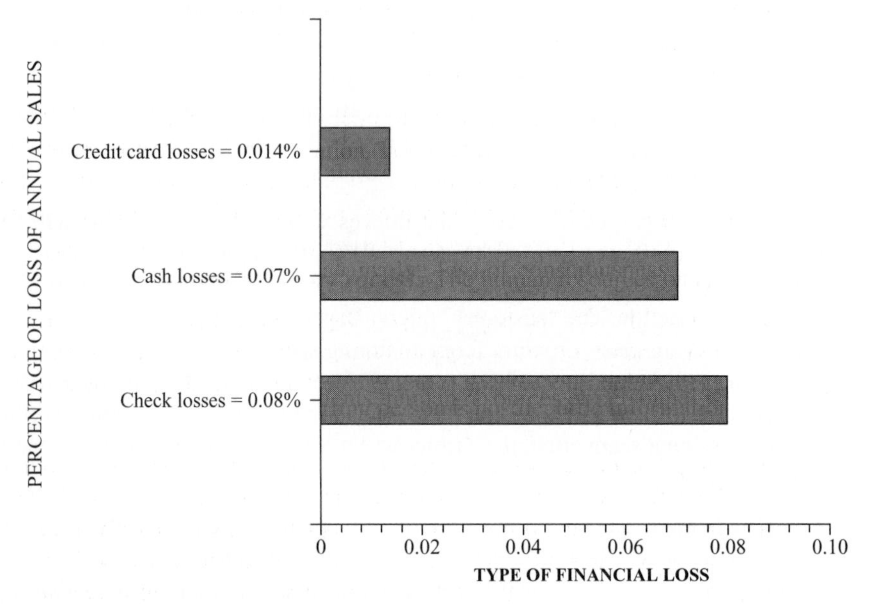

Figure 14-1 Check/cash/credit card losses.

Because most business transactions of some consequence are made by check or credit card, security officers should be well aware of their state laws concerning the issuance of fraudulent checks and the unlawful possession and use of credit cards and debit cards.

Bad Checks

Checks are cashed as a convenience to customers and to encourage new or continued patronage. Therefore, the laxity on the part of the merchant combined with a desire to increase sales volume has caused the incidents of check fraud to increase as it is today. For every merchant who follows strict check-cashing procedures, there are many others who will accept a check without any or few controls whatsoever.

Not all "bad checks" are issued with criminal intent. A check written by a person believing that there is enough money in the account to cover the check, and the check is returned to the retailer as overdrawn, commits no crime. "Floating" or writing a check in hopes or with the intent that funds will be available by the time the retailer deposits it in the bank and it clears, but is returned also for insufficient funds, falls into a gray area and may be hard to prove any criminal intent. These occurrences are not uncommon, and are usually corrected with a phone call to the check-writer and a redeposit of the check. Use care on all bad checks, because the nature of the incident may not be what it seems. For example, a joint account held by a married couple may be overdrawn by one without the knowledge of the other. Also, in a divorce or estranged situation, one may attempt to hurt the other by writing many checks or closing the account. If the retailer cannot recover the loss from the issuer, whatever the problem, civil action may have to be contemplated. Not wishing to proceed in that manner, there are private agencies that will attempt to recover restitution for a fee, usually for a percentage of the amount of the check. See also the section on CIVIL RECOVERY later in this chapter.

However, there is criminal intent in the following instances, and once it is determined as such, the police should be notified.

1. When a check is drawn on an account that the issuer knows will have insufficient funds to cover that check. This is hard to prove unless the bank has advised the account holder in writing that any checks that have been drafted or forthcoming cannot be honored because of insufficient funds. This is a common practice for banks to so advise their account holders, and once a check is written after the issuer has knowledge of this fact, he or she does in fact commit a crime.
2. When a check is returned to the retailer as "account closed," a crime may have in fact been committed if the check was issued after the account holder closed the account himself, or had been notified by the bank that they are closing the account.

Security officers, cash office managers, and cashiers should give special attention when cashing checks after banking hours. Customers cashing checks for large amounts during weekends or after normal banking hours know that the merchant cannot check the bank account for validation. Favorite times for a bad check writer are Friday evenings, Saturday, and Sunday. On questionable checks, procedures may include criss-cross directories, phone listings, and national driver's license directories.

Therefore, a crime has been committed when the issuer of the check has the following knowledge:

- The check the person utters is fraudulent, *and*
- The person intends or believes at the time of utterance that payment will be refused by the bank upon presentation, *or*
- Has knowledge that the checking account has been closed, *or*
- Passes a check knowing that the drawer (the person who has written the check) of the check does not have sufficient funds with the bank to cover it, *and*
- The person believes at the time the check is passed that payment will in fact not be honored by the bank upon presentation.

Check Procedure. Bad check loss is caused because of a lack of adequate check-cashing procedures. These poor procedures will include the following:

- Failure to examine every check
- Failure to record certain information on the check
- Indiscriminate cashing of checks
- Fear that the sale will be lost unless checks are cashed without undue complications
- Inadequate identification of the person cashing the check

Because most of the scams and fraud attempts will be made at the point of sale, the following basic rules should be applied and enforced:

- If possible, the cashing of all checks should be approved by a designated person before completion of the transaction.
- Do not accept a check without two proper forms of identification. This should include a photo ID and a credit card in the same name as the imprinted check.
- Always verify the signatures on the offered identification against the signature on the check. If there is some doubt in the validity, do not accept the check.
- Do not accept a check that already has a signature. Have the customer sign the check in your presence.
- Do not accept a check written for an amount larger than the purchase.
- Do not accept out-of-state checks unless the retailer wishes to take great risk. The police will not follow up on a bad check case out of state for extradition unless it is a felony. Use caution on out-of-area checks.
- Do not accept starter checks (check numbers below 200 or so), or checks that are not imprinted with the name and address of the person involved in the transaction.
- Do not accept third-party checks.
- Do not accept post-dated or past-dated checks.
- Do not accept payroll checks, particularly government checks, without proper identification.
- Do not accept certified or cashier's checks without proper identification.

- Do not accept a check with any handwritten alteration or any alteration in the magnetic numbers on the check.
- Do not be misled if the passer waves to someone, particularly another employee, and offers the "I'm an old customer" routine, or is a big name dropper.
- If the retailer subscribes to a check-cashing verification service, strict compliance with the required procedures must be made to ensure that there will be no loss to the retailer.

Credit Card Fraud

The use of credit cards is becoming the number one means of purchasing power. Consumers are carrying and using credit cards for the convenience and in order to reduce the amount of hard currency they have to carry. Like checks, the merchant must accept credit cards to compete for the customer's business.

In the past, credit card companies and banks mailed out cancellation bulletins on a routine basis noting card cancellations and/or fraudulent card numbers. This program was found to be time-consuming and replete with problems. This program is not popular at this time because credit card companies offer toll-free numbers for a business to call or an electronic swipe of the card for an authorization number. Refusal of an authorization on the transaction may be for an over limit charge, the card has expired or been canceled, numbers appear to be fraudulent, or is not valid for some reason or another.

Federal law mandates that the Secret Service will investigate all financial crimes associated with financial institutions. This includes bank fraud, telecommunication and computer crimes, fraudulent identification, *and credit card and debit card fraud* among others.[3]

Credit Cards Procedure

- Do not accept a credit card that does not contain a signature of the person named on the card.
- Make sure that the signature on the sales receipt is the same as on the card. If there is any doubt, do not accept.
- Do not accept a card for use from one who is not named on the card.
- Do not accept any card that appears to be over-embossed with other numbers or another name.
- Make sure that all the key points that the bank or credit card issuer requires to be checked are completed (expiration date, holograph logo, card numbers, etc.).
- On any sales transaction over a particular amount set by the credit card issuer (usually $50.00), make sure an authorization number/code is provided.
- Prior to the completion of the transaction, if the card is not stolen or canceled and the sale is within the customer's credit limit, an authorization code will be given and the transaction may be completed.
- A bank or a credit card issuer has certain contractual agreements with the retailer as to how a credit card is to be used and offered to consummate a sale. If credit authorization of the sale is refused and the credit card issuer requests that the retailer confiscate the card for whatever reason, the retailer is obligated

under his or her contract to take possession of that card. However, this type of policy usually causes a confrontation. The customer may become argumentative and refuse to give up the card by retaking possession forcefully.

Rather than become involved in an altercation or further confrontation, the cashier or salesperson should request another form of payment to complete the transaction.

Check and Credit Card Identification Procedures

Considering that false identification is the major factor contributing to the losses suffered by retailers resulting from checks and credit cards, the following procedures are generally accepted concerning types of identification.

Acceptable ID

- A valid driver's license with photo of the subject issued by the state in which the retailer is located.
- A valid passport or armed forces/military identification.
- A valid and signed credit card issued by a bank, credit union, or organization offered for that particular sale.
- National retail business credit cards.
- Employee identification cards issued by valid and reputable companies with a photo/signature of the subject.

Unacceptable ID

- Social security cards.
- Gasoline company credit cards.
- Library membership or school identification cards.
- Membership cards issued by assorted fraternal, local, and national social or business associations.

Some Accepted Rules and Procedures for Acceptance. With reference to checks, there are several other ways and procedures that a retailer can use to enhance existing identification techniques. Depending on the type of business and the losses suffered by that business, the extent that the retailer wishes to decrease losses would rest on the costs of these augmented systems. These could include camera systems that photograph the subject along with the ID offered. The film is processed when a check is returned as bad. Another is an individual identification card issued by the retailer to preferred customers. There is also a dry thumbprint system as an aid in identifying serious bad check writers, but this system is out of date, and it is unknown if this procedure is in use at this time by any retailer.

Currently the most popular system is a computerized check verification service that the retailer subscribes to for a fee. This type of system is not a collection agency. It is a "check-alert" type company that will verify the check by examination of the magnetized bank account numbers on the check and the amount of the check online against their database. This service coordinates efforts among all retailers regarding the assemblage of as much information as possible on bad check writers, in order to apprehend and arrest via documentation. If a question arises, the cashier may have to communicate via telephone for further verification. If all is correct, an authorization number will be provided via the computerized register or by voice. The check is now covered for loss by the check-verifying company as long as the required procedures of identification of the subject and the check are completed. These firms also provide an immediate warning system in advising retailers who subscribe to their service of professional bad check writers, submission of stolen money orders, and present geographical areas of operations by these suspects. The cost to the retailer for this service and protection can be little or extensive depending on how often and the number of checks the retailer wishes to verify. To cut costs, the retailer might only request a verification of checks in excess of $50.00 or $100.00. If a bad check is received up to the amount set by the retailer, the loss won't be as serious as it might be if the amount of the check was greater than the set limit. If the check is bad and over the limit that the retailer is contracted for, the check-verifying company takes the loss. Essentially, it is similar to the credit card verification system in which an authorization number is given, except that the issuer of the credit card covers the full value of the credit voucher.

Keep in mind that police departments are not collection agencies, and will pursue a bad check writer only if there is a crime and the retailer is willing to take the necessary action to have the perpetrator arrested and prosecuted. It is not unusual for a bad check artist to suddenly come up with the money and pay the retailer once the check writer is aware that the police are involved. Some police departments will assist the retailer in collecting on a bad check, but this is not common. This is because if the police do collections then the retail employees will become sloppy and lax in following good business practices when it comes to accepting checks. Additionally, the retailer may believe that a crime has been committed, when in fact the police may refer the retailer to civil court for restitution if the facts do not support a *prima facie* case. If a credit card has been accepted without an authorization code or is in fact listed on the register of those cards not to be accepted and was accepted, the retailer will suffer the loss as a "charge back" to their account with that issuer. But if the retailer protected himself by following all of the required key points, the card issuer suffers the loss and they will conduct their own investigation.

If it happens that the retailer does not subscribe to a check authorization service or may suffer a loss not protected by that service, the retailer may wish to recover the loss on his own. One way to attempt recovery on a bad check is for the retailer to contract the services of a collection agency, who will charge a fee from a part of whatever recovery was made by them. However, the loss prevention manager may attempt the same type of recovery through the loss prevention department, if permitted, thereby saving contractual fees for the retailer. If applicable, the manager may wish to research state law for the details concerning "demand for payment of a dishonored check."

Remember that this procedure is for checks that the bank has returned for account closed or insufficient funds on deposit. Also consider that this action should be used only for those customers who issue a check in good faith and not with criminal intent. This is even if they may know or should know that payment of such check will be refused by the bank because of insufficient funds, which cannot be proven.

The above are generally accepted rules for check and credit card acceptance, and depending on the type of retail business that the security officer may be employed, the procedures put in operation may be more or less stringent than those offered here.

For training and identification purposes, the loss prevention department should contact the retailer's bank for information and training guides available to their banking customers on how and what to do on accepting a check. Moreover, all major credit card companies offer the same services, even to the assignment of a representative responding to a short training session for a large group of employees.

Restrictions. The security officer should also be cognizant of the various federal and state laws that a retailer may be required to follow concerning the use of checks and credit cards for the payment of goods and services.

- Some states mandate certain restrictions concerning the recording of personal identification such as the customer's address and telephone number on the credit card transaction form unless such information is required for shipping or delivery purposes.
- The prohibition of a credit card number recorded on the back of a check as a means of identification or some proof of credit-worthiness.
- The prohibition of a demand that a customer present or record the Social Security number for identification and/or as a condition for accepting a check, Traveler's check, gift certificate, money order, or other negotiable instrument in payment for a sales transaction.

CIVIL RECOVERY

Although rarely enforced, the loss prevention manager does have the ability to seek some form of compensation and reparation for a larceny committed on the premises, where he is unable to make a recovery, or unable to sell recovered merchandise because of damage or otherwise. Because of the time and resources involved in such recovery, loss prevention may look to other ways of attempting to make some recovery. Laws about civil recovery are on the books in most of the states, and there are many companies and commercial enterprises that specialize in this type recovery. For a fee based upon the recovery made, they will perform all contacts with the perpetrator, with their actions similar to a collection agency, along with the threat of possible civil action. If recovery is not made, the retailer has the option of pursuing that legal civil action.

Also known as "civil demand," this little known legal process gives the retailer the opportunity to recover all or part of any loss that may have occurred during a larceny. Depending on the state, the law may include an emancipated minor along with an adult who commits a larceny against the property of a retail establishment and will be considered civilly liable. As may be defined in state law, an emancipated minor is a person who is over the age of sixteen at the time of the alleged larceny and was no longer a dependent or in the custody of a parent or legal guardian. The parents or legal guardians of an unemancipated minor shall be civilly liable for said minor who commits a larceny against the property of a retail establishment. These laws usually cover all larceny as defined in the law, and includes not only the theft of property by shoplifting, but also the taking of property by bad check, trick, embezzlement, under false pretenses, etc.

Further, a conviction or plea of guilty at a criminal action does not forego the ability of the retailer to bring a civil suit against the perpetrator, obtain a judgment and collect on that judgment, and does not prohibit or limit the retailer from any other cause of action.

Because recovery is one measurement of a loss prevention department's success, the loss prevention manager may wish to exercise the ability to use this law to the retailer's benefit.

COUNTERFEIT CURRENCY

All retailers face the probability of receiving counterfeit money in return for a purchase. This is particularly so for the large retailer because of the large amount of customers served specifically during sales periods when large crowds gather. There are training guides offered by the United States Secret Service for all businesses. Check the local telephone book for the closest office near your business.

The generally accepted procedure when a customer offers a counterfeit bill is as follows:

- If the bill examined by the cashier is believed to be a counterfeit, the cashier should request a security officer or a cash office manager/supervisor to verify that the bill is in fact bogus.
- If the money offered is counterfeit, retain the bill and advise the customer that the currency is apparently a counterfeit and it will be turned over to the Secret Service as required by law. Do not accept this bill for the purchase.
- Loss prevention or the cash office should have an in-house receipt form that can be given to customer for tax purposes and to identify the subject if the bill is returned by the Secret Service as bona fide. Have the customer produce identification if possible and note it on the receipt. Keep a copy of this receipt and attach it to your incident report.
- A company or in-house form should be compiled and submitted along with the suspected bill to the local Secret Service office or as directed by them. The form sent to the Secret Service along with the suspected bill and customer's receipt copy should contain enough information for the agency to correlate data on suspects, trends, and other statistics. See the Appendix for sample copy of this form. If the suspected currency sent to the Secret Service is found to be valid, it will be returned to the retailer so that the customer can be reimbursed. An incident report should be compiled and copies of the bill and the form sent to the Secret Service, along with the original customer's receipt (if any), should be attached to and made part of the incident report.

If the retailer has no system regarding counterfeit money identified at the point of sale, he may require that his security officers *not* take possession of the money and request that another bill is offered for payment. The problem is that the retailer is required by law to take possession of counterfeit money, or the bogus bill will remain in circulation. If the bogus bill is confiscated and not turned over to the Secret Service (generally police departments do not wish to become involved and will advise that the Secret Service be notified), it may be turned over to the retailer's bank along with the regular deposit, noting such currency to be apparently counterfeit. This procedure presents an uncertainty because when the bank turns all counterfeit money over to the Federal Reserve, it sacrifices all possibility of the Secret Service ascertaining trends and geographical areas where bad money is being offered.

It is understandable that a customer will balk at the suggestion that the bill will be confiscated, particularly if the bill is of a large denomination. It is not uncommon that the customer will say "I just got it from the bank" or "I just got it from an ATM machine. If the bank says it's good, why should I be penalized?" The cash room manager or security officer can advise the customer that the police can be called to the scene for determination. If the police are called, they will usually agree with the retailer because most police officers are not experts and defer to people who handle money routinely as having more expertise than they may have. The police will advise the customer that federal law requires all counterfeit money to be confiscated and turned over to the Secret Service.

However, prior to the presence of the police, a customer, once advised that the bill is counterfeit and will be confiscated, may grab the bill from the cashier's hand retaking custody, and hand over another bill to pay for the purchase. It is suggested that the cashier, manager, or the security officer, if involved, not become entangled in an altercation attempting to regain custody of the suspected bill. Accept the second bill in return and complete the transaction.

If the "customer" is in fact a person who has knowledge that the currency he is attempting to pass is bogus, he will not usually cause any argument, disturbance, or problem of any kind. If this "customer" can't immediately grab back the currency and leave, he will not produce any ID and/or will most likely provide false information so as not to cause any further suspicion. Or he may leave with some excuse before the arrival of a security officer and disappear into the street.

CONTRACTOR AND VENDER LARCENY

Although not considered as serious a loss as other forms of shrinkage, there are two other types of larceny that still have an effect on the bottom line of a business. In both areas, the larceny is usually by surreptitious means, particularly due to the fact that the offender has been given license and privilege to be on board and their activities usually go unnoticed.

Venders who are allowed to be present and stock shelves and cabinets present a workforce savings to the retailer, and as time passes they are generally accepted without much recognition or observation. Contractors who come on board to service equipment and machinery on a routine basis also are generally accepted as part of the normal workforce of the business. Particular notice should be given to those contractors who are present for major renovations or restorations. With their large toolboxes and lunch pails, they have the ability to secrete even the larger items that they wish to steal. However, the customary objects that are stolen usually are small and high end.

Other than routine observation by loss prevention personnel and CCTV, one way to at least keep losses under some control would be for security officers at irregular intervals to inspect vender's cartons or containers as they leave. Moreover, one of the more specific methods in the control of contractor larceny would be to place a provision in the written work contract that the contractor and/or contracted employees are restricted to a certain work area, are subject to visual inspection of any packages or lunch pails upon leaving the work site for any reason, and the wearing of visitor's (contractor) badges while on-site.

SIDEWALK DELIVERY

In this type of larceny scam, the perpetrators purchase a large amount of and/or expensive merchandise and request that it is to be delivered on the sidewalk "in front of 123 Main Street." The merchandise has been prepaid by a bad check or stolen credit card. The excuse that may be given is that they want as little damage to the merchandise as possible, so their "building super" will meet them at the curb and sign for the merchandise. Once the drop is made and signed for, the "super" and "helpers" will bring the merchandise up to the "customer's apartment."

Under no circumstances should truck delivery personnel make what is known as a "sidewalk drop." The "super" and friends will load the merchandise onto another truck as soon as the first truck leaves. Your company trucker must deliver to an exact address and apartment number, with the occupant signing for the merchandise. If the building, apartment, or the people accepting the merchandise are suspicious to the trucker, he or she should inquire further before delivery.

ENDNOTES

1. Training Bulletin, *Introduction to Anti-Robbery Training*, United States Department of the Air Force, originally issued by Headquarters 5th Support Group (ACC) (no date).
2. Op. cit., *2001 National Retail Security Survey—Final Report*, p. 6. Figure 14.1 graph reprinted with permission.
3. *Title 15 USC Chapter 41, §1644*—Fraudulent Use of a Credit Card.

Chapter 15

Loss Prevention and Control

Tactics and Procedures

There are many ways in which a loss prevention department can control or prevent shrinkage to a great extent. Depending on the facility to be protected, many or most of the following methods can be used in varying degrees.

LOSS CONTROL PROCEDURES

The Hiring Process

Although the process of the hiring and investigation of an applicant is a function of the human resources or personnel department, loss prevention should be involved in some of the following processes. This is particularly so when the subject being hired is to be placed in a management level position, being given a sensitive assignment, or when money and/or credit card transactions will be part or all of that person's duties of employment. The screening of employees during the hiring process may be considered one of the most important procedures that a company can practice in spotting a high-risk employee.

The human resources department should require that all newly hired employees receive a written statement of key policies, procedures, and required conduct, and that they acknowledge such receipt by their signature. Giving these new employees the written rules they are to follow, and the risks and consequences that will be taken if improper or dishonest behavior is discovered is a step in the right direction if they should ever have doubts of how to act or if they find themselves in a compromising position. As part of the hiring process, loss prevention should explain to the new hires why employee theft could generate problems for the retailer, and all of the managers and coworkers in the department under suspicion. Detail how managers begin to distrust everyone, innocent coworkers may be implicated, tighter internal controls or procedures are initiated, the manager may lose his or her job or position, and all of the employees within the department may be terminated or transferred under a cloud of suspicion. It should be made easy for employees to come forward and report a theft, a suspicion or their concerns regarding not only security, but also safety. Give them the opportunity to report this information in various ways. Generally, most employees detest the thief who causes the most reaction from management or poor performance where the workload falls on others. The opportunity to address these concerns can be very helpful to management, but employees are fearful of being known or branded a "rat" or "snitch." Anonymous information concerning security and safety can be offered by telephone voice mail to the loss prevention manager (the "hot line"), by electronic mail, by written communication, or in person. In any event, anonymity must be freely given and unknown to others in the workforce; the promise to provide such secrecy must be offered and the informant's identity concealed without fail.

There are several ways that employee theft can be kept in check or at least reduced. Initially, it would be the screening of job applicants during the hiring process. This would include the background check of past employment and verification of education, training, and service elsewhere. With some positions that are more sensitive such as security or loss prevention officers, employees who handle money (cashiers, cash office clerks), employees who handle credit sales, returns and refunds for instance, they must have a more in-depth background investigation. This would include the Department of Motor Vehicles, criminal history checks (local and areas of prior residence), credit checks for good or bad history, and detailed personal interviews of friends, named references, and past employers. Although it is the function of the human resources department of a medium or large company to initiate and conduct the hiring process, the employer should have the loss prevention department involved in the investigation process of those sensitive positions noted above. Association with and making use of local merchants, protective associations, or consumer reporting agencies can be very important in this process because they may maintain records of past employee terminations and/or arrests for theft throughout the industry. These associations are also useful in determining credit history and a record of shoplifters apprehended and/or arrested in other member stores.

Caution must be used, however, concerning business practices and investigations that could negatively affect an applicant for hire. Of concern is the Federal Fair Credit Reporting Act, which was amended in 1996 and retitled *The Consumer Credit Reporting Reform Act.*[1] The revised statute now assures greater privacy protection to the consumer regarding the ability to obtain insurance, credit, or employment. In regards to the hiring process, this act notes certain conditions that must be followed:

1. Before requesting any report relating to evaluation of employment, an authorization request in writing must be obtained from the applicant on a separate sheet of paper and not part of an employment application that the applicant may be required to complete.
2. If a negative report is received and such a report is used wholly or partially in denying employment, a copy of this report must be given to the applicant along with a statement of his or her rights as noted in the statute.
3. Before an employer may use a consumer reporting agency, he or she must certify in writing that he or she has read and understands the obligations under the law and will comply with all requirements as defined.

The security officer must be aware that verification and/or interviews with past employers and references will bring comments that may be subjective in nature. Named references will naturally be those persons that the applicant is certain will give positive remarks on the applicant's background. Past employers or supervisors are reluctant to put pertinent or derogatory information in writing. On the other hand, they may give or lend suspicious hints about the subject in question if that person is not thought well of. If the question of "Would you hire this person again if you had the chance" is passed over lightly, not answered, or dodged in some manner, then you've got your answer. Many will refuse to give any information on the telephone, advising that any inquiry be made on company letterhead. Even then, the information sought after will be minimal, and again subjective, rather than that company place themselves in possible civil liability.

Integrity Screening. The general consensus by human resource management of resumes received from applicants is that a great portion of these "life stories" are false or at least greatly exaggerated, and should be viewed with some concern. It has been said that job applications and resumes contain many embellishment and falsehoods. Therefore, the hiring process should include the following, with such application and attention as may be necessary depending on the position sought by the applicant:

- Past employment verification
- Criminal history checks
- Credit and financial history
- Personal reference checks
- Multiple interviews
- Education, training, and certification verification
- Motor vehicle accident and violations history, as required

Once the subject is hired and becomes part of the company establishment, it is up to the employee's immediate supervisor and/or the department manager to monitor that employee's conduct, particularly so during the probationary period. Along with that, the security officer should constantly be aware of the conduct of all employees, particularly new hires.

Awareness and Training

As we shall see, the first line of defense in reducing losses is the employee and how well that employee reacts to a given circumstance.

It must be the policy of the company to mandate security and safety training for all employees on a routine and timely basis, and such training should fall under the control and direction of the loss prevention department.

The loss prevention manager should be involved in the initial training or orientation class of new hires. This gives the manager the opportunity to meet all new coworkers and to stress the importance of security and safety in the store. The manager should discuss the basic role of loss prevention in the store, the makeup of the department, and the company's policy of investigation, apprehension, and prosecution of shoplifters and dishonest employees. Included should be the discussion on the scope of the security operation and the nature of the business that is protected. The loss prevention manager should stress the accountability and professionalism of the department, its operation and its members, and the need to have the cooperation of each coworker in order to fulfill these responsibilities.

Training is one of the most important responsibilities that a loss prevention department can render in the reduction of losses, whether security or safety in nature.

Loss Prevention Training and Awareness Programs. All or at least many of the following curriculums, programs, and/or strategies should be part of the employee's training and awareness of loss and its prevention, and how it affects the employee, the company, and the customer.

- ***Orientation:*** The initial training and instruction for the new hire.
- ***Rules and regulations:*** The policy and procedure that provides the controls over employees regarding their actions and conduct.
- ***Training and lectures:*** Routine and ongoing in all areas of security and safety. These should include certain personnel who require specific training because of their functions and/or tasks (cashiers, check, credit card and money handlers, etc.).
- ***Bulletin board posters and notices:*** Timely and appropriate notices where employees routinely congregate (time clock, lunchroom).
- ***Company newsletters:*** Articles that pertain to security and safety.
- ***Anonymous telephone hotline:*** For those employees who wish to report company infractions or more serious offenses, but still are inclined to remain anonymous. The telephone extension number must be widely distributed at all training sessions and in all writings.
- ***Honest incentives:*** Cash rewards for those employees whose information leads to an apprehension and/or recovery of assets. Depending on the program in place, the informant may remain anonymous or not.
- ***Routine security and safety inspections and audits:*** These are conducted by loss prevention personnel.
- ***Employee surveys:*** Regarding security and safety with monetary and/or meritorious recognition. This type of information may also be brought to the attention of company management from members of the safety committee at their monthly meetings.

Asset Control

Policy and Procedures. The following areas of concern within the retail establishment require some type of procedures in an attempt to supervise and control intentional and unintentional losses. Moreover, the loss prevention officer must routinely audit and inspect these areas so that both the employee and the customer become acutely aware of the company's commitment to any irregularity. Customarily, procedural controls should be put in writing. Once the procedure is in writing, accepted and placed into effect by the company, it is considered policy.

Primary procedural constraints should include the following:

- Returns and refund controls—cash and credit card procedures and controls
- Credit card and check procedures and controls at point-of-sale (POS)

- Point-of-Sale (POS) Exception Reports
- Point-of-Sale (POS) Bar Coding and Scanning
- Price change and markdown procedures and controls
- Void and register controls
- Access to cash offices or cash handling areas—procedures and controls
- Customer "holds" or layaway areas—procedures and controls
- Stock control/inventory (data entry), bar coding and scanning
- Mini-inventories—daily by department or section
- Use of EAS tags and other monitoring devices
- Unobserved exit controls—use of 24-hour annunciation
- Employee/vender/contractor/visitor package checks
- Property removal procedures for employees
- Trash removal and dumping controls and procedures
- Merchandise receiving and shipping procedures and controls
- Transfers between stores and/or warehouses procedures and controls

The loss prevention department should inspect and audit the above sectors of concern on a routine basis in order to determine that all activities conform to procedures and controls. Written procedures and/or documentation of most of the inspections described above must be compiled and maintained.

INTERNAL AND EXTERNAL THEFT CONTROL

The following suggestions concerning the control of internal and external theft, which have been gathered by the author and retail security professionals, are well-founded methods to address the problem of retail theft. Depending on the type and size of the retail establishment, some or all can be put to good use.

Loss Prevention Systems and Security Personnel

The systems described below have proved worthy in the prevention of theft, but are only as dependable as the personnel who install, maintain, and govern their use:

- Burglary and silent alarm systems
- Closed circuit TV (CCTV)—visible and hidden cameras
- Security guards—uniformed (fixed posts or not)
- Security officers—plainclothes
- Point-of-sale exception based CCTV interface
- Credit card and check controls—training and via database scanning or telecommunications
- Armored car pickups and deliveries
- Drop safes and/or timed entry safes

- EAS tags and merchandise alarms
- Cables, chains, and locks
- Secured displays, cases, and fixtures
- Deterrent signage—shoplifters and employees
- Observation booths or coops
- Routine auditing procedures by management and loss prevention personnel

Employees

1. Employees are not to write up, ring up, or wrap their own purchases.
2. Limit the number of employees or cash registers authorized to ring up other employee's sales, thereby reducing the possibility of collusion.
3. Do not allow any employee to wear or use any merchandise not purchased or written off.
4. Do not, under any circumstance, allow another employee to use an ID card or card-key of another employee.
5. Dishonest employees have been known to slightly damage, rip, or break an item so that they are able to purchase the item at a reduced cost for themselves. Be aware of the possibility that an employee in one department may be in collusion with another coworker elsewhere in the store. This could include dented canned goods to a slight tear in an expensive oriental rug. Use care in your policy concerning employees purchasing damaged goods at greatly reduced or discounted prices.
6. In large retail establishments, all returns for refunds or exchanges by customers should be made at a single location where only one group of employees can control and become aware of various scams. Never allow the employee who made the original sale to also conduct the refund. The "customer" and the employee may be involved in a larcenous situation. This "returns" area also requires written procedures regarding the various circumstances or conditions for a return, including the public posting of the company's refund policy so that the customer is aware of how and when a return, exchange, or refund may be made. The security officer should check with those laws enacted in his state regarding the disclosure of refund policies and/or the required public postings of these policies.
7. Routine questionnaires sent via U.S. mail on the pretense of an inquiry into "customer service" would in fact be one way of determining if any refunds are fraudulent.
8. Set up control procedures at merchandise handout or pickup counters, so those employees cannot hand out unpaid merchandise to friends or relatives.
9. Use care regarding the authority placed in an employee who has the ability to price merchandise. Include and limit those employees who have the ability to use markdown pens, price machines, and sales tickets used for clearance or "as-is" merchandise. Also, smaller or handheld merchandise should be priced with a machine-imprinted sticker, and never handwritten.

10. It should be company policy that loss prevention has the ability and right to inspect all employees' packages, bags, backpacks, briefcases, and lunch boxes upon leaving the store. For purposes of control, all employees should enter and leave through only one door usually called the staff entrance, which should be separate from customers' entrances and exits. If the staff entrance or exit is covered by a security officer, who may also have receptionist or access control duties, bag inspection should be ongoing for all employees leaving the building.
11. There is some debate over whether a woman's handbag may be inspected under these conditions. Check with the store's attorney regarding establishing company policy in this area if it hasn't already been addressed. However, other than an ongoing bag inspection as noted above, if an unannounced inspection is being held at a particular time period, all employees should face the inspection. No one employee should be singled out for a bag inspection unless there is probable cause of a crime being committed and a stop is made for that purpose.
12. Prohibit all lunch boxes, knapsacks, backpacks, or briefcases into the retail workplace. Unless a bag inspection is conducted on a daily basis, the possibility of stolen items leaving in this manner is high. Most large retail establishments have locker rooms for the staff. If not, some type of procedure should be set up. Women's pocketbooks should also be left in a locker, allowing only a small purse to be carried into the work area. If the female employee must carry personal items in a bag larger than a purse, clear plastic bags should be available for use in the store.
13. Regarding bookkeepers or other administration personnel:
    - **a.** Purchase orders should be numbered consecutively in a logbook noting the purchase order number, date of issue, authorization, person issuing, vender, approximate price, and accounting code.
    - **b.** Unless it is a small business or a small retail chain store, money handling and recordkeeping must be separate functions by different employees with audits performed routinely and frequently.
    - **c.** Blank checks should be safely secured from unauthorized access. The checks must be sequentially numbered with an accounting code assigned when it is issued.
    - **d.** Blank checks must never be pre-signed.
    - **e.** Proper and acceptable accounting and bookkeeping procedures must be adhered to.
14. In-house financing for sales of merchandise to employees should have strict controls, with appropriate safeguards if the employee fails to pay, leaves the company, or is terminated. Ideally, routine deductions should be taken from the employee's paycheck. The payroll department, human resources/personnel department, and/or accounts receivable should control and record payroll deduction for purchases.
15. Conduct unexpected audits of all procedures set up to ensure that such company procedures and policy are being carried out as required. Security officers should make their rounds of the interior and exterior of the store on a consistent but irregular manner. This should include all areas of the store, including machinery and mechanical rooms, closets, storage rooms, and warehousing.

This performance by security personnel is not only for the purpose of routine safety and security inspections, but also so that all coworkers observe security's presence throughout the store.

16. Instruct both salespersons and cashiers on the profile and actions of a shoplifter, checks and credit card fraud, and the required procedures.
17. When assisting a customer who is viewing small expensive merchandise at a counter, the salesperson should display only a few items at a time—ideally no more than three items is an acceptable number for control. Also have salespeople arrange displays in a definite pattern, so that if one item is removed, it will become obvious.

Cashiers and Cash Rooms

1. Cashiers must have access to one cash drawer only during their daily workday. No one else should have access to this drawer, including managers or supervisors. During breaks and meal periods, the drawer should be secured in some manner until the return of the cashier. This could be accomplished by dropping off a locked cash drawer in the cash office, or locking up the drawer with the register until the cashier returns. With one cash drawer assigned to only one person who can be held responsible, there will be a true and easier accounting of overages and shortages upon reconciliation.
2. Be alert for all over-rings or voids. A procedure should be placed in effect where on any incident of this type, the cashier must immediately contact the cash office manager or head cashier for confirmation and authorization before continuing with the transaction. All sales shall be rung up and recorded with a sales receipt given to the customer. Upon completion of the cashier's workday, a complete register tally tape and the cash drawer should be deposited in the cash office, along with a true and complete count of all money contained in the drawer. Subsequently, the reconciliation clerk will compare the cash contents of the drawer (and any prior register drains), and any checks and credit card vouchers, against the register tally tape. If there is a discrepancy, certain procedures must be followed. Written policy concerning the parameters of loss and punishment should be made aware to all cashiers upon employment with the company. This policy should be strictly enforced.
3. Maintain a zero-tolerance policy concerning a short register count of cash, and check or credit card voucher loss. Management should set procedures for written warnings or termination concerning minimum and maximum dollar amounts. As to cashier and cash room policy, any cashier who is continually short or over within a set amount allowed ($5.00 as an example) will require retraining or termination. Unless a larceny is at issue, parameters should include a written warning for the first two occurrences. The third occurrence over $5.00 within a particular period of time should be termination. However, any incident in which there is a loss over $100.00 should be cause for immediate termination unless the circumstances are extraordinary. Written warnings by supervisors should be maintained and made part of the employees' personnel record, with each occurrence investigated by the cashier's manager and the loss prevention department as noted below. This policy should be enforced to the letter so that all employees are aware that they must strictly comply with all

procedures concerning the handling of money, and that they will be held accountable.

4. Loss prevention should review and investigate all cash overages or shortages over $5.00 on a daily basis. The review of daily exception reports, including voids, overrings, no sales and refunds for that cashier should be made part of that investigation.
5. In order to reduce the activity of employees approaching one particular cashier who may or is processing "sweetheart" purchases, all employee purchases should be conducted at one specific or centralized register with assigned cashiers rotated daily. If any illegal activity is noted, closer observation can be had at this one location.
6. Never allow a cashier to leave the cash drawer open and turn his or her attention away. The cashier must close the drawer after each transaction, and before another task.
7. Cashiers should be cautioned and trained in the acceptance of money orders. Because many are lost and stolen, acceptance can become a poor risk. As long as correct procedures are followed as dictated by the issuing institution, the retailer is covered for loss.
8. If the retailer makes use of banks of cash register lanes, close and block off those unused cash lanes in an effort to curtail egress (within fire evacuation guidelines for safety).
9. Routinely, the retailer might wish to make use of professional shoppers to make purchases in order to determine that proper cashier procedures are followed. Honesty shoppers should be employed to routinely test the integrity of employees.
10. Cash offices or cash rooms should be separate and secure from all other activity within the store, including customers and employees. Ideally, there should be an outer and inner door with an air lock between, and covered outside each door by CCTV. Entry through each of these doors into the cash room should be activated by an electric-operated locking system. The cash room personnel must be able to monitor each camera before permitting entry through each door. Holdup alarms should be placed strategically within the cash room and possibly the air lock. A certain hand signal may be used by a cashier or other authorized employee indicating that that employee is not under coercion and it is okay to pass through.
11. Cash offices or cash rooms that contain a secured safe should set procedures in regard to what size of a "bank" each cash register drawer should contain when first issued to a cashier. Larger retail establishments may wish to have a substantial "bank" on board for each register and in the safe for making change. For instance, a store with $250,000.00 in gross sales daily and managing ten to fifteen cash registers might wish to maintain approximately $25,000.00 in the safe overnight. In this way, each cash drawer can be allotted $1,500.00 with the balance in reserve for making change.
12. Safe combinations should be available to only those managers and/or employees who are exceptionally responsible, and it is a part of their job to control or have access to the interior of a safe. Once any employee who has knowledge of a safe combination leaves employment for any reason, it should be a routine

procedure to have the combination changed. In any event, safe combinations should be changed routinely, at least once a year. The loss prevention manager should have all safe combinations contained in a sealed envelope, with this envelope safely secured. In case of an emergency where entry into a safe is warranted, loss prevention personnel must have the ability to break open the sealed envelope for the safe combination. Such an emergency could be where the safe must be opened for business, but because of absence for whatever reason, the authorized person/s who know the combination are not present. The security officer who tears open the envelope should note on the envelope the date, time, and reason for access along with the officer's signature. This envelope should be attached to and made part of an incident report compiled on the occurrence. Subsequently, the combination should be changed as soon as possible, with the new combination numbers again sealed in an envelope for future reference by loss prevention.

13. Additionally, routine money deposits should be made on a daily basis from the cash room, whether by armored truck pickup or bank drops. Two reasons exist for daily deposits—it eliminates a greater loss in case of robbery, and it eliminates the possibility of a dishonest employee "floating" large sums of money from day to day for personal purposes.

Stock Control

1. Although a business will have a complete inventory conducted on an annual basis, mini-inventories of various departments or areas are a necessity. Routine mini-inventories conducted throughout the store by *employees other than those who are responsible for the area under inspection* provides the following:
   - **a.** Is used to maintain adequate supplies
   - **b.** Allows management accurate up-to-date information on supply of merchandise and reconciliation of outgoing and incoming merchandise with sales orders
   - **c.** Allows management to spot irregularities and discrepancies between outgoing merchandise and sales, and incoming merchandise and purchase orders or manifests
   - **d.** Has a psychological advantage that thefts or irregularities will be found early
   - **e.** Most importantly, allows management to spot inventory shrinkage almost immediately and to take corrective action before the problem becomes worse
2. All merchandise taken out of stock and used for display or inadvertently damaged should be written off on a special form for the stock control department. Along with acceptable inventory controls, this will give the impression to all employees that loss prevention and management expects a full 100% accounting of all merchandise.
3. Discarded packages, blister packs, and wrappings from which the contents were removed and stolen should be turned over to the loss prevention department in some manner, and reported on a "Known Thefts" form compiled by loss prevention for stock control so that they may be written off. The compilation of these

forms totaled and recorded on a monthly basis will give indications of areas and merchandise of concern for which the security officer is to be aware of.

4. "Hold areas" should *not* be encouraged and maintained if at all possible. These areas are conducive to theft, misplacement, and damage. If used as a convenience for the customer in "holding" merchandise, the area should be secured, controlled, and audited daily by a responsible employee with supporting documentation. Finally, a maximum time should be set for customer pickup.
5. Use caution regarding trash and garbage. Attempt to use clear plastic bags for all trash and garbage if possible. Routinely inspect all trash and garbage bins or dumpsters. Employees are known to dump merchandise in these areas for later retrieval, usually when the store is unoccupied if trash bins and containers are located outside of the building. Watch out for the same employee who routinely is always the last to leave the store at night. If possible, have the trash dumping areas under CCTV surveillance.
6. The display of merchandise or products, particularly high-end items, should not be placed at or near the exit doors so that a shoplifter can easily grab an item upon leaving. If merchandise such as expensive clothing or coats must be placed near or next to an exit, they should be secured by chain through the sleeves or other acceptable manner.

Physical Security

Access Control. Access control is the method of regulating an individual's entry and departure from or within the business facility that is under protection by a security or loss prevention department. This control may be for the purposes of security and protection of people, property, and other assorted assets. Circumstances surrounding a retail establishment is much different than that of an industrial facility where not only all ingress and egress is controlled, but may be surrounded by fencing and/or other barriers. Depending on the facility, truly effective access control will utilize fencing or walls, CCTV, electronic and mechanical locking devices, lighting, and security patrols to name a few. In these instances, entry to workers and visitors are made for operational necessity.

In the retail business, the customer is the main source for income and profits, and therefore, the customer must be given easy access, which the retailer attempts to make appealing, and at times, enticing. Access to the retailer's sales floors therefore must be granted to the general public, but access to stock, warehouse, and receiving areas must be off-limits and strictly controlled. Concerning control, other than reducing the entrances and exits within a retail environment, there is not much that can be done other than EAS devices, CCTV, knowledgeable and cooperative employees, and an effective security force. However, control of employees, delivery people, truckers and their helpers, outside contractors and mechanics, suppliers, and vendors can be controlled to a great degree.

All employees and business visitors must enter and depart from one particular entrance. It may be called a staff, employees, or personnel entrance. This entrance should be controlled by a security guard whose duties may entail receptionist functions. If a receptionist (or receptionist/switchboard operator) is posted at this location, he or she must be part of the loss prevention department so that direct authority and control of that person will be by the loss prevention manager. The duties of the security officer or the receptionist will include the inspection of all packages carried by employees leaving the building. Of course, to do so requires that according to company policy all employees are subject to inspection, and must enter and leave by this one entrance only and no other under any circumstances. All visitors, contractual employees or workers, allowed into the administrative offices or other customer-restricted areas, should be issued a visitor's badge that must be worn at all times within the building. Upon leaving, they are to turn in the badge to the security officer or receptionist. A sign-in log should be maintained for all persons other than employees coming through this entrance if for no other reason than safety during an emergency evacuation of the building. If persons other than employees are subject to a package search upon leaving, such notice must be posted in clear view so that they may be aware of this policy and procedure.

The retail industry tends to have a fast turnover in employment. If the workforce is large and includes full- and part-time workers, it can be difficult at times to know who is who, and who works where. Employees must wear some sort of identification badge if circumstances such as those noted above exist. Moreover, this "badge" is most appropriate for the customer, particularly if no identifying type of uniform or clothing is worn to identify an employee. In addition, many businesses issue an employee ID card-key that contains a bar code or a microchip, which can be used for electronic entry through the staff entrance, and for timeclock entries when reporting or leaving work. For purposes of security and the prevention of loss, this ID card should not be the identifying "badge" worn while at work. In an effort to control the careless loss of these cards, the retailer may wish to fine an employee a fee of $10.00 as an example. This would be for each loss and card replacement, as long as the employee has been previously informed of this written policy.

Loss prevention must constantly inspect and determine that all storage areas, mechanical rooms, closets, warehousing, receiving and shipping areas, and any other space or spaces are locked or secured in some manner in an effort to control access to the public. Consider that this is not only a security reason, but also a safety objective to protect the customer or visitor from injury and subsequent litigation against the company. The security officer should realize that perimeter controls, alarms, and other protective devices are of no use unless properly set up, properly maintained, and most importantly, used to the extent and purpose that they were installed. Control procedures should include the posting of restrictive and "no admittance" signs to all stockrooms, stocking areas, warehouse and receiving dock areas, and non-public (employee only) areas. Moreover, clearly posted warning and advisory signs or other notices reduce or eliminate liability concerns, and offer security officers the ability to control access under the laws of trespass. Written procedures and training should be encouraged for all employees to immediately report to loss prevention any person not an employee observed within these areas.

Unarmed uniformed security guards assigned to entrances and exits can be a psychological deterrent for shoplifters and dishonest employees.

Key Control. All personnel in the loss prevention department should have some training and knowledge in the mechanics and installation of locking devices and key control. This should include padlocks, hasps, hinge pins, the varied types of deadbolts, the proper installation to avoid "slipping" or "shimming" the bolt, face and back plates, and pull-proof and removable cylinder cores. Be aware that local law (fire and building codes) will also determine the use and type of locking devices. The security officer should realize that good hardware is cost-efficient.

The critical factors in key control are the issuance of the key, to whom the key is issued, and what access can be made with that key. In a large facility, which will include many interior and exterior doors, secured offices, cabinets and closets, and the use of padlocks, chains, and cables, some accountability for access to these locks must be considered:

1. Only security officers should have access to perimeter door keys, where they have the authorization to enter during an alarm condition, or opening and/or closing the store for business. For emergency purposes, a determination should be made about who else other than loss prevention should have the ability to enter the store once closed. This is usually the store manager, assistant store manager, and/or the facility engineer or maintenance manager. Of course, whether one possesses a key or not, in order to enter or leave the store at opening or closing will require a passcode to turn off or set the alarm system.
2. Additionally, only loss prevention personnel, the engineer or maintenance manager, and possibly the operations manager should have "grand master" keys so that access to all areas of the store may be easily and quickly made, whether in an emergency or during routine inspections.
3. All existing keys to all locks and mortise cylinders should be located and maintained in a secured fixture such as a master key locker or safe, along with a master key log. This locker should include a spare and/or extra keys to every padlock and cylinder lock in the facility. All keys should be coded or numbered and tagged describing each key and to what lock or locks that key is assigned. Access to this master locker should be restricted to loss prevention personnel only.
4. The master key log should include a listing of all keys distributed and permanently assigned to personnel, and to what door or location. Limit these keys for interior doors only, and to only those managers and employees who require that control. Upon transfer, termination, or any departure from the company, all keys are to be returned and so noted in the log.
5. A separate and secondary key locker and key log sheets should be maintained for those employees who sign out keys for business use on a daily or routine basis, and duly noted when returned. Missing keys must be reported to loss prevention immediately.
6. Keys should be classified and identified as "Grand Master," "Master," "Submaster," and individual key series or keyways.
7. All keys are to be stamped "Do not duplicate" along with the keyway designation and assigned door lock/core number.
8. No lock mortise cylinders should be permitted on the outside of perimeter doors, except for no more than two entry doors. An example would be the main entrance and staff entrance. All mortise cylinders should be standardized with removable cores in the cylinders for easy and inexpensive changes.
9. Those perimeter doors with outside mortise cylinders must have these cylinders attached flush with the door and without a "collar," leaving as little exposed as

possible. The use of a collar would raise the cylinder off the door enough for a burglar using a wrench or large pliers to easily twist or snap off the cylinder for entry.

10. The more popular perimeter door locks (throw bolts) on retail stores today are jimmy resistant, in that they have a round or laminated bolt that operates in a vertical movement with the bolt being surrounded by a sectional hollow strike. Some laminated bolts will have a hook-type configuration on the tip of the bolt to prevent a door from being pried open.

11. Protect the door entry areas from "crash and grab" by the use of superior hardware on perimeter doors, roll-down steel doors or gates, and steel barriers or pipes to deter vehicles ramming the doors for entry.

12. Control the access and egress of customers by securing perimeter doors that cannot be controlled by personnel or electronic means. This would include all fire exits that would be unlocked from within but secured by emergency exit hardware, so as to conform to local fire regulations.

13. Be aware of padlock substitution, where a padlock is located in an area or on a truck to which access can be made at a later time by a burglar. When a padlock is unlocked and left in the open position, a thief can replace a similar looking lock with his own. When an employee secures the padlock upon closing, the burglar will use his own key at a later time to unlock the padlock and enter. The burglar then removes whatever property he wishes to take, replacing his padlock with the original. When the employee returns the next day and unlocks the padlock with his own key, nothing appears amiss. When the loss is discovered at a later time, it will be assumed that the theft occurred internally by dishonest employees. The solution: whether inside or outside the facility, keep all padlocks in a locked position even when not in use.

14. If chains are required for security purposes and to be used in conjunction with a padlock, the links should be 3/8-inch thick and case hardened.

15. Keep all machinery rooms and equipment and storage rooms locked, even in non-public areas.

16. Sensitive keys such as grand masters, masters, sub-masters, and perimeter door keys should remain in control of only specific individuals. Keys to sensitive offices such as cash rooms and computer rooms must be assigned only to those personnel responsible to those areas. Although all keys should be stamped with "Do not duplicate," duplicates can and are made by unethical locksmiths. Therefore, if an employee is assigned one or more of these sensitive keys and leaves the company, no matter under what conditions, all cores or mortise cylinder locks on these doors should be changed. This process should also be considered if these keys are reported lost. This procedure can be simple and completed with personnel on board inexpensively by the use of a core replacement system, and by having an assortment of spare cores, the core is interchangeable in the mortise cylinder with another. A popular key system of this type is the "Best® Core System," in which the core is easily interchangeable or removed from one mortise cylinder to another. In this way, cores can easily be changed if keys are lost or stolen or if an employee leaves employment.

Premises Opening and Closing Procedures

Opening the Facility. Security officers who are scheduled or directed to open the facility may do so when properly authorized. Any manager, loss prevention personnel, or any other employee who may have the ability to do so, who takes it upon himself or herself to enter a building without an adequate or acceptable reason and/or without proper authorization must be held accountable and subject to severe disciplinary action. Unless store policy dictates otherwise, the facility should be opened daily by a security officer, and if possible, in the company of another store employee.

Any entry into the building once secured, other than for the normal opening procedure, must be for good reason. As soon as practical, the employee entering under these conditions, should complete an alarm and entry report, noting the reason/s for entry and submit this report to the loss prevention manager. (See the Appendix for a copy of this report.)

Closing the Facility. *Closing Inspection*—A closing inspection, including a watchman's clock tour, should be conducted on all floors, locations, and spaces in order to determine that no fire or other hazards exist, and that all appropriate safety and security concerns are checked within the building prior to securing the premises for the night. It shall be the responsibility of the loss prevention manager to devise the time and route that the closing security officers must follow.

Alarm System—The alarm system must be functioning normally and on-line prior to the departure of the last security officer to leave the building. Any points that are to be, or must be bypassed at the time of closing must have the authorization of the loss prevention manager or other security supervisor. A security officer should not close the facility alone, and should be accompanied by another security officer or an employee, preferably a manager.

Shipping and Receiving Areas

Receiving and loading docks, trailers, and trailer bays should be considered exceptionally vulnerable to loss by larceny and scams. It is not uncommon for employees, outside truckers, or both acting in collusion to carry out these crimes.

Trailers

1. *King pin locks*—A king pin locking device prohibits an unauthorized tractor (truck) from hooking up to a container (trailer) and removing it from the area. All full containers should have king pin locks attached by receiving personnel, unless in the process of unloading. In particular, king pins should be attached to loaded trailers left overnight. Loss prevention personnel will inspect these receiving areas as directed in order to determine that this procedure is followed.
2. *Missing containers*—When a missing container is discovered, the security officer should make appropriate inquiry and investigation to determine that the container has been simply removed to an incorrect location or apparently stolen. Once it has been determined that a theft has occurred or apparently did occur, a report of the theft should be made to the police. Attempt to determine any markings, logos, or numbers on the containers' sides or rooftop so that the police may be able to identify the container more easily. Include a description and total monetary loss of all contents of the container.

Shipping and Receiving

1. All shipping and receiving bay doors should remain down and locked unless in use. When open and in use, padlocks (if used) should be in the closed and locked position so that no substitution can be made. There should be no exceptions to this rule. All bay doors must be wired to the burglar alarm system.
2. Drivers, their helpers, truck and/or trailer delivery personnel will be controlled at the receiving or shipping docks. Entry will be made only onto the dock and nowhere else. This will not include small hand-carried deliveries by U.S. mail, FedEx, or other messenger services, which may be made to the receptionist. Any merchandise located on the dock that is of no concern to that particular trucker who may be present must be secured as carefully as possible, or kept under observation by CCTV, the receiving supervisor and subordinates. All loading of trucks and trailers should be under observation, or at least the interior checked prior to locking down. Routine inspections by loss prevention must be made to ensure compliance of these procedures.
3. Trucks and trailers must have some type of safeguard for the correct count of contents between the warehouse and the store receiving those contents. Numbered metal or plastic seals that must be cut for entry into the truck or trailer is one way to provide assurance of correct delivery load. Another is the electronic system where once a wire is placed into an electronic receiver and a number is electronically displayed, that same number will be visible upon receipt unless tampered with. In either event, whether at the point of shipping or receiving, the proper verification and the recording of such seal or electronic number must be maintained in some manner. The recording of this number on the truck's manifest would be sufficient.
4. Use care when merchandise or other goods are received via truck or messenger, whether at the truck receiving dock or at the administration offices. On the receiving dock, the truck's manifest should be checked against the contents received immediately upon receipt. This should be done by a responsible store employee, not by the trucker or any helper. If an over-shipment is received, make sure that there are procedures to send it back to the sender or reconciled in some manner. Sporadic and unannounced inspections should be conducted by loss prevention as soon as the receipt of goods are completed and accepted. In this way, a dishonest store employee who is operating alone or in collusion with the trucker can be reduced when it is unknown if and when the manifest will be checked.
5. Regarding the shipping of merchandise in the loading of a vehicle or truck, loss prevention should also conduct routine inspections just before securing the load or leaving the premises, to determine that nothing has been added to the manifest.
6. Don't allow merchandise to be shipped via UPS or the U.S. Post Office unless authorized and recorded in a logbook with all the required identifying information.
7. Hand-carried merchandise transferred to another store or elsewhere must have proper paperwork. This will include any merchandise taken out of the store for trade shows, exhibitions, etc. Any tools or equipment borrowed by an employee, and any scrap or damaged merchandise allocated for trash and properly authorized to be taken out of the store by an employee for personal use, that employee

must possess proper paperwork issued or confirmed by the manager of concern or by loss prevention. An in-house form such as a *property removal slip* would serve as appropriate document for the removal of any property.

Electronic Article Surveillance

The basic idea of electronic article surveillance (EAS) tags is that merchandise will protect itself. It can do away with chains and locks in some instances, and because it acts only against the person who actually is intent on stealing, the honest customer is faced with fewer deterrents. Of course, there can be problems if not properly controlled. All electronic tags—soft, hard, or wafer—must be properly deactivated or removed by store personnel prior to the customer passing a detection monitor when leaving the store. If inadvertently stopped by a security guard or store detective because an EAS tag activated the alarm, the customer could suffer panic, fear, and/or embarrassment. If the customer has in fact suffered any or all of these indications, and civil action is taken, the court can find negligence against the store in a case such as this.

Components of the EAS System

- A detection monitor is located at each door, or any other location within the store.
- This alarm—audio or visual, or in combination—can be remote or at the site of the monitor.
- Electronic wafers or hard tags attached or fastened to the item protected require a special tool to remove without destroying the tag or the merchandise. Electronic soft tags can be attached to or slipped within a sealed package; store personnel must properly deactivate them.
- There are portable verifiers (detection devices) used to confirm the presence of a wafer or tag on the shoplifter once identified by the monitor. It will pinpoint the location of the hidden EAS anywhere on or near the shoplifter.

Benefits of an EAS System

- Inspections of packages are no longer necessary by a security guard.
- Innocent customers need not be stopped and questioned.
- There are less false alarms, and more confidence in challenging by the security officer or guard.
- The "shoplifter" can be immediately located and discreetly called aside for the interview without causing a scene. Caution must be of concern in this instance—unless a larceny has been witnessed, the security officer must consider this "stop" only as an inquiry. No force or restraint can be used if the person stopped wishes to leave.
- The deterrent factor is great. It can be installed boldly to attract attention, or discreetly to avoid detection.
- Discreet or obvious application of soft tags can be made by the manufacturer in the packaging process (for an added fee). The benefit would be the time saved by the employee in the attachment process. Store personnel can deactivate the tags simply and easily in either case.

- If used effectively over a period of time, the EAS system will pay for itself in reducing shrinkage by theft.

Recently there has been a new component added to the detection monitor located at entrance and exits of some retail establishments. If a shopper passes through the electronic monitor, rather than the sounding of bells and whistles, an automatic voice message is uttered from a loudspeaker in the vicinity of the monitor that states the following:

"Attention please. You have set off the alarm denoting that the cashier has not removed the attached inventory tag from your purchase. Please return to the cashier so that it may be removed."

This message, or one similar, is repeated at least twice, and there is no further response or action by any employee. Other than the bewilderment of where the voice is coming from by the person leaving, the general reaction by loss prevention personnel is that the deterrent effect is almost nonexistent.

Ink Dye Tags. These security tags are attached to merchandise, most often to softgoods, and can be removed only by a device. This removal is usually completed at the cash register at the time of the sale. If removed from the premises without being paid for, an alarm will be activated similar to the EAS tags. The tag is adequately secured, and if an attempt is made to remove it by a shoplifter, the tag will break and a heavy permanent type of black or blue ink will ooze from the tag and cover anything the ink will touch. Unfortunately, it will stain not only the perpetrator's hands and clothing, but the merchandise as well. Because of this flaw, this type of security device is not widely used.

Anti-Shoplifting Signage

Some states require that retail stores post anti-shoplifting signs in an effort to obtain certain legal protections. Generally, most states have no such requirement. Depending on the type of retail establishment and the type of customer serviced, it may be left to the retailer or company policy whether to post or not to post. The general consensus among security professionals is that anti-shoplifting signs do deter shoplifting to some degree, and should be part of the anti-shoplifting program. Some stores may not wish to post this type of signage for aesthetic reasons or the unfavorable image that could be perceived by the customer.

However, humorous or other inappropriate signs should never be posted or used in any manner, in any part of the store, and especially in the security office. Offensive signage could place the retailer and the security officer in civil jeopardy. The following is not uncommon:

WE KILL SHOPLIFTERS

SHOPLIFTERS WILL BE BEATEN
BEFORE BEING TURNED OVER TO THE POLICE

Inappropriate signs could cause severe legal and financial repercussions if in fact a shoplifter is shot, beaten, inappropriately treated, or illegally detained during the apprehension or confinement. The connection that could be perceived by someone between the police and the retailer should be of concern to a loss prevention professional. Some retailers hire off-duty police officers for their loss prevention or security department, believing that their training and exposure to criminal activity will make them much more productive than the security officer who may have had no police experience whatsoever. This is discussed in some detail in the section on POLICE OFFICERS HIRED AS SECURITY OFFICERS in Chapter 10. However, those retailers who do hire off-duty police officers may be putting themselves in jeopardy. There have been instances where a security office has had a "humorous" sign posted as follows:

POLICE SUBSTATION

Similarly, an actual police booth or substation located on the property of the retailer, whether leased, rented, or freely given, could cause a plaintiff's attorney to show proof of a conspiracy or collusion between the retailer and the local police. If nothing else, the creation of a "police atmosphere" regarding a booth or substation could be established, thereby placing security officers under the "color of state law." Notwithstanding this, a police booth or substation located in a mall on mall property because of excessive police activity, and that services many retailers within that mall, reasonably would not fall into that category.

Therefore, signs of the type described above and posted as humorous or as a scare tactic can cause problems—don't use them. Serious, truthful, and candid signs that are considered acceptable are as follows:

THESE PREMISES UNDER
CONSTANT TV COVERAGE

SHOPLIFTING IS A CRIME

SHOPLIFTERS ARE SUBJECT
TO ARREST AND PROSECUTION

Some merchants post signs at the entrance of their store requiring that all packages and boxes be checked in and held at a holding or checkpoint area. Other signs may note that all shopping carts and bags are subject to inspection prior to leaving the store. These customer restrictions are permitted in most states and are covered under "license and privilege."

However, caution must be practiced in how, when, and where the "stop" and inspection was conducted, because it might be held in some courts that the restriction placed on customers regarding certain types of searches were not legal, even with posted signs. Consequently, loss prevention or the retailer should be judicious in the type of signage they may wish to use, and if in doubt, legal counsel should be consulted for an opinion.

HELPFUL MANAGEMENT TECHNIQUES FOR SECURITY AND SAFETY

The Role of Loss Prevention

Methods that may be used by loss prevention to enhance the security and safety within a facility could include the following:

1. Loss prevention personnel should be included as a source of information and guidance in the construction or renovation of retail buildings or departments within those buildings. This would include, but not limited to, cash room location, returns area access from outside the store rather than from within, and vacuum tubes from cash registers rather than personally transporting cash.
2. By working with other store and decorating personnel in a cooperative manner, ensure that displays and signage are set up so as not to interfere or conflict with security cameras, employees, and security officers from viewing customers or secluded areas more easily.
3. If a retail store is large in size, make frequent announcements throughout the day over the public address system such as "security to area 30, please," even though the store doesn't have an area 30. This type of an announcement would be helpful particularly during sales days when crowds are much larger. Thieves who may be in the store hearing this announcement will become aware that they may have been spotted and act accordingly. Attempt to keep the knowledge of this procedure from the general store personnel, leaving them to believe that this is an internal code for loss prevention officers.
4. Develop a warning system or code for employees to alert security or other employees of a shoplifter or a suspicious person.
5. High standards should be set and expected of all employees, particularly managers. The loss prevention manager and all security officers must be the role models—above reproach. The security officer must not set a double standard regarding enforcement of store policy and procedures, and moral and ethical conduct. What is required of employees should also be required of managers. If punishment is to be meted out to an offender, all employees, including security officers, must be treated equally. Security officers should treat all customers and employees justly and fairly, as they would expect to be treated in a similar circumstance.

The Role of Management

There are various techniques that the retailer can implement by way of his or her administrators and managers to gain the support of all employees. Morale, communication between managers and subordinates, safety and security issues, employment and business problems, and inquiries are all ongoing subjects of importance where an open discussion can be had among or between all employees.

Although these techniques are not in the realm of authority or control by a security officer, the loss prevention manager and security personnel must realize that the effect on morale and good relationships are directly related to many aspects of the business, particularly safety and security.

Some of these management practices are noted below, and have been proven to be helpful in many retail establishments:

1. Most important of all is that the management of the company must be honest, fair, and ethical in both their business and personal habits, in order to set an example for their employees. This principle must be reiterated and promoted habitually among all management.
2. Management must consider that the employee needs be treated reasonably and justly in all aspects, particularly concerning fair compensation, benefits, and incentives. Have management set reasonable goals and expectations for all employees, making sure that they have both the time and the necessary tools to complete those expectations. Expect that unhappy employees become dissatisfied and begin to experience low morale, which leads to a lapse in safety, security, and customer relations, and in their mind, a justification to steal. Although high morale cannot be equated to less internal theft, many people will not steal from a company or manager they respect.
3. All new employees must be advised and trained in the policies and procedures set by the company, what is and is not required of them, and the repercussions for those employees if there is any violation of the rules. Advise them of the risks of stealing from the business. The fear of termination, apprehension, arrest, and possible jail time is often a positive deterrent to crime.
4. Establish a management advisement team, and a grievance and suggestion process as an outlet for discussion between management and the employees. One type could be a "roundtable committee," which would include an employee representative from all the major departments. This committee would meet on a monthly basis with employees rotating on a routine basis. Minutes would be taken and published for all company personnel to view. Management will attempt to resolve any problem the committee brings to their attention as soon as practical, or advise the committee why such a problem or suggestion cannot be corrected or implemented. Particular issues brought to the retailer's attention by the committee, such as safety or security, should be directed to the safety committee or the loss prevention manager. No reprisals should be taken against any employee, otherwise a free and open discussion will become restrained or suppressed.
5. A safety committee should be established to identify any safety problems in the store and the ability to make the necessary recommendations.
6. All employees should have their work habits and demeanor reviewed and evaluated by their manager at least yearly. This could also include a review of

salaries, benefits, and possible promotion availability. Unfair or unrealistic performance standards for an employee can lead to dissatisfaction, desperation, anger, and finally dishonesty.

7. Delegate some authority or decision-making process to some employees, possibly a lead coworker or valued and experienced employee. Morale is greatly enhanced when an employee is granted some authority and accountability, particularly if this employee's salary is commensurate with the additional responsibilities and duties.
8. Provide an incentive program with appropriate rewards for those employees identifying dishonest employees, or suggesting better or improved security and safety controls.
9. The retailer or store administration should attempt to set up a bonus or incentive plan for employees indicating that if all losses fall below a prescribed amount for the year or some other time period, they will share in a percentage of the savings in the form of a bonus. Having employees involved and sharing in loss reduction with the incentive of a monetary reward at a later time can be highly effective in their attitude toward cutting losses.

The Role of Human Resources

Preemployment Investigation. Preemployment investigation is considered to be one of the most important techniques in the investigative process because this procedure tries to eliminate prospective employees who may later become a security or safety problem.

During the initial interview or screening process of new hires, some applicants may require a more intensive background investigation than others. The private citizen is protected from having certain information revealed without his or her consent. To obtain that consent, all prospective employees must sign a release giving the prospective employer permission to investigate all that may be required for the position that the subject is applying for. This task is usually relegated to the human resources or personnel department of the company.

Those perspective employees who would expect to have an in-depth investigation into their background would include those who would handle any type of money or credit card transactions, security officers, or any person in a sensitive position where harm to the company could result because of that person's actions. For a more detailed examination of preemployment screening, see the section THE HIRING PROCESS on page 218.

Conflicting Issues. Many loss prevention professionals believe that in most large businesses, the human resources department acts as an independent unit from other departments within the business itself. Primarily, the reason for this isolation is that human resources rarely, if ever, shares information with other groups within the establishment. In many instances, personal and private information on an employee must be held as confidential. But this department is an integral part of every employee group, not to share, but to inform and support their own department within the business establishment. In many instances, human resources will not advise loss prevention or other managers when members within their group are involved in wrong or harmful situations, thereby letting minor circumstances grow into serious conditions with the possible increase of loss and/or damage. If information is forthcoming, most often it is very little or cryptic in nature. If a security issue is serious enough that loss prevention must be advised, many times the specifics may be minimal. Even when actions do not require confidentiality, human resources rarely will advise other group managers that some action is pending or under investigation by their department. At times, this isolation can be frustrating and troublesome for the security officer.

In particular, some human resources departments may not view certain actions or incidents as serious as the loss prevention department might. In the case of sexual harassment or civil rights issues, it is most important that all incidents, statements, witnesses, and the people involved be documented along with what action was taken. The human resources manager or the employee involved may believe that after the initial report the incident is or may be of little consequence, and consider the matter taken care of.

Whether or not the victim wishes to pursue the matter or give a written statement, all oral statements should at least be reduced to writing by the investigator and some action initiated. Documentation must be made in all reported incidents.

Every incident of sexual harassment or a violation of civil rights must be investigated so that if reported to an outside agency or attorney at a later time, concerning the occurrence or a subsequent occurrence on the same victim or against any other victim, the loss prevention department can confirm the following:

1. All reported incidents were in fact investigated.
2. Some action was taken.
3. The company followed the law and acted in good faith.

To do otherwise must be considered a serious liability issue.

Considering that even though human resources initially has the responsibility to receive and act on all complaints of this type, the final responsibility of criminal and/or civil liability will fall on loss prevention. This is the most important reason that the loss prevention department should be involved in all reported sexual harassment and/or civil rights cases.

The Employee Termination Process. The human resources or personnel department handles termination of all employees. The exit interview can be a valuable management tool in the personnel security program. This type of interview gives the employee an opportunity to list grievances and to report troublesome situations or illegal actions not previously known. If the departing person is hostile, little information will be forthcoming. But if the subject is leaving under pleasant conditions, a skilled interviewer may obtain information or knowledge unknown to loss prevention or management. Moreover, if the employee leaving the company has knowledge of trade secrets or confidential information and business records, he or she should be warned of their responsibility to keep that information secret. Unless a written agreement was made at the time of hire regarding the taking and distribution of confidential information during or after employment, it would be hoped that the company could rely on the departing employee's honesty to maintain secrecy.

Nevertheless, concerning the plans of a departing employee or the pending termination of an employee, loss prevention should be advised and aware of this course of action. For various security reasons, loss prevention may wish to be informed. These reasons could include the collection of keys, changing of locks and/or safe combinations, computer security, property damage by a disgruntled ex-employee, and the possibility of an ongoing investigation in which the employee may be implicated.

However, there will be times when a manager or security officer must make an immediate dismissal of an employee from the premises for serious safety or security reasons. It must be understood that although the security officer is not a manager, the officer must have the authority to remove or dismiss an employee from the building under certain conditions. The loss prevention manager, the duty manager, and the human resources manager should be made aware of this action and the pertinent reasons as soon as practical, and where applicable, the complete termination process may take place at a later time.

Publicize the Termination? The most effective method of reducing internal theft is to apprehend, terminate, arrest, and prosecute the offender, and advise all other employees of such actions and for what reason. This can be a very strong deterrent on the workforce, however some issues and consequences must be considered.

The question will arise: Should all employees be advised and made aware ultimately of this action on a fellow coworker? There are two schools of thought on this subject. Some retail administrations feel that public knowledge of a termination for cause might result in more harm to the fired employee and/or the fear of some type of civil action because of the notoriety. Other employers feel that all employees should be made aware in some manner or notification so that they will know that the company will not tolerate improper behavior without some type of punishment. Although an arrest can be considered a public record, it cannot be held against the defendant until or unless he or she is convicted. Therefore, the company attorney should be contacted for legal advice and company policy on whether employees should be made aware of a dismissal for cause.

Fair Treatment. During the termination process of any employee where loss prevention has a part and/or is present, fair and equal treatment must be granted to that individual. Be considerate—for example, when compassion should be given to the employee who has committed a "minor" offense. Consider the principles that "justice must be tempered with mercy," and "facts and circumstances alter all situations"—not everything is always black or white. There could be some gray areas in many incidents. Unless a particular employee is given some favor because of a special circumstance at termination or the exit interview, all employees in similar circumstances must be treated equally. It can be said that a termination or a written warning is enough of a deterrent concerning that person's future conduct. Accordingly, some guidelines should be established by the company to determine if it is worth the time and effort to arrest and prosecute for the theft of a few pencils or other inconsequential items—or if these small thefts are adding up to a greater loss and must be curtailed. Decisions such as this may be of some importance to the retailer's anti-theft program, but also to the sympathetic and compassionate treatment of an employee. In many cases, a second chance will produce a more loyal and proficient employee. In any event, a security officer should be present or in the immediate vicinity during a termination for cause in case of aberrant or menacing behavior by the terminated employee. See the section WORKPLACE VIOLENCE in Chapter 18 concerning this problem.

ENDNOTE

1. *Title 15 USC §1681*—The Consumer Credit Reporting Reform Act.

Part 5

EMERGENCIES, THREATS, AND HAZARDS

Chapter 16
Emergencies

THE EMERGENCY PROCEDURE PLAN

Depending on the business establishment, this document may also be titled the emergency safety plan. This plan will assign and fix responsibility, noting those employees who should be accountable during diverse occurrences, and details the procedures to be taken during various emergencies. Every business that employs a tangible amount of personnel, and has as part of their normal business the coming and going of visitors and customers should have an emergency procedure or emergency safety plan to be put into effect by *knowledgeable people* in any emergency. Naturally the larger the facility and the more substantial the number of workers and visitors, the more complex the plan will be.

The loss prevention manager and all security officers within the loss prevention department should be aware of their responsibilities and actions during incidents such as those described on the following pages. It is therefore incumbent for the company to have a written emergency procedure plan in effect detailing what is an emergency, how it is to be handled, and who does what and when. First aid responders and fire brigade members should have emergency training and/or certification within their scope of duties. Additionally, all employees of the retail establishment should have training in fire safety and emergency evacuation procedures soon after being hired, with subsequent yearly retraining. This should also include the required hazard communication and bloodborne pathogen training mandated by OSHA.

Every loss prevention department must consider emergency response as one of the most important functions that will be assigned to them.

Emergency Planning

The emergency plan must be in writing. It must be precise and specific in nature, defining the normal to emergency modes in terms of the organization for each incident required. The plan is developed to protect and save lives, minimize injuries, protect property, and reduce the exposure of shutdown and restoration procedures.

The key elements of the emergency procedure plan for the emergency responder are what to do, when to do it, and who should do it!

The emergency plan should describe in detail the following areas of concern:

- The company's policy
- Risk assessment
- Description of each emergency or serious incident that could occur, and details regarding the procedures for each
- Evacuation and shutdown procedures
- A list of all emergency equipment available on-site
- A list of all employees who are first aid responders, members of the fire brigade, and all personnel who are to respond depending on the particular incident
- A list of all mutual aid agreements or procedures (police, fire, ambulance, electric, gas, and telephone emergency response; heat and cooling systems; elevator repair; glass replacement; alarm maintenance; etc.)
- A list of all management and administrative personnel of concern who are to be notified depending on the incident, including their emergency telephone and pager numbers

The emergency plan should detail every emergency that could occur within the facility, which would include but are not limited to fire, gas leaks, bomb threats, explosions, natural disasters, blackouts and brownouts, and lost or found children.

The emergency procedure plan should include the following procedures:

- Who should respond to that emergency or serious incident, when, where, and how?
- What duties or responsibilities are assigned and to whom?
- Who becomes "in charge" of the scene or the incident?
- What decisions and notifications are to be made, when, and by whom?
- Who will make public announcements or act as the spokesperson if and when the media becomes involved?

Because company policy is not policy unless it is written, a thorough and detailed written emergency procedure plan will serve as a directive and guide for all employees in an emergency. In particular, it will be a guide for the security officer, who will be part of the response team in most, if not all, emergencies.

Emergency Response Team

Note that not all members of the response team will be on duty or present at the time of the emergency, but there should be at least a minimal group of emergency responders who can handle the occurrence.

The employees listed below may be considered part or all of the emergency response team depending on the type and severity of the emergency to which they are assigned to respond.

In a retail environment, in which the emergency procedure plan will describe their duties, the "knowledgeable people" who will be a part of the emergency response team are the following:

- The store manager
- The operations manager or assistant store manager (as applicable)
- The duty manager (the senior manager for the day, if applicable)
- The loss prevention or security manager
- All security supervisors, security officers, and security guards on duty
- All employees assigned to the fire brigade
- All first aid responders
- The engineer or maintenance manager and/or supervisors
- All engineering or maintenance employees on duty
- All members of the computer incident response team (CIRT), if applicable

Contingent on the organizational makeup of the company, some of the above managers or employees may also be first aid responders and/or part of the fire brigade. Whether the security officers are proprietary (employed by the company they are protecting), or contractual (employed by a guard company contracted and hired out to the company they serve), they must be considered part of the emergency plan in which the duties, tasks, and functions are specified.

It is important to reiterate what is noted above—some of the persons above may not be on duty at the same time of a fire or other serious emergency, but an adequate number should be present so that the necessary action may be taken.

Larceny and Liability Concerns During Emergencies. The security officer should be concerned that during any incident where security and store personnel are assisting at a scene of an emergency or otherwise directed elsewhere, the opportunity by others to steal becomes greater than at any other time. It may be a "catch-22" situation, regarding the question of which is considered more important at the time—the emergency itself or a theft that may occur? We can assume that the emergency, no matter how minor, will take priority over the possibility of theft. But it should be part of the training for all store personnel that they should be conscious of thieves who will take advantage of this type of situation in order to commit a larceny.

The security officer must remember that in any emergency, the primary concern is the safety of life, limb, and property. The specific response by the security officer will depend on the type of emergency and what duties and responsibilities he or she is authorized and required to perform.

Concerning the actions and response of a security officer to any emergency, no matter how insignificant, if the retailer requires that certain actions be taken or entered into by a security officer in response to that emergency, and the security officer fails to act in a reasonable manner, civil litigation could be sought by one who has been damaged in some way.

In essence, if security officers are obligated by their employer and/or through their employment to have a duty to act, and do in fact fail to act, the officer and the employer could be held liable for civil damages sought by a plaintiff.

For further details see the section LEGAL DUTY in Chapter 17.

Consider also those security officers who have been trained and are knowledgeable about their duties in responding to various emergency situations. They are an asset to their employer. The officer's professional competence and demeanor during an emergency situation will have a calming effect on all those people in and around the facility—supervisors, coworkers, customers, and visitors. If the officer becomes excited or agitated in reaction to or during the course of the emergency, both employees and customers will view the officer as incompetent, or the occurrence as more serious than it may be, and if nothing else, will become overly concerned, fearful, and possibly panic.

NATURAL AND MAN-MADE DISASTERS

Categorizing Disasters

Public safety agencies place disasters into defined categories. Basically these categories may be identified as natural, accidental, or man-made.

Natural disasters may include environmental factors such as severe weather conditions and come in many forms. Excessive rain, flooding, hurricane, tornado, and earthquake are a few that can cause property damage and business interruption, and therefore, loss of assets. Adding to the seriousness of any one of these natural disasters would be the geographic location or national region of the business in question as it relates to the susceptibility or seriousness of that particular disaster.

Accidental occurrences could include fire, gas leaks, chemical and toxic spills, and structural damage. Man-made incidents are also a threat to the business enterprise, in that arson fire and criminal and terrorist acts can seriously affect persons and property to a great extent. How much damage is caused, how much of a loss is suffered, and how long the business closure or suspension will be, if any, will determine the reaction of employees and the security force. The role here for the security officer is the protection from further damage to property and merchandise, and the tally of the damage and its cost so that some recovery can be made through insurance or write-offs.

Depending on the extent of these disasters, the seriousness of death, injury, and destruction of property must be considered as an essential part of the emergency procedure plan.

Most importantly, if the disaster takes place during business hours, the initial basic response by security officers is the immediate concern for the safety of customers, visitors, and store personnel.

Fire Emergency

Many business establishments may be unique in the type of materials contained on premises that may cause or fuel a serious fire. Some may have more flammable and combustible materials on-site than another type of enterprise, and must incorporate special firefighting apparatus, hardware, and training.

As an example, some retail department stores contain warehouses, storerooms, and closets that house far more combustibles and are more exposed to fire than supermarkets or grocery stores. Plastics, wood, wood composition, and plastic foam contained in furniture and bedding ignite and melt easily, generate high heat, and produce toxic fumes and heavy smoke. High piled palletized stock in racking causes the probability of being heavily fireloaded. Sprinklers in the warehouse racking are considered a necessity. Fire-resistant buildings, completely sprinklered and constructed in sections with fire containment walls and doors between major portions of the building, is a major deterrent to the spread of fire until the arrival of the fire department.

The local fire department should have the availability to have routine walk-through inspections, particularly during business hours. This is most important when the building engages in routine construction and renovation. Local fire or building codes will dictate the amount, type, and placement of fire extinguishers and/or hardware. Such codes will also note the amount and type of fire exits that will be required, how and when they are or are not to be secured, and how all perimeter doors will operate. Housekeeping is most important to fire prevention. Clean and orderly areas throughout the store reduces the probability of fire. But fires do happen. From a tilted lampshade that comes in contact with a hot electric lightbulb to an electrical short in a fixture, store personnel must be prepared to react swiftly.

The Effect of Fire Upon People. No matter how much training, fire protection, and fire equipment that may be brought to or contained in a facility, we cannot control people once a fire has been discovered. People are harder to predict, protect, and control. Whatever the facility, the consequences of a fire are most serious because people can resist fire and its by-products only for a very short period of time.

Depending on the type of fuel involved in the fire and how fast the fire is spreading, the first indication of effects upon the person will be lack of oxygen, superheated air, and the consequence of smoke, toxic gasses, and chemical compounds. Fire uses up oxygen faster than the victim, and suffocation becomes one of the factors for death. Dense smoke becomes an irritant to the eyes, lungs, and air passages. It causes the eyes to water, the nose to run, and irritation to the throat and lungs causing coughing and vomiting. The most common toxic gas is carbon monoxide, and when absorbed into the body, causes brain dysfunction. The person becomes confused and disoriented, and succumbs to carbon monoxide poisoning without ever seeing or coming in contact with the fire. The final factor is heat, by which the body will blister and destroy tissue. When air temperatures reach 200°F, the chances for human survival are minimal to none. The effects on a burn victim cannot be measured in money.

Consider also the factor of panic. Unable to see or exit freely and safely causes people to become frantic in an effort to save themselves. It is not uncommon for people to jump from high-rise windows to their deaths. Many die by piling up against exit doors or are trampled by the rushing mass of people in their frenzied attempt to escape.

So then, generally speaking, because of panic, superheated air, or smoke, people can die even before fire will reach their bodies.

The toll of human tragedy in deaths and injuries, property damage, and public concern often cannot be overcome by the extent of the disaster. Therefore, the importance of fire protection cannot be overstated. Protection of the facility with fire-resistive materials, fire hardware, training, inspection, and enforcement is the key to life safety initially, and property protection following.

Remember that fire prevention is proactive, and fire suppression is reactive.

Fire Safety. Security officers should be an integral part of the fire safety team. In large business establishments, security officers usually have the additional duty of fire inspection as part of their inspection and auditing functions. This includes the routine inspection of all fire hardware—sprinkler systems, fire extinguishers, fire hoses, and fire exits and passageways. Also included would be the inspection of the proper storage of paints, cleaning agents and solvents, gasoline, and kerosene, along with good housekeeping procedures.

Moreover, security officers should be completely aware of the company's emergency procedure in responding to a report of a fire. This will include what their duties are concerning all contingencies specified in the fire safety plan.

Finally, the loss prevention manager must be cognizant that all local and/or state building and fire codes must be fully complied with concerning the location, number, availability, and adequacy of fire extinguishers, alarms, and hardware, as well as fire exits and sprinkler systems.

Every business establishment should have a fire safety strategy as part of the emergency procedure plan in effect for all employees to follow in the event of a fire. This plan should include what an employee should do upon first observing a fire and how to report it, and what and how notifications are made to store employees in order to be aware of a possible emergency and possible evacuation. Additionally, the plan should note the procedure of reporting the fire to the fire department, and the response of an internal fire brigade or other group of trained employees to respond to the scene of the reported fire so that they may be able to extinguish or contain the fire until the arrival of the fire department. If the fire brigade determines that the fire is of a serious nature or is out of control, an evacuation procedure for employees, customers, and/or visitors should be placed in effect.

All employees, but in particular members of the fire brigade and all security officers, should be trained in the following:

- How to prevent a fire—housekeeping procedures and routine inspection
- The science of the chain reaction of heat, fuel, and oxygen
- The four stages of fire development
- The classification of fires—Class A, B, C, and D
- The proper use of a fire extinguisher and the type or agent to use on each class of fire

- The proper response to a report of a fire and evacuation procedures
- The consequences of a fire on a business, people, and property

Fire Extinguishers. Fire extinguishers are seen at home, in vehicles, and at work, and are a common sight in our daily lives. But very few people understand their use or how to work them in effectively fighting a fire.

Fire extinguishers are not designed to fight large or spreading fires. In many cases with small fires, they are useful only under the right conditions. The use of the correct fire extinguisher for the fire being fought is as important as the size of the extinguisher for the fire at hand. An extinguisher must be easily available, in good working order when needed, and large enough to control the fire within reach.

All employees must be given instruction on the types of fires that may occur, the types of fire equipment on the premises, and the correct use of a handheld fire extinguisher.

Fighting the Fire. A member of the fire brigade, a security officer or a trained employee should attempt to fight a fire with a fire extinguisher *only* under the following conditions:

- When everyone has left the area of the fire or is leaving the building.
- When the fire department has been notified and is responding.
- When the fire is small and confined to the immediate area where it started—a wastebasket, small appliance, stuffed chair, stove, etc.
- When the fire can be fought with one's back to a safe exit route.
- When the extinguisher is rated for the type of fire that is being fought and is in good working order.
- When the employee has had adequate training in the use of the fire extinguisher and is confident that he or she can operate it effectively.

Automatic Sprinkler Protection. One of the most effective ways to reduce fire damage is an automatic sprinkler system. According to the National Fire Protection Association (NFPA), automatic fire sprinkler systems are 96% effective in extinguishing or holding fires in check. The remaining percentage (4%) is due to human or mechanical failure by making the sprinkler system ineffective.

Basically, a sprinkler system is an array of water pipes fitted with sprinkler heads, regularly spaced throughout the protected facility. The sprinkler heads are heat activated—when the sprinkler's fusible element reaches a certain temperature, it melts or breaks down so that the valve opens and water begins to jet forth. Fusible elements may include solder type or glass bulb-type fusible links, and are temperature rated.

There are two predominant types of sprinkler systems in the retail environment—wet pipe and dry pipe.

In the *wet pipe system*, which is the most common type, the piping is filled with water under pressure. When the sprinkler is activated, water will discharge and flow immediately. It will continue to discharge water until the system is turned off.

A *dry pipe system* is used to protect unheated areas of a facility where water in the piping might freeze. This system is filled with compressed air with the valve controlling the flow of water usually located in a heated area such as the sprinkler room. The air pressure holds the valve in a closed position, and when the sprinkler is activated, the air pressure is released causing the valve to open and release the water. Some areas of a facility may require a dry system to be turned on manually to certain areas or spaces as the emergency dictates, such as a hospital operating room or a computer room.

There is another type of system known as the *deluge system*, and its purpose is to completely saturate the protected area with water. The piping contains an open sprinkler, which has no cap or fusible element blocking the orifice. The piping contains no water and the water is held back by a valve that is released by a sensor in the fire detecting system installed in the protected area or the facility. This system is very rarely used in retail premises.

Each system has its own inspection, testing, and maintenance requirements. In large facilities, controls and shut-off valves are contained in a secured room. The two basic types of valves used are the gate valve and the butterfly valve. The control valve must remain open at all times except when they are turned off to stop the flow of water, or to facilitate repairs or routine testing and maintenance. All valves in any part of the system should visually indicate whether the valve is open or closed. Access to this sprinkler room should be restricted to engineering, maintenance and security personnel. The National Fire Protection Association sets sprinkler standards that building and fire inspectors follow. Most fire regulations require that the wheels on the valves located in the sprinkler room be chained in an open position protected by a padlock, or possess tamper switches supervised by the fire alarm system in order to discourage sabotage or careless turn-off.

There will be times when a sprinkler system can extinguish a fire, but the primary purpose is to contain or retard the spread of fire until the fire department arrives at the scene. A sprinkler system remains dormant and is there only when it is needed, and again, this also must be fail-safe and fully operational. Most importantly, the sprinkler system must be provided with an adequate and dependable supply of water, both in volume and pressure.

Two weaknesses can affect the operation of a sprinkler system—the flow of water to the system has been shut off or is not working properly, and the fire department is not properly notified for a quick response. Therefore, it can be said that if properly used, automatic sprinkler systems are both effective and efficient as a fire safety tool.

For further information on testing and monitoring procedures, see the section SPRINKLER ALARM SYSTEMS in Chapter 19.

Gas Leaks

Gas leaks must be considered a serious and potentially dangerous situation because of the insidious nature of the substance. Investigate all reports of a possible gas leak or the smell of gas thoroughly, whether inside or outside the premises. If the gas leak is considered significant, the security officer should follow the procedure outlined in the emergency procedure plan.

Basically, the reporting, response, and possible evacuation procedures would be similar to a fire report. In addition to the request of a fire department response to standby in case of an explosion or fire, the local gas company should also be requested to come to your location. The fire brigade and all security officers should be also trained in this type of response in order to not cause a more serious problem with the use of electrical contacts, sparks, cigarettes, flashlights, or mobile radios. Consider all gas leaks as a potential for explosion, fire, serious injury, and death.

Bomb Threats

Determining the credibility of a bomb threat frequently involves a decision to be made by a number of persons. This could include loss prevention personnel, the store manager, building management or ownership, and law enforcement personnel, all who will base their conclusion upon the consideration of several factors. Some of the more common factors might include the following:

- Accessibility to the facility by the public, customers, visitors, and vehicles.
- If the threat was made by phone, did the caller display specific and/or definite knowledge of the facility?
- Was a time limit given and was it realistic?
- Is or has the retailer or the corporate entity been involved in an incident, activity, or publicity that is highly controversial?
- Is the retailer about to or presently involved in union contractual negotiations?
- Are employees presently on a strike against the retailer?
- Have there been previous bomb threats or threats of any type against the retailer or the corporate entity?
- If the corporate entity is large and well known, have there been any threats to the company nationally or internationally?
- Have previous bomb threats resulted in evacuations?
- Does the retailer have any knowledge of a terminated or disgruntled employee having made a prior threat of this type or a similar threat?
- Finally, an examination of the *bomb report checklist* and an interview with the employee who handled the incoming call of the bomb threat.

This information should give loss prevention management a basic understanding of the bomb threat and how to handle the occurrence. One or more of these factors will determine how seriously to consider the threat.

If nothing else, the employee receiving the bomb threat must attempt to determine the following from the caller:

- When the bomb will explode?
- Where the bomb will explode?
- What type of bomb is it?
- How or why it will explode?
- Who is the caller, whom does he represent, or why is he doing this?

Upon completion of the call, the employee should follow the instructions noted on the BOMB REPORT CHECKLIST regarding notifications. See the Appendix for a copy of this checklist.

Types of Bombs. There are basically three types of bombs—mechanical, chemical, and nuclear.

1. **Mechanical.** When there is an intense buildup of heat, gas, and pressure inside a container until it explodes or shatters.

   Small bombs. A small bomb can be very powerful, and can be concealed easily in a briefcase, backpack, handbag, or shopping bag. The bomb may be disguised as a pack of cigarettes or a portable radio, and although small, its consequences can be severe.

   Car or truck bombs. A large bomb can be concealed in any type of vehicle, and when exploded, can cause complete devastation to everything in the vicinity. Any vehicle operated by a person determined on this type of destruction would be difficult to deter unless known beforehand. One way to reduce the damage and injury is to install barriers around a building so that a vehicle would not have the opportunity to park too close.

   Incendiary devices. These devices are normally designed to ignite after the store has closed for business and to start a fire. The usual scenario is where the perpetrator slips or places the device down the sides of upholstered chairs and sofas. Retail stores that carry furniture of this type are at great risk, but it should be remembered that such a device could be placed anywhere so that all businesses are susceptible. Loss prevention must consider that it is almost impossible to prevent a device of this type from being brought onto the retail premises. If an incident such as this happens once, it can be expected that it will happen again. At times when a high risk is anticipated, security officers may be required to conduct as complete search as possible after the store has closed for the evening.

2. **Chemical.** When the explosion is caused by the immediate rapid conversion of a solid or liquid substance into a gas with a much greater volume. Bomb contents using common substances such as fertilizer and other ordinary products are easily purchased and easily transported in bulk.

3. **Nuclear.** The ultimate weapon causing severe and extensive damage to people, businesses, institutions, and property over very large areas. The results can include complete devastation, the mass slaughter and injury to humanity, radiation sickness, and radiation fallout.

Types of Threats. In reality, there are only two types of a bomb threat—the threat without demands, and the threat with demands. In most all instances, these threats will be received by telephone.

Another type of "threat" to business is in actuality no threat at all. It is the terrorist who wishes to cause as much terror and devastation as possible by committing the act by the means of surprise with no prior warning.

Noted below are the various ways in which a retail establishment can become aware of a threat or the presence of a bomb on premises.

Threats Received by Telephone. Generally, the bomb threat will be received by telephone. Any telephone within the store that the outside public can call in and have access to the retailer should be manned by personnel who have been trained to remain as calm as possible and to obtain as much information that can be had from the caller. Additionally, every telephone that can receive incoming calls must have a copy of a BOMB REPORT CHECKLIST handy so that by following directions on this form, the person receiving the call can easily attempt to gain as much information from the caller as possible. The employee receiving the threat most probably will be the switchboard operator, store receptionist, security guard/receptionist, or a customer service representative. They must be trained and directed to write down on the checklist all information that can be elicited from the caller, and whatever can be remembered after the caller hangs up. The assessment of what the caller said, the time the device will go off, the possible location of the device, and how the caller sounded (attitude, speech, and various other indications) may well determine how loss prevention, store administration, and the police will react to the threat.

Bomb Threats Without Demands. The language of the threat is concise and deliberate, short and to the point. The caller gives little warning before the bomb will explode, or may not say when the bomb is to explode. The threat may have been made to a third party—the police, the newspapers, or a telephone operator. As soon as the statement about the bomb is made, the perpetrator hangs up and answers no questions. The warning is short and to the point.

Under these circumstances, the threat may be considered genuine. Call for police assistance immediately. If there is a period of time known or stated before the bomb is to go off, management may decide to wait for the police to arrive. If not, the decision to evacuate or not must be made.

Some of the reasons that the threat may be considered a hoax are that the caller gives more than one hour warning (a timed device), the caller uses slurred speech and may be intoxicated, the threat is made in a joking manner, or the threat is made in a fit of temper where loud, abusive, or foul language is used.

However, considering recent events, if the caller gives the time of the detonation, it may be foolish to accept this time as truthful, and therefore evacuation procedures should be immediately initiated.

Bomb Threat With Demands. This is the bomb threat by extortion, and most often for money. A manager or someone such as an administrator will usually receive the call so that the caller will be able to speak to someone in authority and can expect directions to be carried out. The person receiving this type of call should attempt to delay the delivery for more than an hour advising that only certain people are able to conduct a transaction of this type, and that it will take that long to set up the procedure for such a sum of money. Advise the police immediately after the caller hangs up.

Remember that the extortionist will try to put pressure on the manager in regard to time, but that if the threat is in fact carried out and a bomb does explode, the extortionist has failed to achieve his or her goal. So then, if anything, we have somewhat of an advantage. Any information concerning an extortion of this type should be strictly confidential and information held to only those people who must be involved.

Bombs Received by Mail or Messenger. Written bomb threats that are received by messenger or by mail often provide excellent evidence for the police. Threats of this type are usually made for the purposes of extortion and imply that if the demand is not complied with, an act of terror, most likely a bomb, will befall the company in question. Once a written threat is recognized as such, avoid any further or needless handling in order to preserve fingerprints, handwriting, postmarks, and any other markings on the letter and/or envelope for forensic examination. Loss prevention should notify the police immediately upon discovery. A threat of this type is different than that of a bomb delivered to a retail establishment by mail or messenger, which is described below in some detail.

Letter or package bombs are made to kill and maim when opened. Such devices can be received from terrorists, extortionists, deranged persons, or disgruntled customers. It is not uncommon for this type of hazard to occur, and therefore such threats should not be taken lightly. The employee who receives and/or handles incoming mail or packages by messenger should be aware of the following information.

If a letter or package is received and the mail handler or the recipient has the slightest suspicion that it may contain a bomb, loss prevention should be immediately notified. Once the suspicions have been confirmed or even if there is still some doubt, the police should be called.

If there is any doubt regarding a suspicious letter or package, do not open it.

The envelope or package should be placed and isolated in a locked room away from windows and thin partitioned walls to await the arrival of the police.

Listed below are a number of indications that should alert the mail handler or receiver that the letter or package *might* be considered suspicious:

- Greasy areas or grease marks on the envelope or wrappings.
- The envelope or package may feel overly heavy for its size.
- Uneven weight distribution within the package or the contents appear to be rigid within a flexible envelope.
- A package that has excessive wrapping, or has been very poorly wrapped.
- There may be some type of resistance upon opening.
- Foreign mail, or the amount or type of postage may not agree with the type or class of package mail.
- An odor of almonds or marzipan emanates from the envelope or package.
- There appears to be too many stamps for the weight of the envelope or package.
- The letter or package may appear to have been delivered by hand from an unknown source, and if so, may be a timed device.
- The letter or package contains special markings, unusual endorsements, or restrictions such as fragile, handle with care, private, confidential, personal, addressee's eyes only, please deliver directly to ______, or rush.
- As to the address:

  The handwriting, typing, or the spelling may be very poor.

  It may be addressed incorrectly or have an incomplete correct address.

  No return address may be noted, or the return address is from an unknown or suspicious source.

Finding a Suspicious Object Without Warning. Security officers should realize that not all bomb devices placed in a retail facility would come with a warning, particularly if the bomb is the work of a terrorist. It is essential, therefore, that during the security officers' ongoing routine inspection or walk-through of the facility, that they should be constantly vigilant of any suspicious object or package.

Basically, officers should be concerned about anything:

- That should not be where it is found.
- That cannot be accounted for.
- That appears to be out of place.

If something suspicious is found under these circumstances, it should not be handled, and the police are to be notified immediately. Security officers should be conscious of the particulars or suspicions surrounding this package and their own personal "gut" feelings.

The Terrorist and Other Attacks. Terrorists as a group are not the only people who may make use of a bomb for a particular purpose. The criminal may make actual use or the threat of a bomb for extortion purposes, revenge, a perceived wrong, or simply because the criminal wishes to disrupt normal activities. Unless mentally unstable, a criminal's reasoning is not to injure or cause severe damage, but to elicit money or something of value, or to cause a business interruption. The terrorist will make use of a bomb or other destructive device for another specific purpose. For additional information on this subject see the section TERRORISM in this chapter.

Employee Notification on a Bomb Threat. Other than as noted above, all employees must be trained in the following procedures so that they may be aware and act accordingly:

The Initial Warning. Once the threat has been received, an acceptable notification via the public address system could be made as follows:

This is a (name of company) time check. The time is now ________"

In this manner, upon hearing this announcement, all employees will be aware that a bomb threat has been received, and all radios, pagers, and cordless/cell phones are to be turned off. All assigned employees (including the fire brigade) are to report to the centralized location as directed in the emergency procedure plan for *bomb threat procedures*. The purpose of having certain employees report directly to a centralized location is to make use of their services in assisting the police in a search of the premises. This initial warning may be considered moot if an evacuation is immediate.

However, be aware that those personnel who are to take part in the search are not required to do so, and may refuse to participate because they might be placed or find themselves in a dangerous position. Loss prevention or security officers cannot refuse to assist in a search for a bomb device. They are employed for the protection of life and property. If they fail to respond to this mandate of their occupation, they may face immediate termination.

Remember, unless directed by the police, notification to employees and/or evacuation procedures will be activated according to the emergency procedure plan. Security and building personnel will cooperate with established procedures for an orderly evacuation of the facility.

Bomb Threat Procedure

The following information and basic bomb threat procedure does not cover every bomb threat incident, but will help to direct the efforts of loss prevention officers and building personnel in the handling of such a situation.

Very few bomb threats ever materialize to the extent that an explosive device has been planted or that a bomb will explode, but proper preparation and planning for threats can provide protection of life and property if the situation is in fact real. We cannot overlook the fact that the threat of terrorism within our country's borders is becoming more factual each day. This is particularly true for aggression against large national or international corporations. Therefore, we must take all bomb threats seriously.

Never disregard a threat as a hoax. All threats must be reported.

The protection of life and limb is the primary consideration for security personnel. Following that, the protection of property would be the next concern. In addition, it is important to immediately relay information to the proper authorities, and to initiate accepted procedures in a manner that does not cause panic, concern, or harm among employees, customers, and visitors.

1. When a bomb threat is received, whether by telephone or by letter, all facts regarding the threat and incident should be recorded on a proper form (i.e., BOMB REPORT CHECKLIST). A time log of all occurrences of this type should also be maintained. This time log will include the time of the report, times of all notifications made, time of arrival of public safety personnel, and when all managers, supervisors, and persons of concern arrive at the scene. An incident report should be compiled after the incident is concluded. The bomb incident report form, along with the time log, should be attached to and made part of the incident report.
2. During the telephone conversation and following its conclusion (or upon the receipt of a written communication advising of a bomb threat), the bomb threat checklist should be completed with as much information as possible. Immediately thereafter, the security site supervisor should be notified. The emergency procedure plan should be placed into effect as directed, where key company and building personnel are immediately advised, and where certain actions must be followed. Consider it vital that when a caller makes a bomb threat, as much information as possible should be gathered from the caller. Study the company's BOMB THREAT CHECKLIST, and memorize key points. Keep these forms handy and always available near telephones that take incoming calls. The information contained on this form will be the basis of how the police will conduct their initial actions and subsequent investigation.
3. Based on information received, whether or not the time of detonation for the device is known, the police must be notified immediately after the threat has been received. Depending on the facility's emergency plan based upon company policy and procedure, company management may require an immediate evacuation of all personnel and visitors, or they may elect to wait for the arrival of the police before any action is taken. However, if an explosion of the device occurs, immediate notification to the fire department and the police department and the fire or emergency procedure plan for evacuation of the facility should be activated.

Avoid Undue Panic or Hysteria

4. Although the sight of police and other emergency personnel within the facility will cause concern of those within, attempt to keep the incident as low key as possible. In the event there is no evacuation, prevent the disruption of normal business operations if

possible, but do not refrain to advise if asked by customers and visitors, so that individual decisions can be made to leave the premises until the threat has passed. Be truthful, but if requested by top management not to explain what is happening if asked, conduct yourself accordingly, but make appropriate notations in the incident report.

Keep calm in all emergency situations—think before you act. Your actions and demeanor will have a cause and effect on others.

5. Once the police have responded to the notification of the bomb threat, they will have complete control of the crime scene or "possible" crime scene. Let the professionals in public safety handle the situation. An emergency plan should note by whom and where an interior and exterior search will be made. Generally, a police officer will accompany a security officer, maintenance employee, or other employee who has keys and access to all parts of the facility. A police supervisor or a site security manager should set up and direct the search teams so that the search will be completed in a timely manner with no duplication.
6. All public, employee, and fire stairways and stairwells will be thoroughly searched. Also search all restrooms, stalls, unlocked and locked closets, mechanical rooms, public and private lockers, locker rooms, trash and garbage receptacles (interior and exterior), under displays and desks, and anywhere a suspicious package can be left. Consider any paper bag, briefcase, attaché case, knapsack, backpack, handbag, or item that appears to be out of place or shouldn't be where it is found, as a possible explosive device. With present plastic explosives and technology, a bomb or incendiary device could be as small as a package of cigarettes. If you have doubts, report it as suspicious.

Cautionary Actions

Once a suspicious package is found, no one should touch the object. Call for a police officer to respond if not already present. Evacuate that particular area and safeguard the scene. Only authorized public safety personnel will have the authority to inspect or examine a suspicious package that may contain a bomb device. Do not use a portable radio to transmit a message. All pagers and radios should be turned off and not used once the bomb threat is received. Any transmission of this equipment could possibly activate a device by electronic signal. Be guided by the police or other public safety personnel. Remember that the safety and protection of life and limb are the first considerations of all security personnel.

After a search has been completed and the facility is considered clear by the police and if in fact an evacuation had taken place, reentry by employees and visitors will be authorized only by the police.

This information is basic procedure. Let the professional public safety personnel handle and direct any incident where facts and circumstances may alter the emergency situation, and where only *they* have the legal authority to act under emergency public safety conditions.

TERRORISM

Terrorism may be described as an overt act by a person or a group that causes damage, harm, fear, panic, and apprehension, and that ultimately disrupts the normal working environment of a business or government agency. The most common implement used by the terrorist is the bomb. It is easy to make, easy to transport, and easy to place. The act can usually be accomplished by placing a bomb within or near a building or object so as to bring about the damage and harm they seek. In recent months however, we have also seen fanatical bombers with nefarious intent carrying bomb devices into crowded areas, and blowing themselves up in an attempt to kill and injure as many bystanders as possible.

The intent of a terrorist act is to cause extensive physical damage, personal injury, and death.

It is committed for the purpose of a political, religious, ethnic, cultural, or social agenda.

The ultimate objective is to create fear, panic, and apprehension among the populace in order to bring about a slowdown of movement, social activity, and commerce.

During this period of our country's history, it must be understood that there are many terrorist organizations, both internal and external, that are dedicated to disrupting the American way of life. By causing death, serious injury, and property damage where the destruction causes an economic loss to the country or the business under attack, they in essence cause fear and apprehension among the innocent public at large as we go about our daily routines. They do this with the terrorist's primary weapon of choice—the bomb.

The bomb can be disguised in many ways, and can be designed to cause specific damage and injuries that the terrorist may wish. They can be planted indiscriminately or in specific places depending on the access that the perpetrator may have or the purpose of the terrorist's intent. The terrorist will usually make an attempt at buildings or facilities that contain or will contain large numbers of people. As we have seen in Europe recently, the retail business is a viable and accommodating target. In our country, it is a matter of time when the terrorists will turn their energies away from government facilities or institutions and specifically include the business establishment.

Terrorist activity has increased dramatically in recent years, particularly in Europe and the Middle East. As we have noted, the favorite tool of the terrorist is the bomb, and the basis for such an act is usually for a political, religious, or social agenda. Coercion may also be used as part of the terrorist act, where a demand is made for a specific purpose, such as the release of "political prisoners." If not agreed upon, the terrorists will execute their threats. The threat of a bomb event for the purpose of extortion or to cause damage for some perceived wrong is a different criminal action and should not be classified as a terrorist act.

Recently, our country has also become the target of radicals. Businesses and government have suffered damage to life and property, including the public's apprehension, following such an incident.

Because the terrorist has no compulsion regarding who and how many people will be killed or injured or how much property will be devastated, and the purpose of the terrorist act is to cause fear and apprehension, there will be no warning. If there is any communication to the media or law enforcement authorities, it will be made after the occurrence detailing the purpose of the act.

Past targets of terrorism have included any area where there would be a large concentration of people or national sites, monuments, and institutions.

Remember, besides causing death, injury, and destruction, and to indicate their willingness to advance their cause, the focal point of the terrorist act is to cause fear, panic, and apprehension.

How many of us will enter areas where there is a large congregation of people, travel in an aircraft, shop in crowded malls, or go to any location where a terrorist has previously committed a violent act and may do so in the future? The more the terrorists fulfill their purpose and objective, the more there is a reduction in the commerce and movement of people. As we have seen on September 11, 2001, with the complete devastation of the World Trade Center in New York City, with the surrounding extensive damage and the terrifying loss of life, commerce and movement on our East Coast almost came to a complete standstill. The American psyche was so affected that airline travel, the stock market, and business were reduced tremendously. The attack on the Pentagon on the same day along with an attempt with a fourth aircraft only heightened the consternation. It was a couple of weeks before the public returned to some normalcy in their everyday activities. Today, many months later, the American public is still apprehensive about the possibility of another serious attack by terrorists.

Terrorist activity has also affected American business and businesspeople overseas. Along with that and the bombings of our governmental facilities in foreign lands, and the almost daily suicide bombings conducted in the Middle East, the American public has become sensitive to current events and cautious in making travel and recreational plans.

As noted, the primary weapon for the terrorist has been the bomb, but now we have seen that airplanes have been used in an unmerciful destructive and lethal way. With the treacherous accomplishments that terrorists have committed in the past, we can assume that chemical, biological, and nuclear weapons may be other weapons of choice in the future.

Specific Terrorist Threats. Bombings are not the only threat that may be committed by the terrorist. Other threats may include the following:

- Hijackings of aircraft and other public conveyances (buses, trains, etc.).
- The use of vehicles and aircraft as an instrument to commit further death and destruction.
- Kidnappings, extortions, murder, and/or assassination of business and political leaders or American citizens in general.
- Seizing and holding of buildings, property, and territory.
- Nuclear, chemical, and biological threats against the general public. Consider that the possibility of an attack of this type in the surrounding community will have a devastating effect on any business in the area.

Retail Issues

In regard to a terrorist attack on or within a retail establishment, the retail security officer must be aware that because of the free access given to the public, an aggressive act by someone bent on causing at least some destruction is not exceptional and very hard to challenge. It may be something as simple as a disgruntled customer or employee wishing to cause only damage. Occurrences such as this may be considered an act of sabotage. Such actions have occurred in recent years in large retail stores located in New York City in which small incendiary devices were secreted under the cushions of sofas in the furniture department of the store. Other large explosive devices have found their way in European retail establishments, particularly in England.

Under our present business environment American retail commerce has an open door policy. Other than close scrutiny and observation of people entering the business premises, very little can be done to alleviate the threat.

Precautions. Because the retail establishment gives free access to the public at large, there are few precautions that retail loss prevention could impose on visitors.

Attempting to profile and prevent a potential suspect from placing a bomb device at or within a building or a willing bomber bent on committing suicide in a fanatical effort and belief in furthering their cause is not absolute. Because of this inability to immediately identify any type of bomber entering a building or a mall, we can only protect ourselves in certain areas.

The following are some measures that may be taken to thwart or lessen the effect of a terrorist attack:

Structural Integrity

- Architectural design: The use of structural concepts to make the target less attractive. Easily incorporated into new construction, but can be included into the design of existing structures.
- Excessive glass design: Shards of broken glass can cause injuries far beyond the area of the blast. Laminated or hardened glass can withstand a degree of blast damage.
- The installation of cement or steel stanchions in front of or around the building facility in an attempt to keep a vehicle containing bombs as far as possible away from the building in order to lessen the blast damage.

Internal Security

- Controlled access to heating and air conditioning systems in order to diminish or defeat an attack intent on the distribution of toxic or insidious microorganisms throughout the facility.
- The control of visitor movement in areas not open to the public: Use of a visitor's log, issuance of dated visitor's passes, and the possible use of a security or personal escort to the visitor's destination.
- All employees should be issued and wear identification badges while at work.
- Access control to sensitive areas or those areas not open to the public should be discouraged and challenged including signage, key control, and periodic review.
- All vulnerable areas within the building:

  Restrooms and locker rooms (public and employee)—Trash receptacles should be the wire basket type; dropped ceilings should be secured in some manner; vanities and cabinets should be screwed down; and closets should be kept locked.

  Lobbies—Trash receptacles also should be wire basket type; chairs and couches should have skirts removed for a clear view of the underside; public telephone booths should be removed and should be open and attached to the wall. Product display cases available to the public should be redesigned so that nothing can be placed in or under the case. If fire extinguishers are contained within a wall receptacle, they should be easily and readily observed, such as a locked glass cabinet that must be broken into for emergency use if required.

Doors to storage and custodian closets must be kept locked at all times. All equipment rooms containing telephone, electric, and computer equipment must also be kept locked at all times with access on a controlled basis.

External Security

- If able to do so, attempt to prohibit public and visitor parking in the near vicinity of the building. If possible, reserve parking areas closest or next to the building for trusted employees.
- Install concrete planters or reinforced stanchions between the roadway and the general access areas of the building.
- Access to underground parking, particularly for truck delivery, must be strictly monitored and controlled.

Shopping Malls. Retail establishments located within a mall may face a different type of terrorist or criminal assault than that of a retail business with a facility that is free-standing or is located on a public street. The scope and size of the mall and the complexity of the businesses located within that mall will multiply the problems that a security force will encounter.

As we have noted, a retail business is open to the public for the specific reason of doing business. The retailer gives free access to the masses so that they may purchase and/or browse. A mall locale subjects the retailer with more of a threat than the retailer may be able to control. Crime, large groups of adolescents milling about, accidents, lost people, and vehicular and pedestrian traffic only add to the problems that a retail loss prevention department may face. Special sales events conducted by all or other retailers in the mall may require extra preparation and security officers for the mall and the retailer because of the expectation of large or excessive crowds.

Mall Security. A recent news article noted that the number of suicide bombers attacking various sites in Israel increased during the first half of 2002, and the diversity of the bombers' background in the Islamic world has created concern among terrorist experts that such tactics will soon be found in the United States.[1] Suicide bombers are classified as those who have bomb devices strapped to their bodies or who operate a conveyance containing a bomb.

Also in May 2002, the Israeli Police Commissioner Shlomo Aharonishki, while visiting Washington, D.C., has put shopping malls high on the list of terrorist targets along with any large gathering spots. He believes that by heightening airline security, property protection against vehicle bombs and other types of security, the terrorist has moved into human suicide bombings.[2]

The mall security force should be a centralized separate entity because of the different security and safety issues that are encountered by the retailers. In actuality, mall security has a duty to assist the various retail loss prevention departments within the mall. In that regard, monthly meetings with all retail loss prevention managers or supervisors should take place in order to share problems, special issues, upcoming events, ideas, and resources.

Other than that, security personnel in particular and all employees in general should be trained in identifying persons who look and act suspiciously in their manner, dress or what they carry on their person. Moreover, security personnel must be constantly aware of any suspicious activity or situation that could place people and property in harm's way.

OTHER SERIOUS BUSINESS THREATS

Sabotage and espionage are two particular threats that may be directed against a business establishment for reasons as varied as described below. Note that such acts can also be directed toward a nation as well as a business. Because threats of this type are surreptitious in nature, and unless the retail establishment is forewarned in some manner, attempts by a retail loss prevention department to overcome this type of threat for all practical purposes are nonexistent until after the threat is created.

Sabotage

Sabotage is defined as the intentional damage of property or a product, thereby obstructing or hindering productivity of the normal function. In effect, it is the use of treachery and subversive tactics to cause damage, or to disable equipment and/or property of a business or government agency.

Example

Sabotage may include the destruction or obstruction of telecommunication, gas and electric lines, and the intentional vandalism of property in an attempt to slow down, shut down, or damage the viability of a business or a government entity. This may include libel, slander, or poisoning of a business product in order to harm the reputation of a business. Moreover, a bomb or incendiary device is not uncommon in instances where more damage is planned.

Espionage

Espionage is defined as the act of surveillance, infiltration, and spying on the activities of a business or government agency in order to steal information or something of value for oneself or another such as a competitor or foreign government.

Example

Espionage may include the stealing of proprietary information, business plans and records, secret or technical information and formulas, and/or prototype devices or objects, considered of great value to the owner, and where such a loss may cause a negative effect on a business or jeopardize the safety of a nation.

Natural and Accidental Events

Natural Occurrences

- ***Earthquakes:*** A shaking or violent upheaval of the earth in which property damage can be severe with a great loss of life and which occurs without warning. Predictability of an earthquake event or volcanic eruption is inaccurate at this time.
- ***Tornadoes:*** Cause extensive damage and loss of life to certain areas. Predictability is inaccurate and there is very little warning to the populace prior to the occurrence.
- ***Hurricanes:*** Also cause extensive damage to property and loss of life by wind, rain, and flooding. Predictability is greater for hurricanes than any other natural occurrence.
- ***Rain, snow, flooding, land and mud slides:*** Are generally predictable with a minimal loss of life, but property damage can be extensive.

Accidental Chemical Spills or Exposure. Accidental spills include hazardous materials—any substance that poses a risk to people and the environment even when being handled, used, or made in a reasonable way. Such harmful or toxic substances could cause injurious effects. Occurrences are generally accidental exposures from spills, leaks, or unintentional contact. This contact can occur by inhalation, ingestion, or skin exposure (topically). See also the section on HAZARDS in Chapter 17.

EVACUATIONS

One must consider that in any evacuation scenario, people leaving the premises may become injured because of panic, confusion, or the rush to leave. An injury can take place whether there is an actual emergency or not. Along with that, the likelihood of civil litigation because of an injury and the possible stress and/or anxiety because of the incident cannot be overlooked. There must be written policy about whose order and under what conditions an evacuation of customers, visitors, and employees will take place.

Evacuations may be required under the following various circumstances:

- Fire or a report of fire
- Bomb threat or actual activation of the device
- Gas leak
- Blackout or brownout—loss of electrical service
- Any other emergency that might place the occupants of the building in jeopardy

Because an evacuation is a serious consequence that once it is put into effect cannot be canceled without more confusion, it is most important that all employees be instructed and trained in how to react in this situation. Once the employee is made aware, by coded announcement or otherwise, of a possible emergency situation and a possible evacuation, that employee should comply with the following guidelines:

- Employees should immediately become aware of their location, including where all fire extinguishers and fire exits are located. This should include an approximate headcount of customers in that department.
- Once the evacuation announcement is made, the employee should direct all customers to and out of the closest fire exit, and ask that they remove themselves away from the building.
- They should not have anyone, coworker or customer, use any elevator, but should use the fire exits. They need to remember that fire stairwells are contained areas—regular stairways are conducive to the travel of smoke and heat.
- *Employees must not panic*, otherwise other coworkers and customers will pick up their demeanor. They must be emphatic in directions to customers, but they must attempt to act in a professional manner.
- Before leaving, the employee should make sure that all coworkers and customers have left their area.
- If a customer refuses to leave or act at the employee's direction, loss prevention personnel should be requested immediately for their assistance.
- Once out of the building, the employee should meet and queue up with other coworkers from the same department at a prearranged location, so that their manager or supervisor may take a head count. Anyone not accounted for should be made known to loss prevention.
- To enable management to take a correct head count of all personnel, the receptionist or switchboard operator should leave the building with the book containing all work schedules, the visitor's log, and a bullhorn, which should be handed over to the designated person. The designated person will supervise the personnel count, attempt to make a determination that all visitors from the visitor's log have left the building, and complete any other duties as required in the emergency procedure plan.

Members of the loss prevention department will be informed if employees are missing from the head count and possibly still within the building. The police and/or fire department must be advised accordingly.

Evacuation Drills. Evacuation drills for training purposes should take place for employees at least twice a year, and more preferably every three months. So as not to disrupt the business operation, an acceptable time period for such a training exercise would be just prior to opening the store for business. A proper record of this exercise should be compiled and maintained for future reference (training, liability, and insurance purposes).

RESPONSE, RECOVERY, AND RESTORATION

The purpose of a plan for emergency procedure is to provide a strategy and to reinforce the security officer in his or her role of protecting people and property. The proper training and response of assigned personnel can reduce much or all of the injuries and damage that might occur within a business establishment and, in reality, negate or reduce the amount of liability that may occur.

For serious occurrences in which major damage may be caused by a natural or accidental source, or by an intentional act, the security officer's role is to respond to that emergency, aid the injured, request assistance as required, and secure and protect the scene. Once the immediate emergency is over, the officer's role, along with management, will be *recovery* and *restoration*—to recover as much property as salvageable and to put the business back into operation, if not fully, at least partially.

ENDNOTES

1. "U.S. Fears Use of Belt Bombs—Mid-East Suicide Attacks Difficult to Counter," by David Von Drehle, Staff Writer, *The Washington Post*, Washington DC, May 13, 2002, p. AO1.
2. Ibid.

Chapter 17

Accidental Injuries or Serious Illnesses

CUSTOMER, VISITOR, OR EMPLOYEE

All large retail establishments should have a core of employees who are trained in basic first aid and CPR. All security officers in particular should have this certification because they are normally the first responders. All types of accidents can occur within a retail environment to both employees and to customers. Whether it's an employee who sustains an injury on the receiving dock or while putting up a sales display, or a customer who trips and falls over an object that shouldn't have been in harm's way, the first aid responder should be trained and certified to render care. Security officers should not apply first aid if they are not trained so they do not further aggravate the injury. Remember that their actions, which may cause further harm, *may* be subject to subsequent civil action against the security officers and their company. Then again, their company may be subject to civil action if there are no trained first aid responders to help when a serious injury or illness occurs.

So then, first aid responders should be aware of what they are doing, but there are laws that cover the person against subsequent civil action when they attempt to help an injured person. When there is an emergency there is little time for reflection by a person willing to aid another, whether a certified first aid responder or not. The general rule is that the responder aiding that victim must act as a reasonable person would act in the *same circumstances*. These laws are known as the *Good Samaritan Statutes*, or the *Good Samaritan Law*.

In essence, the law states that a person shall not be held liable for damages for any injury or death sustained by reason of an act or omission in rendering emergency treatment, unless it can be proven that such injury or death was caused by *gross negligence* on the part of the person giving aid.

Most states have enacted laws that exempt professional health-care workers such as physicians, physician's assistants, nurses, etc., from liability for ordinary negligence where they *voluntarily and gratuitously* render aid and emergency treatment to a victim outside of a professional office or health facility. They, like an ordinary citizen, would have liability attached if gross negligence was a factor.

Security officers should check the codes in their own state of employment in order to determine if their state has a Good Samaritan Law that would cover their actions.

Legal Duty

Generally, there is no legal duty that is imposed upon any person to act for the benefit of another. There may be a strong moral duty to act in preventing a harm or a serious threat of a harm to another person, but there is no legal obligation to do so. However, if a person renders aid to another person who has suffered an injury or illness, although no duty is required to do so, the responder or person giving aid must exercise *ordinary care* in that aid, and is held to the standard conduct required of an *ordinary, prudent and reasonable person's* actions.

Conversely, if a person causes an injury to another, he or she is obligated and legally bound to assist that injured party. If a person's negligence places another person in peril, he or she must use *reasonable care* to aid or assist that other person.

Retailers, among others, who invite the public onto their premises for profit-making purposes, have a duty to use *reasonable care* to aid and assist their "guests," to provide a safe premises, and to prevent injury to them from a third party. Moreover, concerning injury from a third party, if the retailer knew or should have known that the third person was likely to commit an injurious act, the retailer has a duty to exercise control over that person and will be held liable if the retailer had actual ability and authority to control the third person's actions. Specifically, employers may be held liable for the actions of their employees.

If the security officer is trained as a first aid and CPR responder, and it is required that the officer render aid to the sick and injured on the premises, the retailer must provide the officer with essential first aid supplies and the necessary personal protection equipment. The officer must also receive the adequate training required under the federal *Bloodborne Pathogen Standard.*[1] By providing this protection and training, the officer may not only administer the proper care to the victim, but it will provide adequate protection to insulate the responder from infection or other health hazards. For further information, see the section on INFECTIONS AND HEALTH HAZARDS later in this chapter.

However, there may come a time when a security officer or another employee will fail to give aid because of a disgusting or repugnant sight, or because of certain conditions the employee may not want to expose himself or herself (and ultimately the employee's family) to any transmittable disease under any circumstance. Upon viewing the victim the security officer may "back off" or fail to aid that person because conditions may exist concerning the possibility of infection to the responder by blood or body fluids. Diseases considered highly transmittable include bloodborne pathogens such as HIV and hepatitus A, B, and C.

Whether a certified first aid responder or not, or whether proper personal protective equipment is provided, there is no legal duty to render aid under conditions that the officer or employee feels may place him or her in danger, or the possibility that the employee could carry such an infection home to his or her family. Other than health-care professionals such as physicians, nurses, certified EMTs, etc. (where professional ethics are involved), there is no law or requirement that a first aid responder, trained or not, must aid the injured person. That decision is left to the individual.

Still, the victim or the victim's family may have a cause for a civil suit against the retailer noting that the security officer failed to act, even though the officer was in fact a certified first aid responder known to and authorized to act accordingly by the officer's company. The employer may terminate the security officer if the officer fails to act in the emergency as trained. Nevertheless, although a civil action could possibly be initiated against the retailer or employer for a wrong or some perceived wrong, there is no legal requirement for a person to render aid whether trained or not in first aid procedures. No civil recourse can be justified, and the officer cannot be held liable.

First Aid Supplies. The loss prevention department should be the department responsible for controlling and maintaining all first aid supplies on the premises. In larger retail establishments, first aid boxes, sufficiently stocked, should be strategically placed throughout the facility for easy access, particularly by first aid responders. The larger the facility, the more box locations will be required on every floor.

An emergency trauma bag containing supplies to be used in the more serious incidents should be centrally located within the building so that it may be brought to the scene quickly. The retailer may wish to employ the services of outside contractor to service and maintain first aid supplies in the boxes and trauma bag on a routine basis. In this way, the first aid boxes and trauma bag will always be well stocked when needed.

The security officer needs to be aware that there will be some employees who will pilfer first aid supplies from the boxes whenever they can, thereby reducing items that may be needed in an emergency. This may include items such as packages of Band-Aids, compresses, bandages, tapes, scissors, and tweezers. Routine inspection of these boxes is essential, especially if the problem of theft is severe. If there is a problem of this type, coworkers should be reminded of the seriousness of inadequate supplies that may be required in an emergency, and that could have a harmful effect on everyone.

Workers' Compensation

Specifically, workers' compensation is an insurance that requires an employer to compensate an employee injured on the job regardless as to who was at fault. This compensation came about in order to protect the relationship between the employer and employee by providing quick and automatic compensation to that employee or the employee's family. Some form of workers' compensation has been adopted in all fifty states of the union. In excess of 90% of the workforce in this country is covered by workers' compensation, although in many states there are some exceptions such as domestic servants, farm workers, or independent contractors. In return for this guaranteed benefit, the injured employee gave up the right to sue the employer for full damages. If there is a third party (other than the employer) who caused or contributed to the accident or accidental injury, the employee may seek civil damages against that party.

However, be aware that there will be fraudulent claims of injuries by some employees that will have a monetary effect on a company. See also the section on INSURANCE FRAUD BY AN EMPLOYEE in Chapter 13.

Employee Injuries. Listed below are the nine basic categories of employee injuries commonly used for insurance and statistical purposes:

1. *Struck by* (vehicle, tool, object)
2. *Struck against* (employee struck or hit object)

3. *Caught-in-between* (fingers, hands, arms caught by nip points or pinch points—squeezed, crushed, loss of . . .)
4. *Body mechanics* (to torso or limbs—strains, back injuries, cumulative trauma)
5. *Laceration/cut/tear/puncture* (by sharp object, tool, etc.)
6. *Fall/trip/slip* (lost balance or other factor or object caused fall)
7. *Contact with temperature extremes* (burns, frostbite)
8. *Eye* (any injury to the eye)
9. *Miscellaneous/other* (any injury not classified)

Accident Records

The Reporting of Accidental Injuries and Illnesses. Any accidental injury reported to or handled by a security officer or an employee of the company must be documented. This report will include the identification of the subject injured or aided; type of injury; date, time, and location; medical aid or assistance rendered; witnesses; and any other information concerning the occurrence.

Anyone, customer or employee, who becomes ill and requires some type of aid or comfort should be handled as importantly and in a similar manner as an injured person. As in an accidental injury, a report of the incident should be compiled and maintained for statistical and insurance purposes. This is particularly so if the person suffering the misfortune or a member of that person's family believes that a negligent act occurred on the premises, or in handling the sick or injured individual and may wish to seek redress in civil court.

Accordingly, a person who suffers some illness on the premises should receive as much care as may be offered to an injured party.

Recording the Incident. Whatever type of personal injury that occurs on the property of the retail establishment, and when that injury is brought to the attention of the retailer in some way (manager, employee, or loss prevention), *a report must be made.* This includes accidents that occur on property inside and outside of the store, as long as it is owned, leased, or controlled by the retailer. No matter how minor the injury to a customer, visitor, or employee, if there is an injury and it is reported, it must be investigated and it must be documented.

All accidents, including illnesses must be reported, investigated, and documented. Most businesses have one form that will encompass the details of an accident or illness for a customer, visitor, or an employee. However, because there are two types of insurance coverage—one for customers and visitors (general liability), and one for employees (workers' compensation)—two types of forms should be used.

All illnesses and accidental injuries to employees must be investigated, if not only for insurance and statistical purposes, but also for incidents that may develop into a workers' compensation case. Customer and visitor accidents must also be of concern, because the possibility of litigation is so prevalent. Therefore, in both categories, the investigation and the report must be complete and accurate. The security officer who investigates the accident, injury, or illness must be cognizant that there will be falsely reported injuries, and illnesses or the exaggeration of minor injuries. If fraud appears to exist, the insurance claims representative or insurance investigator must be advised. Consequently, reporting the accident to the company's insurance carrier will depend on their requirements and procedures. See the Appendix for copies of these reports.

Loss prevention department personnel should be the group that primarily offers medical aid to the injured. Following that, loss prevention must be responsible for the investigation, recording, and documentation of all occurrences of reported injuries and illnesses, whether employee, customer, or visitor related.

In that regard, it should be company policy that all security officers are to be trained and certified as basic first aid and CPR responders.

Loss Runs. One of the important features that an insurance carrier can offer loss prevention and human resources is the *loss run* or *claim report*. Insurance companies are not in business to lose money, and they do not wish to spend their money on your company's losses. Your company pays premiums, and if the losses become too great over a period of time, the insurance company will raise the premiums or cancel any further coverage. Many businesses will set a deductible for their policies that will note an amount the company will cover, and the amount over that specified that the insurance company will cover. Many large retailers will have a $50,000 deductible in most of the risk areas, and therefore are basically self-insured for that amount.

Loss runs include the following categories and was designed to tell the retailer how the company dollars are being spent by your company's insurance company—your company's part as the deductible and their part over the deductible. Each category will also include whether the case is active, closed, and any settlement bestowed or awarded.

- ***General liability (includes operations and premises):*** Encompasses claims made by people outside of or not employed by your business such as personal injuries, accidents, or other incidents.
- ***Property:*** Damage to property such as fire, storm, wind, or flood.
- ***Auto:*** Covers only autos owned or leased by the company and used by employees.
- ***Products liability:*** Covers all claims by people who seek civil action for injury or damage in some manner by or from a product your company had on display or sold to them.
- ***Workers' Compensation:*** Covers employees injured during the course of their employment; it includes medical care, recuperation, and settlement of the claim, if any. Consider also the reimbursement of wages and loss of workdays. In many instances, this is where the greatest monetary loss occurs, and on which loss prevention can have the greatest impact.

Loss runs are usually received from your insurance company on a monthly basis, and are broken down into claims by incident, individual, date, and type of occurrence or injury, all within each of the above categories. It is most important that the loss prevention manager review this information because it will show what, where, when, and how the money is being allocated. Deciphering your loss runs in order to determine the claims activity, and the dollar amounts spent and held in reserve for final determination on that claim among others, requires a detailed study not covered in this book. Your insurance company or broker will be able to give you the necessary information so that you can understand the information and make use of it.

Because accident reporting and loss runs will show where, how, and hopefully why an accident took place, management is able to make the necessary corrective procedures or set up safety programs. In that regard, the loss prevention manager must be responsible for and have the authority to run a safety program. Along with the human resource manager and a top administrative manager, the loss prevention manager must be one of the permanent members on the safety committee.

OCCUPATIONAL SAFETY AND HEALTH ACT

The Occupational Safety and Health Act is administered by the Occupational Safety and Health Administration (also often referred to as OSHA). OSHA is a subdivision of the United States Department of Labor. This act is a federal safety and health law that protects businesses not covered by other federal safety and health laws such as legislation affecting coal mines and nuclear energy. It also excludes coverage of federal, state, and local government employees.

OSHA Injury Records. As required by the Occupational Safety and Health Act, a federal standard, the retailer must initiate and maintain certain records and forms. It requires that the retailer notify the nearest area director, at the Occupational Safety and Health Administration (OSHA), Department of Labor, within 48 hours, if any accident or health hazard results in one or more fatalities or hospitalization of five or more people.

In companies with a large number of employees, the human resources or personnel department usually has the duty of the administration of recordkeeping and notification, with the loss prevention department involved in the initial investigation of the accident or incident.[2]

The most important form that is required by OSHA is the *OSHA 200 Log* (Log and Summary of Occupational Injuries and Illnesses). This form will contain only those injuries and illnesses that concern an occupational death, every nonfatal occupational illness, and those injuries that involve loss of consciousness, restriction of work or motion, transfer to another job position, or medical treatment other than minor injuries where first aid is adequate. Minor injuries where there is no loss of work are not required to be documented on this form.

In larger retail establishments, human resources or personnel will usually compile and maintain this form as required by law. Whoever is responsible for this form, it must be maintained. This log will show all the vital information concerning the injury or occupational illness. It will contain the date of the occurrence, name of the employee, job title, department, and description of injury or illness. If the loss prevention manager uses nothing else for statistical purposes, the information contained in this log can lead to better prevention measures. This form must be retained for five years, with the present year posted with updated information as it occurs. This posting must be conspicuously displayed in the employee areas and subject to an OSHA inspection at any time.

Basically, every employer engaged in a business or industry that affects interstate commerce is required and has the responsibility to observe all OSHA standards applicable to the employer's business, furnish each employee a work area that is free from recognized hazards and/or conditions that can cause physical harm of death, and maintain the premises and work area to comply with all conditions of the OSHA Act.

The Occupational and Safety Health Act General Duty Clause states:

Each *employer* shall furnish to each of his employees, employment and a place of employment which are free from recognized hazards that are causing or likely to cause death or serious physical harm to its employees. Each *employer* shall comply with the Occupational Safety and Health Standards promulgated under this act. Each *employee* shall comply with occupational and safety health standards and all rules, regulations and orders pursuant to this act which are applicable to his own actions and conduct.[3]

Infectious and Health Hazards

Occupational Exposure to Bloodborne Pathogens. Because of the possibility of contamination from bloodborne pathogens (blood or other potentially infectious materials), the first aid responder must be aware of the risk that he or she may face while rendering first aid to an injured person. Moreover, this risk is not only to the responder, but if infected, a possible transmission of the disease to a spouse, children or others could occur. Pathogens include blood and body fluids that carry HIV (commonly known as AIDS), hepatitis A, B, and C, and other assorted infectious diseases.

The federal *Bloodborne Pathogen Standard* (29 CFR §1910.1030) was designed to protect workers from the risk of exposure to those bloodborne pathogens that can cause chronic diseases such as those noted above.

The federal standard (law) requires the following:[4]

- ***Exposure assessment:*** The employer must determine which job classification and specific tasks involve exposure.
- ***Written exposure control plan:*** A site-specific exposure control plan must be developed and in effect.
- ***Hepatitis B vaccination:*** Employees who are at risk to this exposure must be offered free HBV vaccinations.
- ***Education and training:*** The required bloodborne pathogen training sessions for employees at risk must be offered by the employer.
- ***Recordkeeping:*** Medical records of employee exposures and treatment must be retained and kept confidential for the duration of employment plus 30 years.
- ***Hazardous waste disposal:*** The safe cleanup and disposal methods with appropriate biohazard labeling.
- ***Post-exposure incident management:*** The required actions after exposure to an employee, management of after-care, and continuity of records.

With appropriate first aid and CPR training, the security officer and other employees will know the correct procedure to protect themselves. All human blood and body fluids must be treated as if known to be infectious. As long as a barrier (personal protective equipment) is placed between the victim's blood or other body fluids and the first aid responder, and there is the careful disposition of blood, bandages, and other emergency items (proper infection control methods), there is little chance of contamination to the provider.

Hepatitis. Other than HIV exposure, there also is the possibility of other serious viral infections that also can be transmitted via bloodborne pathogens. In particular, hepatitis is to be considered a serious infectious affliction that can cause longlasting illness and death.

Hepatitis is a disease characterized by inflammation of the liver. Viral hepatitis refers to several common diseases caused by viruses that can lead to swelling and tenderness of the liver.

The most common types of viral hepatitis are hepatitis A, hepatitis B, and hepatitis C. There are other forms of hepatitis that are less common including hepatitis D and E, as well three other lesser known viruses. Vaccines exist for types A, B, and D, but there is no vaccine for type C, the most serious of the types.

Hepatitis B and C can lead to serious, permanent liver damage, and is a cause for concern, particularly to those employees who may come into contact with bloodborne pathogens. The retailer is required to conduct bloodborne pathogen training for all first aid responders and all those employees included in the exposure control plan as per the OSHA standard. The standard also requires that all employees included in the exposure control plan should be vaccinated for protection against hepatitis B (HBV). Vaccination and/or testing are to be provided by the retailer free of charge to all employees covered by the standard.

If the employee declines to accept vaccination and/or testing, a declination form must be signed and maintained in the coworker's personnel file, but the employee may request such medical treatment thereafter at any time.

Hazards in the Workplace. There is another federal law that must concern all security officers because of a possible health hazard. The Occupational Safety and Health Administration has set a standard (a law) to ensure that all hazardous and toxic substances produced or brought into a business location are evaluated, and such information concerning their hazard is transmitted to all employees.

This law is the *Hazard Communication Standard*—"The Right to Know Act."[5] All employees have the right to know what hazards and/or harmful substances they might face or may come in contact with in the workplace. This includes all chemicals, solvents, cleaning agents, toxic substances, and environmental hazards. This law also includes the inventory, labeling, training, and the training documentation of all employees. The loss prevention department usually performs these requirements.

Security officers should be aware of all the hazards that may be contained in their workplace. A hazard may be described as follows:

- A *hazardous substance or mixture* is any chemical that is a *physical* or *health hazard.*
- A *physical hazard* is any item that is explosive or flammable, including combustible liquids and compressed gas.

- A *health hazard* is any chemical substance when exposed to a person through the skin, inhalation, or ingestion, may produce acute or chronic effects.
- An *environmental hazard* is any substance, emission, or discharge determined to be hazardous and that poses a danger if released into the environment.

Hazard Communication (Hazcom). As required by the OSHA standard, the company must provide annual training to all employees, no matter how long employed. Additionally, this training must be fully documented concerning participation, and such documentation contained in their personnel file for future reference. This documentation must be available and open for inspection by OSHA.

Known as *The Right to Know Act*, this law covers employee rights while working with hazardous substances. Most retailers may not carry such substances in their product range, but as with other companies may use products that are classified as hazardous. These include everyday items such as paints, cleaners, solvents, cleaning fluids, etc.

All retailers, even as a nonmanufacturing company, are required to conduct an inventory of hazardous substances found or used within their premises. The acute and chronic effects of exposure or overexposure to these hazardous or toxic substances can be found in the material safety data sheets (MSDS) along with the symptoms arising from such exposure and the potential for flammability, explosiveness, and reactivity. A *hazardous substance survey* MSDS form must be individually compiled listing these substances, and this form placed in an area where all coworker notices are normally posted and easily accessible.

The retailer must be committed to providing a safe working environment for all employees, and provide a written training program for all employees who are exposed or may be exposed to hazardous substances or hazardous mixtures found in the work area. The employee is required by law to participate in the training program at least once a year.

Moreover, employees must be made aware of the appropriate emergency procedures in the event of exposure and/or contamination, by a spill, leak, fire, or other accident in the work area when it concerns a hazardous substance. It is the responsibility of all employees to use appropriate protective equipment when handling any hazardous substance, and to ensure that the proper conditions exist for their safe use. Protective equipment and/or clothing must be provided to the employee at no cost by the company.

Conclusion. Many employers oppose governmental interference and the standards mandated by OSHA, because of the expenditures necessary to accommodate or conform to the requirements. However, these mandates are consistent with the basic standards of safety and health, and there is little question regarding the long-term effects obtained from the act.

Loss prevention professionals have come to realize that the *preventive approach to loss*, no matter what type of risk, is the most effective means in its reduction. One of the more important hazards includes injuries to employees.

For further information concerning training requirements for employees, the basic provisions of the act, the obligations and responsibilities of the retailer, and how complaints and OSHA investigations are conducted, see the following booklets printed by the Superintendent of Documents, Government Printing Office, Washington, DC, 20402:—*Federal Occupational Safety and Heath Standards*, and *A Handy Reference Guide*, U.S. Department of Labor, Occupational Safety and Health Administration (OSHA).

CAUTIONARY BEHAVIOR

Security officers should be aware that whether they are certified first aid responders or not, that if the officer or *any employee* comes to the aid of a sick or injured individual and there is a transference or exposure to bloodborne pathogens (blood or body fluids), the exposed officer/employee is covered and protected under the *reporting requirements* of the *Bloodborne Pathogen Exposure Act.* An incident of this type is to be considered a serious exposure and whether or not a subsequent infection of HIV or hepatitus A, B, or C occurs, a workers' compensation report should be considered along with the initial required declarations under the law.

The security officer should also be cognizant of the fact that there will be instances where personal contact will be made with other than an injured or ill person. Whether that contact is by way of an altercation, an arrest by or with the use of force, or some other instance, the possibility is that the officer could be exposed to blood or body fluids, and consequently there might be a possibility of infection. Under these circumstances, the security officer is also protected and covered by the *Bloodborne Pathogen Exposure Act* under the "reporting procedures upon exposure." Therefore, the officer will be treated under this federal law and under workers' compensation regulations.

Americans with Disabilities Act (ADA). The Americans with Disabilities Act is a federal law that affects all American business and in particular retail businesses because these establishments cater to the public with an open door policy. The law was passed a few years ago to prevent Americans with any type of disability from facing various barriers to public accommodations. Compliance enforcement is not carried out by any regulatory agency such as OSHA, but various parts of the act are enforced by the Department of Justice (DOJ), the Equal Employment Opportunity Commission (EEOC), the Federal Communications Commission (FCC), and the Architectural Transportation Compliance Board (ATCB). Their response and subsequent inquiry or investigation is usually based on a complaint made by an individual or a group, and most often concerns some type of a barrier. Particular to retail, these barriers include inadequate or no wheelchair access to entrances, doorways, and hallways, access to another floor of a building, restrooms and its facilities, door handles rather than doorknobs, and no handicap parking.

The law notes that compliance is based on corrections made "readily achievable" and being a "reasonable accommodation." All major businesses have applied the corrective measures required by the law by this time. However, when complaints are made, they are investigated by one of the agencies noted above. If the retailer is advised of a complaint, and it is found to be valid, the retailer should correct the problem rather than face punitive fines. Loss prevention should contact the company attorney for direction and guidelines if notified of an infraction.

THE SAFETY COMMITTEE

As we have noted throughout this book, the obligation of the loss prevention or security officers to their employer and to their profession is to secure a safe environment for the workforce, customers, and visitors alike. This will include the routine inspection, observation, and correction of all hazardous and safety issues in or around the premises. However, there is another most important component in the protection of all those people who will inhabit the facility, and that is the safety committee.

An effective safety committee is the backbone of every successful safety program if the committee is adequate in creating and maintaining an active interest in accident prevention, and serves as a means of safety communication to the workforce. One of the best ways to maintain this high level of interest is to get coworkers involved in participating on the safety committee. Safety committee meetings should be held on a monthly basis without any cancellations. If meetings are frequently canceled, the importance of the committee and the meeting will be diminished. In that sense in order for a safety committee to be effective and acquire the attitude that their function is important, top management should actively participate and serve on the safety committee.

Establishment of a Safety Committee

The structure of the safety committee should be representative of the various departments throughout the store or facility. The members should be knowledgeable and in tune with the various operations within their own department. Department managers or supervisors should be included as members. Membership on the committee should be rotated at least on a semiannual basis, with the rotation structured so that several experienced members remain on the committee at all times. Control of the committee is a management responsibility, and in that manner the operations manager, the human resource manager, or the loss prevention manager should serve as the chairperson of the committee.

Safety committees are only as effective as their meetings. If meetings are too formal, they can stifle creative ideas, meaningful decisions, and most importantly, member interest and participation. On the other hand, if they are too informal, they will almost always end up as simply gripe sessions that achieve little. To keep the meeting on track and meaningful, a basic agenda must be developed to address topics appropriate for each meeting. The order of business should include coworker and customer accident review, inspections and audits, fire and safety violations, near misses, and safety education. Good meetings require discipline, and allow only information related to the topics on the agenda to be discussed at the meeting. If a meeting is open to general discussion, the meeting could last indefinitely with little being accomplished. Set a definite time limit for meetings. Forty-five minutes is common for an effective meeting with a maximum of one hour. All members should be reminded of the time limit and to keep their comments on the topic under discussion.

Minutes of the meeting must be taken and maintained. A copy of the minutes should be distributed to all members of the committee and to all department heads. Additionally, a copy of the minutes should be posted on a bulletin board so that all coworkers may review the business of the committee. All employees are encouraged to approach the safety committee member assigned from their department with any ideas or problems they may view as of interest to the committee.

The selection of safety committee members should be based on the following attributes:

1. ***Willingness.*** To serve and carry out the committee functions.
2. ***Leadership.*** Members chosen should have the respect of their peers, subordinates, and superiors, and have demonstrated the ability to gain respect of new people they work with.
3. ***Technical skill.*** All things being equal, it is best to choose members who have demonstrated safety-related skills. This may include certified first aid responders, volunteer firefighters, etc.

GOALS AND FUNCTIONS OF THE SAFETY COMMITTEE

The function of the safety committee is to create and maintain a high level of interest in the awareness of safety among employees at all levels. To be effective, the safety committee should:

1. Provide a means of communications concerning safety matters between management and the workforce.
2. Develop safety policies and recommend their adoption by top management.
3. Create and maintain an active interest in safety and accident prevention.
4. Identify unsafe work practices and conditions, and suggest appropriate remedies.
5. Encourage support from all levels in all areas of the facility regarding problems, ideas, and solutions relating to safety and health.
6. Assist in accident investigations and develop recommendations to eliminate the accident cause.
7. Recommend and assist in the development of specific safety programs, and further the education/training of coworkers in safety.
8. Assess safety equipment needs.
9. Disseminate safety policy material.
10. Identify specific safety-related problems that seem to be recurring and develop appropriate preventative measures. Inspect for and correct unsafe acts or hazards.

ENDNOTES

1. OSHA—*Bloodborne Pathogens Standard*—29 CFR 1910.1030.
2. To obtain the necessary forms and booklet, *Record Keeping Requirements Under OSHA*, contact the closest Department of Labor Office.
3. Title 29 USC 1900, §5(a)(1), OSHA's *General Duty Clause*.
4. Op. cit., *Bloodborne Pathogens Standard*.
5. OSHA—*Right to Know—Hazard Communication*, 29 CFR 1910.1200.

Chapter 18

Strikes, Violence, Unruly Persons, and Crowds

STRIKES AND PICKETING

One of the more difficult situations that security officers will face will be to confront fellow coworkers who decide to conduct a strike against their employer. This is especially a concern if the security officer is a member of the striking union, or a member of a union that sympathizes with the goals of the striking members.

Depending on the severity of the strike and its effect on the safety and security of people and property, it will be up to the retail administration to reduce its operation, close down the store, or to continue with business as usual. Remember that the retailer has the legal right to remain open for business with as little disruption as possible and the police will enforce that right. Loss prevention's key function during a strike is to control violence, and to protect people and property from harm. However, in the event that the strike may have escalated to some serious extent, the police may request that the retailer curtail certain business operations or services for reason of safety.

The striking union is protected by public law, but it is also required to act within that law. Accordingly, retailers and their employees (including managers and loss prevention personnel) cannot commit strikebreaking tactics.

There are two types of strikes:

- ***Economic:*** The union must give the company 60 days notice of its intent to strike. This period will provide the company with time to negotiate a settlement or to make plans for the strike.
- ***Unfair labor practice:*** This type of strike can take place suddenly and without notice. This would include a "wildcat strike" where there is a walkout or work stoppage, particularly in violation of a valid union contract. The company must react quickly, usually by requesting a court order to return to work.

Security officers must remember that their primary responsibilities are the protection of employees and customers from harm and the protection of property. Retail establishments are susceptible to great loss and damage during a riot or a civil unrest, which may have started as simply as a strike or a demonstration that got out of control.

Therefore, in order to be effective security officers must remain neutral. Security officers may sympathize with the strikers, but their attitude and emotions must be kept to themselves. If the reasons or plight of the strikers will affect how they perform the duties that they were hired to do, they might as well join the picket line. The security or loss prevention manager must have complete loyalty and accountability of all security personnel within this department.

As soon as the security officer (or the immediate security supervisor) learns that a strike will occur or has begun, the loss prevention manager and the retail administration should be advised as soon as practical. Subsequent to that, the loss prevention manager should notify the local police department, particularly if the strike has occurred or is imminent. Strikes and picket behavior are covered under various laws and such laws determine how and what parameters the strikers will operate under. Generally, strikers and pickets may only congregate and picket off the property of the business in question, and under certain lawful conditions may picket only on the public highway (sidewalk, curb, and street). The police will become involved, if nothing else, in order to keep an eye out for any violations of law and keep the peace. If the strikers and/or their supporters become unruly or get out of hand in any way that would cause a disturbance or a business interruption, or attempt to stop or impede the flow of traffic or people onto the business property, the police will be the group to handle the situation and not company security. Security officers must not become involved in physical confrontations with strikers unless an assault takes place on their person or the property they are protecting. Security officers should be guided by the laws of arrest and the use of force as noted elsewhere in this book. The security officer and the retailer can be expected to be directed by police actions in any situation and any request by them during an emergency. This might include the closing down of the premises in order to quiet and/or disperse a mob.

One must remember that protection and access to the facility for customers, visitors, and other employees who wish to continue to work are major concerns. Sabotage may also be a problem because some strikers may become frustrated as time passes and attempt to disrupt business in various ways—some of which may be considered very serious. This could include bomb threats, the obstruction of public utility services (electric, gas, and telecommunications), or outright physical damage to property.

Additional Picketing Issues. Groups or crowds that may form or picket a retail business because of some business practice or circumstance that they feel affects or offends them or others as a group should be handled as that of a strike incident.

An example of such an activity could include issues such as offensive hiring practices, discrimination or harassment practices, animal rights (retail stores that sell furs or animal products), and conduct considered abhorrent to certain religious groups (abortion clinics). If management cannot resolve the situation, the police should be requested. If the occurrence causes a business disruption or their presence is illegal, they can be removed. Caution and discretion in tactics must be considered for fear of bad press and publicity.

UNRULY CROWDS

Unruly crowds can occur at various times and under various conditions. Large groups of people can consolidate into a crowd milling about and bent on one goal—satisfying the reason why they are there. A large amount of customers, at times unexpected, may descend upon a retailer within a short period because of a particular sale or a greatly reduced price on an advertised item. As they become anxious and unruly in an attempt to fight their way to the desired merchandise, tempers will flair and confrontations will occur. Serious problems will arise if the retailer's stock is diminished and cannot service all who are present. As the crowd becomes more cohesive, pushing and shoving people aside, children and the elderly can be severely injured in the rush. Another problem is that damage and larcenous conduct can become the norm under these conditions. Ultimately the reputation of the store will suffer because of customer dissatisfaction and poor press. The retailer never wins in a situation such as this.

Occurrences described above are rare but not uncommon in the retail trade. If the merchandise is depleted with many customers still present, the retailer must make some amends to placate those customers not serviced. Rain checks or the offering of similar or more expensive merchandise at the sale price most often tempers the crowd, at least to some degree. Considerable care and concern must be used at times such as this. The security officer must remember that these are good customers who may have become irritated and angry at a fault committed inadvertently or unknowingly by the retailer.

ABNORMAL, DISTURBED, AND DISGRUNTLED PERSONS

At some time all security officers will be confronted with angry, disgruntled, or disturbed individuals. Minor in nature will be those customers who become angry or annoyed at some company policy such as sales and/or returns, or the attitude or response of a salesperson. These problems can usually be resolved by the store or department manager in placating the customer in some manner, and the security officer should not become involved unless requested to do so.

It is the customer who under no circumstances can be satisfied or persuaded to leave the premises that the security officer must be called to the scene and asked to intervene. It is at these situations that security officers must use all of their personal attributes in affecting an agreeable solution for all concerned. Security officers should consider communication, demeanor, and body language as the positive attributes most likely to succeed. If a solution cannot be found, the retailer/store manager and/or the security officer can ask the customer to leave the store because he or she is causing a scene, a disturbance, or a crowd to collect—all actions that constitute a business interruption and/or a criminal trespass. If the subject refuses to leave, he or she can be advised that the subject is in violation of the law, because after a request to leave the premises and warning has been issued, the subject could be charged with the offense of criminal trespass. Further, the police can be called and the subject removed forcibly and charged with the criminal trespass. If such action is taken in a situation such as this, the security officer or the merchant/store manager must and will act as the complainant to consummate the arrest. Consider that any person taken into custody has been arrested. Subsequently releasing that person for whatever reason thereby failing to continue the arrest onto prosecution places the company employee and the retailer in civil jeopardy.

There will also be instances when a security officer encounters a person who is acting in an erratic or physically threatening manner. This person may be highly argumentative, or exhibit a demeanor that may be considered suicidal, and/or act as though a threat to self, employees, and customers. As a result the security officer may have to resort to physical force.

Responsive actions by a security officer under these situations as are covered in many states by *justification of force* or in the public or mental health laws. The use of physical force upon another person, which would otherwise constitute an offense, may be justifiable and not criminal under certain circumstances. This could include a person acting under a reasonable belief that another person is about to commit suicide or to inflict serious physical injury upon himself or herself, and may use physical force upon such person to the extent that he or she reasonably believes it necessary to thwart such result. Moreover, a person may use physical force upon another person in self-defense or in defense of a third person, or in defense of a premise. Regarding premises, such physical force (other than deadly physical force) upon another may be used when a security officer reasonably believes such force is necessary to prevent or terminate the commission or attempted commission of damage to a premises. Some states include the use of deadly physical force if a person reasonably believes such is necessary to prevent or terminate the commission or attempted commission of arson. Security officers should check with the laws of the state in which they are employed for the rules of conduct in these events.

Generally, it is not necessary for security officers to possess expertise in mental health to determine if a person is mentally disturbed. All that may be required is that *a person (security officer) acting under the reasonable belief* is enough for the security officer to react to the incident. It is not necessary for the security officer to determine if the erratic behavior is caused by alcohol, drugs, or a mental illness, but the actions and/or behavior and the condition of the subject must be observed by the security officer. Third-person information concerning erratic or abnormal behavior is not enough for the officer to act upon—the officer must view and make his or her own interpretation. Caution regarding physical force on the subject should by limited to enough force to prevent harm to the subject or to another.

Subsequent to controlling and placing the subject in custody, the police should be called so that the subject may be removed to a hospital facility for further examination. Police action in these cases is usually for the subject to be treated as a person in need of care, and not as a criminal. Transport from the scene is usually made by ambulance.

In general the courts have found that restraint or detention, reasonable under the circumstances and in time and manner, imposed for the purpose of preventing another from inflicting personal injuries or interfering with or damaging real or personal property in one's lawful possession or custody should not be considered unlawful.

WORKPLACE VIOLENCE

Workplace Violence Defined. The most common conception of workplace violence by the general public are those disputes or confrontations between employee and employer that escalate into serious altercations, and in which serious injury or death may be a consequence. These actions can occur in and around the place of employment or business premises. But as we have seen in recent years, violence can be precipitated by other factors that do not include the employee/employer relationship. Because violence is becoming more prevalent in today's society, particularly in the workplace, it is important that we cover the problem in some detail. As described by the Office of Safety and Health Administration (OSHA), violence in the workplace may fall into three categories:

- **Type I—*stranger violence:*** This type of violence occurs when a stranger, unknown to the occupants of the premises (a business, school, or place of worship), enters with the intent to commit a crime. It could include an armed robbery or a sexual assault upon an employee, customer, or visitor. Moreover, it might include a deranged or hate-filled individual who believes that his or her actions will bring him or her some type of recognition, whether reasonable or not. It is estimated that this type of violence accounts for 60% of all workplace homicides.

- **Type II—*customer/client violence:*** Occurrences such as these may take place when a client attacks an employee during the course of a business transaction. This could include a welfare recipient attacking a social worker, a patient striking a heath-care worker, or a disgruntled customer attacking a salesperson. It is estimated that 30% of all homicides fall into this category.
- **Type III—*employee violence:*** Although this area accounts for only 10% of workplace homicides, it appears to be the most prevailing form of aggression as perceived by the general public. It will include employee versus employee; employee attacks upon supervisors, managers, and bosses; and domestic violence. The subjects of the conflict can also include former employees, temporary or contractual employees, or subcontractors who may spend a significant amount of their workday on your premises.

Workplace Violence—a Perspective. Although percentages noted above have been the well-accepted statistics, recent criminal activity is rewriting the percentages and the types of violence within each category.

Workplace violence can strike anywhere—from supermarkets, shopping malls, retail department stores, offices, government buildings, schools, banks, libraries, and even restaurants. The escalation of violence in these accessible open public locales places not only the employee at danger but also the visitor. The assault may be random in nature, or it may include targeted individuals.

The occurrence of violence in Type I and Type II as described above is exceptionally hard to predict, because these assailants will be strangers and there will be no prior knowledge of that individual. When that person enters your premises, it will usually be the first time you will have any interaction. Other than certain safeguards that will reduce crimes such as robbery, and specific actions by an employee to reduce or curtail an attack, it will never be possible to completely eliminate the threat.

However, there is one area in which some effort can be made to address the problem of violence. That area is *Type III—Employee Violence*. Because there can be no inquiry into a person's private life during the hiring process, the employer must depend completely on prior employment criminal and financial inquiry and hope that the information received is complete and forthcoming. Other than that, the employer has no further recourse other than to observe the demeanor and performance of the newly hired employee during the probationary period. If not observed during this period, sooner or later there will be obvious warning signs to alert an observant supervisor or boss to possible serious behavior problems. Although the employer may view workplace violence as minor and an additional problem to face, there is also the problem of compliance under federal law, which states that the employer must provide a safe and healthful work environment for all employees.[1]

Other than the social or physical disorders that could identify a violent person, we should be more concerned with the Type III category so we may be able to recognize this behavior to some degree. This individual may be a disgruntled or former employee, or a person who is or becomes uncontrollable or erratic because of alcohol or drugs. In addition, it is not uncommon for an angry or irate spouse or lover of an employee to cause an altercation in and around the business premises.

Employee Violence

Although workplace violence between coworkers would not normally be considered an emergency where retail security officers must become physically involved to control the situation, it does happen. There is little doubt that violence in the workplace is on the increase, and it can occur under various conditions. Anger, frustrations, competitiveness, theft between coworkers, and stress, for example, can make emotions and tempers escalate into physical confrontations. Moreover, minor or negligible problems can also simmer and increase to where harm or destruction most likely can occur. In that respect, this is why security officers must have their eyes and ears tuned to the employee community, where fellowship and silence is most often the norm.

As a security officer, the first and most important step in anticipating workplace violence is to know your employees. Hopefully the human resources or personnel department has gone beyond a cursory check of prospective employees during the hiring process so that those persons who have a troubled or violent background can be identified and refused employment.

Petty instances can lead to serious overt actions, therefore, security officers must be aware of everything around them. Unless the occurrence has already become critical, it is in the company's best interest for them to bring these minor instances to the attention of the human resources or personnel manager as soon as they are made aware. Theft of personal property by one coworker from another is not only a cause for concern by loss prevention, but also whether the culprit is truly identified or not can lead to serious physical violence. Moreover, there will be times when tempers flare and fists fly for no other reason than jealousy, work habits, or girlfriend-boyfriend situations.

In addition, certain business situations or events may trigger a violent incident among workers, including negative performance ratings, disciplinary actions, terminations, strikes, downsizing, love triangles, and just plain personality dislikes. Depending on the seriousness of the situation, some immediate action must be taken, ranging from some type of consultation by managers to immediate dismissal. In most occurrences, a warning and subsequent close attention of the combatants will suffice. But in the more critical events, the security officers must remember that even the most docile employee will react to mob behavior during labor actions or strife, simply because a person's livelihood may be at stake. During these serious situations, loss prevention must protect those employees and management personnel still on the job and the facility itself from any risk or harm. When an employee is threatened with bodily harm on the premises, or threatened off premises and an assault takes place within the facility, loss prevention should attempt to have the threatened employee make a police report of the incident.

During all terminations for cause, a security officer should be present or in close proximity in case the situation becomes loud, abusive, or physical. The terminated employee should be escorted to his or her locker for confiscation of company property or to gather his or her own private property if necessary and immediately escorted off premises. The terminated employee should be given a trespass warning if the company feels that it is a necessity, written if possible, noting that he or she is not to enter into any area of the store other than that area open to the public. Further, the terminated employee is not to contact former coworkers while they are working and disrupt them while at work. He or she should be advised that any violation of this trespass notice could result in an arrest.

Caution should also be used in how and when reason for termination or evidence is presented to the employee. Do not give the impression, if possible, that another employee assisted, gave help, or in any way caused the termination of the fired employee. If the terminated employee believes that another coworker is in fact involved in his or her dismissal, attempt to dissuade or deny such belief. If the security officer feels that the fired employee may take some retribution against another, advise him or her that if such action is taken, he or she will be arrested and charged with the appropriate crime. For further information concerning this matter, see the section on THE EMPLOYEE TERMINATION PROCESS in Chapter 15.

Additionally, security officers must consider the possibility of an incident that could occur and may provoke an employee so intensely as to seriously injure or kill people that the subject believed were or could have been the cause of his or her predicament. A random act of this type and/or the possibility of a hostage situation on premises call for the immediate assistance of the police and emergency medical assistance if required. Security officers should not become involved directly with the person committing the assault or the hostage taking—their only duty is to protect as many employees and customers as possible by removing them from the crime scene. Whether the subject remains on premises or is involved with a hostage, the police will be the controlling factor once they arrive, and the security officer will stand by to give whatever assistance or information the police may require during the incident.

Identifying the Potential Perpetrator. Several early warning signs may be considered in attempting to identify the employee with propensity toward violence. Some of these traits can be identified during the hiring process, whereas others may not be observable until the subject has been employed for a period of time. These could include the following traits and/or personal history of an individual:

1. A migratory work history, which might involve an involvement in serious disagreements or violence in prior employment. A criminal history of violence, or any history of violence outside of the workplace. A substance abuser—alcohol or drugs.
2. A history of domestic or child abuse, or as a victim of abuse. A history of psychological problems or personality disorders, resolved or not. This would include obsessive compulsive behavior, and abnormal, inappropriate or odd and erratic behavior. Romantic or sexual obsessions, particularly if observable.
3. A loner or a socially isolated individual with no or very few friends. Paranoid or has an unwarranted sense of entitlement. Views change, coworker promotion, or little or no wage increases as a personal indignity. Chronically disgruntled, always complaining. Does not accept criticism, has contempt and disdain for authority. Holds grudges against anyone who has "offended" him or her. Externalizes blame, will never accept or own up to self shortcomings.
4. Easily justifies other acts of violence or violence elsewhere as permissible. Views intimidation, force, fury, or violence as legitimate and acceptable. A

bigot and/or a devotee to racial, political, religious, ethnic, or cultural biases. An obsession with, access to, or possession of weapons, including attraction to or participation in paramilitary groups or training.

Results of Violence in the Workplace. Any serious incident of violence occurring on a business property can cause the following aftereffects:

- Business disruption
- Civil law suits and legal expenses
- Need for increased security
- Property damage
- Employee trauma
- An effect on productivity or a reduction in the business enterprise
- An effect on the company's image

ENDNOTE

1. Op. cit., *OSHA's General Duty Clause*.

Part 6

ALARMS AND INSPECTIONS

INTRODUCTION

Consider the following description of burglar and fire alarms to be a basic introduction into these systems. If proprietary security officers were employed in a facility where they are responsible in some way in the control, operation, maintenance, and repair of these devices, they should have complete knowledge of those systems on board.

Maintenance of Alarm Hardware

Proprietary ownership of all burglary and fire panels, equipment, controls, and devices can be maintained and serviced by the facility's own personnel, or by the manufacturer of the equipment under a separate contractual agreement. If the system is installed and leased to the retailer, upkeep and maintenance may also be part of that lease agreement between the retailer and the central station provider. Both systems, burglar and fire, must be maintained in good working order. However, whoever maintains these systems, security officers must be completely familiar with all contingencies that may occur. Having the knowledge, training, and expertise prior to an emergency, and how to act and respond to an alarm during such an incident will serve them well in the reliability and confidence given to them by their superiors.

Chapter 19
Alarm Systems

BURGLAR ALARMS

The burglar alarm system consists of a continuous flow of low-voltage electricity throughout the alarm circuit. Any interruption or break in this electrical flow or current will activate the alarm. Various detection devices connected to this electric circuit are designed to interrupt the electric current when triggered, and when triggered sends a signal out notifying that there is a break or movement within the protected premises.

All certified alarm systems must have a standby source of power, such as battery packs for both the alarm circuit and electronic devices in order to maintain operation in case of power failure. Various combinations of sensing devices, alarm controls, and alarm signal equipment can be applied and/or modified to any business premises. Whatever sophistication or combination of equipment used will depend on the risk, the structure, occupancy, the value of the property to be protected, and the cost.

Accordingly, the key elements of a reliable alarm system are the proper equipment for the protection required, the proper application and response to that system, and an effective central station.

Alarm Design, Protection, and Hardware

Burglar alarm systems are composed of three parts—sensing devices, alarm control, and alarm signal.

Sensing Devices. Sensing devices are used in the actual detection of the intruder, and provide

- *Perimeter protection*—point of entry,
- *Area protection*—spaces within the premises, and
- *Object or spot protection*—direct or individual coverage.

Perimeter Protection. Includes devices protecting any point of entry: perimeter doors, windows, roof hatches, skylights, and vents. Because most illegal entries occur at these locations, it is most important that protection includes these areas. The most common device is the magnetic contact switch. This item can be attached to a door or window in such a way that if opened, the contact is broken and will activate the alarm. These contacts can be surface mounted, recessed, or concealed, and are available in all varieties.

Metallic foil or window tape had been widely used in the past. But because of its inherent problems, it has just about been discontinued. Foil tape can be accidentally broken or intentionally damaged by a would-be burglar. For example someone could use a razor blade to create a very fine "line" break in the foil, causing time and energy attempting to find and correct the break in order to keep that point of entry on-line and not bypassed. This foil tape was applied to glass doors and windows, and required frequent maintenance, particularly on doors with heavy traffic. Today glass doors and large glass panels and windows are protected by glass breakage sensors, which are usually attached to the ceiling, facing toward and set back from the glass depending on the coverage required. When the noise of breaking glass is detected, the glass breakage sensor will activate the alarm.

Other devices include wooden screens and lacing. Wooden screens are made of wooden dowels assembled in a cage-like fashion with fine brittle wire within the dowels and frame, and made to cover a particular opening. Any break in this screen or frame would trigger an alarm. It is primitive, but effective. The term *lacing* is where walls, roofs, or ceilings are protected by weaving a lace-like pattern of metallic foil or fine brittle wire and is placed within and covered by wallboard, plaster, or wood paneling. Breaking through a roof, ceiling, or wall would then trigger an alarm.

Area Protection. Includes devices that guard the interior spaces of the building against intrusion and any movement within. Any perimeter break not covered by other devices, such as an entry through the roof or an outside wall, would pick up any movement within. These devices provide protection to any space or area that an establishment may wish to protect, and would include highly sensitive and/or an invisible means of detection in high-risk areas. These sensors are also effective against a "lock-in" burglar, who hides within the building until everyone leaves, takes what he or she wishes and breaks out. A good system can provide central station an exact location of the intruder, even to the extent of "following" the intruder throughout the building as the intruder passes each sensor. A disadvantage to these sensors is that they must be adjusted to sensitivity or protection of movement because of the possibility of frequent false alarms. Movement of flags, banners, balloons, or other hanging objects; air emanating from heating or cooling ducts; and the movement of birds flying in large buildings or the body heat of a mouse can activate the sensor.

Various sensors can be used for the purpose of area protection, and the use of any one of them will depend on the protection desired or required and the particular device to be used. The following are some examples:

Photoelectric eyes or beams—these devices transmit a beam of light across a protected area. When an intruder interrupts this beam, an alarm is activated. Originally a light sent to a reflector such as a mirror, today's photoelectric eyes use light-emitting diodes, a beam invisible to the naked eye. They can have a range in excess of one thousand feet and provide excellent protection.

Ultrasonic detectors—these devices are part of the motion detector group. Mounted high on walls or ceilings, they can protect a three-dimensional area with an invisible pattern. Any movement by an intruder within the protected area of this device disrupts a high-pitched (ultrasonic) sound, which will activate an alarm. These devices can be subject to false alarms because of the movement of air currents and ultrasonic noises from mechanical equipment.

Infrared detectors—these devices detect heat from the body of the intruder. Once any rise in temperature is met, an alarm is activated.

Microwave detectors—this type of motion detector uses high-frequency radio waves to detect movement and has a greater range than ultrasonic. Because it does not use sound (air), microwave is not prone to false alarms caused by air currents. Because microwaves can penetrate materials such as glass or reflect metal objects, their installation should be properly positioned.

The most common motion detector in use today combines the use of infrared and microwave. In this way, both heat and movement can be detected. These devices can be had in varying ranges of width and distance for the coverage required and can be mounted anywhere.

Object or Spot Protection. Provides direct or individual protection to a particular item or thing such as a safe, expensive equipment, sensitive documents, or something of great value. Other than common devices such as magnetic contacts on a safe door, or a sensitive pad located under a rug in front of a protected item, sophisticated devices include the following:

Capacitance detectors—these are also called proximity detectors, in which the object that is protected becomes an antenna electronically linked to an alarm control. Depending on the sensitivity level desired, anyone approaching the object causes an unbalance to an electrostatic field and the alarm is activated. Only metal objects such as safes can be protected in this manner.

Vibration detectors—electronic vibration detectors (EVD) utilize a highly sensitive and specialized microphone that is attached directly to anything such as a safe, cabinet, or art object. It can also be attached to surfaces such as a wall, ceilings, and windows, and can be adjusted to detect a sledgehammer on a concrete wall or the delicate penetration of a glass surface. Vibration detectors have an advantage over capacitance detectors because they can protect all objects, not just metal, and will alarm only when the object is moved or a vibration is detected.

Alarm Control. Alarm control is the method in which the alarm detection is activated or turned off. Whoever has complete control over the alarm system has complete power of security protection over the facility. The person or persons who control that system have the power to turn on and off the system at will, have the ability to bypass points of entry or protection, change opening or closing times, and add or delete passcodes. Burglaries have occurred because someone failed to set the system, or bypassed a point because of laziness and failed to make an attempt to correct the problem. Therefore, it is important that only high-level, dedicated, and loyal employees have access to the alarm system, and then assigned only to the extent or level of access that may be required. Alarm controls fall into two categories, and are described as follows:

Keyed (local) alarm controls—this method is the original procedure for controlling an alarm system and is commonly used in small businesses. Simply put, it is an alarm that is set with the use of a key upon leaving the premises. It is turned "on" when leaving and "off" when opening the business the next day. Keyed controls are economical and very easy to operate, and when set off usually activates an audible alarm outside of the building in an attempt to alert passersby, neighbors, or the police. Shortcomings include forgetting to set the alarm, the loss of the key, or the key can be easily stolen or duplicated, and locks can be "picked." Moreover, there is no written record of exit or entry and by whom. This is not the system to use in a large retail establishment.

Remote (central station) alarm controls—with a central station system, all activations and/or signals are electrically sent to a central station burglar alarm system provider. Any access or keyboard entry, whether it is setting or deactivating the alarm, bypassing points or areas, changing opening or closing times, and who has access and what passcode was used is recorded for future reference. Hard-copy printouts of all signals can be furnished by the central station provider or by the facility's own printer. Because a central station monitors all signals, any irregularity will receive prompt response. Police will be asked to respond to any signal outside of the parameters that are agreed upon between the central station provider and the retailer. This type of system includes the central station being connected via telephone lines or radio. Some systems use telephone lines with a radio backup, but in any event, battery packs are used as a backup in the event of an electrical power failure. A telephone line break will cause a request for police response.

Central station providers also offer installation, maintenance, and repair of the complete burglar alarm system, and radio response of their own security patrol if required. Some people may consider the procedures required by the provider to be cumbersome and annoying at times, but the protection of tighter security far outweighs any inconvenience. Of course, the services provided by a central station are only as good as their timely response to an activation of an alarm or occurrence, response for maintenance repair, and the quality of the people employed by them.

Alarm Signal. The alarm signal is an annunciator or reporting method in which central station, police, or other responsible parties are notified when the alarm detection system has been activated or when there is another problem that should be attended to.

Alarm signals are of two types and are described as follows:

Local alarm signaling—this system is used by both small and large businesses where a large bell or other audible alarm is set off on the outside of the building in question. Problems with this type of alarm have been noted earlier and there is no assurance that the responsible parties will be notified when the alarm sounds. This is particularly evident today, when local residents are becoming accustomed to alarms going off at all times of the day and often for no reason. The basic reasoning for this type of alarm is first to scare off the burglar or intruder upon hearing the alarm, and then, hopefully notification. In order to improve upon this fundamental system, some communities have allowed businesses to be connected to a police station via telephone lines. In large communities, this has been found to be impractical because of so many false alarms and the required police action.

Remote (central station) alarm signaling—the transmission of an alarm signal via telephone line or radio to a certified (Underwriters Laboratories listed) central station is generally regarded as the most reliable method of notification and reducing a loss. Central station includes trained operators on duty 24 hours a day who supervise, notify, record, and maintain alarms, and are supervised by competent managers. They make proper notifications to the subscriber and police upon receipt of an alarm or other condition, response of an armed guard (if contracted), and response of maintenance repair if required. Proper transmission of the alarm signal to a central station is essential. At this time, the direct wire system is considered the most reliable for high-risk locations. This is a single direct (dedicated) telephone line from the subscriber to the central station. When phone lines short out or are broken, problems will arise, but providers accept these problems routinely and should be well equipped for rapid response. Burglars are becoming more sophisticated in the use of electronics and electricity, thereby generating special line security systems that are necessary to prevent "shunting" or "jumping" a telephone line. Moreover, as secured electronic satellite systems become more enhanced and reliable, wireless alarms will become more prevalent in business establishments.

Types of Burglar Alarm Systems

Central station systems are those in which the operations of electrical protection circuits and devices are signaled automatically to, recorded in, maintained, and supervised from a central area or station having trained operators and guards in attendance at all times. They are sometimes called a *silent alarm*. They are independently owned and engaged in furnishing protective signaling service and should have no interest in the property being protected.

Local alarm systems are those systems in which the protective circuits and devices are connected to an enclosed tamper-protected bell or other audible alarm attached to the exterior (and possibly the interior) of the facility. The alarm system is under the control and maintenance of the store proprietor or the owner of the building. If there is a need, and the business has contracted for the service, this audible alarm will sound off along with silent notification to the central station.

Proprietary systems are those in which the store proprietor owns all the protective equipment and all devices within the facility, but are serviced under contract to a central station provider for central station service and maintenance of the equipment.

Contractual systems are those systems in which all equipment and devices are installed, owned, and maintained by an outside provider under a contract with the retailer. Because no central station service is provided, a central station service must be contracted separately. However, some central station companies may also provide this type of equipment service along with central station communications.

A police station-connected system is one in which a signal, initiated at the protected premises, is received and monitored at a police station. Some audible alarms may have a delay of up to five minutes so that the police may respond to the premises before the alarm sounds off.

Class and Grade of the System. For the purpose of clarification, there are three classes of burglar alarm systems. The system class indicates the kind of property that the burglar system protects. They include *mercantile premises*, *mercantile safe and vault alarm*, and *bank safe and vault alarm*.

System installations are identified according to type, grade, and extent of protection by a certificate issued by Underwriters Laboratories, Inc. Grades of alarm systems encompass several categories depending on the type of system. It includes protection against tampering, time of response to an alarm, and wiring fault. The certificate will certify the type of protection and installation provided, which will include complete or partial protection and the class of installation. Insurance coverage will or may depend on the protection certified.

FIRE ALARMS

Fire detection systems are generally classified according to the location where the alarm signal is received.

- ***Local systems***—those in which the alarm registers inside and outside of the protected premises, and is primarily a sounding notification for the occupants.
- ***Auxiliary systems***—those in which the signal is received at the municipal or local fire department. The connecting devices at the protected facility are owned by the facility, and all other equipment connecting to the fire department circuits are owned or leased by the municipality. This system is limited to the signal transmission only, and will not supervise sprinkler systems.
- ***Central station systems***—those in which the service is similar to that provided for burglary coverage, where the signal is registered in an office of a private agency located away from the facility. This agency is in operation 24 hours a day with trained personnel and acts on the signal as required—whether the facility is occupied or not, and who and when notification is made depending on what type of signal. The agency may own all devices within the facility and conduct business on a leased service basis. Maintenance can be provided on a contractual agreement by a fire system and maintenance service with reporting requirements provided by a central station.

  The central station system is common for large establishments, but the quality of service depends on the effective and efficient service provided by the agency. ADT Security Systems and Honeywell International are two examples of large national agency providers. As with burglar alarm protection, the protection that the retailer relies upon is only as good as the central station service provided.

Alarm Design and Hardware

The basic fire alarm system consists of three fundamental components—initiating devices, a control panel, and audible signal devices.

Initiating Devices. These devices initiate an alarm signal and can be manual or automatic, coded or noncoded. The conventional fire alarm pull box is an example of a manual initiating device. Pressure switches, smoke and heat (thermal) fire detectors, and waterflow switches are examples of automatic initiating devices.

Manual fire alarm boxes are manually activated, because there must be someone available to actually pull or set off by hand the sensor in the box to initiate an alarm in case of a fire. These boxes are usually strategically located throughout the facility, both public and nonpublic areas for easy access. They are painted red and are easily identified for the purpose they serve. They serve no purpose during hours when the facility is closed and unoccupied.

Automatic fire detectors come in various forms and are able to cover areas that are attended or not for the purpose of detecting smoke, heat, or flames. Whether in occupied areas or not, the automatic detector increases the speed in which the alarm will be transmitted. Because no single signaling device will be 100% effective in all situations, a professional fire survey should be taken to disclose the correct devices or combination of devices and spacing required for the protection of life and property. These detectors can respond to heat, visible smoke, flames, and invisible or visible products such as dust and tobacco smoke.

Control Panel. All fire alarm systems must always be armed and ready for an emergency. They must also be fail-safe so that in an emergency they will perform without fail. Therefore, the fire control panel must supervise all circuits and provide a "trouble" signal in any abnormal or failing condition. This would include a power failure, open circuit, or a ground fault. Generally, the fire control panel will indicate by audible or visible signal that there is a malfunction in the system that would interfere with the proper transmission of an alarm signal.

Another function of the fire control panel is to provide a terminal or transfer point to accept signals from alarm-initiating circuits, and through relays or other circuits operate audible signal devices (bells and horns), in addition to auxiliary devices such as activation of fire doors (release) and the shutdown of fans, heating, and air conditioning. And most importantly, the signal is transmitted to a central station.

Audible Signal Devices. These include any device that responds to the actuation of the fire alarm system by sounding the alarm. This will include bells, horns, buzzers, sirens, and taped voice messages sent through the public address system. These audible signals or sounds will occur upon activation at any time of the day, whether open for business or not.

SPRINKLER ALARM SYSTEMS

All parts of the sprinkler system must include a waterflow alarm service. The monitoring of only part of the system will not be satisfactory in terms of hazard control and acceptance by a rating bureau.

All devices attached to the system for monitoring remain inactive for long periods or until an emergency arises. In an effort to ensure that all alarm detection, supervisory, and transmission equipment is in operational order, tests must be conducted on-site routinely as required. A central station agency or a certified private contractor usually performs this service, and will also provide written certification of such testing.

Approvals and/or certification are provided by Underwriters Laboratories, fire insurance associations, insurance groups, and local rating bureaus. All follow the recommendations of the Fire Protection Association (NFPA) and similar organizations.

Central station monitoring provides two types of services for the facility with a sprinkler system:

1. ***Supervisory Service.*** Makes sure that the sprinkler system is in operation at all times for full coverage. Sensors will detect such unsafe conditions as closed valves (sabotage or accidental), poor or insufficient water pressure, freezing temperatures, and power failure at the fire pump. These supervisory sensors detect the unsafe conditions and notify the central station where it is recorded. Central station operators will make the proper notifications to responsible personnel for quick repairs and restoration of the system for protection.

   Supervisory service will include the following:

   - Gate valve/butterfly valve
   - Post-indicator valve
   - Area temperature
   - High or low air or water pressure
   - Water levels and temperatures of secondary water supply
   - Fire pump operation
   - Power to fire pumps
   - Tamper sensors

2. ***Waterflow service.*** Protects against sprinkler leakage caused by damage to the sprinkler head or the outbreak of fire. The flow of water through the system activates a fire alarm signal to the central station. Whether the building is occupied or not, central station operators will advise the fire department and the subscriber.

Waterflow monitoring will include the following types of systems, which were also discussed in the segment on AUTOMATIC SPRINKLER PROTECTION in Chapter 16.

- ***Wet-pipe alarm systems:*** systems in which all sprinkler piping contains water throughout the system under pressure, and water is released through each sprinkler head as each head is activated by heat or flames individually. Premises with normal or high occupancy are protected by a wet system in approximately 75% of all systems.
- ***Dry-pipe alarm systems:*** systems that employ air under pressure throughout the system, and allow water to flow to the sprinkler heads after the air pressure is released upon activation.
- ***Combination systems:*** systems in which both of the above are in use depending on the requirements of the facility.

There are also other types of systems such as the *pre-action* and *deluge* systems, which may be found in industrial and manufacturing facilities, and are generally not found in a retail establishment. Hospitals or penal institutions may require a pre-action system, in that a manual or electronic signal is needed to start the flow of water through the piping. Cold storage, freezer areas, or unheated spaces subject to freezing temperatures will also require a dry system.

Chapter 20

Systems Inspection, Testing, Maintenance, and Recordkeeping

FIRE INSPECTIONS

During any daily routine tour of a facility, some discrepancies are bound to be detected. Because of this, fire readiness must be maintained year-round. This is done every day by a regular visual inspection tour by security officers and by a complete fire inspection throughout the building at least monthly. On-site inspection is considered a primary tool in fire protection.

Fire code compliance is based heavily on building design and construction. Certain safety requirements must be met in order to obtain a certificate of occupancy issued by the local authorities and established by their building codes. Fire inspections are conducted to enforce compliance to these building and fire codes. The inspection will be conducted by local building inspectors, county or city fire marshals, or a local firefighter or fire inspector. They have the authority to issue citations returnable in local courts for any violation of these codes.

The loss prevention manager should accompany the inspector on this tour. In this way, the fire inspector can impart first-hand knowledge of any violations and acceptable ways to correct them. The inspector can also give knowledge of fire safety to the manager during the inspection. But most of all, by witnessing the inspection, the manager demonstrates to the inspector a willingness to cooperate and agree to any recommendations that may be offered, and thereby builds a friendly relationship for future inspections.

The insurance companies can also force compliance on the retailer. Insurance companies may conduct fire inspections before a policy is underwritten, and may do so periodically thereafter. Insurance companies cannot demand correction of fire violations as local authorities do, but they can exert considerable influence in denying insurance coverage for any business with inadequate fire protection or unacceptable fire hazards. On the other hand, insurance companies will offer reductions in premiums for the retailer when it can be shown that fire risks are reduced significantly. Some of the ways that this can be accomplished is by regular inspections of all fire equipment, fire stairways, fire exits, buildup of trash or garbage while on routine patrol, in-depth monthly fire inspection of the facility, and the obligatory systematic training of employees in fire safety.

Routine testing, inspection, and maintenance of the facility's water pressure and sprinkler systems, the routine testing and maintenance of the complete fire alarm system, and the routine inspection, recharging, or replacement of all fire hardware is usually completed by outside service agencies or businesses authorized to issue inspection and certification endorsements. These certificates and regulated inspections are or may be required by local codes or insurance companies.

A methodical fire inspection should be carried out by loss prevention. The loss prevention manager or a security supervisor should perform this fire inspection on a monthly basis. The purpose is to determine the fire readiness of the facility. It involves a thorough and systematic check of the entire premises, equipment, processes, operations, and fire protection systems. If the loss prevention manager wishes to assign this duty to a security officer, the officer should have some knowledge of fire safety and fire hardware. The use of a security officer who is also a volunteer firefighter would be an excellent choice. This is not to say that all members of loss prevention should not be aware and inspect everything as they walk within and outside the facility on a daily basis. See the Appendix for a sample FIRE INSPECTION form.

Areas of Inspection

Do not consider the suggestions for fire inspection noted below as complete, because the extent of inspections will depend on the type of facility, its construction, the nature of the business, and its contents. However, on a monthly basis, the following suggestions for a general fire inspection can be considered as a good standard:

General Areas

- All smoking is prohibited unless the store has a designated safe smoking area for employees. Visitors and outside contractors should be advised of the no smoking rules.
- Good housekeeping practices—rubbish and waste material does not accumulate, combustibles are safely and correctly stored, kitchen filters and exhaust systems are checked and cleaned regularly, and all passageways, aisles, and doorways are kept clean and clear, particularly fire exits and fire stairways.

Storage Areas

- Unused pallets should not be stacked more than six feet high in areas protected by sprinklers or outside the facility if there is no sprinkler protection.
- No material should be stored closer in height than eighteen inches from the sprinkler head so that the effectiveness of the water shower from the sprinkler is not obstructed.
- All outdoor storage should have adequate clearance from the building.
- Prohibit all storage in stairwells, and in electrical, mechanical, telephone, and computer hardware rooms.

Electrical Equipment

- Check that all fuse and control boxes are clean and closed; junction boxes are covered; no frayed, loose, or exposed wiring from junction boxes, receptacles, or fixtures. The maintenance or engineering departments along with loss prevention should be alert to any hazards of this type.

- Determine that all fixtures in the facility are in good condition and properly supported, particularly all lampshades are properly affixed.
- Determine that all free-standing or floor electrical lighting fixtures on display do not encroach into areas where an unsafe electrical condition can be created, or where a person may trip and fall or catch some part of their body thereby causing an accidental injury.
- Prohibit the use of portable space heaters if possible. If allowed, they should be strictly regulated and inspected routinely.
- Ovens, stoves, fryers, and electric space heaters should be part of the closing procedures to determine that all are shut down.

Although not part of an alarm system, many large retail businesses maintain an electrical generator on premises that will start up automatically in the event of a blackout, brownout, or other electrical problem. These generators are fueled by diesel oil or gasoline and produce enough electricity for computers, cash registers, and emergency lighting for the safety of all occupants in the building. Proper maintenance of this equipment must be a routine activity.*

Fire Extinguishing Systems and Equipment. Unless inconsistent with local fire and building codes that require circumscribed routine inspections, the following should be considered:

- The sprinkler system should be tested completely, including pressure gauges and valves, at least annually and certified.
- The fire pump should be run weekly with a full test annually and certified.*
- Routine inspection and care to any part of internal piping or the water mains to prevent obstruction or clogging from foreign material.*
- Determine if fire pump gauge readings are to be noted daily.*
- Standpipe hoses should be inspected monthly for proper placement and damage.
- Make sure standpipe connections are not obstructed.
- The fire alarm system should be tested monthly to determine if it is operational and if all interior alarms, fire doors, etc., are in good working order. This should include all manual pull stations and smoke and heat alarms.
- Portable extinguishers must be visually inspected for damage, leakage, correctly charged, and operational at least once a month. Determine that proper placement is made according to local codes. At least an annual inspection, recharging, and routine maintenance with a certifying tag attached should be completed by a fire hardware servicer.
- The kitchen and/or cafeteria extinguishing systems should be serviced and inspected semiannually.

* These tests should be conducted by the maintenance or engineering departments with appropriate endorsed reports.

Employee and Customer Safety

- A fire drill with full evacuation procedures should take place preferably every three months so that employees are reinforced in their classroom fire safety training. This will also determine the operational order of the fire alarm system and the public address system.
- Determine that all doors to stairwells and fire stairways are self-closing and unobstructed, all stairways are unobstructed, all exit routes are kept clear and unobstructed, all directional fire exit lighting is operational, and that all emergency lighting and/or emergency generators are operational.

In addition, the loss prevention manager should make available to the fire department a set of master keys and floor plans of the facility so that in responding to a report of a fire, the firefighters won't have to break in or knock down doors to gain entry into the building or interior spaces. A safe and secure method would be to place the store's master keys and floor plan in a Knox Box® located outside a perimeter door, and in which *only* the fire chief or fire company will have a key to access this Knox Box®. Under this system, no employee of the company, not even members of the loss prevention department, may have access to this box, except for the loss prevention manager. Connection of this box to the burglar alarm system would advise central station of any illegal entry.

ALARM SYSTEMS TESTING

All loss prevention personnel should be familiar with and aware that the building's alarm systems should be tested as a matter of course. Documented routine testing is usually required by insurance carriers and may also offer protection from liability and damages arising out of a civil law suit. Some or all store employees may be asked to assist in these tests.

The following schedule for testing is suggested for the average retail facility and will include the central station agency as may be applicable:

- Holdup alarms—at least once every three months, with routine review of robbery procedures for cash office personnel
- Burglar intrusion and motion alarms—tested at least twice a year
- Fire alarms—the entire fire system tested once every three months
- Evacuation procedure—a full evacuation of the store. A test of this type during business hours will naturally cause a business disruption, and possible trepidation and injuries to customers and visitors during the evacuation procedure. Therefore, it is recommended that this test be conducted with employees present but prior to the opening of the store to the public. Evacuation tests should take place every three months preferably, with six-month intervals at the least.

ALARM RECORDS

An ALARM AND ENTRY REPORT should be compiled and submitted by the security officer on all reported incidents occurring after hours when the store is closed. The maintenance of these reports serves two purposes:

1. It records the response to an alarm condition whether the store is open for business or not, as well as determining the reason for the alarm, actions and/or corrections taken, and who responded.
2. It records problems that may become inherent in the system over a period of time, or require attention and investigation to correct the issue in question.

   (See the Appendix for a copy of this report.)

Maintenance of Records. Proper recordkeeping is a must for recording all alarm signals, supervisory signals, and trouble signals by the loss prevention department. This should include all records concerning routine supervisory procedures and testing requirements by the maintenance or engineering department if these systems are part of their building support.

Remember that these records may be open for review by local fire marshals, fire inspectors, rating bureaus, and insurance carriers. The security officer must keep in mind that these records provide a method of alerting those of concern to potential problems before they become serious, and assurance that the responsibilities of central station and the facility's personnel are being properly carried out.

Other than records of certification, repairs, inspections, etc., maintained by the maintenance or engineering department of the facility, loss prevention should compile and maintain a fire incident report on all alarms and signals pertaining to the fire alarm system. These reports should include all routine tests and evacuation drills for insurance purposes.

ALARM SYSTEM RESPONSE

Burglary and Fire Response: After Hours

A security officer may be dispatched to a facility via a central station, a fire department or by other means. Unless it is a fire response where firefighters will be at the scene, the officer should not enter the building alone, particularly if the notification has been initiated by the burglary alarm. Cautionary measures dictate that the security officer must enter the building with a police officer. There are some burglar alarm systems where, depending on the location and the devices that are set off individually or in sequence, it can be determined prior to entry if the alarm sent was a mechanical problem, set off internally by innocent means, or false. Unless the responding security officer is confident that this may be the case, and also has been advised that the initiating device is not a perimeter door or window, the officer should enter with a police officer. There should be no exception to this policy. It is often easy to fall into the mindset that all alarms are false alarms when many, many times they are in fact false. However, this is a dangerous practice to fall into.

When responding to *other* than a fire report, the security officer should:

1. Enter the building with a police officer—do not place yourself in danger.
2. Proceed to the alarm station or control board and verify the location/s of the alarm.
3. Describe the area/s of the alarm or intrusion to the police officer and assist in the search of the facility.

4. If an actual break-in has occurred, they should follow the direction given by the police.
5. In the case of a false alarm, or if unable to determine the cause of the alarm, attempt to correct the problem and reset the system. The officer should advise central station that they are on premises and about to reset and leave. If the system cannot be set without bypassing a point or points, contact the security supervisor or manager for instruction. The security officer may be directed to stay on premises, or wait for the arrival of a mechanic from the alarm company or central station maintenance so that the corrections can be made, or a temporary trap set up so that the premises can be secured.

Robbery and Fire Response: During Business Hours

Cash Office Holdup Alarm. It is assumed that the cash office or cash room of a retail establishment has one or more holdup triggering devices that can be activated by cash office personnel when a robbery takes place. If possible, the authenticity of the alarm should be verified. The cash office should be observed from a distance by the responding security officers. It is often a serious mistake when inexperienced security officers run into a cash office without prior observation and become involved in the incident where injury might be the result. Security officers should be able to direct the police to the cash office area. If security officers should find themselves in the midst of a robbery situation, it must be clearly understood that security officers will comply with any demands made during the robbery, and if possible, should ensure that the cash office staff will cooperate as well. The most important point to remember during situations such as this is that the protection of life takes priority over all other considerations. The loss of other assets is of little importance when compared to personal safety. Experienced security officers will attempt to gain complete descriptions of the perpetrators, weapons used, method of operation, method and direction of escape, and description of auto used, if any. See also the discussion of *anti-robbery procedures* in the section ROBBERY in Chapter 14.

Fire Response. Upon a report of a fire, in whatever manner, the fire safety plan should be placed into effect as described in the emergency procedure plan.

24-Hour Alarms. Initiating devices for 24-hour alarms are generally affixed to exterior or emergency exits that are left in an active mode throughout the course of the day. The activation of this type of alarm without authorization should be investigated immediately by loss prevention. Shoplifters, persons committing vandalism, dishonest employees, or visitors often use these exits for a fast means of escape or to pass through stolen property. Any employee who opens and sets off a daytime annunciation device without good reason should be severely disciplined.

Part 7

RELEVANT TOPICS OF CONCERN FOR THE RETAIL LOSS PREVENTION DEPARTMENT

Chapter 21

Report Writing

THE PREPARATION AND MAINTENANCE OF INCIDENT OR CASE REPORTS

Because report writing is one of the more important tasks that a security officer will do as part of his duties, we will take some time to explain how a good report is put together.

The accepted ABC's of report writing are:

- ***Accuracy:*** Attempt to be as accurate as possible in all aspects in the report. This will include correct times, dates, spelling of names, correct addresses and phone numbers, and anything else more or less important. Be accurate particularly to the facts in the case.
- ***Brevity:*** Be brief and to the point, but not so much that the report suffers.
- ***Clarity and completeness:*** The text should flow so it can be easily read and understood. The report should be complete with all the facts that were gathered. Although brevity is important, it would be wise to cover and satisfy any questions that the reader may have on reading the report.

In addition, every complete report must contain the following elements:

- ***Who:*** The report must include everyone who is involved in the incident, including all participants and witnesses.
- ***What:*** The situation must be described as the officer observed it, and any action taken. Or, if applicable, the incident must be described as given by the participant or witness.
- ***Where:*** The location of the incident must be specific, and to include the security officer's whereabouts during the event, how advised, and any actions.
- ***When:*** This relates to the specific time of the incident, or if not exactly known, reported as closely as possible to the occurrence, using the terminology "at about XXXX hours." Include the time of all actions, arrivals, and departures pertaining to the incident.
- ***Why:*** This should be reported if known, which may indicate a motive for the criminal act or the cause of the accident. It may also justify the officer's actions during and after the incident if he is involved.
- ***How:*** If the facts warrant it or the officer has some insight, by reporting how the incident may have occurred or developed, he or she may be able to confirm the necessity for security or safety corrections.

The security officer should always carry a notebook or pad for any notes to be written down at the scene of an incident. These are also known as taking "field notes." These notes concerning facts and comments, in effect anything of value, will be used for the final and formal report of that incident. If note-taking cannot be done at the scene of occurrence, it should be done as soon as practical rather than rely on one's memory. In more important or serious incidents, attempt to maintain all field notes for future reference, as they may be needed in court to confirm your truthfulness or to verify what is contained in the company's formal or official report.

The final report should be clear, readable, and complete, and all the information contained in the report should be chronological using military time. The officer should attempt to use the correct spelling and grammar throughout any report. If the spelling of a word is in doubt, use a dictionary. A poorly worded and misspelled report can make a competent security officer look as if the officer was ignorant and unprofessional. Any imperfections noted by the reader will reflect on the security officer's position and expertise as a professional and as an investigator.

> Remember, no matter what type of a report, it should contain the following information:
> *Who, What, Where, When, Why, and How.*

RECORDKEEPING

Dependable recordkeeping by the loss prevention department is a primary function. The security officer should compile and complete a form with all-pertinent known facts and/or details for any incident the officer is involved in or that comes to the officer's attention. There are important and varying reasons for the assembling and maintenance of records:

- Accurate records must be completed and maintained over long periods as required by law. For loss prevention, this includes state, federal and OSHA requirements.
- Research, inquiry, and submission to the company's insurance carrier or in court of records or reports pertaining to customer or employee accidents, property damage, liability and civil actions, apprehensions and arrests, or any other incident that will or may require some future scrutiny.
- For upper management to accept the need for loss prevention as a necessity by recording substantial and irrefutable evidence compiled and statistically presented. In this way, management at corporate headquarters can formulate yearly, quarterly, or monthly analysis of all tasks and functions of that department.

This would include the following:

1. Number of incidents or occurrences by type and location—identifies trends and areas of loss or problems.
2. Customer and employee accidents or property damage—type, number, location, and disposition.

3. Criminal apprehensions and arrests, external/internal—by type, number, property involved and recovered, and disposition.
4. Inspections and audits.
5. Mandated routine security and safety issues, inventory, and safety committee meetings.
6. Investigations, internal/external—by type and disposition.
7. Training, both security and safety—by type, mandated by law and by company policy.
8. Civil and criminal actions—all litigation pending or closed by type, disposition, recovery, and loss if any.
9. Recovery by type, monetary or merchandise—by value and type and if external and internal.

Regarding recovery, the computation and maintenance of recovery figures is a necessity in establishing a cost-benefit ratio—the cost of the loss prevention payroll, or the loss prevention payroll plus the cost of all security systems and devices, compared to total recovery and work activity.

Logs

Logs should be maintained for each type of report, or at least the more important reports, which will show a compilation or listing of each incident in an orderly manner for easy inquiry. A log with the date, type of incident, name of subject if any, and numerically assigned in the log and on the report would easily control acceptable research and filing procedures. The more important reports that should be logged numerically would be the incident report, the customer accident report, and the employee accident report, with all other report forms attached to and made part of the incident report as required.

THE SIGNIFICANCE OF THE REPORT

Although writing a report of an incident or an investigation is the least favorite task of an investigator, it should be considered one of the most important. The written report is usually the only evidence that an investigation took place, or that a reported incident did occur and was in fact examined and documented. Security officers and their employer will find that this report is most important if required for future reference, particularly in criminal or civil court actions, and for insurance purposes.

Security officers must have the ability and be required to record any incident that occurs during their watch, no matter how minor. For the more important occurrences, in which times, dates, locations, notifications, people, and facts must be noted in detail for future reference or possible litigation, an incident report must be compiled. It should note who, what, when, where, why, and how, and should be complete as possible. The report should be maintained and filed numerically. If no number is assigned to the incident, it should at least be maintained chronologically. It also should be signed and dated by the security officer completing the form. A master log record detailing date, time, incident briefly described, and number assigned should be maintained for easy reference. Remember, accurate and complete reports regarding observation, specific dates and times, actions, statements, and where and how property was located and recovered can reduce the chance of lost criminal cases, and prevent and/or reduce the filings of civil actions. The loss prevention department should maintain all apprehension and arrest cases for at least three years after the completion of any court action. In fact, the retailer should preserve all records compiled by loss prevention permanently for future reference if at all possible.

In addition, we may consider another important reason to compile a report on all occurrences. We have detailed in varied ways throughout this book that the security officer is employed to protect the company and its assets, and along with assorted security systems, is to a great degree a deterrent.

But how does one measure that? Security officers do not manufacture anything. They don't sell anything. How does a security officer or a security force add to the company's value, determine its worth, or justify its existence?

The security force does that by reporting every incident or interaction, including the required audits, inspections, and reporting procedures. It is a way of justifying the need and significance that can be had by the use of an effective security force. It could be said that it is a cost vs. benefit, which can be measured by the quantity and quality of activity achieved by that force.

Custodial Responsibility of the Report

If someone is involved in an incident, particularly if there is an arrest or an accidental injury that has occurred, and they, their attorney, or outside investigators request a copy of the report for whatever reason, advise them that a formal report will or has been compiled of the incident, but company policy forbids a copy to be issued. It should be considered reasonable that the security officer's name, names of witnesses, and company managers be given if requested. If a copy of the formal report is requested at a later time, it would be most probably at a discovery/EBT hearing or by subpoena, and at which time, an attorney representing the officer or the officer's company would be involved in that action.

Remember that any report compiled by the security officer is an "in-house" company report and loss prevention is under no legal obligation to offer or give a copy on demand. Consider also that any report compiled by members of the loss prevention department are to be retained as confidential records with only certain company employees privy to their contents.

One other important point should be covered here. Many investigators will add personal comments or opinions to a report. Others feel that this is wrong—that only the facts should be contained in the report and that the investigator's opinions have no place in being recorded. In reality, these written comments will only come back and "haunt the writer" at a later time.

Moreover, if any civil action follows concerning an incident, the insurance or retailer's attorney will not look favorably on the officers' actions after they become aware of comments on reports that will or might be detrimental to the presentation of their case. If security officers or investigators feel strongly that they have a comment or opinion that is based on their experience and expertise, or of some knowledge they believe that should be made part of report, officers can proceed in two ways:

1. Compile a separate or supplementary page containing whatever information the officers feel should be in the report. Maintain this page with the report but do not attach and make it part of the report. Consider this page for the officer's reference only, but also realize that such writing may be subject to discovery at a later time. If these personal observations and his or her competence are used in court, the security officer's attorney may have to offer the officer's years in security service, training, education, prior criminal justice employment if any, expertise and experience concerning the matter in question in order to support this "professional opinion." Without these credentials or proof of expertise, consider this supplemental information as detrimental.
2. Put no comments and/or opinions of this type in writing—they have no place in the report. This practice should be considered disadvantageous upon examination by others or if the report is produced at a hearing. However, if the case is reportable to the company's insurance carrier or legal representative outside of the company, the security officer should contact and advise these people of this information, noting your belief of its importance and that the officer would rather not put it in writing.

Realize that anything in writing—field notes, personal notes, the original report, and any information that is covered in point 1 above—is open for discovery by an attorney at a later time. If the question is asked, "Did you compile or produce any other report, part of a report, or anything that you made part of original or main report?" "Do you have any other notes or writings that were generated by or for this incident?" the security officer will have to answer truthfully and produce whatever the officer has written. Consider then, the seriousness of one's "opinion" when made part of a report.

It must be emphasized at this point for the security officer to be cognizant that any report compiled and submitted must be as truthful to the facts as possible. The security officer must remember that he or she may have to swear under oath before a court or a hearing that all contained in the report is the truth. To compile a report that contains untruths is a falsification, and to testify to that false report as the truth is perjury.

Consider also, that any formal written report compiled by a security officer as required by his or her employer is a "business record," and to intentionally falsify a business record may constitute an additional crime

The Time Record

Of great importance in certain occurrences and emergencies is the compilation of a time record. Whether incorporated into or separately compiled and attached to and made part of the incident report, time entries can be effective and substantial in subsequent criminal or civil procedures. Along with the required reports such as the arrest/apprehension report or a bomb threat checklist, time entries add to the complete and professional appearance of the total reporting process.

Security officers assigned to formerly report the incident in question should consider whether a time record is to be started if the circumstances so warrant. If unable to do so because of other tasks, another security officer or responsible employee should be assigned this duty.

Other than that noted elsewhere regarding a time record on an arrest or apprehension, the following time entries should be considered part of the report on any serious incident or as may be applicable:

- Time of occurrence, or time of the initial report.
- Time that police were notified and requested (as applicable), time that police are present (include name and shield number of each officer and supervisor).
- Time that the fire department was notified and requested (as applicable), time that the fire department are present (include name of fire officer or chief in charge).
- Time proper notifications made to loss prevention supervisor, and other management personnel as required in the emergency procedure plan.
- Time of evacuation (if any).
- Time of permission given by police/fire officer to reenter the facility (as applicable).
- Time of management/administration personnel present or in contact.
- Time of any other important development during the incident.

Keep in mind that the more serious the occurrence that takes place within or around the business establishment the security officer is assigned to protect, the more a time record will be considered an important supplement to any report.

DOCUMENTATION

The instances above show how important and consequential the taking of a report can be. No matter how minor an incident or how minimal the information gathered for the report, whether an apprehension, a personal injury, lost child, or a disgruntled customer, a specific formal report should be compiled and maintained for future reference. To reiterate, however insignificant an incident may be, if any action is taken by a security officer, it should be documented in some form.

Chapter 22
Training

THE LOSS PREVENTION MANAGER'S ROLE IN TRAINING

One of the most important functions of the loss prevention manager's job is the training of managers and employees of the company. Although this manager is most directly charged with the training of loss prevention personnel, the responsibility goes further. The loss prevention manager must also become involved in the training of other employees in security and safety-related matters. This will include, but are not limited to, employment policies and rules of conduct as described in the company's employee handbook, fire safety, check and credit card acceptance procedures, internal and external theft, and in essence, the protection of all assets.

Loss prevention supervisors and senior or lead security officers who have the ability and expertise may be assigned to conduct instruction in many of the following areas.

Required Training for Employees

All new hires should be given some training by the loss prevention department as soon as possible after starting the new job. Initial instruction and introduction into security and safety should, in fact, be part of the hiring and orientation process. Subsequent training sessions should include, among others, fire safety, evacuation procedures, other safety issues, and the cause and effect of civil litigation. But more importantly, certain employees, because of their positions, should have more comprehensive training in a particular area. This would include employees such as cashiers and cash room workers who handle money and credit cards. Also, there are certain training requirements that are mandated by the federal Office of Safety and Health Administration (OSHA). This includes bloodborne pathogen training for those employees who are enumerated in the company's exposure control plan, and hazard communication training required of all employees. Although some establishments assign these OSHA training classes to the human resources or personnel department, it would be most proper for the security or loss prevention department to train and control the process because it will be that department that will be involved in any violations, investigations, and obligatory reporting.

Depending on the retail establishment and the company's commitment to training, the following procedures and factual information should be brought to the attention of all new employees as soon as possible after they are hired, some of which may be required by federal and/or state law:

- Review of the company's policy, procedures, rules, and regulations concerning safety and security for the employee.
- The role of the loss prevention department, the identification of risks and the prevention of shrinkage, theft, and other losses, and how it affects the company, the employee, and the customer.
- The employee's duty and loyalty to the company and to fellow coworkers in reporting unlawful and unsafe conditions.
- The employee's role in how to report an incident or emergency, and how to act at the scene of an accident or emergency.
- Fire safety and the use of fire hardware. How to react to a fire or similar emergency notification according to the company's procedures.
- A critique on evacuation procedures for employees, customers, and visitors.
- Hazards and safety in the workplace, including their "right to know" (Hazcom—hazard communication) concerning hazardous substances on premises, and the required OSHA bloodborne pathogen exposure training for certain employees.
- The effects of civil litigation on the company and the individual, and how to avoid liability.

The human resources or personnel department is usually the office that will initially coordinate orientation, coworker conduct and exposure of the company to new hires, and ongoing training classes regarding the business of the company. Nevertheless, the loss prevention manager must be the one manager mandated to conduct and supervise all training concerning health, safety, and security issues. Subordinates of the loss prevention manager should be assigned as trainers to assist in the training process, as long as they have the expertise and the knowledge to train and communicate the required information.

Training should be continuous, from the date of hire and routinely thereafter. This is to include security and safety, not only for the members of loss prevention, but all employees. Along with training as a tool for awareness, the loss prevention and/or human resources departments should set up programs that will keep the employee mindful of their responsibilities as a partner in loss prevention. This could include the following:

- Videos and hand out materials
- A column in the company newsletter
- Honesty incentives
- Safety incentives
- Bulletin board posters, notifications, etc.
- The posting of the minutes of the safety committee and round table meetings

The loss prevention manager should be involved in the initial orientation training class of new coworkers. This provides the loss prevention manager the opportunity to meet all new employees and stress the importance of security and safety in the store. During this meeting, the loss prevention manager should discuss the makeup of the loss prevention department, describe the security personnel attached to the department, the company policy regarding shoplifters and crimes committed by employees, and the role that all employees play in security and safety. The following topics must be covered:

Protection of life—explain that there is no greater responsibility than the protection of employees and customers. This will include not only protection of life, but protection from injury.

Protection of property—includes all of the company's assets. Explain the responsibility of protecting the building, the warehouse stock, the merchandise, and the equipment and supplies contained within to operate the business.

Prevention of loss—loss prevention is responsible for any loss to the company other than losses due to poor merchandise or operating decisions. The areas of responsibility include security and safety by routine auditing and inspection, claims and investigation of employee and customer accidents, check and credit card fraud, product liability claims and investigation, building security, shoplifting, internal larcenies, burglary, robbery, and fire safety.

Shrinkage. The introduction should cover what shrinkage is and how it is determined, that is, stock loss, or, paper vs. physical. Discussion should include the need for all employees to be involved in the protection of inventory. Include the following areas that compromise shrinkage and the employees' responsibility in each of the following:

Shoplifting. Discuss company policy on shoplifting. Stress that no employee other than loss prevention officers is permitted to stop a shoplifter, or anyone whom they believe may have committed or attempted to commit a larceny. Be sure that all employees understand that security officers will not stop a suspected shoplifter unless they witness the crime. Also explain to the employees how critical it is to the success of the security program that they call for loss prevention whenever they witness or suspect any theft or any suspicious situation. All employees should understand the impact of shoplifting on their lives and livelihood, both as an employee and as a consumer.

Advise the employees of the award program if the company has one instituted for rewarding employees who give information to loss prevention, which results in a recovery of property or money caused by a ticket switch or shoplifting. Also explain the awarding of cash for credit card recovery if the company has an award program in conjunction with various credit card companies.

Internal Theft. A discussion of internal theft should be frank, but recognize and advise the fact to each new hire that most employees are honest and sincere in their work. They detest witnessing a theft or having knowledge of a theft by another coworker, because it places them in a situation of keeping quiet or informing on that person. Stress the need for honesty among coworkers because of the trust that the company is placing in them. Remind them that an employee who is taking things from a company may also take things from other coworkers. An important point to make is that employees who are stealing from the company take from each of us individually—through reduced profits that have an effect on increased pricing, reduced benefits or pay raises, and in some cases, loss of jobs due to cost reductions. Explain the company's policy on internal theft. Discuss the employees' responsibility to report all known or suspected thefts to loss prevention. Discuss what "sweethearting" at the cash register is and how loss prevention attempts to control it. Also explain what controls are used at merchandise pick-up and the use of coworker package inspections.

Discuss the problem of dishonest employees. An employee may wish to meet with the loss prevention manager off premises to discuss a possible crime or situation. On the other hand, an employee may wish to remain anonymous and still report information to loss prevention that he or she may feel should be reported. In this case, the loss prevention department should set up a reporting system such as telephone voice mail with a particular telephone extension dedicated to such matters. Accordingly, a reward system should also be instituted as policy so that if an apprehension or termination is made because of information received, that employee, anonymous or not, would receive the award. However, it should be noted that the award should be significant enough to induce even the reluctant informant to contact loss prevention. Moreover, it must be stressed that any information, however received, including the name of the informant if known, will be held in the strictest confidence.

Coworker Errors. Discuss the importance of accuracy in the employee's work and the need to correct errors that are made as soon as practical. Also explain the need to compile the required forms regarding displays or damaged merchandise so that stock control may "write-off" these items from inventory. Use examples of how errors or poor reporting reflect on inventory recovery and profit.

Damaged Property and/or Merchandise. Explain to the employee that any property or merchandise intentionally damaged or misused where the company suffers a loss will not be tolerated, whether by a customer or an employee. Damage to merchandise caused unintentionally must be written off. Further, that any sabotage leading to the destruction or attempted destruction of company property or the obstruction of business operations will be considered a serious offense and dealt with according to law.

Advise the employee how "known thefts" are handled and that their manager will train them how and when to report the loss or "write off" an item of merchandise.

Accidents. All new hires will be advised on how to handle an accident, what to do, and how to report it. This includes both employee and customer accidents and illnesses. They will also be advised that in case an employee is exposed to someone else's human blood, that they fall under the BLOODBORNE PATHOGEN EXPOSURE CONTROL PLAN for bloodborne pathogens. The employees' right to know under the HAZARD COMMUNICATION STANDARD must be addressed. Additionally, they must be instructed on what not to say or do when in the presence of the injured party or other witnesses.

Other Issues. The loss prevention manager must also cover the following:

Employee conduct—explain the need for policy and rules of conduct as described in the employees' handbook or other document. Discuss the importance of reading this policy and understanding the rules of conduct in particular. Encourage them to ask human resources or loss prevention if they have any questions about the rules or policy.

CCTV—explain where the cameras are located, under what legal provisions or restrictions that the company operates these cameras under, and the purposes for which they are used.

Checks and credit cards—advise employees of the company's basic check acceptance policy and credit card procedure, and that cashiers, in particular, will be given detailed instruction in these two areas.

Robbery, disorderly or disgruntled customers—all employees should be instructed on what to do in the event of a robbery. Be certain that everyone understands that they are never to resist anyone with a weapon or a perceived weapon. They must cooperate fully. The safety of the person is to be considered above that of property. In the case of a disorderly or disgruntled customer who may or may not be causing a scene, advise the employee to request a security officer immediately.

Safety Training

The loss prevention manager will be responsible that the following training classes are conducted as required:

Pre-training—preliminary safety instruction for all employees upon hire (OSHA required).

Fire safety and evacuation procedures—required of all employees per OSHA and company policy, soon after hire.

Hazard communication training—required of all employees per OSHA, to include annual retraining.

First aid/CPR training and certification—required of all first aid responders assigned by and per company policy, and may include other pertinent personnel as needed. Contractual training and certification may be provided as required.

Bloodborne pathogens training—required of all first aid responders, or by occupational exposure per the OSHA Standard. To include instruction in the exposure control plan and hepatitis A, B, and C. Includes documentation for hepatitis B vaccination required of those coworkers noted in the exposure control plan. Basic introduction of this standard to all employees who may be exposed as part of their Hazcom training.

Back safety instruction—should be required of all warehouse, receiving, and shipping employees in particular, and may include customer handout, customer service coworkers, and any other employee as directed by their manager.

Loss Prevention Officer Training

As far as the training required of security officers, it is expected that they would have attended all training given and required by the loss prevention department. Moreover, the security officer should be certified in first aid and CPR so that he or she may be available to respond to any accidental emergency in which the officer will be of use. In fact, other than the security officer being registered and/or licensed as may be required by the state in which the officer is employed, his or her job description should also include all training that is applicable to and required of that position.

The loss prevention manager should conduct orientation training in security and safety for all newly hired security officers, and ongoing training of all present security officers on a routine basis. All training for security personnel must be documented for proficiency, professionalism, and liability purposes. This training will include, but is not limited to, the following:

- Knowledge of pertinent local and federal laws
- Knowledge of company policy and procedures, rules and regulations
- Detection of safety violations and apparent or possible criminal activity—internal or external
- Investigative procedures and techniques, including interview and interrogation techniques
- Apprehension, restraint, and detention procedures
- Report writing—including the proper use, compilation, and maintenance of reports
- Statistical analysis of all loss, recovery, restitution, arrest/apprehensions, etc.
- Accident investigation, accident analysis, and statistical reporting
- Procedures for dealing with local law enforcement and other investigative agencies, attorneys, banks, and credit card companies
- Case preparation and court testimony
- Knowledge and review of alarm systems and building procedures
- Complete knowledge of the contents of the emergency procedure plan, which will include emergency procedures for natural and accidental disasters, bomb threats, terrorist activity, brownouts, blackouts, fires and gas leaks, with emphasis in the emergency operation and control of the sprinkler system and the electric producing generator system
- Instruction in inspection and auditing procedures and individual assignment to areas of responsibility
- Legal and proper use and installation of CCTV equipment

PERFORMANCE EVALUATION

Although human resources will be the department that will direct and coordinate the employee evaluation program with the necessary forms and attestations, the loss prevention manager should be cognizant of the following elements that should be contained in the format.

The performance of each employee from the loss prevention department should be accurately evaluated, *and it must be based on the written job description* for each grade or position. Therefore, consider that the written performance evaluations will cover loss prevention or security officers and security guards, and anyone else assigned to that department. The objectives of a performance evaluation are the following:

1. To assist in the career development of the employee
2. To communicate feedback on the employee's performance
3. To set goals and individual objectives
4. To provide documentation of performance based on observable behavior and actions
5. To determine any training requirements that may be needed
6. To determine the suitability and effectiveness of the employee's present assignment
7. To determine the employee's ability to accept additional responsibility and future assignments
8. To determine suitability for promotion and/or wage increase

Evaluation should take place at three months (an acceptable probationary period), at the sixth month after the initial hiring, and annually thereafter. The employee's immediate security supervisor should conduct the evaluation, with concurrence or disagreement of such evaluation by the department manager so noted on the form.

The form should include the essential functions and tasks as detailed in the employee's job description, the level of performance expected of the employee depending on his or her experience and position, and the evaluation rating criteria. In addition, it should also contain the mutually agreed upon goals and objectives agreed to and consistent with the employee's job description. The level and completion of required training should also be made part of this form.

The completed evaluation should be reviewed by the supervisor and the employee, and may include the previous evaluation period (if any) concerning earlier established goals and performance. The supervisor must include specific comments on whether the employee has met, exceeded, or failed to meet performance standards in each criterion. After completion, review, and discussion with the supervisor, the employee should acknowledge the comments contained in the evaluation with his or her signature. Employees may also add their own comments, pro or con, to the form in the area provided. If for whatever reason, the employee refuses to sign and acknowledge the completed evaluation in the space provided, the supervisor rating that employee shall note "refused to sign" in such space. Any appeal by the employee contesting the evaluation should be made to the human resources department.

The security officer, security guard, or any other loss prevention personnel, who performs unsatisfactory between evaluations or commits a company infraction should be notified in writing by his or her supervisor or manager of such action, including corrections and/or admonishments as may be required. It shall be acknowledged by the signature of the employee and placed in the employee's personnel file along with all past evaluations.

Supervisors and managers of the loss prevention department must realize that routine performance evaluations of employees within their department can be an exceptional tool in training, career development, evaluation, and supervision. Moreover, it serves both the individual and management by fostering fair and impartial personnel decisions that must be made from time to time.

Appendix

1. INCIDENT/CASE REPORT 318
2. LOSS PREVENTION CONTINUATION/SUPPLEMENTAL REPORT 319
3. LOSS PREVENTION ARREST/APPREHENSION REPORT 320
4. WRITTEN CONFESSION SAMPLE 321
5. RELEASE FORM 322
6. TRESPASS WARNING 323
7. CONSENT TO SEARCH 324
8. BOMB REPORT CHECKLIST 325
9. CUSTOMER/VISITOR ACCIDENT REPORT 326
10. CUSTOMER/VISITOR ILLNESS REPORT 327
11. EMPLOYEE ACCIDENT/ILLNESS REPORT 328
12. ALARM AND ENTRY REPORT 329
13. MONTHLY FIRE SAFETY INSPECTION REPORT 330
14. WEEKLY BUILDING SAFETY INSPECTION REPORT 331
15. LOSS PREVENTION PROPERTY RECOVERY REPORT 332
16. COUNTERFEIT CURRENCY NOTIFICATION TO SECRET SERVICE 333
17. FOUND PROPERTY REPORT 334
18. ETHICS AND CONDUCT FOR THE SECURITY OFFICER 335

The reports and/or forms contained in this section may be used as presented, or may be modified to fit a particular retail establishment or loss prevention department.

INCIDENT/CASE REPORT

STORE NUMBER/LOCATION ______________________ **REPORT NUMBER** ____________

DATE OF REPORT ____________ DATE OF INCIDENT ____________ TIME OF INCIDENT __________

LOCATION OF INCIDENT ____

____

TYPE OF INCIDENT: *Check all that apply*

THEFT

- ☐ LARCENY
  - ☐ SHOPLIFTER
  - ☐ INTERNAL
- ☐ BY CHECK
- ☐ BY CREDIT CARD
- ☐ FROM EMPLOYEE
- ☐ FROM CUSTOMER
- ☐ ROBBERY
- ☐ BURGLARY

CASH VARIANCES

- ☐ REGISTER
- ☐ SAFE/VAULT
- ☐ CASH DRAWER
- ☐ DEPOSIT
- ☐ BY FORCE
- ☐ BY SCAM
- ☐ OTHER

SHORTAGES

- ☐ TRANSFERS
- ☐ DISTRIBUTION
- ☐ OTHER

ASSAULT

- ☐ CUSTOMER
- ☐ EMPLOYEE

MISCELLANEOUS

- ☐ CRIMINAL MISCHIEF
- ☐ TRESPASS
- ☐ DAMAGE TO PROPERTY
- ☐ UNKNOWN DISAPPEARANCE
- ☐ OTHER (explain in detail)

CRIME..... ☐ ATTEMPTED ? ☐ COMPLETED ?

ARREST... ☐ Y ☐ N Attach Arrest/Apprehension Report

DETAILS OF INCIDENT ____

____

____

____

____

____

____

____

____

____

DISPOSITION ____

____

____

______________________________ POLICE REPORT # *(If any)* ______________

______________________________ ______________________________

REPORT PREPARED BY APPROVED BY

USE CONTINUATION/SUPPLEMENTARY PAGE FOR FURTHER DETAILS, COMMENTS, WITNESSES, ETC., AS REQUIRED

LOSS PREVENTION

CONTINUATION/SUPPLEMENTAL REPORT

REFERENCE TO REPORT: ____

REPORT NUMBER: ______________ DATED: ____________ PAGE: ________ of __________

DETAILS: ____

☐ CASE ACTIVE ☐ ARREST ☐ NO ARREST ☐ RESTITUTION ☐ CASE CLOSED

REPORT PREPARED BY ______________________________ TITLE ________________

DATE OF THIS REPORT ________________ APPROVED BY ________________________

This report is to be attached to and made part of the original report and numbered in sequence.

LOSS PREVENTION

ARREST/APPREHENSION REPORT

Refer to Incident Report Number ____________

Date of Occurrence ________ ________ ______ Time of Occurrence __________ Date of This Report ________________
Month Day Year

Location of Occurrence ____

Original Report by ______________________________ Dep't ______________

Classification of Crime ____________________________ No. of Subjects _____ This Subject No. ______

Name of Subject ______________________________ Aliases/AKA______________

Age _____ Date of Birth ______________ Social Security # _____ ___ _____ Home Tel. # ______________

Home Address ____

Business Name/Address ______________________________ Tel.#______________

Height ______ Weight ______ Build ______ Race ______Complexion ______ Eye color _____ Hair color _____

Hair length/type _________ Mustache/type/color ________________ Beard/type/color __________________

Brief physical description ____

Witnesses ________________ ________________ ________________

Police involved? Y ___ N ___ Time called ______ Time of arrival _______ Police Report # ______________

Police Officer/s Name ______________________ ______________________

Shield No. _______ Shield No. _______

Subject released: To Police ____ To Parent ______________________________

Other (explain below) _____ Time of release ______________

Brief details of occurrence ____

____

____

____

______________________________ ______________________________

Security Officer Assigned Approved By

Use continuation/supplemental report for complete details, witnesses, etc. Attach originals to incident/case report.

WRITTEN CONFESSION SAMPLE

The following example of a written declaration may be used in court as evidence against a defendant charged with the crime of larceny.

STATEMENT OF JOHN DOE

My name is John Doe, am 35 years of age being born on December 16, 1966. I live at 421 Halestone Street, Morristown, NH 12345 with my wife, Jane, and my two children, John Jr., age 6, and Jennifer, age 8. I am employed by ABC Contractors in Morristown as a carpenter.

Today, Monday, June 26th, 2001, at about 1:30 PM I was in Henshaw's Department Store, Maple Street Mall, Anytown, NH with my wife. My kids were home being cared for by my mother-in-law, Martha Jones. While in the store on the first floor, I decided to take a man's ring that I saw laying on the counter in the jewelry department. I describe this ring as yellow gold with a large white stone on the face. I believed this ring to be expensive. I always wanted one like it, but I could never afford it. I put the ring in my jacket pocket and continued to shop with my wife in the store. After she made several purchases, we were about to leave the store when someone stopped me. This person said he was a security officer and he wanted me to go with him to the security office. When I asked why, he said I was under arrest for stealing some jewelry. In the office, the security officer found the ring that I took in my jacket pocket where I had put it. I have been told that this ring is valued at $1249.00, and that the white stone on the ring is actually a diamond.

I realize now that what I did was wrong, and I'm sorry that I took this ring. I want to say that my wife, Jean, was unaware that I did it. She had nothing to do with it. I did it on my own.

I give this statement to George Smith who is writing it for me and it is the truth. I have not been threatened or harmed in any way, or given any promises for giving this statement.

WITNESSED:	X John Doe
George Smith	421 Halestone St.
Security Officer	Morristown, NH 12345
Ted Blackstone	(123) 456-7890
Loss Prevention Manager	June 26, 2001

***

Comments:

Notice that the first paragraph completely describes and identifies who the subject is.

The second paragraph notes the date, time, and the place of occurrence, why he was present and who was present with him. Included also, the opportunity, his intent and desire to commit the larceny, describing from where and what he stole, and where he placed the stolen object on his person. He describes the arrest and where the security officer found and recovered the stolen property. Notice that the value of the ring is noted (which constitutes grand larceny, a felony), but he is not advised at any time that he will be charged with the felony, only that he is to be arrested.

The third paragraph shows that he is sorry (shows remorse) for committing the crime, and lays blame on himself.

In the final paragraph, the subject states that he was not threatened, harmed, or given a promise for this statement, that it was given voluntarily, and that all the above is the truth. Note that if a police officer were taking this confession, a Miranda warning *and a caveat would be included; that making or giving a false statement is a crime and the subject could be charged as such. As civilians, security officers need not include these admonitions.*

If possible, the security officer writing the statement should make one or two spelling or grammatical mistakes in the text. When the subject reads the finished statement before signing, the mistakes should be brought to his attention and requested that he cross out, correct and initial those corrections. This is an indication he has read the statement and acknowledged or made the corrections himself.

The statement must be signed by the subject along with him noting his address, telephone number, and the date. When the statement is signed by the subject, it should be witnessed by at least two persons and so noted by their signatures.

A. B. HENSHAW AND COMPANY
456 MAPLE STREET MALL
ANYTOWN, STATE 98765

RELEASE FORM

I, ________________________________, have been taken into custody by
Print name

company employees for committing a theft on the premises of A. B. Henshaw and Co. at

456 Maple Street Mall, Anytown, State, 98765 on ______________________________,
month day year

at ________________. I hereby admit that I did take and attempt to carry away property
time of day

belonging to A. B. Henshaw and Co. without purchasing it. I describe this property as...

____, valued at $______________.
describe item taken

I have been told that I will not be arrested or prosecuted for this theft and that I will be released. I give this written statement of my own free will. I have not suffered any injury or any harm while in custody. Also, I have been given the promise that whether I sign this admission and release or not, I will still be released without any further action against me. By giving this release however, I do realize and promise not to initiate any criminal or civil action by myself or on my behalf against A. B. Henshaw and Co. and/or their employees for my actions in this incident described herein.

Witnessed by: **Signed** ______________________________________

______________________ Home address ______________________________

______________________________. Tel.#__________

______________________ Today's date____________________

The above release form is a simple sample of what should be included. Use caution in this area: the retail security officer should always adhere to company policy and procedures regarding legal issues such as the compilation of a release, and what may be required in various occurrences.

A. B. HENSHAW AND COMPANY
456 MAPLE STREET MALL
ANYTOWN, STATE 98765

TRESPASS WARNING

I ______________________________ hereby acknowledge by signing this document that on this date I was personally informed by ______________________________ who is a Security Officer or Manager employed by A. B. HENSHAW AND COMPANY, that any license or privilege, permission or any authority granted to me prior to this date to enter an/or remain upon these premises, 456 Maple Street Mall, Anytown, State, 98765 or any other premises owned and/or operated by A. B. HENSHAW AND COMPANY in this state or any other state has been revoked, and that if I enter any A. B. HENSHAW AND COMPANY store from this time on for any reason whatsoever, I will be committing a criminal trespass as defined under this state's laws (or the laws of the state of concern), and will be subject to arrest and criminal prosecution. I have also been advised that this form will be kept on file for future reference and will be used against me if I do in fact commit a trespass as defined herein.

X______________________________
Signature

WITNESSED:

____
Print Name

____
Signature

____
Address

__________ __________
Title Date

______________________________ ______________
Today's Date

____
Signature

______________ ______________
Date of Birth Home Telephone Number

__________ __________
Title Date

____
Social Security Number

* * * * * * * * * * * * * * * * *

VERBAL TRESPASS WARNING

I have personally advised the above identified subject who has refused to sign the aforementioned agreement of the trespass law in this state, and have so ordered said subject never to enter this store or any other A. B. HENSHAW AND COMPANY store at any time and for whatever reason, and if he does so enter this or any other Henshaw company store, he is subject to arrest for criminal trespass. He/she acknowledged this verbal warning that it was understood by stating "YES."

____
Witness to verbal warning

____
Signature of person giving the verbal warning

__________ __________
Title Date

__________ __________
Title Date

Original to trespass file, attach copy to arrest/apprehension report and incident report

A. B. HENSHAW AND COMPANY
456 MAPLE STREET MALL
ANYTOWN, STATE 98765

CONSENT TO SEARCH

I, ____ having been informed that I have
(PRINT NAME)
a constitutional right not to give permission for a search of my personal property or any property owned by me, possessed by me, or under my control, including any motor vehicle in my possession, and that I have the right to refuse consent for any type of search by any security officer of the Loss Prevention Department of A. B. Henshaw and Company, or any search by a manager employed by that company.

Having been so advised, I hereby authorize ________________________________

a Security Officer to conduct a complete search of ________________________________

located at ____

I understand that any property found and seized as a result of this search may be used against me in any legal hearing or court of law.

This written permission is being given by me freely and voluntarily, and without threats or any promises made to me of any kind.

TODAY'S DATE ____________________

PRINT NAME ____________________ SIGN NAME ____________________

DATE OF BIRTH ____________________ HOME ADDRESS ____________________

____________________ TELEPHONE # ____________________

WITNESS ____________________ WITNESS ____________________

TITLE ____________ DATE ____________ TITLE ____________ DATE ____________

File original with incident report. If an arrest is made, attach original to police report and file copy with incident report.

BOMB REPORT CHECKLIST

GENERAL TELEPHONE INSTRUCTIONS UPON RECEIVING A BOMB THREAT

LISTEN – DO NOT INTERRUPT THE CALLER. BE CALM. BE COURTEOUS.
TAPE RECORD THE CONVERSATION IF POSSIBLE.
ATTEMPT TO WRITE OUT THE COMPLETE MESSAGE GIVEN BY THE CALLER. PROLONG THE CONVERSATION.
DETERMINE AND NOTE AS MUCH OF THE FOLLOWING INFORMATION AS POSSIBLE.

EXACT WORDS OF CALLER ____

____

____

____

TODAY'S
DATE: ______________________ ORIGIN OF CALL: Local ___Long Distance ___Booth ___Within Bldg.___ Unknown__

TIME OF CALL: ________________CALLER'S IDENTITY: Male ___ Female ___ Juvenile ___ Approx. Age: ______

BOMB FACTS

PRETEND DIFFICULTY HEARING THE CONVERSATION. KEEP CALLER TALKING.
IF CALLER SEEMS AGREEABLE TO FURTHER CONVERSATION, ASK QUESTIONS SUCH AS THE FOLLOWING – BUT DO NOT ANGER THE CALLER.

When will the bomb go off? __________________ Hour? ____________ How much time remaining?________________

Where is it located? ____What area of the bldg.? ________________________

How do you know so much about the bomb? ____

Why are you doing this? ____

Where are you now? ____

What is your name/address? ____

IF THE BUILDING IS OCCUPIED, INFORM THE CALLER THAT DETONATION COULD CAUSE INJURY OR DEATH.

CHARACTERISTICS OF CALLER

Check off all that apply

VOICE	SPEECH	ACCENT	LANGUAGE	MANNER
___Familiar	___Fast	___Local	___Excellent	___Calm
___High pitched	___Slow	___Not local	___Good	___Rational
___Deep	___Distinct	___Foreign	___Fair	___Coherent
___Raspy	___Stutter	Type?________	___Poor	___Deliberate
___Intoxicated?	___Slurred	___Race?	___Foul	___Righteous
___Loud	___Nasal	___Region	___Other	___Angry
___Soft	___Distorted			___Irrational
___Pleasant	___Lisp			___Emotional
___Other?	___Other?			___Incoherent
				___Laughing

FAMILIARITY WITH THIS FACILITY?
___Much: Explain ______________________
___Some: ___________________________
___None

BACKGROUND NOISE

___Factory machines	___Office machines
___Bedlam	___Mixed/noisy
___Music	___Street traffic
___Trains	___Animals
___Voices	___Airplanes
___Party atmosphere	___Quiet

POLICE NOTIFIED? Yes ____ No ____ Time Ntfd.______________

Time of Arrival ______________________

PERSON REPORTING _________________________________

Use other side of this form for further information if needed. Attach copy to incident report; original to police.

NOTIFY YOUR SUPERVISOR IMMEDIATELY OR FOLLOW THE EMERGENCY PROCEDURE PLAN.

CUSTOMER/VISITOR
ACCIDENT REPORT

ACCIDENT NUMBER: CA-__________

DATE AND TIME OF ACCIDENT ____________________ DATE OF REPORT ____________________

INITIAL REPORT BY ____________________ DEPT ASSIGNED ____________________

REPORT TAKEN BY ____________________ TITLE ____________________

CUSTOMER/VISITOR INFORMATION

NAME ____________________ SEX: M F DOB __________ AGE ______

HOME ADDRESS ____________________ *(Apt.)* ______

(City/Town) ____________________ *(State)* __________ *(Zip)* ______

TELEPHONE NUMBER: (Home) (____)______________ (Business/other) (____)______________

PARENT/GUARDIAN: *(If Juvenile)* ____________________

ACCIDENT LOCATION ____________________

DESCRIPTION OF ACCIDENT SITE ____________________

TYPE OF FLOOR ____________________ WEATHER CONDITIONS *(If applicable)* __________

LIGHTING CONDITIONS: Good ___ Fair ___ Poor ___ Explain: ____________________

CUSTOMER'S DESCRIPTION OF ACCIDENT ____________________

____

____

____

DESCRIPTION OF CLOTHING/SHOE TYPE WORN ____________________

____

DESCRIPTION OF TREATMENT *(Note if treatment refused)* ____________________

____

CUSTOMER LEAVE STORE UNDER OWN POWER? YES ___ NO ___ EXPLAIN: ____________________

____________________ VIA: □ Private conveyance

REMOVED TO HOSPITAL? *(Name/Location)* ____________________ □ Company conveyance

____________________ □ Ambulance

WITNESS/S NAME ____________________ ____________________

ADDRESS/S ____________________ ____________________

TELEPHONE/S ____________________ ____________________

PRODUCT INVOLVED? YES ___ NO ___ ARTICLE No./DESCRIPTION ____________________

____

ACTION TAKEN ____________________

COMMENTS ____________________

____

USE CONTINUATION PAGE FOR FURTHER DETAILS, COMMENTS, WITNESSES, ETC., AS REQUIRED.

CUSTOMER/VISITOR
ILLNESS REPORT

REPORT NUMBER: CI-______________

DATE OF INCIDENT______________________________ DATE OF REPORT ______________________

TIME OF INCIDENT __________ INITIAL REPORT BY ______________________DEPT ____________

REPORT TAKEN BY ______________________________________ TITLE ______________________

VISITOR INFORMATION

NAME ______________________________________ SEX: M F DOB _____________ AGE ______

HOME ADDRESS ____ (Apt.#) _________

(City/Town) ____ (State) __________ (zip) ___________

TELEPHONE # (Home) ______________________________ (Business/other) _______________________

PARENT/GUARDIAN (If Juvenile) ____

ADDRESS ____

LOCATION OF ILLNESS ____

____

DESCRIPTION/CONDITION OF LOCATION ____

____

DESCRIPTION OF ILLNESS SUFFERED ____

____

____

DESCRIPTION OF TREATMENT (Note if treatment refused) ___________________________________

____

DID PERSON LEAVE STORE UNDER OWN POWER ? YES __ NO __ EXPLAIN ________________________

____

REMOVED TO HOSPITAL? YES __ NO __ NAME/LOCATION _____________________________________

____VIA: AUTO ___ AMBULANCE ________________

WITNESS/S _________________________________ _________________________________

_________________________________ _________________________________

COMMENTS ____

____

Use continuation page for further details, comments, witnesses, etc., as required.

EMPLOYEE ACCIDENT/ILLNESS REPORT

ACCIDENT NUMBER: E- ___________

DATE OF THIS REPORT ____________________ DATE OF ACCIDENT ____________________

EMPLOYEES NAME ________________________________ TIME OF ACCIDENT __________

AGE ______ DOB ________________ SS# ______-______-________ EMP.# ________________

HOME ADDRESS ____

HOME TELEPHONE ______________ DEP'T/POSITION ____________________ HIRE DATE ________

ACCIDENT LOCATION ____

DESCRIPTION OF INJURY/ILLNESS ____

____

HOW TREATED? ____

DESCRIBE HOW INJURY/ILLNESS OCCURRED ______________________________________

____

WHAT WAS EMPLOYEE DOING PRIOR TO INJURY/ILLNESS? __________________________

____

____

WITNESS/S ____

____

REMAINED AT WORK? YES ___ NO ___ ASSIGNED LIGHT DUTY? YES ___ NO ___

EXPLAIN ____

REMOVED TO HOME? ___ HOSPITAL? ___ VIA: AMBULANCE ____________

LOCATION ______________________________________ COMPANY CONVEYANCE _____

____ PRIVATE CONVEYANCE _____

TREATED BY DOCTOR ____

ACCIDENT DUE TO UNSAFE PRACTICE? *(If yes, explain):* ______________________________

____

STATE CORRECTIVE ACTION TAKEN AND DATE ____________________________________

____

______________________________________ ______________________________

EMPLOYEE'S SIGNATURE ATTESTING TO THE TRUTHFULNESS OF THE INFORMATION CONTAINED IN THIS REPORT.

SIGNATURE OF PERSON TAKING THIS REPORT

Original to human resources, copy to loss prevention files. Use continuation/supplemental report for additional information.

ALARM AND ENTRY REPORT

DATE OF OCCURRENCE ____________________ TIME OF NOTIFICATION ________________

ARRIVAL TIME ON PREMISES ________________ TIME LEFT PREMISES __________________

TYPE OF OCCURRENCE/NOTIFICATION

□ Burglary report

□ Fire report
- □ False alarm
- □ Smoke/heat head
- □ Sprinkler head
- □ Fire board trouble alarm
- □ Fire board supervisory alarm
- □ Other

□ Damage to property (explain)

NOTIFICATION BY

□ Central Station
Time of alarm signal __________
□ Fire Department; at scene? □ Y □ N
□ Police Department; at scene? □ Y □ N
□ Mall Security; at scene? □ Y □ N
□ Other (explain below)

□ ENTRY OTHER THAN ALARM CONDITION
(note reason and authorization below)

INCIDENT REPORT No.____________________
(if applicable)

DETAILS/COMMENTS ____

____

____

____

____

____

____

____

____

REMAINED ON PREMISES? □ Y □ N

REASON?
Mechanical alarm repair: □ Burglar □ Fire
Perimeter repair: □
Interior repair/cleanup: □

PREMISES SECURED? □ Y □ N

ALL ALARMS RESET? □ Y □ N
Burglar Alarm Points Bypassed? □ Y □ N
Authorized by ___________________________
Point #'s ______________________________

NOTIFICATIONS MADE TO ____

____

________________________________ ________________________________
Reported by Approved

This report is to be compiled and submitted to the loss prevention manager on all building entries after business hours. Check off all that applies. Attach copy to incident report if applicable.

FIRE PROTECTION

MONTHLY FIRE SAFETY INSPECTION REPORT

This fire safety inspection report will be completed by a loss prevention officer on a monthly basis and the original retained for statistical, insurance, and auditing purposes.
NOTE ANY CHANGES OR CORRECTIONS REQUIRED OR COMPLETED UNDER COMMENTS

1. FIRE EXTINGUISHERS

A. Readily accessible and visible? □ Y □ N
B. Fully charged? □ Y □ N
C. Cylinder shows damage? □ Y □ N
D. Seals, hose intact? □ Y □ N
E. Tags indicate required certification? □ Y □ N

2. SPRINKLERS

A. Main sprinkler valves open and clear of obstruction? □ Y □ N

B. Sprinklers unobstructed and at least 18" from stored items? □ Y □ N

C. Is fire pump tested as required? □ Y □ N

3. FIRE DOORS

A. All fire doors in good condition? □ Y □ N (incl. alarms)

B. Clear so that they can close properly? □ Y □ N

C. Doors blocked open or secured in open position? □ Y □ N

4. FIRE ALARMS

A. Tested and found in good working order? □ Y □ N

B. Can be heard in all areas? □ Y □ N

C. Pre-recorded evacuation announcement reliable and available? □ Y □ N

D. PA System tested daily? □ Y □ N

E. PA System connected to emergency generator? □ Y □ N

5. EVACUATION

A. Are emergency exits located as required by building code? □ Y □ N

B. Fire exit doors easy to open/unblocked? □ Y □ N

C. Evacuation routes and passageways/stairways clear and well marked? □ Y □ N

D. All emergency exit lights in working order? □ Y □ N

6. EMERG. GENERATOR

A. Tested weekly? □ Y □ N

B. Emergency lighting and fire exit lighting connected and functional? □ Y □ N

C. Routine maintenance log up-to-date? □ Y □ N

4. HOUSEKEEPING

A. Excess combustible trash removed on a routine basis? □ Y □ N

B. Adequate trash containers and/or dumpsters provided? □ Y □ N

C. Excess pallets stored and removed as required? □ Y □ N

COMMENTS/ACTION TAKEN ____

____

____

____

______________________ Date of inspection

______________________ Signature of person completing inspection

Copy to: Operations Manager? □ *Y* □ *N Engineering/Maintenance Manager?* □ *Y* □ *N Incident Report # (if applicable)*______

USE OTHER SIDE FOR FURTHER COMMENTS OR DETAILS.

BUILDING SAFETY

WEEKLY SAFETY INSPECTION REPORT
CUSTOMER AREAS

This safety inspection report will be compiled by a loss prevention officer on a weekly basis and the original retained for statistical, insurance and auditing purposes.

PARKING LOT/SIDEWALKS

Sidewalks and paved areas free of cracks, holes, depressions, and obstructions? Y N

Curbs, ramps and parking areas visibly marked as required? Y N

Curbs, sidewalks, ramps free of litter/trash/debris? Y N

Fire hydrants free of blockage? Y N

Ice/snow removal adequate? Y N

Shopping carts removed from lots and sidewalks routinely? Y N

ENTRANCES/EXITS

All doors in safe operating condition? Y N

All exterior glass found secure? Y N

Floor mats and/or cones in place when raining as required? Y N

Exterior of emergency exits marked/free of obstructions? Y N

Interior of fire exit door; panic hardware OK and access unblocked? Y N

Food and liquid spills adequately removed? Y N

REST ROOMS

Rest rooms clean and presentable? Y N

Well stocked with soap/paper goods? Y N

Floor surfaces in good, clean and dry condition? Y N

Trash cans emptied on a regular basis? Y N

SIDEWALKS/CURBCUTS, ENTRANCES/EXITS AND RESTROOMS **ADA** COMPLIANT?
Y N (explain)

CUSTOMER AND SALES AREAS

Floors free of broken tiles, cracks, or holes? Y N

Transition molding does not create a tripping hazard? Y N

Throw rugs provided with slip-proof matting? Y N

Sales floor clear of unattended pallets, carts, dollies, and boxes? Y N

Wrapping, banding, litter removed from floors? Y N

Floors dry and clear? Y N

Stairways/escalators free and clear of litter/obstructions? Y N

Elevators clean and in good running order? Y N

All free standing displays secured and/or safe? Y N

Displays free of sharp edges? Y N

Shelving displays secured to wall? Y N

Swinging/suspended signage secured from striking customers? Y N

Floor lamps tilt proof? Y N

Electric cords removed from aisles? Y N

Display jars/display knives sealed or secured in holders? Y N

Knife displays above 48”? Y N

Sharp edges of knives protected and guarded? Y N

Stacked glassware and dinnerware/dishes secure from tipping or falling? Y N

Furniture pieces displayed on shelving adequately secured? Y N

Hanging pictures and mirrors adequately secure? Y N

RESTAURANT/KITCHEN

Floor surfaces free of spills and litter? Y N

Tables/chairs in good condition? Y N

Health hazards observed? Y N

Kitchen clean, orderly and appears safely operated? Y N

____
Date of inspection

____
Signature of person completing inspection

Copy to: Operations Manager? □ Y □ N Department Head/mgr. responsible? □ Y □ N Other? ______________

NOTE ANY COMMENTS, REMARKS, AND ACTION TAKEN ON THE REVERSE SIDE OF THIS FORM.

LOSS PREVENTION

PROPERTY RECOVERY FORM

STORE NUMBER AND LOCATION ______________________________ PAGE _____ of _____

DATE/TIME OF INCIDENT ______________________ REFER TO INCIDENT REPORT # __________

ARREST? ☐ N ☐ Y (Attach Arrest Report)

LIST ALL MERCHANDISE RECOVERED:

DESCRIPTION	ARTICLE #	QUANTITY	UNIT PRICE	$ TOTAL

Continue to page two if required.

SUB-TOTAL THIS PAGE: __________

TOTAL RECOVERY: __________

BRIEFLY DESCRIBE INCIDENT: ____

REPORT PREPARED BY ______________________________ TITLE ______________________

Original to recovery book/file. Attach one copy to incident report.

(*COMPANY LETTERHEAD*)

UNITED STATES SECRET SERVICE
123 MAIN STREET
SUITE 123
ANYCITY, STATE 12345

RE: CONFISCATED COUNTERFEIT BILL/S

DATE ______________________________

THE ENCLOSED COUNTERFEIT BILL/S WERE OFFERED FOR MERCHANDISE AT OUR LOCATION AND WERE CONFISCATED ON ___________________________________AT ABOUT __________HRS.

Denomination	#1. ____________	#2. ____________	#3. ____________	#4. __________
Federal Reserve Bank & Letter	____________	____________	____________	__________
Series (Yr.)	____________	____________	____________	__________
Serial No.	____________	____________	____________	__________
Letter/Quadrant No.	____________	____________	____________	__________
Letter Face Plate No.	____________	____________	____________	__________
Back Plate No.	____________	____________	____________	__________

IDENTIFICATION OF SUBJECT, IF ANY: ____

____

TYPE OF IDENTIFICATION: ____

COMMENTS/DETAILS ____

____

____

____

IF ANY FURTHER INFORMATION IS REQUIRED, PLEASE CONTACT:

____

JOHN JONES
LOSS PREVENTION MANAGER

REFER TO OUR
INCIDENT REPORT NUMBER: __________

COMPANY NAME
456 MAPLE STREET MALL
ANYTOWN, STATE 98765
Telephone (XXX) XXX-XXXX

FOUND PROPERTY REPORT

FOUND BY ________________________________ DATE ______________ TIME ____________

LOCATION____

RECEIVED BY ______________________________ DATE ______________ TIME ____________

DESCRIPTION OF PROPERTY ____

____

____

____

PROPERTY RETURNED TO BY ________________________________

☐ OWNER DATE ______________TIME ____________

- ☐ PRESENT
- ☐ PROVIDED ID
- ☐ DESCRIBED ARTICLE/CONTENTS

☐ OWNER'S REPRESENTATIVE

- ☐ PRESENT
- ☐ PROVIDED ID
- ☐ PROVIDED WRITTEN AUTHORIZATION (copy attached)
- ☐ DESCRIBED ARTICLE/CONTENTS

The owner or recipient must complete the following upon return of property:

☐ THE PROPERTY AS DESCRIBED ABOVE HAS BEEN RETURNED TO ME IN FULL WITH NOTHING MISSING.

☐ THE PROPERTY AS DESCRIBED ABOVE HAS BEEN RETURNED TO ME BUT THE FOLLOWING ITEM/S ARE MISSING:

____

____

____

☐ I REQUEST THAT A POLICE REPORT OF THE LOST OR STOLEN ITEM/S BE MADE AT THIS TIME.

☐ I DO NOT WISH TO MAKE A POLICE REPORT AT THIS TIME.

____ ______________________

Signature of property owner/representative Date

____ ______________________

Witnessed by Date

ETHICS AND CONDUCT
FOR THE
SECURITY OFFICER

ETHICS ARE RULES OF CONDUCT in which a profession or a group set standards so as to regulate and/or guide themselves and their conduct in their contact with others. The rules of ethics are to be considered a responsibility to be followed by those who belong to the profession or group. In this regard, a Code of Ethics may be formulated by which standards, when followed by a security officer, will only have a favorable impact upon the employer and the public contacts that the officer makes.

THE STANDARDS OF ETHICS AND CONDUCT

COURTESY—The respect and cordiality shown to fellow coworkers and all persons with whom the security officer comes in contact. Courtesy is most conspicuous to the beholder. A negative attitude only begets a negative response. At times, an antisocial or negative person will place a security officer in a trying situation. The officer must remember to act in a professional and businesslike manner, no matter how the other person acts. A response in kind to the subject usually only escalates the situation to where it could lead to an argument or altercation.

RESPONSIBILITY—Responsibility is a personal attribute. Maturity can also be considered a factor in assuming responsibility. It includes dignity and pride in ones demeanor, work habits, uniform, and workplace. Self-pride and self-worth begets self-respect. An officer who is not punctual in responding to his or her post ready for work, or is late in any of his or her assignments or reports, reflects a lack of responsibility. A security officer must be prompt, efficient, attentive, and accurate. His or her employer, or the client who has contracted his or her employer, if any, relies on the security officers' responsibility.

FAIRNESS—A security officer should act in a just and objective manner toward everyone. All persons coming in contact with the officer are to be treated with equal reasonableness. Respect the rights of others. Being subjective in one's duty gives more right or benefit to some, and denies that right to others. Whether through thoughtlessness, misjudgment, and misfortune or by malicious intent, an occurrence of this type could cause conflict and possible litigation for all concerned. Remember that respect toward another reflects a state of mind.

COOPERATION—Service and assistance to other security employees and supervisors, and to all others only reflects the desire to do a good job. Cooperation and willingness to work with others only enhances one's good image.

PERSONAL INTEGRITY—A standard where a security officer conducts his or her personal and business life in an exemplary fashion, and above reproach in terms of stability, fidelity, and morality.

Self-respect	the dignity and pride in one's self and in what one does.
Honesty	in words as well as in deeds.
Cleanliness	personal habits of good grooming and neatness in body and clothing.
Stability	ability to routinely act fairly, including actions under pressure, and the control of one's temper.
Loyalty	steadfast and true dedication to the officer's position, profession, organization, and coworkers.
Morality	a poor reputation and a low moral standard are difficult to reverse. Low morals attract attention to the detriment of the person and the organization.
Attitude	a person's conduct and bearing toward another or actions on the job site. A good attitude produces a good reaction in all contacts; it is a key to success or failure.

Glossary

ABBREVIATIONS As found in law citations:

A.D.2d	Appellate Division Reports, 2d series
Aff'd.	Affirmed
Cal.Rptr.	California Reporter
Cir.	Federal Circuit Court of Appeals
C.F.R.	Code of Federal Regulations (Federal Law)
DCNJ	District Court New Jersey (Federal)
E.D.	Eastern District (Federal)
EDNY	Eastern District New York (Federal)
F.Supp.	Federal supplement
F. 2nd	Second Circuit
NDNY	Northern District New York (Federal)
NLRB	National Labor Relations Board
N.Y.2d	New York Court of Appeals Reports, Second Series
N.Y.S.2d	New York Supplement Reporter, Second Series
SC	United States Supreme Court
S.Ct.	United States Supreme Court Reporter
SDNY	Southern District New York (Federal)
Sup.	Supplement
Sup.Ct.	United States Supreme Court
U.S.	United States Supreme Court
USC	United States Code (Federal Law)
U.S.C.A.	United States Code Annotated (Federal Law)

ACCESSORY Although not the principal actor in the commission of an offense, a person who solicits, requests, commands, or intentionally aids the principal actor to engage in the commission of such offense. Accessories are divided into two classes—one who before the fact aids, abets, or procures another to commit the crime, and one who after the facts, knowing the crime has been committed, receives or assists the criminal.

ACCOMPLICE A person who is liable to prosecution for the identical offense charged against the defendant on trial. One who is so connected with a crime that he might himself be convicted as a principal to the crime (e.g., acting in concert).

ARRAIGNMENT Calling or bringing a defendant before the court to answer an accusation or complaint.

ARREST To take a person into custody for the purpose of holding that person so as to answer to a criminal charge or civil demand.

ASSAULT Any intentional, unlawful offer, attempt or threat of corporal injury to another by force, or force unlawfully directed to the person of another, under such circumstances as to create a well-founded fear of imminent peril, coupled with the apparent present ability to effectuate the attempt if not prevented. An attempt to offer or beat another, without touching him, as if one lifts up his fist in a threatening manner at another. The least touching of another's person, if done willfully or in anger, constitutes battery. Also, intentionally, recklessly or with criminal negligence causing physical injury to another person.

ASSAULT & BATTERY Always includes an assault, thus the two terms are used together and combined as assault and battery. An unlawful touching of the person of another by the aggressor, or by some substance put in motion by him.

BATTERY Intentional and wrongful physical contact with a person without his or her consent, that entails some injury or offensive touching. Unlawful beating or unlawful touching of the person by another.

BENCH WARRANT A court order, in which a criminal action is pending, directing a *police officer*, or a *uniformed court officer*, to take custody of the defendant in such action, and bring him before the court.

BURGLARY To knowingly enter or remain unlawfully in a building with the intent to commit a crime therein.

CASE LAW The application of a particular case opinion with those facts as close to the facts as possible in the current case before the court. To be of use, the former opinion must have relevancy, value, precedent, or persuasive authority to the present case. The closer the facts are to each case, the more authority the former case will provide for that case now before the court.
See also *Holding*, *Precedent*, and *Persuasive Authority*.

CIVIL ACTION Action brought to enforce, redress, or protect private rights. In general, all types of actions other than criminal proceedings.

CIVIL LAW A body of statutory and common law with private rights and remedies available to a citizen; regulates arrangements, contracts, and claims between individuals and corporations.

COMMON LAW Introduced and carried over into the United States of America from England by early settlers. Law that originated from usage and custom prior to statutory (written) law. Judicial decisions were based on or incorporated the customs of society at the time. Today, common law includes those non-statutory precedents, customs, and traditions that may be used as a guide in the judicial process.

COMPENSATORY DAMAGES Those damages directly referable to a breach or tortious act, and which can be readily proven to have been sustained, and for which the injured party should be compensated as a matter of right.

CONSENT SEARCH A search that is carried out with the voluntary authorization of the subject of the search; permission is granted by the subject. It can be given orally or in writing.

COOP Any location where a security officer can be hidden from view, and where the officer can observe the conduct and behavior of customers, visitors, and company personnel. The location may be within an interior wall, closet, or other contrivance, and where a two-way mirror may be put to use for the purpose of covert observation.

CRIME A crime is an act or omission forbidden by law, and punishable upon conviction by some penalty, such as a fine, imprisonment, or death.

CRIMINAL LAW The body of statutory (written) law that proscribes those acts or omissions as crimes committed by or against the individual and/or the state, and the punishment to be dispensed after conviction for those offenses or actions detrimental to the state (the people). A distinct body of rules governing the definition, trial, and punishment of crimes.

CRIMINAL TRESPASS To knowingly enter or remain unlawfully in or upon premises. A person commits a trespass when he does not have license and privilege to enter therein. Usually a misdemeanor, but depending on local law a simple trespass may be considered a lesser offense.

DAMAGES An award sought after by the plaintiff for some "wrong" that has been committed against him. The award is usually in the form of money, but not necessarily so.

DEADLY PHYSICAL FORCE Defined as physical force, which under the circumstances in which it is used, is readily capable of causing *death* or a *serious physical injury*. To commit deadly physical force upon another, a person may use such force when he or she reasonably believes it to be necessary to defend him or herself, or a third person in imminent fear of death or serious physical injury. Also, such force may be used against a perpetrator to prevent or terminate the commission or attempted commission of murder, kidnapping, forcible rape, forcible sodomy, robbery, arson, and certain burglaries. Some states may have more severe restrictions on a private person using deadly physical force. Check your state criminal codes in which you are employed for further clarification.
See also *Physical Force*.

DECISION A determination arrived at after consideration of facts, and, in legal context, law (the courts judgement).

DEFAMATION Words or written material that were said or made known with malice and caused special damages. See *Libel* and *Slander*.

DEFENDANT The adverse party to an action. In a criminal case, one who has committed the crime; in a civil action, one who has committed the wrong and who the plaintiff seeks damages from.

DURESS Any illegal imprisonment, or legal imprisonment, used for an illegal purpose, or threats of bodily or other harm, or other means amounting to or tending to coerce the will of another, and actually inducing him/her to do an act contrary to his/her free will.

EVIDENCE

Testimonial evidence: Oral testimony of a sworn witness; subject to cross-examination. There are two types: direct and circumstantial.

Direct—Actual knowledge of facts using one's senses, i.e., eyeball witness.

Circumstantial—Evidence used to prove a fact, i.e., fingerprints, blood.

Best evidence: Concerns documents or writings. Simply means to produce the original.

Circumstantial evidence: Evidence of facts and circumstances as distinguished from direct proof, which circumstances, when established, lead the mind to certain conclusions.

Continuity of evidence: That evidence secured or kept in custody and how it was passed from one to another—an unbroken chain that protects the integrity of the evidence.

Corroborating evidence: Evidence supplementary to that already given and tending to strengthen or confirm it.

Direct evidence: Evidence that, if believed, proves a fact or matter in issue without the intervention of proof of any other fact, or without any inference or presumption. Testimony by a witness who actually saw, heard, or touched the subject or issue of interrogation.

Documentary evidence: Evidence supplied by papers, books, writings, etc. (a type of real evidence).

Hearsay evidence: Evidence of what some other person has been heard to say. This is usually excluded unless it falls within one of the recognized exceptions, i.e., dying declaration, a spontaneous utterance or admission, etc.

Material evidence: Sufficiently important; it is not trivial.

Opinion evidence: Generally, witness testimony based on the expertise of the witness.

Physical evidence: Evidence that proves that a crime was in fact committed, and can be connected to the perpetrator. Any item or physical thing that may be found that has a connection to the crime. Examples are fingerprints, a bullet, a weapon, personal property left at the scene, tool marks, recovered stolen property in possession of the perpetrator, VCR tapes of the act.

Presumptive evidence: Evidence that is not direct and positive; evidence afforded by circumstances from which a presumption may be drawn.

Real evidence: Objects or persons; something that can be seen, heard, or observed by the court.

Relevant evidence: Direct bearing on the fact in issue, pertinent and worthy of consideration.

EXCLUSIONARY RULE Evidence obtained unlawfully and excluded from the court proceeding; evidence that cannot be used.

FALSE ARREST An unlawful arrest; an unlawful imprisonment.

FALSE IMPRISONMENT Detention of a subject without justification. The same as false arrest; the terms are synonymous.

FINDING The result of the deliberations of a jury or a court (judge or jury).

FELONY A crime punishable by more than one year in a state prison or correctional facility.

FRAUD A false representation of a matter of fact, whether by words or conduct, by false or misleading allegations, or by concealment of that which should have been disclosed, which deceives and is intended to deceive another, and thereby causes injury to that person. See also *Injury*.

GYPSY Also Gypsies, Gipsy. 1. A secret criminal organization in Europe and the United States, operating since about 1000 A.D. 2. A self-perpetuating, structured, and disciplined association of individuals and groups, combined together for the purpose of obtaining monetary gains, wholly, or in part by illegal means, while protecting their criminal activities through a pattern of graft and corruption.

HOLDING A decision by the court; a holding is a legal principle to be drawn from the opinion (decision) of the court. See *Finding*.

INJURY Any damage done to another's person. It includes that person's rights, reputation, property, or physical and mental harm.

INTENTIONAL TORT A tort or wrong perpetrated by one who intends to do that which the law has declared wrong; also cited as a *Willful Tort*. (In contrast with a negligent act in which the tortfeasor fails to exercise that degree of care in doing what is otherwise permissible.)

JUDGMENT Decision or sentence of the law given by a court, justice, or other tribunal on the claims of parties to a litigation.

LARCENY A person with intent to wrongfully take, obtain, withhold, defraud, deprive, or appropriate property of another for himself or a third person by trick, false pretenses, or embezzlement or has control over property not his own, commits a larceny.

LIBEL A malicious publication in printing, writing, signs or pictures tending to blacken the reputation of one who is dead, or the reputation of one who is living.

MALICE A willful intent to do mischief; ill will. A wrongful act done intentionally and without just cause or excuse.

MALICIOUS PROSECUTION A prosecution that is begun with malice and without probable cause.

MISDEMEANOR A crime punishable by no more than a year in jail. Time is usually served in a local or county jail.

NEGLIGENCE The failure to exercise a degree of care that a reasonable person would exercise given the same circumstances, and thereby causing injury and/or damage. Negligence could be equated to carelessness (negligent tort).

NEGLIGENCE PER SE Conduct, whether of action or omission, which may be declared or treated as negligence without any argument or proof as to the particular surrounding circumstances, because it is contrary to the law.

NLRB The National Labor Relations Board—a federal agency.

NIOSH National Institute for Occupational Safety and Health—a federal agency.

OSHA Occupational Safety and Health Administration—a Federal agency.

PEACE OFFICER Distinct from a police officer; powers are not as broad. Limited to certain lawful acts of authority or jurisdiction. Ex: parole or probation officers, court officers, corrections or prison officers, game wardens, bay constables, fire inspectors. Powers may be further defined in the various state laws. Some states may differ in that some police officers are also peace officers.

PERJURY The act of a person under oath who knowingly and willfully swears falsely in a matter material to the issue or point in question. Perjury is a crime.

PILR The Property Insurance Loss Register—a national data registry in which insurance underwriters may inquire of subjects under investigation for prior excessive claims or insurance fraud.

PHYSICAL FORCE Physical force is justifiable and not considered an offense when used in defense of himself or another person, in defense of a premises, in order to prevent a larceny or criminal mischief to property, or in order to effect an arrest, and/or to prevent an escape from custody. Such force must be reasonable under the circumstances and not excessive. Check with your state criminal codes, which may be more or less restrictive in the interpretation of the use of physical force upon another.

See also *Deadly Physical Force.*

PHYSICAL INJURIES A *physical injury* may be defined as an impairment of a physical condition or substantial pain (bloody lip, black eye, swollen facial injuries, minor lacerations, or loss of teeth that require medical attention, etc.). A *serious physical injury* is defined as an injury that creates a substantial risk of death, causes death or serious and protracted disfigurement, impairment of health, or the loss or impairment of the function of any bodily organ or extremity (loss of an eye, arm, leg, bullet wound, knife puncture, broken bones, paralysis, etc.).

POLICE OFFICER A person employed by the state, municipality, a special district or public authority; a member of a *force* sworn to protect the community and maintain public order, safety, morals, and health. To prevent and detect crime, and to uphold and enforce all laws and regulations, with the power to arrest, control and direct, all within his "geographic area of employment." May also be known as a *sworn police officer.*

PLAINTIFF One who brings suit, bill, or complaint against another; one who seeks damages for some wrong.

POSSESS As defined; "means to have physical possession or otherwise to exercise dominion or control over tangible property." (Has been defined as to whether on his person or not.)

PERSUASIVE AUTHORITY May be cited as an excellent analysis of the legal issues and provide guidance for any court that happens to read it; is considered "persuasive authority." It is not binding in another state court, but may be considered.

PRECEDENT A decision from an earlier case that is relevant to the present case being decided. If there is nothing to distinguish the circumstances or facts of the current case from the case already decided, the earlier holding is considered binding on the court. A holding from one state is not binding upon another state but may be considered.

PRIMA FACIE CASE A case made out of evidence sufficient to counterbalance the general presumption of innocence. Enough presentable evidence for an arrest or a case to proceed in court. Also *prima facie* evidence; evidence showing the existence of the facts, and which if uncontradicted is sufficient to maintain the proposition affirmed.

PRODUCT/S LIABILITY The legal liability of manufacturers and sellers of a product to compensate buyers and users, which can also include browsers and bystanders, for damages or injuries suffered because of a defect or defects in the goods purchased or for sale.

PROBABLE CAUSE Those facts and circumstances that would lead a reasonably prudent person in like circumstances to believe that a crime has been committed and that the person committing such act is guilty.

PUNITIVE DAMAGES Compensation in excess of *Compensatory Damages*, which serves as a form of punishment to the wrongdoer who has exhibited malicious and willful conduct.

REASONABLE GROUNDS Knowledge (reasonable belief) that a person has possession of stolen merchandise on his person that belongs to the retail establishment. Such knowledge may be based on probable cause.

REASONABLE TIME The manner in which a suspect is handled based on lawful and reasonable custodial and arrest tactics; a reasonable time and manner for imprisonment with no intentional delaying tactics prior to turning the subject over to the police.

ROMANY OR "ROM" Also Romanies. 1. Of India, its people, or their language. 2. A native or inhabitant of India, or a person of Indian descent. 3. The language spoken by the gypsies. 4. The gypsies collectively. See also *Gypsy*.

ROUGH SHADOWING Shadowing that is done in such a manner as to cause the subject under observation to be aware he has been discovered, causing discomfort or annoyance, or to interfere with him in any way. Generally used to make the subject uncomfortable enough to leave the store. Also Shadowing—an unobserved close watch of a subject; a subject under surveillance.

SHOPLIFTING A form of larceny, a type of theft. The theft of merchandise or property from a retail merchant. The offender is charged with the crime of larceny, not "shoplifting."

SURVEILLANCE To keep close and constant watch over someone or something. Certain types are not permitted or considered decent and appropriate, such as in some situations with CCTV.

SLANDER Defamation by words spoken; malicious and defamatory words tending to the damage of another.

SPO Special Police Officer (as in New York State). Additionally, in some states a citizen who is not a police or peace officer may be given police powers under certain circumstances.

SUBPOENA A writ or order requiring the attendance of a person at a particular time and place to testify and/or present himself as a witness.

SUBPOENA DUCES TECUM A subpoena commanding a person to attend and produce some book, paper, or a document that is pertinent to the issue in question; the court's order to produce the record.

TORT A willful/negligent wrong committed against a person by another. A private or civil wrong or injury, for which the court will provide a remedy in the form of an action for damages.

UTTER, UTTERING Putting into circulation; offering. To deliver, offer, or put into circulation a note (counterfeit currency) or check known not to be legal and/or genuine.

WILLFUL TORT See *Intentional Tort*.

VICARIOUS LIABILITY Where liability is not only attributed to the wrongdoer, but to his trainer, his supervisor, and employer; one who has delegated authority to the wrongdoer, or who has all or some authority over the wrongdoer's actions. An attempt by the plaintiff to bring as many subjects as can be held responsible into the lawsuit in order to broaden the culpability and increase the monetary damages awarded.

Selected References

Bare, William K. *Fundamentals of Fire Prevention*, (New York: John Wiley & Sons, Wiley Series of Fire Science, 1977).

Barker, Lucius J., and Barker, Twiley W., Jr. *Civil Liberties and the Constitution*, 6th ed. (Englewood Cliffs, N.J.: Prentice Hall, 1990).

Black, Henry Campbell. *Blacks Law Dictionary*, 7th ed. (St. Paul, Minn: West Publishing Co., 1999).

Cushman, Robert F. *Leading Constitutional Decisions*, 18th ed. (Englewood Cliffs, N.J.: Prentice Hall, 1992).

Lieberman, Jethro K. *The Evolving Constitution*, (New York: Random House, 1992).

McDonagh, Michael E., Esq., handout and the authors personal notes from a 1993 lecture on *The Legal ABC's of Retail Security*, at a New York City seminar sponsored by The Retail Loss Prevention Association, Smithtown, NY. Mr. McDonagh is a partner in the law firm of Lester Schwab Katz & Dwyer, New York City, and is a specialist in retail litigation defense.

McKinney's Consolidated Laws of New York—Annotated (with 1998 supplements), including annotations from state and federal courts and state agencies. (St. Paul, Minn.: West Publishing Co., 1998).

New York Consolidated Laws Service—Annotated Statutes (with 1998 supplements) (Charlottesville, Va.: Lexis Law Publishing, 1998).

New York State *Criminal Procedure Law*.

New York State *Family Court Act*.

New York State *General Business Law*.

New York State *Labor Law*.

New York State *Penal Law*.

The Reid Technique of Interviewing and Interrogation®, ©1993. Workbook and course materials presented at training seminars conducted by John E. Reid Associates, Inc., 250 South Wacker Drive., Suite 1100, Chicago, Illinois, 60606.

United States Code Service—Lawyers Edition, Volume 42 USCS—The Public Health and Welfare §1983—1998 supplement. (Charlottesville, Va.: Lexis Law Publishing, 1998).

2001 National Retail Security Survey—Final Report, University of Florida, Security Research Project, Department of Sociology and the Center for Studies in Criminology and Law, Gainesville, Florida, 32611–7330, by Richard C. Hollinger, PhD., Director, and Jason L. Davis, Graduate Research Associate, ©2002.

Webb, Garn H., LL.B. *Plain Language Law—Civil Wrongs (Torts)*, (Atlanta, Ga.: Professional Impressions, Inc., 1981).

Websites of Interest

Websites are routinely redesigned and file names may change. Home pages that are popular today may not be found tomorrow. Noted below are the more popular sites that have been in service for some time or are national in status. They are continually updated with current information.

TERRORISM

http://www.fema.gov/library/terror.htm

FEMA—Federal Emergency Management Agency

Terrorism defined, terrorism facts prior to Sept. 11, 2001, natural disasters, hazardous materials.

http://www.state.gov/s/ct/rls/pgtrpt/2000

United States Department of State

Global terrorism, incidents, and patterns.

http://www.fbi.gov/terrorinfo/terrism.htm

Federal Bureau of Investigation

Domestic terrorism.

http://www.bt.cdc.gov

Centers for Disease Control and Prevention

Terrorism and the public health; biological, chemical, and radiological contamination and exposure.

http://www.lib.umich.edu/govdocs/index.html

http://www.lib.umich.edu/govdocs/usterror.html

University of Michigan Documents Center

Exceptional research site for all phases of terrorism. Complete resource on 9/11 attack, post 9/11 attacks against Americans here and abroad, counterterrorism, weapons of mass destruction, and background research.

HAZARDS AND INFECTIOUS DISEASES

http://www.osha.gov

U.S. Department of Labor, Occupational Safety and Health Administration

The law, controls, and training for Bloodborne Pathogen Exposure including hepatitis infection and workplace hazards.

WORKPLACE VIOLENCE

http://www.osha-slc.gov/SLTC/workplaceviolence/index.html
OSHA—Occupational Safety and Health Administration
Criminal violence in the workplace, workplace violence.

http://www.cdc.gov/niosh/homepage.html
CDC—Centers for Disease Control and Prevention
NIOSH—National Institute for Occupational Safety and Health
Assaults in the workplace, risk factors, hazards, implementing workplace prevention strategies and programs.

http://www.behaviormanagement.org/disorders.asp

http://www.mhsource.com
Behavior Management Systems and Mental Health Infosource
Personality disorders, aggressive behavior, aggression and transference, plus other mental abnormalities.

RETAIL SECURITY

http://www.nrf.com/search
National Retail Association
Abstracts on loss prevention issues concerning disaster management, risk management, shoplifting methods and controls, etc.

http://www.soc.ufl.edu/srp.htm
University of Florida; Department of Sociology and the Center for Studies in Criminology and Law,
Publishes the National Retail Security Survey; annual research in retail losses and strategies.

INDEX

A

Abnormal, disturbed and disgruntled persons, 81
Access control, 228
Accidental illness:
- HIV, HBV, 273–274

Accidental injuries, 267
- customer/visitor, 267
- employee injuries, 269
- first aid supplies, 269
- legal duty, 268
- records, 270
- Worker's Compensation, 138, 269

Accident investigations, 123
Accident records, 270
- loss runs, 271

Accomplices, 173
Admissions, 38–41
Alarms:
- alarm records, 299
- alarm response, 300
  - burglary, fire after hours, 300
  - robbery, fire during business hours, 301
- burglar alarm systems, 288
  - type, class and grade, 292
  - design, protection and hardware, 288
- fire alarm systems, 293
  - classification, 293
  - design, hardware, 293
  - sprinkler alarm systems, 294
- hardware maintenance, 287

Alarm tests, 299
Americans with Disability Act, 276
Anti-security item, 80
Armored car services, 135
Arrest, 52
- authority to arrest, 55
- arrest by a private citizen, 56
- cautionary release, 175
- compassion vs. prosecution, 175
- conditions required, 57
- culpability, 54
- defenses, 54, 80
- defined, 52
- evidence to support an arrest, 52
- false arrest, 17
- false imprisonment, 17
- offenses defined, 55
- "private citizen" concept, 57
- resisting arrest, 62
- use of force, 59–62

Assault and battery
- assault defined, 32
- battery defined, 32
- elements of, 32

Asset control, 221
Attempt to commit a crime, 84
Awareness and training, 220

B

Bad checks, 208–211
Bank drops, 205
Batons, 101
Battery, 31
Burglar alarm systems (*See* Alarms)
Burglary, 82, 198
Bombs:
- bomb threat procedure, 257
- bomb threats, 252
- bomb types, 253
- evacuation, 264–265
- notification to employees, 256
- suspicious objects, 255
- types of threats, 253–256

C

Case law, 4
Cashiers, 178, 225
Cashier theft, 189
Cautionary releases, 175
Cautionary remarks, 41, 49, 119
CCTV, 66, 115, 116
Check fraud, 208–209
Check procedure, 210, 212
Chemical sprays, 101
Children:
  found, 150
  lost/missing, 148
Civil court, 37
Civil law, 6
Civil liability, 9
  intentional wrongs, 9
  invasion of privacy and defamation, 31, 119
  negligent wrongs, 9
  privacy and privilege, 120
Civil litigation, 35, 42
Civil recovery, 214
Civil rights, 66–69
  Civil Rights acts, 66–69
  Color of State Law," 68
  defined, 67
  enforcement, 67
  invasion of, right to privacy, 71
  sexual harassment, 69
Civil wrong, 8
Claim of right, 80
Color of State Law," 68
Common law, 4
Compassion vs. prosecution, 175
Compensatory damages, 28
Computer emergencies, 192
  security precautions, 192
Computer response team, 192
Computer theft and sabotage, 191–194
Confessions, 38–41
  threats or promises, 39, 41, 114
Confidential information, 120, 306
Cons, 123
Consent to search, 64
Contractor/vender larceny, 216
Contractual services, 130
  armored car services, 135
  assorted services, 139–140
  insurance/fidelity bonding, 137
  polygraph, 135–137
  undercover detectives, 130
    beneficial consequences, 132
    the use of the UC, 131
  undercover operations, 130
    honesty shoppers, 132
  watchclock systems, 133
Controls, theft, 222–237
Cost/value/benefit analysis, 157
Counterfeit currency, 215
Court system, 36
  civil court, 37
  criminal court, 36
  Grand Jury, 36
  trial process, 37
Credit card procedure, 211–212
Credit cards and debit cards, 86
  confiscation, 88
Credit card fraud, 86, 208, 211
Crime (*See also* External crimes; Criminal law):
  attempt to commit, 84
  felony, 56
  misdemeanor, 56
Criminal and civil litigation, 35
Criminal court, 36
Criminal justice system, 35–36
Criminal liability, 17
Criminal law, 5, 51, 55–66
  arrest, 52
  attempt to commit a crime, 84
  burglary, 82, 198
  embezzlement, 187
  larceny, 78
    anti-security item, 80
    defined, 79
    defense by defendant, 80
    possession stolen property, 85
    theft of services, 86, 188
    value of stolen property, 79
  legal powers/limitations, 52
  robbery, 200
  trespass, 13, 81–82, 83

Criminal possession of stolen property, 85
Culpability, 54, 79, 97

D

Damage:
 graffiti, 191
 intentional/unintentional, 191
Damages, civil:
 for assault/battery, 32
 awarding of, 29
 defined, 28
 compensatory, 28
 for malicious prosecution, 29
 suffered by plaintiff, 28
 punitive, 29
Damaging remarks, 41, 49, 119
Defamation, 31, 119
 libel, 31, 119
 slander, 31, 119
Defenses:
 against civil suit, 15, 54
 claim of right, 80
 by criminal defendant, 80
 for lawful detention, 19
Depositions, 46
Deterrence, 108–109
Disasters, 247
Disclosure of confidential information, 120, 306
Discovery, 45
Dishonest employee, 155, 179
 computer theft and sabotage, 191–194
 covert actions in curtailing, 186
 employee theft, 179–181
 how they steal, 185
 indicators of theft, 186
 insurance fraud, 139, 189
 intentional damage, 191
 types of internal theft, 187
  cashier theft, 189
  computer theft, 191
  embezzlement, 187
  pilferage, 190
  theft of services, 188
 where they steal, 184
 why they steal, 183
Dishonest security officer, 194
Documentation, 44, 308
Drugs on premises, 146
Drug testing, 146

E

Eavesdropping/recordings, 117
Embezzlement, 187
Emergencies, 244
 accidental events, 264
 accidental injuries; employee, customer, 267–270
 accident records, 270
 bomb threat, 252
 employee injuries, 267, 269
 evacuations, 264
 fire, 248
 first aid supplies, 269
 gas, 251
 legal duty, 268
 natural disasters, 247, 264
 sabotage, 263
 terrorism, 258
Emergency procedure plan, 244
 emergency planning, 244
 emergency response team, 245
 larceny and liability concerns, 246
Employees (*See also* Dishonest employee; Internal theft):
 cashiers, 178, 225
 drug testing, 146
 fair treatment, 241
 hiring process, 218
 injuries, 267, 269
 relations with the security officer, 99
 role of the employee, 176
 salespeople, 177
 search of the person, 66, 118
 security risk, as a, 182
 theft, 179–181
  how they steal, 185
  where they steal, 184
  why they steal, 183
 theft control, 223
 training, 177, 309–314
 violence, 284

Espionage, 263
Ethics and conduct (*See* Appendix)
Evacuations, 264–265
Evidence (*See also* Glossary):
  confessions/admissions, 38
    obtaining, 38
    threats or promises, 39, 41
  damaging remarks, 41, 49, 119
    incident/case reports, 306
    interview attempts, 41
  preserving, 38
  rules of evidence, 49
    burden of proof, 50
    defined, 49
    exclusionary rule, 50
    motion to suppress, 50
Examinations before trial, 46
Exterior patrol, 141
  assessment/prevention, 142, 143
External crimes or threats:
  bad checks, 208–209
  bank drops; robbery/larceny of, 205
  burglary
    defined, 82, 198
    facility/asset protection, 199
  cons, scams, etc., 123, 206
  contractor and vender larceny, 216
  counterfeit currency, 215
  credit card fraud, 86, 208, 211
  criminal possession of stolen property, 85
  larceny, 78, 79
  returns and refunds, 206
  robbery:
    anti-robbery procedures, 202
    defined, 200
    employee procedures, 203
    officer response, 204
  sidewalk delivery, 217
  till taps and scams, 207

F

False arrest/imprisonment, 17
  damages awarded, 28
  defined, 17
  elements of:
    awareness of confinement, 18
    confinement not privileged, 19
    intent to confine, 18
    merchant's privilege, 19
    no consent to confinement, 19
Federal standards (law):
  Americans with Disability Act, 276
  bloodborne pathogens, 273
  hazard communication, 275
  OSHA, 272
Felony defined, 56
Fingerprints/photos, 58
Fire alarm systems, 293
  classification, 293
  design and devices, 293
  sprinkler alarm systems, 294
Firearms, 100
Fire department access, 299
Fire drills/evacuations, 299
Fire emergency, 248
  automatic sprinkler system, 250
  effect of fire on people, 248
  fighting the fire, 250
  fire extinguishers, 250
  fire safety, 249
Fire inspections, 296
  areas of inspection, 297
Flim-flams," 123
Force (*See* Use of force)
Forms and reports (*See* Appendix)
Fraud:
  bad check, 208–211
  credit card, 86, 208, 211
  identification procedures, 212

G

Gas leaks, 251
General releases, 32
Good faith, 26
Grand Jury, 36
Grand larceny, 205

H

Handcuffs, 100
Hazard communication, 275
  training, 275

Health and infectious hazards, 273
Hepatitus infection, 274
Hiring process, 218, 239
Honesty shoppers, 132
Human resources, 239
  pre-employment investigation, 239
  termination process, 240

I

Identification errors, 26
Illness on premises, 267
Incident reports, 303
Infections and health hazards, 273
  bloodborne pathogens, 273
  hazards, 274
Informants, 115
Information, reliance on, 26
Injuries (*See* Accidental injuries)
Inspections and Audits:
  alarm tests, 299
  areas of inspections, 297
  building inspections (*See* Form; Appendix)
  evacuation drills, 264–265
  fire inspections, 296
  inventory control, 227
  (*See also* Stock control)
Insurance/fidelity bonding, 137
Insurance fraud, 123, 189
Insurance fraud by employee, 189
Integrity screening, 220
Integrity testing, 194–197
Intentional wrongs, 9
Interviews and interrogations, 125
  interviews defined, 125–126
  interrogations defined, 125–126
  juveniles, 75, 128
  Miranda warning and other issues, 127
  the "Reid 9 step system," 126
  unions, 128
Internal and external theft control (*See* Theft control)
Internal theft:
  cashier theft, 189
  computer theft, 191–194
  contractor/vender, 216
  covert actions/curtailing, 186
  embezzlement, 187
  indicators, 186
  insurance fraud, 139, 189
  pilferage, 190
  theft of services, 188
Invasion of privacy and defamation, 31, 119
  defamation, 31, 119
  disclosure of confidential information, 120, 306
Inventory loss, 156
Investigation at the scene, 121
  collection of evidence, 122
Investigative techniques, 111
  conducting the investigation, 112
  overt/covert, 111
    CCTV, 115, 116
    covert surveillance, 116
    drug testing, 146
    employee searches, 66, 118
    informants, 115
    insurance fraud and accident
      cons, scams, 123
      investigation, 123
    internal investigation, 112
    interviews, 125, 126
    loss, theft, shrinkage, 111
    pre-employment invest., 239
    privacy and defamation, 31, 120
    wiretaps and telephone recordings, 117
Invitee, 12

J

Justification of Force, 59
Juvenile
  apprehension of, 71
  defined, 72
  custodial procedures, 74
  juveniles and the courts, 72
  parental notification, 76
  questioning of, 75

K

Key control, 229
Knox box, 299

L

Larceny, 78
  contractor/vender, 216
  defined, 79
  criminal possession, 85
  from the person/no force, 205
  value of stolen property, 79
Law:
  case law, 4
  civil law, 6
  common law, 4
  criminal law, 6
  history of, 2
  introduction to, 2
  precedent, 4
  redress, right for, 5
  stare decisis, 4
  statutory law, 3
Lawsuit, civil , 42
  basis for, 14
  role of loss prevention, 44
  service of, 43
Legal duty, 268
Legal powers, 52
Legitimate interest, 120
Liability, 5, 8, 12–15
Libel, 31
License and privilege, 12, 81
  invitee, 12
  licensee, 12
  privileged access, 82
  trespasser, 13, 82
    burglary defined, 82
    trespass defined, 12, 82
    use of the trespass warning, 83
Lighting, 143
Litigation, 36, 42
  civil lawsuit, 42
  court system, the, 36
    civil, 37
    criminal, 36
  criminal justice system, the, 36
  discovery, 45
    depositions/interrogatories, 46
    examination before trial, 46
  preponderance of evidence, 50
  reasonable doubt, 50
  role of loss prevention, 44, 107
  trial process, the, 37
    testifying at trial, 47–49
  (*See also* Pre-litigation)
Loss control (*See* Theft control)
Loss control procedures, 218–237
Loss prevention:
  defined, 92
  justification of, 306
  retail loss prevention, 90, 92, 237
Loss prevention officer, 90, 94
Loss prevention tactics, 218–237
  asset control, 221
  awareness training, 220, 221
  hiring process, 218
  reactive vs. proactive, 109
  systems and loss prevention personnel, 222
Loss runs, 271
Lost and found children, 148–150
Lost and found property, 150

M

Malice, 25–28
  defined, 27
Malicious prosecution, 25
  absence of probable cause, 26
  commencement or continuation of a proceeding, 25
  damages suffered, 29
  elements of, 25
  proceeding terminated in favor of the plaintiff, 26
Malls, 262
Management:
  effect on morale, safety and security issues, 238
Management techniques;
  role of loss prevention, 237
  role of management, 237
  role of human resources, 239
Media, 153
Merchant's privilege, 19
  defense to lawful detention, 19

Miranda warning, 39, 41, 127
Misdemeanor defined, 56
Motivation by actual malice, 27
  vicarious liability, 30

N

Natural disasters, 264
Negligence:
  defined, 13
  proximate cause, 13
  ordinary care, 13
Negligent:
  hiring practices, 10
  retention practices, 10
Negligent wrongs, 9

O

Occupational exposure to bloodborne pathogens, 273
Offenses:
  defined, 55
  felony, 56
  infractions, 55
  misdemeanor, 56
  violations, 55
Opening/closing procedures, 232
OSHA, 272
  employer and employee training requirements, 273, 275
  required injury records, 272

P

Parental notifications, 76
Parking fields, 141
Patrol, exterior, 141–144
Performance evaluation, 314
Photographs, 58
Physical evidence, 38
Physical force, use of, 59–62
Physical security, 228 (*See also* Asset; Theft control)
Picketing issues, 279–280
Pilferage, 190
Plain-view"doctrine, 65
Police officers, 58, 151
  aiding, 62
  hired as security officers, 152
  obstruction of, 151
  police cooperation, 151
  resisting, 62
Polygraph, 135–137
  restrictions, 136
Possession of stolen property, 85
Precedent, 4
Pre-litigation, 36 (*See also* Litigation)
Premises liability, 12
Prints and photos, 58
Privacy defined, 71, 120
Privacy; expectation of, 66
Private-citizen" concept, 57
Privilege defined, 120
Privileged access, 82
Probable cause, 20
  defined, 21
  factors, leading to, 24
  presumptions/burden of proof, 223
  reasonable grounds, 22
  reasonable time and manner, 23
  shoplifting offenses, 169
Products Liability, 14
Profiling, 160–162
  shoplifter; the, 162
Property:
  lost and found, 150
  stolen, 79, 85
Prosecution vs. compassion, 175
Prosecution, selective, 174–176
Proximate cause, 13
Public address systems, 102
Punitive damages, 29

R

Radios, 102
Reactive vs. proactive, 109
Reasonable doubt, 50
Recordkeeping, 304
Records, 304
  accident, 270

Records *(continued)*
alarm, 300
loss runs, 271
OSHA (required), 272
time record, 307
Recovery, 266
Redress, right for, 54
Releases:
cautionary, 175
general, 33
in lieu of, 33
Reports and forms (*See* Appendix)
Reports:
custodial responsibility, 42, 306
significance of, 42, 44, 305, 306
Report writing, 42, 98, 303
Resisting arrest (police only), 62
Response, recovery and restoration, 266
Restraints, 100
Retail security:
loss prevention defined, 92
media and, 153
reactive vs. proactive, 109
responsibility of, 107
Returns and refunds, 206
Right to privacy, 66, 71, 119
Right for redress, 4
Risk analysis/threat potential, 103
loss prevention surveys, 103
deterrence as a factor, 108
examination and inquiry, 104
responsibility, 107
Robbery:
anti-robbery procedures, 202
defined, 200
employee procedures, 203
officer response, 204
Rules of evidence, 49

S

Sabotage, 263
Safes:
fire safe, 144
money safe, 145
Safety committee, 276
Safety defined, 92, 98
Sales receipts, 207
Scams and schemes, 123, 206
Scope of employment, 14
Search and seizure, 62
consent to search, 64
criminal possession of stolen property, 85
employee searches, 66, 118
incidental to a lawful arrest, 63
search after arrest, 62
plain-view" doctrine, 65
fruit of the poisoned tree" concept, 66
search of the person, 64
Security and civil law, 52
Security defined, 92
Security guard defined, 94
Security and safety defined, 92
Security negligence, 12
Security officer, and the employee, 99
basic responsibilities, 95
culpability of, 54
defined, 94
disclosure of confidential information, 120, 153, 306
dishonest, 194
functions of, 96
legal powers and limitations, 52
performance evaluation, 314
privacy and defamation, 119
privacy and privilege, 120
private-citizen" concept, 57
role in security and safety, 95
detect, 96
deter, 97
report, 98
testifying at trial, 47
behavior on witness stand, 47–49
cautionary remarks, 49
weapons/devices/controls, 100
Security officer and the employee, 99
Selective prosecution, 174–176
Self defense, 59
Sexual harassment, 69
conduct of, 69
Shrinkage, 111, 155
Sidewalk delivery, 217

Signage, 235
Shoplifter, 155, 159
  actions that encourage, 165
  actions that discourage, 166
  classification, 159
  cost/benefit/value, 157
    accomplices, 173
  detainment and detention, 172
  primary rules, 169
  profile of, 162
    the art, 163
    characteristics, 164
  profiling the offender, 160
  protective devices, 166–167
  releases, 33–34, 175
  selective prosecution, 174
  social issues, 159
  the stop, 171
  ticket switch, 167
  witnessing the crime, 169
Slander, 31
Sprinkler;
  auto protection, 250
  alarm systems, 294
  monitoring, testing and classification, 295
Statements, 39
  oral, 39
  written, 39–41
Statuary law, 3
Stare decisis; rule of, 4
Stock control, 227
Stolen property:
  possession, 85
  value, 79
Strikes and picketing, 279–280
  abnormal, disturbed and disgruntled persons, 281
  unruly crowds, 280
Surveys; loss, 103–105

T

Termination of employee, 240
Terrorism, 258
  malls/security, 262
  precautions, 261
  retail issues, 260
  specific threats, 260
Testimony:
  depositions, 46
  at trial, 47–48
Theft (*See* Internal theft; Larceny; Shoplifter)
Theft control; 222–237
  anti-shoplifting signage, 235
  cashiers and cash rooms, 225
  employees, 223
  helpful management techniques, 237–242
  internal and external, 222
  stock control, 227
  systems and security personnel, 222
  tactics and procedures, 218–237
  physical security:
    access control, 228
    anti-shoplifting signage, 235
    CCTV, 66, 115
    EAS tags, 234
    key control, 229
    opening and closing procedures, 232
    shipping/receiving areas, 233
    stock control, 227
    trailers, 232
  procedures, 218
Theft of services, 86, 188
Threat potential (*See* Risk analysis)
Ticket switch, 167
Till taps and scams, 207
Time record, 173, 307
Torts (wrongs):
  intentional (willful), 9
  negligent, 9
Training, 309
  awareness, 220, 221
  cashiers, 178
  hazard communication, 275
  loss prevention, 313
  loss prevention managers role in, 309
  orientation, 309
  required training for employees, 309
  safety, 313
  salespersons, 177

Trespass, 13, 81–82, 83
Trial process, 37 (*See also* Litigation)

U

Use of force, 59–62
  deadly physical force, 60, 61
  defined, 59, 61
  defense of another, 59
  justification, 59
  self defense, 59
Unions, 128
Unruly crowds, 280

V

Value of stolen property, 79
Vicarious liability, 14, 29
Violence (*See* Workplace Violence; Strikes)

W

Weapons, 100
  batons and jacks, 101
  chemical sprays and electronic devices, 101
  firearms, 100
Wiretaps, 117, 118
Worker's Compensation, 138, 269
Workplace violence:
  abnormal, disturbed persons, 281
  defined, 282
  employee violence, 284
  identifying the potential perpetrator, 285
  results of violence, 286
Wrongs (*See* Torts)

DATE DUE

GAYLORD			PRINTED IN U.S.A.